Marcel Broodthaers and Film: A Second of Eternity

MARCEL BROODTHAERS AND FILM
A SECOND OF ETERNITY

EDITED BY STEVEN JACOBS AND RAF WOLLAERT

LEUVEN UNIVERSITY PRESS

Published with the support of the KU Leuven Fund for Fair Open Access, and FWO (Research Foundation – Flanders)

Published in 2024 by Leuven University Press / Presses Universitaires de Louvain / Universitaire Pers Leuven. Minderbroedersstraat 4, B-3000 Leuven (Belgium).

Selection and editorial matter © 2024, Steven Jacobs and Raf Wollaert
Individual chapters © 2024, The respective authors

This book is published under a Creative Commons Attribution Non-Commercial Non-Derivative 4.0 License. For more information, please visit https://creativecommons.org/share-your-work/cclicenses/
Attribution should include the following information:

Steven Jacobs and Raf Wollaert (eds), *Marcel Broodthaers and Film: A Second of Eternity*.
Leuven: Leuven University Press, 2024. (CC BY-NC-ND 4.0)
Unless otherwise indicated all images are reproduced with the permission of the rightsholders acknowledged in captions. All images are expressly excluded from the CC BY-NC-ND 4.0 license covering the rest of this publication. Permission for reuse should be sought from the rights-holders.

ISBN 978 94 6270 431 2 (Paperback)
ISBN 978 94 6166 577 5 (ePDF)
ISBN 978 94 6166 620 8 (ePUB)
https://doi.org/10.11116/9789461665775
D/2024/1869/25
NUR: 674

Design: Theo van Beurden Studio
Cover illustration: *Berlin oder ein Traum mit Sahne*. 16mm film. 1974. Courtesy Berliner Künstlerprogramm des DAAD. © Estate of Marcel Broodthaers, c/o SABAM Belgium 2024

CONTENTS

Preface	7
Introduction The Cinema Models of Marcel Broodthaers Steven Jacobs and Raf Wollaert	11
René and Marcel at the Movies **Preliminary Remarks** Bruce Jenkins	63
***La Séance* and Other Assemblies** Eric C. H. de Bruyn	75
Broodthaers's Cinepoetic Concretions Christophe Wall-Romana	105
A Denounced Tautology On *Une Seconde d'éternité (D'après une idée de Charles Baudelaire)* **(1970)** Andrew Chesher	123
***Le Corbeau et le renard* in Knokke-le-Zoute** Notes on the Production and Projection at EXPRMNTL 4, December 1967 Xavier García Bardón	145
Traveling Words and Images Found Postcards in the Films of Marcel Broodthaers Deborah Schultz	169
Marcel Broodthaers's Underground Cinema *Au-delà de cette limite* **(1971)** Charlotte Friling	189
Broodthaers, Bentham, and Pygmalion *Figures of Wax* **(1974)** Steven Jacobs	207

In The Eye of the Storm 221
Berlin oder ein Traum mit Sahne **(1974)**
Raf Wollaert

Filmography 245
Raf Wollaert

Contributors and Editors 261

Index 265

PREFACE

At the centennial anniversary of Marcel Broodthaers (1924–76), a fresh opportunity emerges to revisit his enduring artistic legacy. Having garnered substantial institutional and scholarly recognition since his passing in 1976, Broodthaers has been acknowledged in many a capacity covering the extensive scope of his endeavors: poet, journalist, neo-Dadaist, conceptual artist, fictional museum director, post-medium epitome, et cetera. Surprisingly absent from this list, however, is his role as a filmmaker.

Given Broodthaers's prolific output of at least fifty short films, it is remarkable indeed that only a select few aficionados are acquainted with the extraordinary extent of his filmic practice. Yet cinema, both as a medium and principle, was crucial to Broodthaers's artistry. This is the central premise of this edited volume.

To a large extent, this book is the result of a research project sponsored by the Research Foundation – Flanders (FWO) that enabled Raf Wollaert to write his PhD thesis on Marcel Broodthaers and cinema under the supervision of Steven Jacobs at the University of Antwerp. We would like to thank FWO for making this possible, as well as our colleagues at the University of Antwerp, in particular the members of the Visual Poetics research group. At the university we also thank the Department of Literature for its financial support of this publication.

In addition, we would like to express our gratitude to all individuals and institutions whose support, both direct and indirect, has been instrumental in the realization of this book as well as the symposium and film program that paved the way for it. First of all, we would like to thank Maria Gilissen for her generous support throughout the research project. Her lifelong commitment to Broodthaers's oeuvre has been essential for the preparatory work that went into this volume.

We also wish to convey our deepest appreciation to Cinematek Brussels, whose unwavering dedication to preserving Marcel Broodthaers's films and facilitating their accessibility provided an indispensable foundation to our research. Our special thanks go out to a remarkable cadre of individuals at Cinematek, including Bruno Mestdagh, Victor De Vocht, Christophe Piette, Elise Boudjema, Steven Van Impe, Regina De Martelaere, Mikke Somers, Arianna Turci, Tomas Leyers, and all their colleagues who have supported our research or facilitated the screenings we organized.

Cinematek also hosted the "Marcel Broodthaers & Cinema" symposium and the accompanying film program in June 2022, which enjoyed the support of the University of Antwerp and the WIELS Contemporary Art Centre in Brussels. We would like to thank all participants, chairs, and audience members for their contributions and valuable comments. Some of the authors represented in this book based their chapters on their lectures at the 2022 symposium but we would like to acknowledge all speakers at that event regardless of whether their lectures are featured here, particularly Maria Elena Minuto, Gabriele Mackert, Jennifer Wild, and Joris D'Hooghe for their illuminating presentations as well as Nico Dockx and gerlach en koop for their widely acclaimed artistic intervention. In addition, we express our appreciation to Tom Paulus, Elvira Crois, Dirk Snauwaert, and Els Van Riel for their support in organizing the symposium and film program.

We also owe thanks to various organizers of exhibitions, lectures, symposia, and film screenings in which some of our still-evolving ideas were presented and discussed, including the "Soleil politique" and "LIVINUS – voor de TOEKOMST" exhibitions that took place at the M HKA Antwerp respectively in 2019 and 2021; the program dedicated to Broodthaers's films at De Cinema Antwerp in January 2020; the "Industrial Poems" exhibition held at WIELS Brussels in 2021; the "London's Art Networks and Marcel Broodthaers" conference at the Chelsea College of Art in June 2023; the "Filmer l'art" conference at INHA Paris in October 2023; the *Berlin oder ein Traum mit Sahne* screening and panel talk hosted by the DAAD and Akademie der Künste in Berlin in November 2023; and finally the "Marcel Broodthaers: Portrait de groupe" podcast series set up by ISELP in the fall of 2023.

Furthermore, our research benefited from the collaborative support of other institutions and organizations such as Cinea Brussels, Dirk Dejonghe Film Laboratory in Kortrijk, FOMU Antwerp, Ghent University, and the MACBA Museum in Barcelona, as well as individuals including Lotte Beckwé, Constantin Broodthaers & Yola Minatchy, Enrico Camporesi, Xavier Canonne, Frank Castelyns, Jan Ceuleers, Christophe Chérix, Cathérine David, Liesbeth Decan, Sofie Dederen, Yves Depelsenaire, Gerrit Jan de Rook, Liliane Dewachter, Nico Dockx, Saskia Gevaert, Marie-Pascale Gildemyn, Marge Goldwater, Rachel Gruijters, Adriaan Raemdonck, Michal Ron, Anne Rorimer, Joe Scanlan, Marion Schmid, Dieter Schwarz, Trevor Stark, Ernest Van Buynder, Levina van de Bundt & Mike Floothuis, Piet Van Hecke, Margaux Van Uytvanck, Bart Versteirt, Stefaan Vervoort, Patricia Villon Ledesma, Michael Walsh, and Matthew Witkovsky.

We also extend our heartfelt thanks to institutions that have contributed to the ongoing updating of Broodthaers's filmography and granted access to their archives, which include the Centre Pompidou in Paris, RKD in The Hague, S.M.A.K. in Ghent, Archives et Musée de la Littérature in Brussels, Kunstmuseum in Basel, Hoffmann Foundation in Basel, the Tate in London,

Museum Abteiberg in Mönchengladbach, WDR in Cologne, Staatliche Museen in Berlin, DAAD Berliner Künstlerprogramma in Berlin, MoMA in New York, Broodthaers Society of America in New York, the Walker Art Center in Minneapolis, and especially the MACBA in Barcelona, with special thanks to Patricia Sorroche and Núria Montclús for their invaluable assistance. We are also deeply appreciative of Broodthaers's contemporaries who are keeping his memory alive, in particular Jean Harlez, David Lamelas, Anny De Decker, Yves Gevaert, Michel Baudson, Jacques Charlier, Lynda Morris, David Lamelas, Michael Werner, Benjamin Buchloh, Folker Skulima, Terry Sheldon, and Noel Cronin. Furthermore, we wish to express our thanks to Broodthaers's dedicated collectors for their unbridled generosity, especially Ivo Van Vaerenbergh, Johan Smets, and The Friends of the M HKA. Special thanks in this regard are owed to Barbara and Lola Herbig, whose support was vital concerning all the above endeavors.

Finally, we would like to express our heartfelt thanks to Leuven University Press and its acquisitions editor Mirjam Truwant for making this book possible as well as to all authors who contributed to this volume with a series of fascinating essays.

September 2024
Steven Jacobs and Raf Wollaert

INTRODUCTION
THE CINEMA MODELS OF MARCEL BROODTHAERS

Steven Jacobs and Raf Wollaert

BROODTHAERS AS A FILMMAKER

The origin myth of Marcel Broodthaers's artistic career has been told over and over. He appeared on the scene in the late 1940s as a poet orbiting the Belgian Surréalisme révolutionnaire and communist movements and turned from poet into visual artist in 1964 with *Pense-Bête*, a stack of unsold, eponymous poetry collections transformed into a sculptural object. In tandem with the famous invitation card for his first solo exhibition—"I too, wondered whether I could not sell something and succeed in life"—this work is commonly approached as the Rosetta stone for Broodthaers's subsequent twelve-year journey through the art world, ending with his passing in 1976 and comprising an oeuvre that has been linked with trends, currents, and phenomena such as (Post)Surrealism, Neo-Dada, Pop Art, Nouveau Réalisme, Conceptual Art, and Institutional Critique.

It is less common to conceive of Broodthaers as a filmmaker, although he made more than fifty short films, shot in 35mm and 16mm, meeting labels as diverse as fiction, documentary, experimental, drama, comedy, home movie, and animation. What's more, Broodthaers's first film was made in 1957, more than seven years before his self-staged appearance as an artist. Even apart from his substantial filmography, Broodthaers's literary and artistic oeuvre is inconceivable without film. Both his writings and visual works include many allusions to cinema, its history, technology, and paraphernalia, with explicit or implicit references to classical cinema and directors such as Jean Vigo, Alain Resnais, or Alfred Hitchcock, to early cinema to silent slapstick cinema, and to film theorists such as Georges Sadoul, who authored the *Histoire générale du cinéma* (1946–54). The first volume of Sadoul's survey features in one of Broodthaers's

Joaquín Romero Frías. Portrait of Marcel Broodthaers. c. 1971. © Estate of Marcel Broodthaers

iconic self-portraits, in which he wears a mask evoking Fantômas, the master criminal made famous by Louis Feuillade's film serial (1913–14). The photograph is only one of many indications that Broodthaers's films are inherently connected with his entire artistry, intertwined with numerous other works. Moreover, this interest in film would affect Broodthaers throughout his entire career, from his first poems published in the late 1940s to various photographic works and the so-called *Décors* of the 1960s and 1970s. Last but not least, his grand fictitious museum project, the *Musée d'Art Moderne, Département des Aigles*, spanning several years and works, also included a *Section Cinéma*, serving as the décor for the abovementioned portrait.

The themes, motifs, and source materials of Broodthaers's films are often identical to those he used in his books, prints, objects, inscriptions, and installations. While it is impossible to study Broodthaers's films without referring to Broodthaers "the artist," it is also absurd to discuss his artworks and ideas without considering his substantial cinematic production. Nonetheless, Broodthaers's role as a filmmaker has been significantly undervalued and understudied, which may be mostly due to the relative inaccessibility of his filmic oeuvre. This resulted in the remarkable situation of only a few aficionados being acquainted with the true extent of Broodthaers's filmmaking. The Broodthaers scholarship, too, which has taken significant proportions over the last decades, usually tends to downsize his cinematic output to a limited selection of better-known titles such *La Pluie* (The Rain) (1969) or neglect it altogether.

Paradoxically, the close interconnection between his films and other works made the former somewhat invisible to art historians—an effect no doubt triggered by a misunderstanding of Broodthaers's oft-quoted statement that he was "not a filmmaker."[1] According to Eric de Bruyn, "film is constituted as a procedure by Broodthaers, not as an auxiliary means of representation; a procedure moreover that pervades his whole practice as an artist [...] fully integrated within the total field of artistic production."[2] It would be consequently myopic or absurd to discuss Broodthaers's films separately—especially after an entire wave of film historians has emphasized the inherent hybrid nature of cinema while revealing its intermedial connections with the visual arts.[3]

In light of this, it comes as no surprise that Broodthaers and his works are omitted in most if not all surveys of cinema, even in those focusing on experimental or avant-garde film. Although Broodthaers's cinema can be labeled as highly idiosyncratic and more related to his works in other media than to contemporaneous tendencies in (avant-garde) cinema, many of his films do share themes or stylistic traits with divergent trends and currents in experimental film from the 1940s to the 1970s, such as Post-Surrealist essay films, lyrical art documentaries, Lettrist and Situationist film, film experiments by various Fluxus artists, and Structural cinema. Although Broodthaers no doubt shared with the filmmakers of these tendencies their disapproval of commercial cinema's complicity with the "society of the spectacle," the sentiment did all but lead him to pursue experiments with abstract film or "anti-cinema" in the vein of the endeavors by the Lettrist offspring on the one hand or a provocative, radically political cinema à la Jean-Luc Godard on the other. True to his skepticism regarding cinema's future, Broodthaers neither embraced "new techniques of the image" to reinvent cinema nor sought to redeem it from the pull of authority and commodity.[4] Moreover, video left him cold entirely, precisely at the time when many artists cherished the new technology's possibilities and anticipated democratic appeal. Just at the moment when the famous Portapak was launched, Broodthaers empathically (re)embraced celluloid film while denouncing the label "experimental" altogether.[5]

The omission of Broodthaers in surveys of avant-garde cinema is unmistakably related to the fact that he mostly worked outside experimental film circles, outside the sphere of coops, ciné-clubs, and specialized film festivals, entrenching his cinematic output within the realm of the visual arts with its circuit of museums and art galleries. When asking permission to film on the premises of University College London for *Figures of Wax* (1974), he tellingly noted, "While not a filmmaker in the generally accepted sense, film has been an important part of my medium as an artist. My films are usually quite short, of only ten minutes or so duration. They are not made to be exhibited commercially and the interests they have is as works of art—their audience is that for poetry and painting."[6]

While his work was completely disconnected from commercial cinema, Broodthaers's separation from the world of avant-garde film needs to be nuanced as he contributed to the second and fourth editions of the *EXPMRNTL* film festival in 1958 and 1967 respectively. He also had many contacts in various film circles—albeit these were rather in his capacity of a cinephile, journalist, or screen- and dialogue writer than as a creative filmmaker.

Although he had no doubt inherited a sense of cinephilia from some of his early Surrealist associates like Paul Nougé, Christian Dotremont, or René Magritte, Broodthaers's earliest encounters should mostly be situated within the Brussels ciné-club scene. At the Brussels Palais des Beaux-Arts in the 1950s, Broodthaers regularly attended the screenings of film classics organized by the *Écran du Séminaire des Beaux-Arts* in particular. Occasionally, he was also involved in the organization of specific screenings, curating and introducing programs compiled of (appropriated) *actualités* and (art) documentaries, a practice that would reverberate throughout his later career, as several of his "installations" also included film programs with his own works as well as appropriated footage. Founded in 1944 by Henri d'Ursel, Henri Storck, Charles Dekeukeleire, and André Thirifays, all of whom were in some way steeped in the prewar Surrealist Belgian avant-garde, the *Écran* was the preeminent place to watch film classics in Belgium before the opening of the Cinémathèque royale, which emerged from it in 1962. In addition, Broodthaers shared an artistic network with filmmakers such as Henri Storck, Luc de Heusch, and Paul Haesaerts, as well as with critics such as André Thirifays and Paul Davay, all of whom were involved in the film club and contributed to the development of the prolific Belgian scene for art documentaries in the postwar years.[7]

Before and immediately after his entry into the art world, Broodthaers was even professionally involved in film production. In the early 1960s, for instance, he worked as a screenwriter for a dozen of documentary shorts addressing a variety of topics—including tourism, leisure, and cultural affairs—by directors such as Patrick Ledoux, Philippe Collette, and Henri Kessels.[8] In 1961, he also took care of the dialogues in Jean Coignon's animation film *Le Poirier de misère* (The Pear Tree of Misery, 1961). While these projects might have been inspired by a desire to channel his writerly capacities to the fullest extent within the public sphere in line with his concurrent forays into journalism, they also indicate his interest in the film medium and his contacts with Belgian documentary filmmakers, although his position within these circles was marginal. Nevertheless, it was in this context and at this time that Broodthaers met the two cameramen who would greatly assist him throughout his filmic career: Paul De Fru and above all Jean Harlez.

Despite his contacts with cinephile film clubs and professional filmmakers, Broodthaers's own films largely remained within the realm of the visual arts, cherished as a kind of fragile *Fremdkörper* in museums and art galleries, which often lacked the infrastructure to screen them, thus presenting his films as canned objects in showcases rather than projected on a screen—a fact that definitely hindered their exposure and public awareness for decades and probably also thwarted a more active attention to the films in the Broodthaers *Forschung*. On the other hand, the intimate entanglement between Broodthaers's cinema and visual arts practice has been posing significant challenges to curators and film programmers until now, resulting in curatorial choices that either did not or simply could not always honor the distinct viewing conditions that some of his films demand. Anyone endeavoring to show a representative selection of Broodthaers's filmmaking will have no choice but to deal with the issue of pre-painted screens and the question of whether highly specific environments can and should be faithfully restaged.

These issues are even further complicated by the fact that the artist himself would often assume the roles that are typically reserved for future interpreters of his work. He not only edited his catalogs and curated his own retrospectives but also took care of his own film anthologies according to the principle of "new tricks, new scams." A final issue is enfolded within the specifically social dimension of many of Broodthaers's enterprises—the *Musée d'Art Moderne* in particular—which equally asserted itself within his filmic séances. As this represents the most ephemeral quality of his work, it leaves the most room for speculation and is easily lost from sight, if it can be restaged at all. As Trevor Stark argues, any retrospective of the artist is "haunted by the possibility that the fragile connective tissue of social relations that was Broodthaers's medium is simply no longer accessible to immediate experience," an effect that is even enhanced by the persisting challenges that his work poses to the art institution's curatorial apparatus, and which may well be called the most enduring trait of his legacy.[9]

Despite this, Broodthaers enjoys the status of what Stark has come to term an "art historian's artist," as witnessed by the plethora of scholarly accounts that have appeared on his work since his death. After the pioneering work of Michael Compton, Benjamin Buchloh, and Marie-Pascale Gildemyn,[10] key monographs such as the ones authored by Deborah Schultz and Rachel Haidu touched upon Broodthaers's cinema only in a rather tangential manner, whereas other scholarly articles, despite their theoretical breadth, generally limit their scope to a set of rather well-known titles or installations.[11] Furthermore, a first attempt to collect some of the dispersed scholarship on Broodthaers's cinema was undertaken in 2001 with the volume titled *Vorträge zum filmischen Werk von Marcel Broodthaers*, featuring proceedings by Rainer Borgemeister, Birgit Pelzer, Julia Schmidt, and Dorothea Zwirner. This collection, however, only appeared in German and remained all in all quite fragmentary in its outlook.[12] Likewise, *Cinéma modèle*, published in German and French in 2013, discusses only five of Broodthaers's key films.[13] Two exceptionally comprehensive accounts have been proposed by Bruce Jenkins and Eric de Bruyn and reflect their groundbreaking engagement with the subject.[14] Jenkins was among the first curators to recover and champion Broodthaers's films and co-pioneered the presentation of his work in the United States, while de Bruyn first introduced this fundamental part of Broodthaers's oeuvre to the emerging theoretical scholarship on his work.[15] For this reason, it is all the more significant to have new contributions by these authors included in the present volume.

The numerous catalogs of the posthumous retrospectives of Broodthaers's work, on the other hand, do show some awareness of the artist's filmic oeuvre, witness the frequent occurrence of, alas, mostly incomplete filmographies. Of course, the richly illustrated 1997 catalog of the first exhibition exclusively dedicated to Broodthaers's cinema, edited by Manuel Borja-Villel, represents nothing short of a milestone in this regard. However unprecedented in its enterprise to map this body of work, this key publication too overlooked some films and remained rather descriptive in its treatment of some titles. As it is still an indispensable source for studying and exhibiting Broodhaers's cinema, this volume seeks to build further upon both its topographic and critical endeavor. It provides an updated filmography based on an inventory of the current holdings of some major institutions in Europe and the United States on the one hand and a minute comparative study of all major preceding filmographies on the other. Furthermore, this volume generously complements the essays by Jenkins and Jean-Christophe Royoux included in the 1997 Barcelona catalog on the one hand, and those by de Bruyn on the other. This previous "wave" of scholarship on Broodthaers's cinema mostly emphasized the ways in which the artist's cinema addressed the medium's history and (material) ontology against the background of its "museumification" within the walls of the gallery space (instead of in cinema theaters) on the one hand, and the emergence of digital film and moving image installations on the other. A quarter century later, we celebrate the artist's centenary within the context of an unprecedented ubiquity, proximity, and performativity of the moving image, bringing about entirely new regimes of visibility once again. In this sense, it remains as opportune as ever to revisit the models that Broodthaers advanced in his Sisyphean attempt to conceive of a critical cinema emerging out of the cracks between stasis and movement, absence and presence, historicity and immediacy.

CINÉMA MODÈLE (1970-71)

Cinéma modèle marks the first retrospective that Broodthaers dedicated to his own filmmaking. It ran between October 1970 and January 1971 in a basement in Düsseldorf, before it would be transformed into *Section cinéma*. Under the heading of *Cinéma modèle, Programme La Fontaine*, five films were shown that the artist had made by then: *La Clef de l'horloge* (1957), *Le Corbeau et le renard* (1967), *La Pipe* (1969), *La Pluie* (1969), and *Un Film de Charles Baudelaire* (1970).[16] As a retrospective, *Cinéma modèle* not only looked back on Broodthaers's own filmic production but also explicitly involved a series of historical artists and authors whom the abovementioned films were supposedly based on or dedicated to, respectively the German Dadaist Kurt Schwitters, seventeenth-century French fabulist Jean de La Fontaine, renowned Belgian Surrealist René Magritte, and nineteenth-century poet Charles Baudelaire. This practice of attribution signals two important traits that permeate both the artist's visual work and his filmmaking: a predilection for the past and the outdated on the one hand and a keen sense for citation on the other. In addition, *Cinéma modèle* and the five titles included in its film program are exemplary of Broodthaers's entire cinematic output. The themes and topics as well the "stylistic" aspects of *La Clef de l'horloge, Le Corbeau et le renard, La Pipe, La Pluie*, and *Un Film de Charles Baudelaire* reappear in many of his other films. Furthermore, *Cinéma modèle* is not so much a film program of theatrical screenings in the usual sense; it was first and foremost an "exhibition of cinema," thus responding to the notion of a "film installation," a concept that also fits the *Section cinéma* (1972) of his *Musée d'Art Moderne, Département des Aigles* and the various *Décors* of the early 1970s. Because *Cinéma modèle* is so paradigmatic of the themes, forms, and practices of Broodthaers's cinema, its films constitute the framework of this introductory essay.

LA CLEF DE L'HORLOGE: THE ANALYSIS OF PAINTINGS

Broodthaers made his first film, *La Clef de l'horloge (poème cinématographique en l'honneur de Kurt Schwitters)* (The Key to the Clock; Cinematic Poem in Honor of Kurt Schwitters) in 1956–58,[17] about six or seven years before he famously presented himself as a visual artist with *Pense-Bête* (1964). Just as many of his artworks have been interpreted as visual extensions of his literary activities, his films, too, can be considered a continuation of a poetic project by cinematic means. Broodthaers would later state that "film is an extension of language."[18] Sometimes demonstrating an underlying cinematic imaginary, his poems of the 1940s and 1950s almost prefigured his shift to film, creating a kind of "cinepoetry," an attempt, in the words of Christophe Wall-Romana, to conceive poetry through the lens of cinema.[19] This close connection between film and poetry also resonates in the film's subtitle "poème cinématographique"—an ambiguous concept, since it denotes a twofold avant-garde tradition yielding both poetry and films, reaching back to the 1920s.[20]

Shot in 16mm, the seven-minute film is a personal report of the Kurt Schwitters retrospective that took place at the Palais des Beaux Arts in Brussels in the fall of 1956.[21] By means of a series of close-ups and panning shots, Broodthaers scrutinizes various works by Schwitters. Repeatedly adjusting its focus, the camera scans the surfaces, emphasizing the tactile qualities and objecthood of Schwitters's *Merzbilder*. In so doing, *La Clef de l'horloge* is

La Clef de l'horloge (Poème cinématographique en l'honneur de Kurt Schwitters). 16mm. 1957.
© Estate of Marcel Broodthaers, c/o SABAM Belgium 2024

a type of "art documentary," although it hardly seems to answer to the conventions of the genre. Despite its highly idiosyncratic nature, the film can be situated in a tradition of midcentury lyrical art documentaries that were produced in France, Italy, and most notably Belgium during the 1940s, and 1950s.[22] Belgian filmmakers such as Henri Storck and Paul Haesaerts made poetic, reflexive, and experimental films on art, often self-consciously emphasizing the encounter between the original artwork and the film medium. Like the work of Haesaerts and Storck, Broodthaers's debut film employs the capabilities of the cinematic medium to develop a formal analysis, for instance revealing the circles and materials in Schwitters's works. Furthermore, like his midcentury predecessors, Broodthaers does not present his film as a mere duplication of the artworks but precisely makes clear that film transforms or remediates them. There is no doubt that Broodthaers must have been familiar with the films by Storck and Haesaerts, which were screened at the L'Écran du Séminaire des Arts, the film club at the Brussels Palais des Beaux Arts that Broodthaers frequented. While *La Clef de l'horloge* takes the transformative powers of cinema to another level, other Broodthaers film projects were much more indebted to films such as Storck's *Le Monde de Paul Delvaux* (1946) or Haesaerts's *De Renoir à Picasso* (1950). *Bruegel et Goya, journalistes* (1964), for instance, clearly echoes the practices of midcentury lyrical art documentaries. The film was made by photographer Henri Kessels, with Broodthaers writing the scenario (as indicated in the credits) and, according to some sources, a voice-over commentary as well.[23]

To a large extent, however, *La Clef de l'horloge* fails to "document" Schwitters's works. Broodthaers does not offer us a clear view of the artworks, often showing them from an oblique angle, never revealing their frames. Schwitters's works are even turned upside down and shrouded in darkness, only revealed by a flashlight restlessly moving over them as Broodthaers made the film after the opening hours, with the help of the night guard of the Palais des Beaux-Arts. Instead of a regular museum visitor, he rather impersonates a nocturnal intruder, suggesting the uncanny atmosphere of a noir thriller or gothic melodrama, in which haunted portraits are explored with the help of flashlights or flickering candles.[24] In *La Clef de l'horloge* the moving light creates a sense of intrigue, supported by the soundtrack comprising a voice-over commentary that opens the film with brief information on Schwitters and Merz. However, the commentary soon switches to a nonsensical dialogue between a man and a woman, a "love poem" with references to clocks but also to the moon and stars, to his hands on her skin, et cetera.[25]

Revealing objects and surfaces by means of projected light, Broodthaers's film hypostasizes the logics of cinema, occasionally even using negative images, thus turning Schwitters's *Merzbilder* into something immaterial created by moving light. The flashlight's circular shape does not only interact with the circles in Schwitters's work (including a wheel that is actually turning), it also evokes an eye, a staple motif in Surrealism that also marks some of Broodthaers's sculptural installations such as *La Tour visuelle* (1966). First and foremost, Broodthaers's circular light on Schwitters's wheels refers to the interconnected cogs, wheels, and disks of the clock mechanism indicated in the film's title.[26]

It is striking that Broodthaers himself and his critics did not present *La Clef de l'horloge* as the "Opus no. 1" of his career as a visual artist. On the contrary, the film has rather been seen as something that should be situated outside his artistic oeuvre. This is remarkable as the subject of the film, the 1956 Schwitters retrospective in Brussels, can be considered a watershed moment for Broodthaers, marking his shift from Surrealism toward a more "Pop" or Neo-Dada approach to the everyday, as well as his transition from poetry to the visual arts.[27] Furthermore, Broodthaers remained highly interested in Schwitters. He did not only include *La Clef de l'horloge* in the *Cinéma modèle* film program in Düsseldorf in 1970, he also wrote a text for the catalog of a Kurt Schwitters exhibition at Kunsthalle Düsseldorf in 1971.[28]

The importance of *La Clef de l'horloge* for the further development of Broodthaers's career is also indicated by several themes that recur in many of his later works and films. First of all, there is the Dadaist-Surrealist lineage, exemplified here by the *Merzbilder* by Schwitters, favoring everyday objects and detritus—an element that permeates Broodthaers's oeuvre, which is filled with mundane and inexpensive objects such as mussels and egg shells. Second, focusing on artworks, *La Clef de l'horloge* prefigures many if not most of Broodthaers's succeeding films as they take static images (maps, postcards, clippings from newspapers and journals, inscriptions, signage, wax figures, ventriloquist dummies, et cetera) as their subjects. Some of his films also focus on paintings such as *Analyse d'une peinture* (Analysis of a Painting, 1973) featuring an anonymous seascape with a small fleet of fisher boats, probably painted around 1900.[29] The film consists of a montage of scenes showing the basic elements of the painting: the picture itself, a series of its details, its gilded frame, a blank canvas, and a black background. Broodthaers hypostasizes the encounter between painting and film by the conflation between canvas and film screen. The film contains a scene in which the artist rolls up the canvas destined to be painted. This gesture is confounded with the gesture of rolling up the same screen onto which the image has been projected.

The same painting also features in *A Voyage on the North Sea* (1973–74), combining two different depictions of the sea. On the one hand, the film contains color reproductions of the aforementioned oil painting. On the other, *A Voyage on the North Sea* includes black-and-white photographs of a pleasure yacht. The film therefore juxtaposes not only photography with painting but also the twentieth century with the nineteenth, labor with leisure, the real with the fictitious, black-and-white with color, et cetera. Strikingly, in both films, extreme close-ups turn the painting into abstract images reminiscent of Tachisme or modernist monochrome painting. Similarly, blowups of the photographs evoke the grain of their reproduction.

Apart from images of the painting and the photographs, *Voyage on the North Sea* also includes references to page numbers, emphasizing its intermedial dimensions, as the work also exists in the form of a book.[30] The relation between book and film is ambivalent: we can consider the book as a kind of script for the film, while the film can be interpreted as a recording of the book. Furthermore, both manifestations seem to have swapped some of the characteristics of each medium: while the film, which also contains intertitles indicating page numbers, is highly static, the book suggests some kind of movement with the help of the page layout, breaking up the images, recomposing its fragments into a sequence. In doing so, *Voyage on the North Sea*, which is based on a juxtaposition of two different images in itself, precisely meditates on the relations and transformations between different media as well as on the role of mechanical reproductions. It is in this perspective that Rosalind Krauss, in her 1999 book *A Voyage on the North Sea*, presented Broodthaers as the ultimate embodiment of a "post-medium" condition, dismissing the pursuit of medium specificity so cherished by modernist art.[31] Conflating painting, photography, illustrated book, and film, Broodthaers does not aspire to reach the essence of the mediums he employs—certainly not that of film, which he considered a

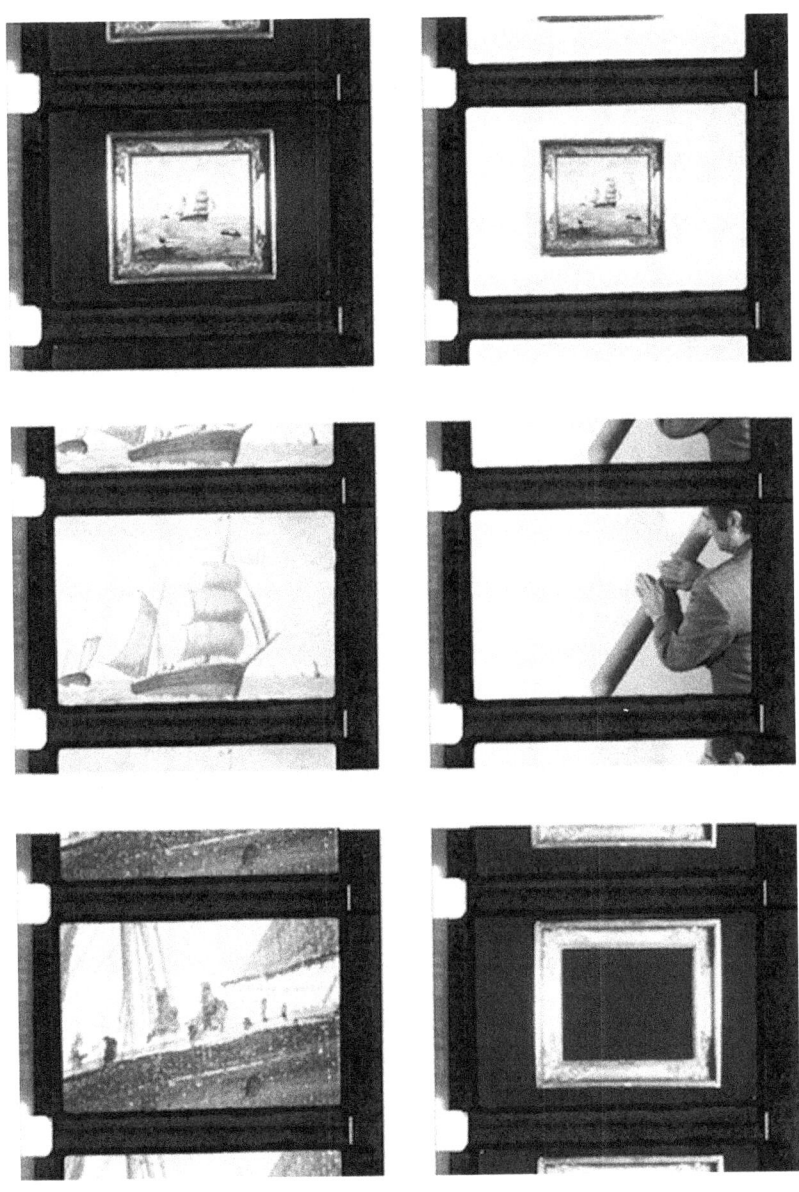

Analyse d'une peinture. 16mm. 1973. © Estate of Marcel Broodthaers, c/o SABAM Belgium 2024

Material related to *A Voyage on the North Sea*. 16mm. 1973-74. Photo Rachel Gruijters. Collection Ivo and Monique Van Vaerenbergh. Photo Rachel Gruijters. © Estate of Marcel Broodthaers, c/o SABAM Belgium 2024

heterogenous or impure medium from its inception. Paradoxically, he touches upon the essence of the media involved by combining and juxtaposing them. His extreme close-ups draw our attention to the materiality of the paint and to the brush strokes in the painting, so cherished by previous generations of artists. The "essence" of painting is thus revealed by means of the powers of cinema (in the film) or those of photography and mechanical printing (in case of the book and the film).

What's more, with these images of ships at sea, Broodthaers also touches upon the alleged "essences" of the film medium, as the sea and water surfaces are veritably "cinematic" motifs, which were cherished by early filmmakers and French avant-garde film of the 1920s. In the eyes of filmmakers such as Henri Chomette or Jean Epstein, water, with its endless and unpredictable combination of unexpected rhythms and ever-changing light reflections, answered to their conception of the *photogénie* as it was something that only the medium of film could represent. Broodthaers himself tackled the "impressionist" fascination for moving, capricious, fleeting, and ephemeral motifs such as water or smoke in films such as *La Pipe* (The Pipe) (1969) and *La Pluie*.

In *Voyage on the North Sea*, Broodthaers did not film the sea, however, but a painted and photographic representation of it. The moving image of cinema was thus used to evoke not movement but stasis instead. While *La Clef de l'horloge* brings the painting of Schwitters to life with its restless moving lights, camera movements, and rhythmic montage, *A Voyage on the North Sea* underscores a (potential) movement that is halted or frozen. It is also telling that Broodthaers did not use the opportunity to show us the act of browsing through the book, for instance. On the contrary, the inserts with page numbers avoid continuity and halt any cinematic flow. Given this perspective, many of Broodthaers's films, despite their highly idiosyncratic qualities, tally with so many avant-garde films of the 1960s, including those of Andy Warhol, Michael Snow, Hollis Frampton, and many Fluxus artists, which arrest images for prolonged periods of time.[32] The only movement used in *Voyage on the North Sea* is the extension of the film itself in time. In so doing, *Voyage on the North Sea* is also the key of a clock, a "clef de l'horloge."

However, there are also important differences between *La Clef de l'horloge* and Broodthaers's succeeding films dealing with artworks. Emphasizing the mobility of cinema by its encounter with a static medium, *La Clef de l'horloge* embraces the dynamics of cinema with its restlessly moving search light, rhythmic montage, and actual on-camera mobility (such as a turning wheel). In addition, the film uses some striking camera movements, though the majority of shots are taken with a static camera. Many of Broodthaers's succeeding films are also made with a static camera, but in contrast to the restless mobility and speed that characterize *La Clef de l'horloge*, they are marked by a slow editing rhythm, emphasizing rather than neglecting the static qualities of the source images.

La Clef de l'horloge is also an exemplary Broodthaers work as it deals with time in the historical sense. According to Benjamin Buchloh, the film provides a "sign of what would come" insofar as the film is underpinned by the "construction of a dialectical space between the cultural practices of the present and those of the past."[33] Broodthaers's take on Schwitters tallies with this aspect. Schwitters (who died in 1948 and worked until the end of his life) can be considered a "contemporary" artist for Broodthaers, who made this film in 1956–58. However, in his later years, Schwitters was often repairing or re-creating his prewar Merz constructions, rearticulating or reinterpreting his radical works from the Weimar period. Furthermore, the creation of *La Clef de l'horloge* coincided with the rediscovery of Schwitters's earlier collages with proto–pop mass media images by younger artists such as Eduardo Paolozzi and Robert Rauschenberg. Schwitters was thus an artist of the past and Broodthaers, instead of merely paying homage (despite the film's subheading), rather proposes a speculative, cinematic reenactment of the artistic and literary "model" developed by Schwitters. Looking back to his 1956–58 film, Broodthaers stated in the early 1970s that for him, the banal objects in Schwitters's collages and assemblages "were like superb stars when in fact they are bits of wood, rags, and old bus tickets. [...] For the people of my father's generation, the objects played the servile role of dashes of color or brushstrokes intended to strengthen the composition. While for me, too, the object was divested of its character, it thereby became the sign of a spoken lyricism."[34]

Though he subtitled his film "homage," it was clear for Broodthaers that Schwitters's art could not be "represented" or "reproduced" but needed to be rearticulated through the means of cinema. In line with Surrealism's fascination with the obsolete and outmoded, Broodthaers invoked cinema as a means to preserve things of the past or as a tool to construct a counterhistory, revealing the utopian potentials of past moments.

UN FILM DE CHARLES BAUDELAIRE: BROODTHAERS AND COUNTERMEMORY

In *Camera Lucida*, Roland Barthes famously recalled how cinema's earliest beginnings had roots in the "techniques of cabinetmaking and the machinery of precision." No doubt thinking about Étienne-Jules Marey and Edward Muybridge's chrono-photography, he argued that "cameras were essentially clocks for seeing."[35] Broodthaers too insisted on the static essence of the cinematic image and would many times probe into the precinematic nebula from which the filmic medium would eventually consolidate near the end of the nineteenth century. In the abovementioned picture taken by Joaquín Romera Frías, Broodthaers, dressed up as Fantômas, holds up a copy of Sadoul's *L'Invention du cinéma* while releasing a whisp of smoke from the corner of his mouth. Despite what the book's title suggests, the first volume of Sadoul's renowned *Histoire générale du cinéma* does not start but ends with the invention of cinema, discussing the plethora of devices and spectacles that preceded it. Throughout his career, Broodthaers revisited the composite sphere of the pre- and early cinema era as it allowed him to perceive of and speculate on an alternative history of the medium that remained hidden from view by the integral and absorptive logic of the classical cinematic apparatus. He would likely agree with Barthes's view of photography, and thus cinema in an extended sense, as an amnesic rather than mnemonic medium, as such qualifying as a "counter-memory."[36] About a decade earlier, in 1971, Michel Foucault had conceptualized the latter term as "a use of history that severs its connection to memory, its metaphysical and anthropological model."[37] However, rather than an erasure of memory altogether, his notion of a countermemory implied a critical practice seeking above all to challenge the teleological or normative frameworks of "monumental history" through parody, dissociation, or outright sacrilege, in order to transform it into a "totally different form of time."[38] Touched upon earlier by Buchloh and de Bruyn, this conception of a "countermemory" allows for the fathoming of the often-anomalous temporality of Broodthaers's cinema and the historical speculations it repeatedly stages.

As mentioned above, *La Clef de l'horloge* acquires its prognostic dimension regarding Broodthaers's subsequent filmmaking due to its anachronistic cinematography and recourse to citation, among other things. This raises the important question of whether Broodthaers sought to draw a connection between these two, or to put it differently: Was *La Clef de l'horloge* made with the aim of creating an "imaginary film relic," *as if* Schwitters had operated the camera and cut the film himself?[39] This issue becomes even more complicated when considering a film that was supposedly made before the very birth of cinema, at least if its title is taken at face value: *Un Film de Charles Baudelaire* (A Film by Charles Baudelaire) (1970). About the latter, Broodthaers expressed himself as follows:

> *Un Film de Charles Baudelaire* is not a film for cinephiles. Why not? Because it was shot in the nineteenth century. And because the cinephiles have never seen reels dating from the time when Muybridge, the Lumière brothers, and Edison were still unborn or were taking their first steps under the watchful eyes of their industrialist mamas and papas.[40]

According to Trevor Stark, *Un Film de Charles Baudelaire* "has the merit of almost being technically possible to have been produced in the 1850s as a magic lantern show."[41] Although Broodthaers seldom emulated the camera and editing techniques of early cinema in a literal way, many of his films evoke the atmosphere of what Tom Gunning called the "cinema of attractions" of the 1895–1907 era as well as cinema's prehistory, a kind of proto-cinema akin to magic lantern shows and phenakistiscopes, which makes "Un Film de Charles Baudelaire" a quite plausible and a less anachronistic idea.[42] Apparently made under the influence of a line taken from Baudelaire's poem *La Beauté* (Beauty)—"I hate the movement that shifts the lines"—the film, in Stark's view, empathically "stalls the affordances of technologies of the image."[43] Dispensing with the moving image altogether, *Un Film de Charles Baudelaire* basically consists of black leader, alternated with still images and close-ups of a contemporary (i.e., twentieth-century) world map. In so doing, the film is both thematically and formally in line with many of Broodthaers's other works. For instance, it features a map, an object appearing frequently in his oeuvre, but first and foremost a subject that is immobile and "uncinematic," like the paintings or inscriptions that also persistently feature in his (filmic) work. Furthermore, it deals with a maritime voyage, another Broodthaersian topic, evoking nineteenth-century colonial expansion and the lure of exotic adventure that he addressed in works featuring palms and exotic animals.

 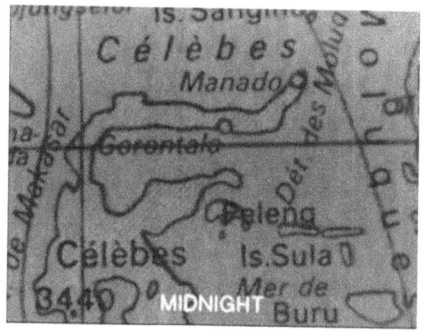

Un film de Charles Baudelaire (English version). 16/35mm. 1970.
Courtesy of the Walker Art Center's Ruben/Bentson Moving Image Collection.
© Estate of Marcel Broodthaers, c/o SABAM Belgium 2024

Broodthaers made two versions of the film in 1970. Next to an English one, a French version exists that was supposedly never shown during Broodthaers's lifetime. Except for the language of their subtitles, the films differ as to the words themselves appearing in them. The English version reels off a sequence of seemingly random dates running between January 3 and December 17, 1850, at regular intervals, before displaying them in reverse order until March 31. Interspersed with these dates are a series of ominous, single words reminiscent of adventure novels: "knife," "scurvy," "shark," "torment," et cetera. Combined with the synced sequence of images of the world map, *Un Film de Charles Baudelaire* evokes the idea of a dispersed "travel diary." In keeping with the film's title, it is usually interpreted as a fictional travelogue of the voyage that Baudelaire embarked upon when he was sent off to Calcutta aboard of an ocean liner by his stepfather in an attempt to put an end to his debauched lifestyle. The reluctant traveler, however, refused to go further than Mauritius and the Île de Bourbon (Réunion) before returning to France. Strikingly, Baudelaire's voyage to the Indian Ocean took place between June 1841 and February 1842, nine years prior to the dates indicated in Broodthaers's film.[44] The film thus rather evokes the idea that Baudelaire made a film in memory of his voyage. Apart from the dates, the geography also does not match Baudelaire's biography. An overall view of the world map is followed by details, one of them showing Europe and another one only the sea without landmass within the lines of longitudes and latitudes and the inscription "Equateur," which Baudelaire actually crossed in the Atlantic Ocean before reaching the African coast. Other close-ups of the map show us Celebes (in Indonesia) and the Chilean island of Sala y Gómez, regions that Baudelaire never visited but which were apparently incorporated in his filmic recollection of his voyage.

For Broodthaers, Baudelaire is one of various nineteenth-century artists (Grandville, Mallarmé, et cetera) coming to terms with the conditions of industrial modernity. A "poète maudit" who presented the industrial metropolis as a suitable subject for lyrical poetry, Baudelaire conflated timeless ideas on beauty and remnants of the Romantic Sublime with the banal aspects (from gas lamps to asphalt) of modernity, which he famously defined as "le transitoire, le fugitif, le contingent, la moitié de l'art, dont l'autre moitié est l'éternel et l'immuable."[45] *Un Film de Charles Baudelaire*, tellingly, avoids the transitory, fugitive, and contingent, fixing ephemeral memories of voyages into immobile images of a static map. Jean-Christophe Royoux has suggested that Broodthaers's fascination with immobility, and the dialectic between movement and stasis that underpins his cinema in general, took Baudelaire's aesthetics as a "model."[46] For *La Beauté* points out that beauty, personified as a statue addressing the reader of the poem like an "unguessed sphinx," is "mute and noble as matter itself."[47]

Broodthaers's take on Baudelaire can be compared with the ideas of Walter Benjamin, who presented Baudelaire as the modern artist par excellence, a flâneur fully immersed in the intoxication of the modern metropolis organized according to the logics of consumer capitalism on the one hand, while keeping an aesthetic distance at all times on the other.[48] Although there is no indication that Broodthaers elaborately read and studied Walter Benjamin (he referred to Benjamin only once in a 1975 interview published after his death),[49] particularly since Benjamin's writings only resurfaced from the late 1970s onward with only a small corpus of texts available in French and English, his entire oeuvre seems a perfect illustration of Benjamin's ideas on the phantasmagoria of industrial capitalism with its plethora of devices of visual display. Broodthaers also evokes Benjamin with his outspoken interest in the development of techniques of mechanical reproduction that destroyed or at least redefined the "aura" of works of art. Broodthaers's "Benjaminian" fascination for the nineteenth century and its visual culture encompassing zoos, museums, waxworks, worlds' fairs, Épinal prints, magic lanterns, shadow plays, photography, and film also inspired a whole strand of scholars, including Benjamin Buchloh, Douglas Crimp, and Rosalind Krauss, among others, to employ Benjamin as a convenient and successful methodological framework to study Broodthaers's oeuvre in general as well as specific projects.

While Broodthaers's knowledge of Benjamin's writings was rather limited, he was certainly aware of György Lukács's notion of reification, particularly through the writings and lectures of Marxist philosopher Lucien Goldmann, a Lukács disciple who was best known for his sociology of literature. In 1969–70, Broodthaers attended Goldmann's seminar on Baudelaire at the University of Brussels and the French version of his Baudelaire film was Broodthaers's contribution to this seminar—the equivalent of a written thesis.[50] Goldmann's "structural genetic" approach consisted in identifying a series of essential oppositions underpinning Baudelaire's poetry that could ultimately be traced back to the "double déchirure" (double tear) represented by the insurmountable gap between a fundamentally insufficient *here* and an unattainable, idealized *elsewhere* cast in both spatial and temporal terms.[51] Lukács's notion of "transcendental homelessness," which implies a nostalgia for utopian perfection, clearly resonates with this empathically melancholic worldview. His fierce criticism of naturalism, which he extended to the realm of the "new industry" of photography, could also be derived from it: "I consider it useless and tedious to represent what *exists*, because nothing that *exists* satisfies me. Nature is ugly, and I prefer the monsters of my fantasy to what is positively trivial."[52] This kind of hostility appears to resurface in Broodthaers's early stance on cinema, as expressed in the 1958 note "Ma mémoire est un film en couleur" (My Memory Is a Film in Color):

> My memory is a film in color, one that is technically superior to commercial films. I have yet to see a color on film with tones vivid and rich enough to compare with mine. So I go to the cinema when I feel like it, but this cinematographic facileness rather bores me.[53]

It could be asked, then, to what extent the anachronism and stasis that permeate Broodthaers's films should be read as the seals of a distinct anti-cinema. However, "an anti-film is still film,"[54] according to Broodthaers. Like the artist, we are left to speculate about Baudelaire's position on cinema, leaving room for accounts that at least nuance the author's assumed animosity toward the filmic medium as a further corruption of art under the aegis of the "exact reproduction of nature." For according to Christophe Wall-Romana, Baudelaire "contributed to reveal a precinematic imaginary," as he "sought a new integration of the Romantic imagination with vision and the material image via specific sensorimotor experiences."[55] Heralding the literary practices that Wall-Romana has subsumed under the banner of *cinepoetry*, Baudelaire conceived of an imagination capable of making static images move, as such introducing the idea of a cinema of the mind.

Significantly, one of Broodthaers's earliest poems, titled "Projet pour un film" (Project for a Film, 1948), published about a decade before his first "actual" film was shot, appears to stem from exactly this kind of cinema-infused imaginary, painting the picture as an "immobile landscape" that is suddenly animated by a fly penetrating it.[56] In keeping with Wall-Romana's interpretation of cinepoetry, it can be considered a text "written from the purview of or as a treatment of an imaginary movie."[57] The years between "Projet pour un film" and *Un Film de Charles Baudelaire* would see the emergence of a handful of similar, unpublished (prose) texts testifying to a cinema-informed imaginary, which may (implicitly) be informed by Baudelaire's "model" of an "imaginary cinema." Although it is certainly incorrect to cast Broodthaers's oeuvre as essentially post-Surrealist, early poems such as "Projet pour un film" can nevertheless be situated in a Surrealist tradition that reveled in such "cinepoetic" experiments. Wall-Romana has shown how André Breton quickly sought to co-opt cinepoetry as a literary practice channeling a whole generation's enchantment with the filmic medium.[58] Since Guillaume Apollinaire, who coined the term "surrealism" in 1917, famously stated that "the epic poet shall express himself with the cinema," an assertion that was soon followed by the first explicit cinepoem, *Indifférence, Poème cinématographique* (1918) by Philippe Soupault, numerous authors empathically embraced cinepoetic writing, some of whom would later become affiliated with Surrealism.[59] During the interwar years, cinepoetry not only flourished in France but also came to fruition in Belgian Surrealist circles, albeit to a more limited extent. Mainly virtual scenarios by authors such as Fernand Dumont, Irène Hamoir, Eric de Haulleville, Henri Storck, or even Magritte survive. In 1965 Broodthaers further contributed to the subgenre of the virtual scenario with *Évolution ou L'Œuf film* (Evolution or The Egg Film).

However, as Royoux has noted, Baudelaire's preoccupation with immobility also expresses the desire to "escape from the sensation of time, and its social conception,"[60] reified time, in other words, which has taken shape according to the needs of the emerging industrial society. According to de Bruyn, *Un Film de Charles Baudelaire* should be read in this vein. He describes how it was screened at *Prospekt 71: Projection* in the Düsseldorf Kunsthalle, a group show dedicated to art's encounter with the media of technical reproduction: photography, slides, film, and video. The exhibition, which included works by Hanne Darboven, Gilbert & George, Dan Graham, David Lamelas, and Tony Morgan among many others, hailed film (and video) as "a transparent support for the artist's message," thus establishing what de Bruyn identifies as the "the model of 'conceptual film.'"[61] Needless to say, Broodthaers's cinema was completely at odds with this model. In a 1969 text titled "Projet pour un texte," in which he lines up the (im)possible avenues for a future cinema no longer "defined as a discipline of movement," his critique of Conceptualism's instrumentalization of cinema reads as follows:

in certain kinds of Conceptual Art, the film is often a banal intermediary in which the idea plays the main role of subject. But is not the subject diminished by this flatness in the style of transmission, if not absorbed and relegated to a documentary on received ideas that is sometimes original?[62]

Un Film de Charles Baudelaire may be said to criticize Conceptualism's naïve and reductionist belief in objectified, transparent language by its deliberate hermeticism and the suggestive aura of its subtitles. The *détournement* to which Broodthaers subjects the device of the subtitle, a recurrent feature in the films that appeared in the immediate wake of *Un Film de Charles Baudelaire*, has been described by Rachel Haidu as a "disruption of verbocentrism," as the artist uses text to "implant doubt, confusion and uncertainty where language is usually used to erect standards of referentiality, veracity, and objectivity."[63]

In *Un Film de Charles Baudelaire*, the words in the subtitle section probably call on multiple sources within Broodthaers's "archive." As an arcane intertextual reference, they are reminiscent of Edgar Allan Poe's *Narrative of Arthur Gordon Pym of Nantucket* (1838), which Baudelaire translated to French in 1858, a connection pointed out by Stark and supported by the notes from the American art critic Barbara Reise belonging to Broodthaers's inner circle in London. However, most of all *Un film de Charles Baudelaire*'s puzzling subtitles seem to draw on Broodthaers's own poetic universe, which is a priori of a highly intertextual nature. Belonging to a vast repertory that was subjected to a constant process of rewriting, reassembly, and reuse, the words in the film's subtitles can be traced back all the way to some poems written both before and after his entry into the artworld;[64] they would also resurface in other "constellations" several years later. Severed from these literary contexts, they "shine like *solitaires*,"[65] not only in *Un Film de Charles Baudelaire* but also in the second open letter that Broodthaers published on June 27, 1968, and in *Académie I* and *II*, the first works in a series of thirty-six vacuum-formed plates, the so-called *Industrial Poems* or *Plaques*, which the artist produced between 1968 and 1972.[66] *Académie I* and *II* basically present a text divided into three paragraphs, the middle one reading as follows:

> Silence. The species marches on with chattering eyes. A green cube. A blue sphere. A white pyramid. A black cylinder. Like dreams you can hardly remember; worlds where shark, knife, cook are synonyms. A black cube. A black pyramid.[67]

If this stanza enfolds a tongue-in-cheek criticism of the reductionist aesthetics of Minimal and Conceptual Art, as characterized by primary forms and objective language, *Un Film de Charles Baudelaire*, then, can be read as a countermove against the reductionist approaches of cinema that are associated with these movements. This is even more obvious, given that in the French version of the film, most of the words are replaced by exactly the geometrical figures mentioned, while serial numbers appear instead of the dates, ascending from 000000 to 90000, before counting down again.

According to de Bruyn, it was mostly the "spectacular corrosion of historical memory" advocated by the "literalist" phenomenologies of Minimal and Conceptual Art that represented the main target of *Un Film de Charles Baudelaire* and perhaps in much of Broodthaers's cinema in general.[68] *Un Film de Charles Baudelaire* "pits the reversibility of a fully reified time—the abstract chronology of a clock or calendar—against the forgetfulness of an existence locked in a perpetual present."[69] According to this vision, the construction of a countermemory implies not so much saving specific (literary) legacies from oblivion but rather rescuing historicity itself. As *Un Film de Charles Baudelaire*'s silence is only broken by a clock striking twelve times and the ticking of a metronome, Broodthaers appears to remind the film's viewers of the imperative expressed in Baudelaire's poem titled "The Clock": "Impressive clock! Terrifying, sinister God, whose finger threatens us and says: *"Remember!"*[70]

As Broodthaers was well aware of, the latter also functions as the credo of the museum. Two years before *Un Film de Charles Baudelaire* was shot, Broodthaers initiated *Musée d'Art Moderne. Département des Aigles*, a fictional museum that knew twelve instalments between 1968 and 1972 and which is widely considered to represent one of the highlights of Institutional Critique. *Un Film de Charles Baudelaire* also appears to be linked to this critical endeavor, as one of the shots features the gilded inscription "Musée-Museum" against a black background and the words "Enfants non admis" (Children not allowed) are audible on the soundtrack. Just as Broodthaers envisioned how Baudelaire should have made a film, museums rearticulate, reconceptualize, and create memories and histories rather than simply preserving them, which implies that the construction of "countermemories" or fictional travelogs, like *Un Film de Charles Baudelaire*, can be complemented by a "counter-museums," an avenue that Broodthaers would develop in depth with *Section cinéma* (1971–72).

LA PIPE: MAGRITTE'S SMOKE SCREEN

Looking back on his itinerary through the art world in 1974, Broodthaers revealed that it was René Magritte's pipe that instigated his "adventure."[71] As a filmmaker too, Broodthaers referred to Magritte's icon, with several versions of a film featuring a pipe made between 1969 and 1972. As *La Trahison des images* (1928–29)—"Ceci n'est pas une pipe" (This is not a pipe)—is not only considered Magritte's most renowned painting but also as one of the very icons of Surrealism, Broodthaers's reference to it raises the question about his relationship with Surrealism, which had been important and fruitful in Belgium during the interwar period but remained also highly influential in the first decades following the Second World War. Although he publicly distanced himself from Surrealism, his stance was certainly more ambiguous than the oppositional model that is commonly put forward in this respect. Although his artistic, literary, and cinephile cradle stood at the center of the Belgian Surrealist avant-garde, "a house with many rooms" as Xavier Canonne aptly put it, Broodthaers ever remained at the fringe of the movement.[72] Nevertheless, his visual and filmic oeuvre betray an underlying Surrealist legacy that can hardly be dismissed, were it only for the fact of some obvious Surrealist tropes that occasionally surface in his work under various guises, of which his reference to Magritte's *Trahison des images* represents the most obvious example.

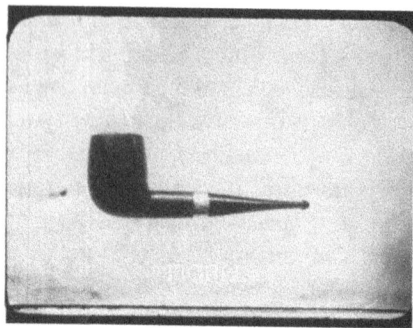

La Pipe (Figure blanche). 16/35mm. 1969-71. Courtesy of the Walker Art Center's Ruben/Bentson Moving Image Collection. © Estate of Marcel Broodthaers, c/o SABAM Belgium 2024

Although he and Magritte would only sporadically meet, mostly during the 1960s, Broodthaers appears to demonstrate the latter's seminal influence on his work through numerous citations in which the figure of the pipe plays a central role. In keeping with Baudelaire's eponymous poem, in which the pipe belongs to and may be said to represent an author, Broodthaers used the figure of the pipe to cast Magritte as a "man of letters,"[73] rather than a painter. Shortly after Magritte's passing in 1967, the iconic pipe would occur in various forms in Broodthaers's work, most notably in a series of *Plaques* made between 1968 and 1970,[74] and in the film *La Pipe* (The Pipe), of which several versions were produced between 1969 and 1972. Essentially representing a transposition of the motif from painting to the indexical medium of cinema, the film consists of a succession of static shots showing an actual pipe against the background of a whitewashed brick wall, both enveloped in and releasing clouds of smoke. This image is supplemented by sequences showing a clock and the (empty) background wall. In *La Pipe satire* (1969), another spinoff of the *La Pipe* corpus, the smoking pipe is shown sitting in the pubic region of a naked woman, while Broodthaers himself enters the picture wearing a Fantômas mask once again, while playing the accordion. As such, this version exactly conveys the amateurish ambiance and burlesque comedy of the numerous farcical shorts that Magritte himself would shoot with his wife and Surrealist associates at his home during the 1950s and '60s, as mentioned in Bruce Jenkins's essay in this volume.[75] In this quality, *La Pipe satire* may qualify as the most Surrealist title of Broodthaers's entire filmography. Although some of his films unmistakably feature some of the common traits of what has come to be seen as "Surrealist cinema," such as sound-image disjunctions, slapstick gags, or narrative incongruities, Broodthaers's cinema by no means fits the label "Surrealist" formally, thematically, or historically speaking. In Broodthaers's cinematic oeuvre, for instance, we cannot find any dream narratives or mythopoetic associations, supported by associative montages or shocking disjunctions. *La Pipe* too, despite its literal representation of one of the movement's hallmarks, should not be read as a mere homage to or recovery of Surrealism.

On the contrary, Broodthaers's reception of Magritte's pipe represents a strategy to advance an alternative "model" of Magritte, which, according to Broodthaers, risks becoming obscured by the latter's canonization as a Surrealist painter, well underway at that time. Thus, *La Pipe* too presents a countermemory by filmic means. Similar to how *La Clef de l'horloge* sought to reanimate Schwitter's poetry of "instability, fragility, and menace" in defiance of the emerging formalistic and critically sterile reception of his work,[76] *La Pipe* may be said to rescue Magritte's poetic subversiveness against a consolidation of his oeuvre in mere aesthetical terms or within the popularized imagery of historical Surrealism.[77] In an open letter published in 1968, Broodthaers wrote, "I saw the curtain, woven by the Surrealists and which hides the topical value of his work, open before my eyes."[78] Thus, on the one hand, he believed that "Ceci n'est pas une pipe" differentiated Magritte's intellectual approach from the caprices of his Surrealist fellows. On the other hand, however, the "topical quality" that Broodthaers assigned to his work suggests that his "rediscovery of Magritte," as expressed by *La Pipe*, was also prompted by certain developments on the contemporaneous artistic scene.

Interestingly, Broodthaers appears to have revisited Magritte's legacy at pivotal moments throughout his artistic development. In turn, the content of his reception of Magritte seems directly related to the artistic context of his practice, as Marie-Pascale Gildemyn has pointed out.[79] Emphasizing the precedence of Magritte's imagery of vernacular and often oversized objects to the iconography of artists like George Segal, Claes Oldenburg, or Jim Dine, Broodthaers fashioned him as the unlikely and involuntary precursor of Pop Art and Nouveau Réalisme, significantly around the time when he ventured into the art world himself, exactly by appropriating their vocabulary.[80] A few years later, the reception of *La Trahison des images* heralded a new "topical value" against the backdrop of the combined emergence of Conceptual Art and the spread of (Post)-Structuralism and Semiotics.

Whereas the advent of Pop and Nouveau Réalisme had moved Broodthaers to shift his artistic endeavors toward the domain of visual arts, the renewed critical interest in language, linguistics, and literature may have rekindled his original vocation as a "man of letters," steering his practice into new directions, which involved a critical engagement with the above tendencies on the one hand and the reintroduction of the material signifier into his work on the other, as illustrated by the emergence of the *Industrial Poems* or some post-1967 films, such as *Le Corbeau et le renard, Un Film de Charles Baudelaire,* or several of his so-called Postcard films (discussed in the chapter written by Deborah Schultz). Within this context, Broodthaers revisited Magritte and *La Trahison des Images*, not only as a "model" for his own language-oriented practice but as a "countermodel" against Conceptual Art's complacent claims concerning "language as art," or "Art as idea as idea," as Joseph Kosuth would have it.

Allegedly, it was Magritte who inspired André Breton and Paul Éluard in 1936 to posit that "poetry is a pipe" as a sardonic response to Paul Valéry's designation of poetry as "a relic."[81] If the "pipe principle" is truly elevated to a full-fledged *Ars Poetica*, then poetry is essentially conceived as a radical negation of the contingent ties between word, image, and object; the subsequent "debacle of the intellect" (as Breton and Éluard would have it)[82] leaving the signifier as a merely tautological residue, as an empty shell. In a 1968 unpublished manuscript, Broodthaers appeared to subscribe to this "model" by situating Magritte "at the origin of an art that plays on the ambiguity of the image and its representation—on the signifier and signified."[83] This statement could indeed be read as a cursory account of *La Trahison des images*. For the same reason, Magritte's painting appeared on the radar of (post)structurualism, which Broodthaers was also aware of. "At [this] time," he wrote, "it was not merely fashionable to refer to the relations between the signifier and the signified, but moreover, these still had a few surprises in stock."[84] In 1968, Michel Foucault published the essay "Ceci n'est pas une pipe," in which the author pursued a minute analysis of the nature of Magritte's subversive strategy underpinning *La Trahison des images*. Without delving into the specifics of his argument, we can say that Foucault concluded that Magritte thoroughly disturbed affirmative discourse and its corollary (historical) regime of "resemblance" by multiplying "similitudes" that undercut the latter's hierarchy as they "circulate the simulacrum as an indefinite and reversible relation of the similar to the similar."[85]

This play with the arbitrariness of the sign would turn out to be a major takeaway for Broodthaers, who was also aware of Foucault's "Ceci n'est pas une pipe" and envisaged a (never achieved) critical edition of it, replete with his proper commentaries, published under the auspices of the Literary Section of the *Musée d'Art Moderne* between 1969 and 1972.[86] At the same time, Broodthaers reworked *La Pipe* by adding subtitles to it: "Figure I," "Figure II," "Figure III," and "Figures" in *Ceci ne serait pas une pipe* (1969–71) and "Gestalt," "Abbildung," "Figur," and "Bild" in *La Pipe (Gestalt, Abbilding, Figur, Bild)* (1969–72). In addition to the mentioned films, the "figure" or "fig.," as a familiar referential token within a didactic system, made a marked appearance in many of Broodthaers's books, *Plaques*, slide projections, ensembles, other films, and drawings from 1966 through his last works, peaking at the turn of the 1960s and '70s.[87] Since the "Fig." signs often occur in tandem with the image of a pipe (and the motif of smoke), not only in *Ceci ne serait pas une pipe* but also in *Industrial Poems* such as *Livre tableau ou Pipes et forms académiques* as well as in *Section cinéma* (as we will see), it is evident that Broodthaers took his cue from *La Trahison des images*' undercutting of linguistic codes to set up an arbitrary, and thus entirely self-referential system of "figures." Offering a *détournement* of an established discursive order, Broodthaers's "Fig." sign can be considered a textual equivalent of Magritte's pipe, making use of the same "literalism," as Foucault would have it. Undermining referentiality and upsetting the viewer, pipe and "fig." function as empty or floating signifiers, no longer able to maintain their grip on meaning.

Additionally, the "Figures," like the pipe, are conceived as the emblems of a critique against any reductionist and idealist metaphysics/phenomenology in general, and those advocated by Conceptual and Minimal Art in particular. As Broodthaers described it, "There remains the linguistic matrix (a play on the very concept of container and content) which will be recorded as a hypocritical lamentation about the destruction of the object by linguistics and at the same time as an attempt to achieve a relationship between the figure as visual representation of a form an the figure as representation of language."[88] The strategies of negation that Broodthaers pursued through pipe and "figure" ultimately appear to restage the romantic *pipe dream* of a pure, unmediated, and *objective* experience of reality, untainted by any category. Broodthaers acknowledged around the same time that it was a quite similar utopian aura, "redolent of the mystery of attics," that he sought to recover from Schwitters's oeuvre in *La Clef de l'horloge*, which, moreover, appears to underpin a neo-romantic poetics: "The contradiction we find in Schwitters's works between the universe of fantasy and that of mathematical rigor undoubtedly opens the door to poetic interpretations."[89]

The poetic principle, in other words, appears to reside within the fold between cognition and perception, or the imaginary and symbolic order, to put it in Lacanian terms.[90] Upon closer investigation, this gap is thematized in many of Broodthaers's films produced between the end of the 1960s and the beginning of the 1970s. For instance, all the titles comprised in *Cinéma Modèle* can be said to revolve to some extent around the tension between unruly, amorphous substances and subjective experience on the one hand and deficient categories trying to harness these on the other. In *La Pipe*, the pipe is shown to be unable to contain the smoke threatening to obscure it from view altogether. It is the smoke that brings the image of the pipe into a physical or sensory reality in contrast with the pictorial space of Magritte's *La Trahison des images* or the pipe-shaped signs in the *Plaques*. In addition, the smoke adds texture to the image as well as cinematic depth. Furthermore, it conveniently obscures the cuts between the shots while also giving an ethereal and even ghostly presence to the pipe and the Fantômas figure. Like the motif of water that features in several of Broodthaers's other films, the smoke presents itself as an ephemeral and therefore a veritably "cinematic" substance—something that can only be represented by the medium of cinema, which is capable of registering its constantly morphing appearances. As smoke is seen to blanket the clock as well, it appears as a metaphor for time eluding the reified logic imposed by the latter. As we have seen, *Un Film de Charles Baudelaire* also thematizes the incongruity between the subjective experience of space and time and the measuring systems conceived to mold it according to the interests of the industrial society.

As Thomas McEvilley has argued, "the idea of language's control over reality was a prominent theme in the 1960s and 70s" conveyed by numerous artistic practices and theoretical discourses.[91] Careful not to reproduce the lingo of the "totally administered world," a specter which some conceptual practices ended up affirming, Broodthaers marshalled Magritte's "model." In so doing, he not only sought to tap into a legacy that gained currency within a specific theoretical context but also rekindled its anarchic import, which should not be lost from sight. In their subversion of didactics, films such as *La Pipe* and *Le Corbeau et le renard* definitely target authoritative speech too. This strategy also goes to the heart of *Au-delà de cette limite* (Across This Border) (1971). As Charlotte Friling points out in her essay, the film questions the invisible, yet performative borders that are set in place by an administrative, impersonal discursive order. Subsequently, this "speculation on the borders of the gallery and of society" was extended within the confines of the gallery space. As such, Broodthaers pits a "poetic violence" against institutional and authoritative violence.

However, the "age of drifting signifiers" that he sought to come terms with had long been underway, even at the time of *La Trahison des images*. Quoting Jean-Joseph Goux, Cathérine David has shown how "the rupture between sign and thing at the end of the nineteenth century" was part of a global collapse of the "values regulating [not only] linguistic, [but also] economic and symbolic exchange."[92] Along came a *crisis of verse* too, of which the poetic oeuvre of French symbolist author Stéphane Mallarmé may be said to represent the very pinnacle. It is no coincidence that Broodthaers's reappraisal of Magritte's *La Trahison des images* coincided with the rediscovery of Stéphane Mallarmé's *Igitur* and *Un Coup de dés jamais n'abolira le hasard* (A Throw of the Dice Will Never Abolish Chance), his famous 1897 poem with an unusual typographic layout that Broodthaers allegedly received from Magritte around 1945–46.[93] It is clear from a 1969 interview that Broodthaers considered Magritte not only as a practical but also as an intellectual intermediary of the "model" of Mallarmé. Moreover, Broodthaers underscored Magritte's reception of Mallarmé in a strategic attempt to distinguish him from mainstream Surrealism:

Look, the poetic model of Magritte was Mallarmé and Mallarmé has never been the poetic model of the Surrealists. This was rather Rimbaud or Lautréamont, but it was not Mallarmé. It was not this kind of cold reason that guided a sentimental endeavor. For Magritte, it was about analyzing the poetic relationships between objects, or throughout them with a new method. This is much more a learned approach than a naïve by the way.[94]

Broodthaers's reception of Magritte, most paradigmatically conveyed by *La Pipe*, thus enfolded a "modèle Mallarmé" that would turn out to be even more significant for his subsequent work. The connection that Broodthaers drew between the two became most apparent in the *Pipe alphabet* series (1969) of *Industrial Poems*, first exhibited at the "Exposition littéraire autour de Stéphane Mallarmé," in which the pipe ideogram was integrated in a space, both that of the exhibition and the *plaque* itself, conceived as a spatialization of Mallarmé's poetics. A similar reenactment of the author's legacy, this time by filmic means, can be traced in *La Pluie*.

LA PLUIE: THE POETIC PRINCIPLE AND THE ACT OF WRITING

Shot in the garden of his house in the rue de la Pépinière in Brussels where he founded his *Musée d'Art Moderne, Département des Aigles* one year earlier, the 1969 two-minute film *La Pluie* shows Broodthaers sitting at a small crate in front of a whitened brick garden wall on which the words "Département des Aigles" are stenciled—the very same location where *La Pipe* was shot. In a little notebook, he writes with an old-fashioned penholder that he dips in an ink well. Suddenly, it starts to rain, thick raindrops are falling. Unmistakably staged with some kind of artificial rain poured with a watering can, the film shows only a very local rain shower—at a certain moment, it seems as if the rain only hits the artist and his table. By staging a rain shower, Broodthaers willy-nilly touches upon the limits of the craft of filmmaking: though a rain shower might be a highly "photogenic" topic that resonates with Broodthaers's emphatic interest in water and the sea in numerous films, in practice, it turns out to be something that is difficult to film as the droplets of natural rain are too small and falling too fast, usually resulting in nothing more than a haze on film. In the world of professional film, scenes situated in the rain usually require the skills of entire special-effects departments—even a neorealist filmmaker such as Vittorio De Sica needed the assistance of the Roman fire department to shoot the rain in his *Ladri di biciclette* (1948).[95] *La Pluie* rather evokes the emphatically artificial rain showers or water bursts we encounter in 1920s avant-garde cinema such as in Hans Richter's *Vormittagsspuk* (1928) and particularly in René Clair's *Entr'acte* (1924), in which a rain shower thwarts the chess game of Marcel Duchamp and Man Ray on a Paris rooftop.

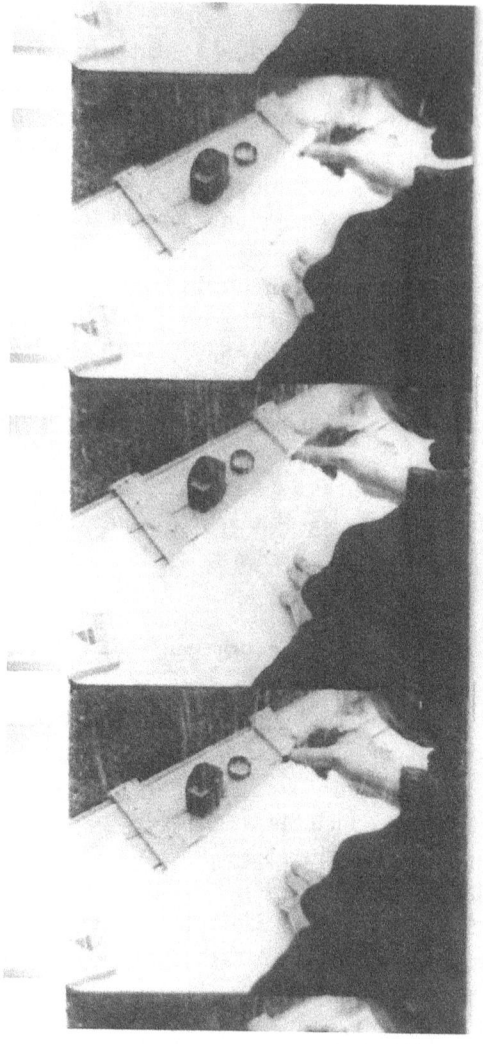

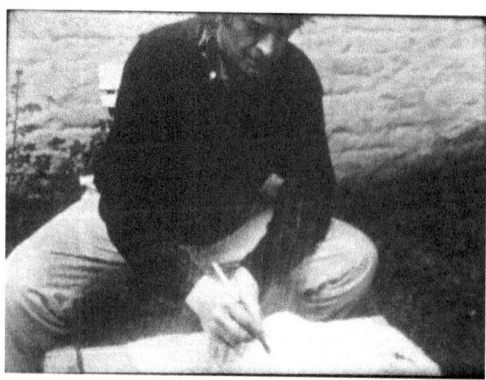

La Pluie (projet pour un texte). 16mm.
1969. Courtesy Centre Pompidou,
MNAM-CCI/Dist. GrandPalaisRmn.
© Estate of Marcel Broodthaers,
c/o SABAM Belgium 2024

In contrast with the histrionic reaction of Duchamp and Man Ray, who abort their play, Broodthaers seems undisturbed in *La Pluie*. While the rain is pouring down, he continues writing despite the impossible circumstances as the shower intensifies, with the ink well overflowing and everything becoming soaking wet. Broodthaers attempts to neglect the forces of nature but, in the end, writing something down with pen and ink turns out to be impossible. After the film fades to black, revealing the intertitle "Projet pour un texte" (Project for a text), he gives up, puts down his pen, and leaves the frame.

This intrepid but also futile and somewhat tragicomic act reminds us of silent slapstick cinema, which contains quite a few remarkable scenes with rain showers, including Charlie Chaplin's *Between Showers* (1914), *Caught in the Rain* (1914), and *Payday* (1922), Harry Langdon's *The Head Guy* (1930), and Laurel and Hardy's *Scram!* (1932). It is, however, particularly Buster Keaton who became immortal with rain-soaked scenes in *One Week* (1924), *College* (1927), *Steamboat Bill Jr* (1928), and *The Cameraman* (1929), his body undergoing the violent forces of nature (as those of modern machinery in other scenes) without losing his deadpan expression. In so doing, Broodthaers situates himself in a long tradition of European intellectuals and avant-garde artists cherishing silent slapstick cinema, René Magritte being one of them.[96] These artists interpreted slapstick cinema as a perfect allegory of industrial modernity and its cult of speed, the jerky movements of slapstick comedians embodying the rhythms of the cinematic apparatus. In addition, they cherished slapstick cinema's surreal logic, neglecting and transgressing not only bourgeois morality but also the laws of gravity. Broodthaers's interest in slapstick cinema recurs in several of his films, from the motif of the pie in the face in *Berlin oder ein Traum mit Sahne* (1974) to a more explicit appropriation in *Charlie als Filmstar* (1971), in which a Chaplin short was projected on a screen on which Broodthaers's characteristic "fig." signs were printed. Furthermore, Broodthaers's fascination with slapstick cinema is, of course, part of his love of early cinema in general, which pervades many of his films as well as works in other media. Though slapstick cinema had already originated in Europe (particularly in France) shortly after 1900 and despite the fact that Mack Sennett founded one of the first studios in Hollywood to produce films according to the logics of serial manufacture and an efficiency-induced division of labor, Hollywood silent slapstick cinema of the 1910s and 1920s has been interpreted as an extension of the non-narrative logic of early cinema, or what Tom Gunning labeled "the cinema of attractions," which dominated film production up until 1907.[97] For Gunning and other scholars, slapstick cinema was the film genre in which the logics of the "cinema of attractions" favoring a succession of shock moments was appropriated and elaborated, unlike the increasing interest in narrative development in the feature-length movies of the classical era. Like many early films, *La Pluie* focuses on a single action, without further narrative advancement or character development. It is a film that shows

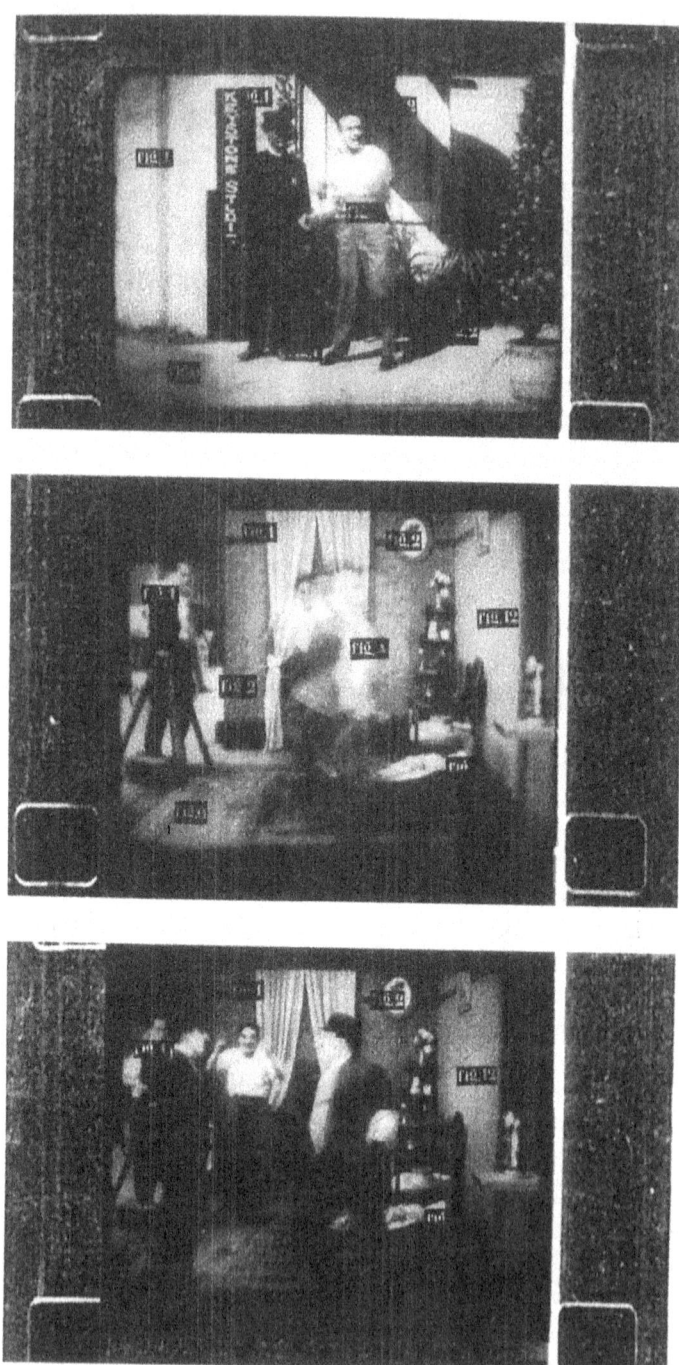

Charlie als Filmstar. 16mm. 1971. © Estate of Marcel Broodthaers, c/o SABAM Belgium 2024

rather than tells. Consisting of ten shots, the film is marked by a "primitive" or deskilled style, using "functional" positions for the handheld camera that seems to adjust its focus at various moments.

At the same time, the film is rich with allusions and has a thematic complexity that resonates with several topics in Broodthaers's broader oeuvre. First and foremost, *La Pluie* is designated as a "projet pour un texte"; it is about text, words, letters, and the act of writing—an element that recurs in other Broodthaers films, from *Une Seconde d'éternité* (A Second of Eternity) (1970), consisting of the inscription of the artist's signature within a second and the topic of Andrew Chesher's essay in this volume; to several films showing inscriptions on shop windows such as *Crime à Cologne* (A Crime in Cologne) (1971); various postcard films discussed in Deborah Schultz's contribution; and *Au delà de cette limite* (1971), dealing with the signage in the Paris metro as discussed in Frilling's chapter. As *La Pluie*, *Le Corbeau et le renard*, and the *Plaques* illustrate, Broodthaers's work often emphatically returned to issues of écriture, especially at the time of *Cinéma modèle*. This has led a host of scholars to consider his art practice as a visual reprise of the issues he dealt with as a former "man of letters," which perfectly fits the popular image, dear to many of his contemporaries, that Broodthaers essentially remained a poet, notwithstanding his explicit self-fashioning as an artist and his equally explicit denial of being a filmmaker. According to Rachel Haidu, his practice presents itself as a critical engagement with a contemporaneous (literary) modernism steeped in negation, seeking to strip language from its communicative, performative, and authorial character, as such reducing it to a kind of "zero degree of writing" after the seminal work of Roland Barthes. It should be asked, then, how Broodthaers's cinema is informed by a "poetic principle"? What is then "the outsized role of text" that Haidu observes to permeate his filmic oeuvre?[98]

Indeed, from the very outset of his career, well before he entered the art world, Broodthaers's poetry and films seem to belong to a single continuum facilitating an intensive intermedial exchange, which is exemplified by his 1948 poem *Projet pour un film* functioning as a virtual film, and *La Clef de l'horloge* being subtitled "a cinematographic poem." Likewise, after his so-called objects-period coming to a close, his second achieved film, *Le Corbeau et le renard* (1967), heralds a host of filmic works in which a literary commitment is omnipresent, as embodied by performances of (failed) speech or writing acts as in *La Pluie* but also by found text in several of his "postcard films"; references to monuments of (French) literary history (e.g., *Un Film de Charles Baudelaire*, 1970); and last but not least, the material signifier as a recurring motif in many titles. Precisely at the moment when French intellectual discourse fell increasingly under the spell of literary theory, as represented by the scholarly accounts of philosophers such as Goldmann, Barthes, Blanchot, Lacan, et cetera, Broodthaers's films appear to contemplate the contemporary predicament of the "poetic principle" by pitting (counter)historical poetical "models" against the current state of affairs. While the presence of words, letters, and inscriptions in Broodthaers's films may coincide with an interest in the same topics among other avant-garde filmmakers, from Lettrist cinema to Paul Sharits's *Word Movie* (1966) and Hollis Frampton's *Zorns Lemma* (1970), the historical dimension of Broodthaers's critical enterprise "should never be lost out of sight."[99]

Crime à Cologne. 16/35mm 1971. © Estate of Marcel Broodthaers, c/o SABAM Belgium 2024

At the time when *La Pluie* was shot, the case of Mallarmé had gained an extraordinary centrality in French critical theory to the extent that the cream of contemporary philosophers—Sartre, Blanchot, Derrida, Foucault, Sollers, and Deleuze, to name only a few—had been advancing "their" Mallarmés at a steady pace, a tendency that did not escape Broodthaers's attention. "*Un Coup de Dés...* currently many references," he ironically commented in an open letter distributed at the opening of an "Une exposition littéraire autour de Stéphane Mallarmé" in December 1969.[100] In his well-known artist book based on the latter poem, Broodthaers covered all of its words by black strips corresponding to Mallarmé's characteristic typographic layout in order to highlight the visual and material significance that is granted to the linguistic signifier in this work. Through this venture, Broodthaers seemed to appropriate Mallarmé—the "inventor of the space of modern art" and, significantly, one of the fountainheads of cinepoetry according to Christophe Wall-Romana[101]—too, as a prism through which to consider the notions of erasure and deferral, which had moved to the center of critical attention, as witnessed by their underpinning of popular concepts such as "the death of the author," "the zero degree of writing," or "différance."

In *La Pluie* too, apparently dedicated to Mallarmé, text is essentially erased, the act of writing annulled. Words become images as the rain "shifts the lines and changes the words into watery ink dots." The effect is reminiscent of the calligraphic imagery of abstract expressionist painting or the experiments conflating writing, drawing, and painting by Belgian artists such as Christian Dotremont or Pierre Alechinsky in the 1950s—an effect that was particularly suited for cinema as demonstrated by the various films related to CoBrA showing artists at work: Alechinsky's *Calligraphie japonaise* (Japanese Calligraphy, 1955), Jan Vrijman's *De werkelijkheid van Karel Appel* (The Reality of Karel Appel, 1962), Johan van der Keuken's *Een film voor Lucebert/Lucebert, tijd en afscheid* (A Film for Lucebert/Lucebert, Time and Farewell, 1962/1967/1994), and Luc de Heusch's *Alechinsky d'après nature* (Alechinsky from Life, 1970) and *Dotremont: Les Logogrammes* (Dotremont: The Logograms, 1972).[102]

Hence, like *Pense-Bête*, *La Pluie* too can be read as a metaphor for Broodthaers's transition from poet to visual artist. In a similar vein, Christophe Viart reads *La Pluie* as the "accomplishment of what he had begun some years earlier, in 1964, when he left literature behind in order to move toward the visual arts."[103] While *Pense-Bête* (1964), a sculpture made of books, obstructed the act of reading, *La Pluie* deals with the obstruction of the act of writing. In both works, the deconstruction of one artistic activity becomes the basis for another one. Though highly different activities connected to different artistic disciplines or media, both writing and painting are activities or processes that evolve in time—their durational aspects make them "cinematic;" this in contrast to the already-written and already-printed texts that feature in many of his other films such as *Le Corbeau et le renard*, which was also screened in the *Cinéma modèle* program in 1970.

FROM *LE CORBEAU ET LE RENARD* TO THE *DÉCORS*: THE EXHIBITION OF CINEMA

Although *Le Corbeau et le renard* (The Raven and the Fox) (1967) was only Broodthaers's second film, produced a decade after *La Clef de l'horloge*, it is widely considered a key work within both his cinematic and visual oeuvre. It exemplifies a cinematic practice conceived as a continuous effort to de- and rematerialize the filmic medium within the pluriform spaces opening up between "writing," "the object," and "the image."[104] As such, *Le Corbeau et le renard* is rightly considered to be paradigmatic of the distinctly intermedial path that Broodthaers's oeuvre in general took, which brings us to the last feature that this introductory essay seeks to highlight.

Like *La Pluie*, *Le Corbeau et le renard* too marks the resurfacing of text, writing, and language at the center of the artist's concerns, albeit in a considerably different vein. The film is named after the eponymous fable by seventeenth-century French author Jean de La Fontaine; its genesis essentially recounts the iteration of this hypotext through different stages of rewriting (*réécriture*) and remediation. This process was initiated by Broodthaers's transformation of de La Fontaine's source text, which, it should be mentioned, is itself an adaptation of the moralizing story by the ancient Greek fabulist Aesop. The resulting "personal writing (poetry)," alternatively titled "Le D est plus grand que le T" (The D is bigger than the T) essentially yields a text "made up of clichés, borrowings from elementary writing lessons and personal inventions."[105] Unsurprisingly then, Broodthaers presented *Le Corbeau et le renard* as an "exercise in reading,"[106] rather than "an experimental film." The text from which the work would emerge first featured as part of a visual artwork significantly titled *Lecture*, which was shown in Broodthaers's first retrospective, *Court-Circuit* (short circuit) held at the Palais des Beaux-Arts in 1967. It constitutes a printed canvas mounted on a shelf bearing an empty glass jar. In his review of the exhibition, Jean Dypréau, a leading art critic, and one of the early supporters of Broodthaers's work, cast it as follows:

> The poet writes a fable, *Le Corbeau et le renard*, full of typographical obsessions, colored images, constructivist allusions, (there is even an architect involved), and the visual artist makes it into a painting. One does no longer read text, as one beholds signs taking possession of a space, and that what Michel Tapié called "structures of repetition" is proposed to the reader-turned-spectator.[107]

More specifically, Dypréau remarked how the procedures of mechanical reproduction permeated *Court-Circuit*, as exemplified by printed and photographic canvases representing earlier artworks and some allusions to the means of reproduction, notably camera tripods. The exhibition itself was actually captured on film by Jean Harlez, a Brussels cameraman and director who would shoot many of Broodthaers's films.[108] In the resulting film, titled *Objet* (Object) (1967), *Lecture* is put to use as a miniature set staging a stop motion sequence of some of Broodthaers's typical vernacular objects (eggshells, glass jars, mussel pots, etc.) against the backdrop of the appropriated text. Of course, this setup invites a "reading" of the work along the lines of the "*La Pipe*-model," or to put it in Dypréau's words, "Who said that today poetry is everywhere except in poems. Marcel Broodthaers has written poems, he has remained a poet, but to him the poetic act has principally become a plastic act."[109]

However, *Le Corbeau et le renard* was not only a harbinger of the earlier discussed poetry "of a theoretic character" that would mark subsequent films,[110] such as *La Pipe*, but more importantly signaled the structural analysis of the cinematic apparatus—as a specific "language"—that Broodthaers would pursue throughout the years to come. On the one hand, cinema is approached as a mere "procedure,"[111] thus as a means to express the poet-turned-artist's

Le Corbeau et le renard. 16mm film projected on a painted screen. 1967.
Exhibition view "Marcel Broodthaers" Fridericianum, 2015. © photo: Achim Hatzius.
© Estate of Marcel Broodthaers, c/o SABAM Belgium 2024

"poetic principle" rather than an end in itself. However, on the other hand, *Le Corbeau et le renard*'s upsetting of codes no doubt targets those of language and readership as much as those of cinema and spectatorship. In an effort to bolster the latter endeavor, Broodthaers famously decided to use a painted screen, featuring a section of the text on which *Le Corbeau et le renard* was based, to have his film projected on. Through the introduction of an altered screen, the work succeeds in subjectifying the public on multiple levels, since the latter's traditional disembodied and integrated experience of cinema is now relegated to a material and composite setup of largely tautological devices. In *Section cinéma* too, Broodthaers would make use of altered screens as part of his pursuit to breach the "absorptive nature and diegetic universe of classical cinema," as Eric de Bruyn would have it.[112] By projecting the film on a plane that was no longer the usual virgin white surface, Broodthaers materialized the traditionally invisible or transparent projection screen.

Nevertheless, *Le Corbeau et le renard*'s self-referential dimension and its deconstruction of the traditional *dispositif* of cinema should by no means be perceived as a modernist pursuit toward purism or medium-specificity, for Rosalind Krauss stated that "Broodthaers honored the differential condition of film" (instead of relegating it to any material crux).[113] Contrary to his Structuralists contemporaries' filmic essentialism, that is a cinema reduced to a set of medium-specific properties, Broodthaers perceived cinema's very "impurity" as its most fundamental characteristic; "aggregative, a matter of interlocking supports and layered conventions," as Krauss would have it.[114] Screened in the margin of the fourth *EXPRMNTL* festival for experimental cinema—because of the altered screen, Broodthaers's film was not admitted to the official selection—*Le Corbeau et le renard* featured next to Michael Snow's *Wavelength* (1967), which won the first prize. Broodthaers ironically characterized *Wavelength*, now considered as one of the unmistakable highlights of Structural Cinema, as "a painter's film," or even as "a cinema of the sound object," once more emphasizing cinema's intermedial nature, as if anticipating the essentialist claims that were yet to be made by the later theorists' of Structural Film, P. Adams Sitney in particular.[115]

By hypostasizing the film screen and revealing the spatial setup of the film screening, *Le Corbeau et le renard* presents itself as a "film installation," as such answering to Gene Youngblood's concept of an "expanded cinema" that implies the notion of the artist as an "ecologist," involved with an environment rather than with objects.[116] Broodthaers, in his capacity as a filmmaker in the late 1960s and 1970s, does not only share the fascination of many contemporaneous avant-garde filmmakers for the temporal or durational aspects of cinema (exemplified by the abundant use of extended long takes and the use of immobile or static subjects), he would also reflect on the spatial aspects of the film screening not unlike filmmakers and video artists such as Michael Snow, Anthony McCall, Lutz Mommartz, Dan Graham, Bruce Nauman, and Dennis Oppenheim.[117]

This also becomes apparent in the *Section cinéma* (1972), the seventh installment of Broodthaers's *Musée d'Art Moderne*, which he started in 1968. Eric de Bruyn has argued that *Section cinéma* "functioned as "both a foundational and archaeological site, which continuously wavered between a state of construction and dismantlement," while "fulfilling the concrete function of storage facility, meeting place, production studio, film theater, and museum space."[118] Interestingly, *Section cinéma* emerged parallel to other artist-run spaces that met some of these categories but above all shared the aim of capturing social interactions as art, freed from the constraints of any institutional straitjacket. Located only a few houses away, "Restaurant Spoerri" had become an important meeting place for artists in the Düsseldorf scene, while "Produkt Kino," established by the artist Tony Morgan (with whom Broodthaers shared an apartment in Düsseldorf), was conceived as an alternative institution for the production, commissioning, distribution, and screening of artist's films.[119] However, the social underpinning of Broodthaers's *Séances*, as exemplified by *Section Cinéma*, differed fundamentally from countercultural pursuits such as Restaurant Spoerri and Produkt Kino: rather than accommodating Fluxus-informed "life as art" happenings, it functioned as a "museum of attractions," a "theatre of memory that could not reverse the erosion of social experience," to put it in Eric de Bruyn's words.[120]

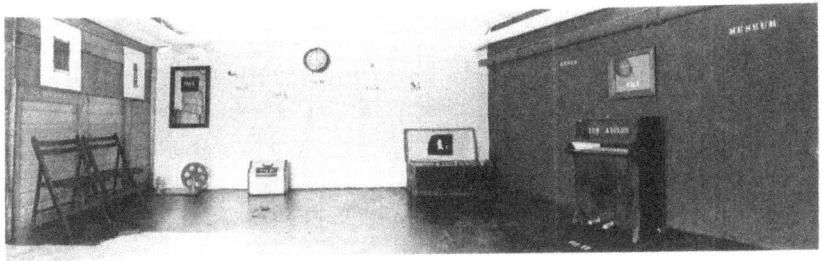

Installation views of *Section Cinéma*. Düsseldorf, 1971–72.
© Estate of Marcel Broodthaers, c/o SABAM Belgium 2024

First of all, *Section cinéma* screened some footage documenting the activities of the first section of the *Musée*, combined with three found film segments acquired at a local photoshop: a compilation of sequences from a Chaplin film, a touristic documentary film about Brussels, and a frantic succession of outdated newsreels randomly spliced together. The latter were projected on a stenciled wall bearing the artist's characteristic "Fig." signs. The connection between Broodthaers's own filmmaking and early cinema also underpins the "ensemble of objects," titled *Théorie des Figures*, that featured alongside the film program, replete with the same "Fig." inscriptions featuring on the wall. A first set of twelve objects included a mirror, a winder, a smoke bomb, a pipe, and a mask, among other things. A second set of eleven similar objects was placed into an open antique chest at the end of the same wall. While some of them reference the paraphernalia of early cinema, others, such as the pipe, the clock, or the mask, featured as props in Broodthaers's own films.

As an installment of his vast museum fiction of the *Musée d'Art Moderne, Département des Aigles*, *Section cinéma* can also be seen as a component of

Broodthaers's "Institutional Critique" of museum institutions, which involved a systematic as well as poetic inquiry into the social, formal, and organizational conditions of art galleries.[121] Like artists such as Hans Haacke, Daniel Buren, and Michael Asher, Broodthaers did not express ambitions to abolish or destroy all museums; rather, he sought to unveil the false neutrality of the museum and to lay bare its invisible institutional logic. This Foucauldian or Althusserian critique of institutions and their ideological foundations and assumptions also marked the so-called apparatus theory of film, more or less simultaneously developed in the late 1960s and early 1970s by theorists such as Jean-Louis Baudry and Jean-Louis Comolli.[122] For Baudry, the film screen was not an unmediated frame onto the world but rather a "meta-psychological mirror" fulfilling the spectator's whish for fullness, transcendental unity, and meaning. Precisely because of its specific layout or its "dispositif"—the dark enclosed viewing conditions reminiscent of Plato's cave—cinema imposes an idealist ideology, which masks the illusion of the film production.

While Broodthaers's *Musée d'Art Moderne, Département des Aigles* made us aware that the conventional museum setting (both in its classical and modernist manifestations as an enfilade of palatial rooms or a "white cube" respectively) is a historically and politically contingent "installation" as well, his entire film production, too, emphasizes the material, spatial, and apparatus-like aspects of cinema. As most if not all of his films were and are usually screened in the "white cube" of a gallery setting rather than in the "black box" of a cinema theater, the cinematic apparatus (screen, projector, electric cables) becomes an inherent part of the work, once more exemplified by *Section cinéma*'s recourse to painted screens and its exhibition of the paraphernalia of filmmaking. One could argue, in line with observations made by Raymond Bellour, that Broodthaers demonstrated that the "dispositif" of classical cinema is just an installation as well.[123]

Broodthaers's films and film installations can thus be seen as attempts to reveal, and thus counter, the ideological effects of the apparatus. However, by moving to the art gallery, he not only disconnected the film medium of its mass cultural appeal and its preference for spectacularization but also turned film into an object of aesthetic contemplation. What's more, enclosed in the museum, film now appropriated the special presence, or the "aura" once accorded to the unique work of art—the very process Broodthaers critiqued in his so-called museum fictions and in many of his other works questioning artists' signatures or the monetary value of precious artworks. While Walter Benjamin famously saw in the means of mechanical reproduction a possibility for the destruction of the traditional cult value and the "aura" of the work of art, cinema's migration to the gallery resulted in the almost opposite phenomenon of the aestheticization of film. In a paradoxical effort to overcome the fatal predicament of cinema, Broodthaers may be said to have reified it in an allegorical way.[124] Nonetheless, by avoiding spectacle, character identification, linear narrative development, voyeuristic pleasure, and immersive experiences, Broodthaers's films and film installations tally with the materialist approach that marked both the paradigms of institutional critique and apparatus theory.

The practice of "exhibiting" films would become a major concern of Broodthaers during the 1970s, more particularly in his so-called *Décors*. In 1972, when the *Musée* cycle came to a close at Documenta 5, Broodthaers removed *Section cinéma* from the list of fictional museums that he had been staging over the preceding four years, since in his view, it simply constituted a "subjective environment."[125] In retrospect, this seemingly trivial, administrative intervention nevertheless signaled the advent of a final phase in the artist's practice in which cinema itself would become a generative, intermedial "model." Between 1974 and his death in 1976, Broodthaers staged six wayward retrospective exhibitions in Brussels, Basel, Berlin, Oxford, and London. Having become known as *Décors*, they display earlier pieces by the artist together with appropriated objects, or even rented props in ever freshly conceived and site-specific constellations. Conceived to defy the retrospective's typical aim to consolidate and thus merchandise the artist's oeuvre, they question the format's logic through their reinsertion of Broodthaers's artworks in apparently fictional and anachronistic environments. The *Décors* are usually perceived as the final and conclusive move of a series of dazzling somersaults that drove Broodthaers from poetry into the art world, from the object to the museum, and from the intimacy of the page toward the "conquest of space."

However, next to poetry and visual art, cinema was definitely as integral to this denouement. For one thing, this is because Broodthaers's *Décors* roughly coincide with a prolific period in the artist's filmmaking. His cinema practice reached a very pinnacle, both in terms of quantitative output and in terms of its stylistic sophistication and conceptual breadth. Films such as *Figures of Wax (Jeremy Bentham)* (1974), *Berlin oder ein Traum mit Sahne* (1974–1975), or *La Bataille de Waterloo* (1975) are longer and more developed in a technical sense. Upon staging his penultimate *Décor*, titled "Décor: A Conquest by Marcel Broodthaers," at the London Institute of Contemporary Arts' New Gallery in the early summer of 1975, Broodthaers reportedly even told curator Barry Barker that "once he fulfilled his commitment to the exhibition *L'Angelus de Daumier* at the Centre National d'Art Contemporain, Hôtel Rothschild, Paris, in October 1975, he would give up making objects and exhibitions and concentrate on making films."[126] Whether or not this resolution, curtailed by the artist's untimely death, would have come true, this quote speaks volumes about the centrality of cinema within Broodthaers's late practice.

Obviously, the filmic connotation of the word *Décor*—a film set—already betrays this significance and has provided Cathleen Chaffee and Rachel Haidu a concrete handhold to cast the artist's late exhibition practice within a cinematic perspective.[127] Two of Broodthaers's exhibits in fact fulfilled the function of a film set—"Un Jardin d'hiver [I]" for *Un Jardin d'hiver (A B C)* (1974), and

"Décor: A Conquest by Marcel Broodthaers" for *La Bataille de Waterloo* (1975)—while some of the other *Décors* definitely conveyed the image of "deserted sound stages," without necessarily having served as film locations.[128] Conversely, props from films shot outside the exhibition space would be included in *Décors* as autonomous artworks. "Invitation pour une exposition bourgeoise" (1975), for instance, displayed a stuffed parrot playing a key role in *Berlin oder ein Traum mit Sahne*. Finally, some *Décors* denoted not only the site of a film shooting but also moviegoing as they provided a venue for the screening of specific titles or anthologies by Broodthaers. These would either take place in a site-specific "environment," such as *Un Jardin d'hiver [II]* in "Catalogue Catalogus," or in a dedicated cinema room, or "Salle noire," after the title of this kind of space in *L'Angélus de Daumier*.

The conception of the exhibition space as a site hovering between (filmic) production and consumption on the one hand and physicality and representation on the other, which defines Broodthaers's *Décors*, can be traced back to *Le Corbeau et le renard*'s expansion of the filmic apparatus. However, it was above all *Section cinéma* that provided the prime "model" for the *Décors*. As Douglas Crimp pointed out, "the formation of a *collection*" first emerged under the guise of *Théorie des figures*, the collection of exhibited film props, and, significantly, as an anthology of films themselves under the banner of *Section cinéma*'s immediate predecessor: *Cinéma modèle*.[129] Hence, if *Section cinéma* "functioned as both a foundational and archaeological site," according to de Bruyn,[130] it certainly enjoys this status concerning Broodthaers's future practice in its capacity of a testing ground for the entanglements between cinema and exhibition that the artist would pursue under the aegis of *Décor*.

Programme, set up in the Antwerp Wide White Space Gallery in January 1973, can be considered a second exhibit announcing the *Décors*.[131] Once again, a spatial constellation sprang from an initial intention to host the screening of a filmic anthology, in this case *Rendez-vous mit Jacques Offenbach* (1972), which had been shown at the Palais des Beaux-Arts about one month earlier. Here, a trestle table on which four stacks of (film) posters were displayed under a plexiglass cover created a specific context for the compilation film. Illuminated by a floor lamp and flanked by two potted palm trees, the arrangement recalled the average information stand at a film festival, however, without providing any background information to the film program, as the posters remained fully blank save for a printed border and the words "Programme; Fig. 1."[132]

Like *Section cinéma*, *Programme* was immersed in a specific fiction. Whereas props, director's chairs, and a winder made for the former's ambiance of a film set and editing room, other objects were selected for the latter exhibit. Among others, the palm tree that would become one of the hallmarks of the *Décors* makes its first appearance in *Programme* as a figure of banality, an obligatory piece of decoration used for making all kinds of events a bit more festive or respectable. Formulaic as a punctuation mark, it remains as invisible

Installation views of *Décor: A Conquest by Marcel Broodthaers*. ICA, London, 1975.
© Estate of Marcel Broodthaers, c/o SABAM Belgium 2024

as it is a prerequisite for a clear understanding of the constellation it structures. Only such recognizable clichés like the palm tree allowed Broodthaers to assemble calculated fictions with a minimum of appropriated objects, turned into "plastic means."[133] This principle of efficiency and an emphasis on semiotics is not only reminiscent of his early poetry but relates to filmmaking in general, especially as perceived through the lens of the prewar avant-garde. *Section cinéma* and *Programme* thus demonstrate how Broodthaers's *Décor* practice was informed by cinema from its very origin. This is not only because the first retrospectives by the artist were basically conceived as *expanded* film anthologies but even more fundamentally because they were permeated by an "idea of cinema" both thematically and structurally. Jean-Christophe Royoux also noted this, stating that Broodhtaers's "transition from poetry to the plastic arts seems to be redoubled by a more fundamental transition to the expanded cinema of exhibition."[134]

This observation allows to approach (some of) Broodthaers's *Décors* as a form of "cinema by other means," after the definition advanced by the avant-garde film scholar Pavle Levi: "a practice of positing cinema as a system of relations directly inspired by the workings of the film apparatus but evoked through the material and technological properties of original non-filmic media."[135] As for the exhibitions that actually served as film sets, such as "Décor: A Conquest by Marcel Broodthaers," in which the beholder suddenly takes on the role of an actor, this stance obviously kicks at an open door. After all, Broodthaers's kaleidoscopic procedure involving a constant remediation and reshuffling equally applied to the filmic and visual art realm, making the artist's approach to the *Décors* similar to the work done at the editing table, including all the latter's serendipity and trouvailles. This cinematic blueprint not only manifests itself within the *Décors'* experience and setup but extends well into their scenography and paratexts. While the announcement poster of "*Éloge du sujet*" was designed so as to "make cinema," [136] one of the projects for its invitation card featuring a drawn film strip may be read as an oblique reference to the sequence 8 (+1) same-sized galleries, "unfurling like a reel," in which the exhibition took place.[137] Similarly, the *coupures* or breakdowns of the "L'Angélus de Daumier" exhibition into thematic rooms were intended to resemble a kind of découpage or method of film editing.[138] Broodthaers's *Décors* thus not only constituted concrete sites of/for cinema but also reflected a filmic logic across the whole of their conception and articulation.

In this sense then, Broodthaers's cinema appears to come full circle. Whereas at the beginning of his career, cinema served as a model for poetry, his last works use film as a model for exhibitions. Furthermore, several of Broodthaers's key film installations reflect on his development as a filmmaker. While *Cinéma modèle* offers a "museal" retrospective of Broodthaers's own films, the *Section cinéma* can even be regarded as the artist's "own idea of a film museum,"[139] as Xavier García Bardón points out in his essay. Moreover, *Section cinéma* offers "a 'mise-en-scène' of the composite public sphere of early cinema,"[140] which precisely presented the cinematic apparatus as an attraction in itself: the sudden appearance of the light beam, the rattling sound of the cranking of a projector, the rewinding of film reels resulting in reverse motion, the freezing and mobilization of projected images dependent on the pace of the projectionist, et cetera—all were essential parts of the "attraction" of the early film experience, which resonates in Broodthaers's anachronistic self-fashioning as an early cinema showman in the *Section cinéma*.

Installation view of *Programme*. Wide White Space Gallery, Antwerp, 1973.
Photo Jos Van den Bempt. © Estate of Marcel Broodthaers, c/o SABAM Belgium 2024

As Bruce Jenkins has argued, Broodthaers's cinema was "both phenomenologically and ideologically cast in the past tense."[141] His entire film production is marked by an interest in the earliest stages of cinema, when the new medium had utopian potential, before it got entirely subjected to a Fordist mode of production, producing standardized commodities that fully answered to the logics of capitalist reification (with the phenomenon of the "film star" as its most exemplary manifestation). This becomes apparent in his implicit and explicit references to Lumière, Feuillade, Keaton, and Chaplin, or the atmosphere of early serials visualized in *Ein Eisenbahnüberfall* (1972), a "film without celluloid," made as a series of staged photographs though emphatically invoking cinema by the depiction of sprocket holes on the edges as if the work consists of frames of a 35mm print. *Ein Eisenbahnüberfall* is another example of Broodthaers's interest in the above-mentioned "cinema by other means," while his films proper are often marked by a deskilled "primitivism" that can be found throughout the history of avant-garde cinema, from the Dadaist and Surrealist appropriation of Méliès, early trick films, and Feuillade to Structural filmmakers and Fluxus artists.

The *promesse de bonheur* of early cinema that Broodthaers invokes in many of his works stands in sharp contrast to his skepticism toward any attempt to (re)animate some avant-garde legacies. For Broodthaers, the increasing erosion of cinema's original utopian prospects by the forces of the culture industry could not be undone by any subsequent avant-garde claiming to introduce a new kind of cinema. Yet in 1969, he still considered film, in a vein similar to André Bazin's "myth of a total cinema," as "a project," leaving open the possibility of (temporarily) reinventing it.[142]

His nostalgia for early cinema, his distance vis-à-vis contemporaneous experimental film subcultures, and the striking absence of references to modernist art house cinema in his works and writings turn Broodthaers into an artist who looks at cinema as if it were a phenomenon of the past. In so doing, Broodthaers can be considered a precursor of the migration from the cinema to the museum by filmmakers such as Jean-Luc Godard, Chris Marker, Chantal Akerman, Pedro Costa, Atom Egoyan, Peter Greenaway, Abbas Kiarostami, and Apichatpong Weerasethakul, who (occasionally or frequently) started making film installations in the 1990s or early 2000s, after having made films for the cinema theater. Conversely, cinema's centennial anniversary in the 1990s also saw an entire generation of visual artists, including Pierre Huyghe, Douglas Gordon, and Tacita Dean, among many others, who intensively engaged with the historical and material aspects of the cinematic apparatus. Since the turn of the century, their efforts were, rightly or wrongly, subsumed under the label "Post-Cinema," a phenomenon that was often driven by a desire to salvage the popular medium of the twentieth century par excellence, as the latter was perceived to be jeopardized by the death of arthouse cinema as well as by the literal disappearance of (celluloid) film in favor of digital formats. This redemptive aspect was particularly prominent in the work of Tacita Dean, who made the melancholic lament for the waning materiality of film a central theme in her oeuvre while she also honored Broodthaers in her film *Section Cinema* (2002), which explores the Düsseldorf venue where Broodthaers had installed his *Section Cinéma*.

As media-archaeological devices, Broodthaers's films and film installations also indicate the close connections and the formal and organizational similarities between the phenomena of post-cinema, early film, and pre-cinema. Broodthaers's films therefore remind us of Raymond Bellour's observation that the era of (classical) cinema can be seen as just an intermediary phase lasting about a century, situated in between all kinds of proto-cinematic contraptions (magic lanterns, phenakistiscopes, zoetropes, chrono-photography, et cetera) on the one hand and the vast array of post-cinematic experiments by artists on the other.

Broodthaers's unique way of traversing the history of film is extensively covered in the following pages of this book. His vast production is listed in an updated filmography, which closes a collection of nine essays, each dealing with a specific topic, a particular film, or a cluster of closely related films. The chapter series opens with an essay by Bruce Jenkins, who has earlier published some of the key texts on Broodthaers's cinema. Jenkins discusses the artist's films in relation to his indebtedness to René Magritte's persona and works, particularly his home movies of the 1940s, 1950s, and 1960s. In addition, Jenkins discusses Broodthaers's films against the background of the institutionalization of experimental cinema, particularly the 1958 and 1967 editions of the EXPRMNTL film festival where Broodthaers's first and second film were screened. Broodthaers's use of obsolete film practices is also a crucial topic in Eric de Bruyn's chapter, which focuses on the notion of the séance, denoting both a "screening" and a form of "discussion," or "public sphere," appropriating early cinema's performative mode of presentation while also reinvigorating practices of "assembly" that developed in the wake of May '68.

Next, chapters by Christophe Wall-Romana and Andrew Chesher take Broodthaers's literary-informed engagement as a basis to reassess some of Broodthaers's films and para-cinematic projects. Wall-Romana's essay revisits Broodthaers's intervention on Mallarmé's poetry to interpret Broodthaers as a Mallarméan artist. Entitled Broodthaers's "Cinepoetic Concretions" and dealing with films such as *L'Œuf film* (1965), *Une Seconde d'éternité* (1970), and *Projet pour un poisson* (1970–71), Wall-Romana's essay implicitly refers to Roland Barthes's notion of *concrétude* (the way words are refashioned into material operators of experience rather than tokens of signification) as well as evoking Broodthaers as an artist whose entire oeuvre is a form of cinepoetry, including many works that address visual projection, point of view, visual motion, photography, text-image relations, magic lantern, and screen—the prototype setup for cinema.

Focusing on *Une Seconde d'éternité*, Chesher, too, discusses Broodthaers's indebtedness to Mallarmé and his interest in several practices that resonate with concepts articulated by Barthes such as the "degrée zero" of writing, the act of writing as a "narcissistic activity," and the notion of a "writerly text." In so doing, Chesher unfolds the complex relationships between Broodthaers, Barthes, Baudelaire, and Mallarmé, while also drawing attention to the contexts in which *Une Seconde d'éternité* has been shown, revealing a network that also includes artists such as Gilbert and George, Panamarenko, Piero Manzoni, and Daniel Buren.

The important role of text in Broodthaers's films is also evident in *Le Corbeau et le renard* (1967), which is the focus of the chapter by Xavier García Bardón, who analyzes its screening at the EXPRMNTL 4 film festival in December 1967 at Knokke-le-Zoute. García Bardón demonstrates how Broodthaers's film, which broke and expanded the standard use of the medium on several levels, resonates with the development of 1960s experimental cinema.

Finally, the contributions by Charlotte Friling, Deborah Schultz, Steven Jacobs, and Raf Wollaert delve into a number of films that until now have largely been neglected or remained devoid of critical appraisal, such as *Au-delà de cette limite* (1971), Broodthaers's so-called postcard films (1971–72), *Figures of Wax (Jeremy Bentham)* (1974), and *Berlin oder ein Traum mit Sahne* (1974–1975). According to Friling, *Au-delà de cette limite*, which deals with the signage of the Paris metro in the aftermath of May '68, marks Broodthaers's transition from poetic films—in which signs, writing, and images are his main subject matter submitted to the plastic dynamic mobilization of montage—to several films in which photo-mimetic images are confronted to graphic signs as well as printed, reproduced, or written texts.

The relation between printed images and written text is also crucial in some of Broodthaers's "post-card films" such as *Histoire d'amour (Dr. A Huismans)* (1971) and *Chère petite sœur (La Tempête)* (1972), discussed in the chapter by Deborah Schultz, who relates Broodthaers's cinematic treatment of postcards to his use of found objects in his practice more widely. In so doing, she investigates how these films are indicative of the complex relationship between the verbal and visual arts, animating existing objects and opening up their narrative suggestions.

The dialectics between stasis and motion marks *Figures of Wax (Jeremy Bentham)* (1974), the topic of the chapter by Steven Jacobs, who relates Broodthaers's filmic portrait of utilitarian philosopher Jeremy Bentham to the latter's ideas on the "auto-icon" as well as to a Surrealist fascination for wax-figure cabinets, mannequin dolls, and Pygmalion effects. In addition, Jacobs presents *Figures of Wax* as a postcapitalist city symphony, which juxtaposes a display case containing Bentham's corpse with London shop windows filled with mannequins, linking the film with Broodthaers's interests in processes of reification expressed in many of his other works.

Finally, in his analysis of *Berlin oder Traum mit Sahne* (1974–75), Raf Wollaert dissects the film's reciprocal relationship to the Broodthaers's exhibition-as-medium practice, the so-called *Décors*, and shows how its idyllic imagery is ultimately permeated by concerns over the impending reification of his work and persona.

NOTES

1. Marcel Broodthaers, "Interview with Trépied," trans., *Marcel Broodthaers: Cinéma*, ed. Manuel Borja-Villel & Michael Compton, exh. cat. (Barcelona: Fundació Antoni Tàpies, 1997), 319.
2. Eric de Bruyn, "Marcel Broodthaers: Cinéma Modèle," *Texte zur Kunst* 29 (March 1998): 33.
3. See Angela DalleVacche (ed.), *Film, Art, New Media: Museum without Walls?* (London: Palgrave Macmillan, 2012); Brigitte Peucker, *Incorporating Images: Film and the Rival Arts* (Princeton: Princeton University Press, 2014); Susan Felleman, *Art in the Cinematic Imagination* (Austin: University of Texas Press, 2010); Steven Jacobs, *Framing Pictures: Film and the Visual Arts* (Edinburgh: Edinburgh University Pres, 2011); and Agnes Pethö, *Cinema and Intermediality: The Passion for the In-between* (Cambridge: Cambridge Scholars Publishing, 2011).
4. Broodthaers, "Draft for a Text," trans., *Broodthaers. Cinéma*, 322.
5. Broodthaers, "D Is Bigger than T," trans., ibid., 319.
6. Marcel Broodthaers in a letter addressed to the secretary of University College London (9 December 1973), in Cathleen Ann Chaffee, "Figures of Wax: Marcel Broodthaers in Conversation with Jeremy Bentham" (master's thesis, Courtauld Institute, University of London, 2001), appendix I: Letters.
7. See Steven Jacobs, *Art & Cinema: Belgian Art Documentaries* (Brussels: Cinematek, 2013); Steven Jacobs, "A Concise History and Theory of Documentaries on the Visual Arts," in Joshua Malitsky (ed.), *A Companion to Documentary Film History* (London: Wiley-Blackwell, 2021), 291–310.
8. For a (non-exhaustive) list of the films on which Broodthaers would collaborate as a screen- and dialogue writer, see the filmography in this volume.
9. Trevor Stark, "Marcel Broodthaers, Art Historian's Artist," *Texte zur Kunst* 103 (September 2016): 227.
10. Michael Compton, "Marcel Broodthaers," in *Marcel Broodthaers*, exh. cat. (London: Tate, 1980); Benjamin Buchloh, "Marcel Broodthaers: Allegories of the Avant-garde," *Artforum* 18, no. 9 (May 1980): 52–59; Marie-Pascale Gildemyn, "Marcel Broodthaers (1924–1976): Monografie" (master's thesis, Ghent University, 1978).
11. Deborah Schultz, *Marcel Broodthaers: Strategy and Dialogue* (London: Peter Lang, 2007); Rachel Haidu, *The Absence of Work: Marcel Broodthaers, 1964–1976* (Cambridge, Mass.: MIT Press, 2010).
12. *Vorträge zum filmischen Werk von Marcel Broodthaers*, ed. Christian Posthofen (Berlin: Nationalgalerie, 2001).
13. Dieter Schwarz (ed.), *Marcel Broodthaers: Cinéma Modèle* (Düsseldorf: Richter Verlag, 2013).
14. Bruce Jenkins, "CB: Cinema Broodthaers," in *Marcel Broodthaers*, exh. cat. (Minneapolis: Walker Art Center, 1998), 92–109; Eric de Bruyn, "Cinéma Modèle," op. cit.
15. Enno Patalas (1929–2018) from the Munich Film Museum was another crucial pioneer in this regard.
16. See Schwarz, *Cinéma modèle*.
17. *La Clef de l'horloge* was shot in 1956 during a Kurt Schwitters retrospective that ran at the Brussels Palais des Beaux-Arts between 13 October and 11 November. Apparently, a soundtrack was only added in 1958. In the end, Broodthaers dated the film to 1957.
18. Broodthaers, "Interview with Trépied," trans., *Broodthaers: Cinéma*, 319.
19. See Christophe Wall-Romana, *Cinepoetry: Imaginary Cinemas in French Poetry* (New York: Fordham University Press, 2013).

20. While on the one hand films by Henri Chomette or *L'Étoile de mer* (1928) by Man Ray and Robert Desnos have been cast as "poems," Philippe Soupault would publish "poèmes cinématographiques" from 1917 on, that is, poems written from the purview of cinema. With *Projet pour un film* (1948) and *La Clef de l'horloge*, Broodthaers engaged in both of these traditions.
21. The Schwitters exhibition at the Brussels Palais des Beaux-Arts took place from 13 October to 11 November 1956. Other venues of this traveling show included Hannover, Bern, Amsterdam, and Liège.
22. Steven Jacobs, Dimitrios Latsis, and Birgit Cleppe (eds.), *Art in the Cinema: The Mid-Century Art Documentary* (London: Bloomsbury Academic, 2020).
23. Marcel Broodthaers, "Bruegel and Goya, Journalists, 1964," in Gloria Moure (ed.), *Marcel Broodthaers: Collected Writings* (Barcelona: Ediciones Poligrafa, 2012), 133.
24. Steven Jacobs and Lisa Colpaert, *The Dark Galleries: A Museum Guide to Painted Portraits in Film Noir, Gothic Melodramas, and Ghost Stories of the 1940s and 1950s* (Ghent: AraMER, 2013).
25. The text of the sound track has been published in *Broodthaers: Collected Writings*, 63. See also Broodthaers, EXPRMNTL catalog, reproduced in *Cinéma*, 23.
26. *Broodthaers: Collected Writings*, 63. French version.
27. *Broodthaers: Collected Writings*, 65; *Marcel Broodthaers: Cinéma*, 24. As Broodthaers clarified himself in an unpublished text with references to works by René Magritte and Daniel Spoerri, *La Clef de l'horloge* marked his preoccupation of the interconnections between words, images, and objects.
28. Marcel Broodthaers, "Die Null-Figur," in *Kurt Schwitters* (Düsseldorf: Städtische Kunsthalle Düsseldorf, 1971), 15. *Collected Writings*, 66.
29. See "Interview with Marcel Broodthaers on His Film 'Analysis of a Painting' by B.H.D. Buchloh and Michael Oppitz," reproduced in *Cinéma*, 230–31.
30. See Cathleen Chaffee, "Marcel Broodthaers's *Un voyage en Mer du Nord*," *Yale University Art Gallery Bulletin* (2011): 61–63; Steven Jacobs, "A Voyage on the North Sea, Marcel Broodthaers," in Tamara Berghmans (ed.), *Photobook Belge, 1854–Now* (Antwerp/Veurne: FoMu/Hannibal, 2019), 257.
31. Rosalind Krauss, *A Voyage on the North Sea* (London: Thames and Hudson, 1999).
32. See Justin Remes, *Motion(less) Pictures: The Cinema of Stasis* (New York: Columbia University Press, 2015).
33. Benjamin Buchloh, "Marcel Broodthaers's Section Cinéma," in *Marcel Broodthaers, Section Cinéma du Musée d'Art Moderne, Département des Aigles* (New York: Marian Goodman Gallery, 2010), 8.
34. Marcel Broodthaers, "Die Null-Figur," in *Kurt Schwitters* (Städtische Kunsthalle Düsseldorf, 1971), 15. See "La Figure 0," trans., *Broodthaers: Collected Writings*, 66.
35. Roland Barthes, *Camera Lucida, Reflections on Photography*, trans. Richard Howard (London: Vintage Books, 2000), 15.
36. Ibid., 91.
37. Michel Foucault, "Nietzsche, Genealogy, History," in Donald F. Bouchard (ed. and trans.), *Michel Foucault; Language, Counter-memory, Practice; Selected Essays and Interviews* (Ithaca: Cornell University Press, 1977), 160.
38. Ibid., 160–64.
39. Bruce Jenkins, "Un Peu Tard: Citation in the Cinema of Marcel Broodthaers," in *Broodthaers: Cinéma*, 291
40. Broodthaers, "Un Film de Charles Baudelaire," trans., *Broodthaers: Collected Writings*, 429.
41. Trevor Stark, "Reification and Worldview in Marcel Broodthaers' Maps," video lecture on Vimeo, February 19, 2021, 08:15, https://vimeo.com/514192880#_=_.

42. See Tom Gunning, "The Cinema of Attraction: Early Film, Its Spectator, and the Avant-Garde" (1986), in Thomas Elsaesser (ed.), *Early Cinema: Space, Frame, Narrative* (London: BFI, 1990), 56–62.
43. Broodthaers, "Draft for a Text," *Cinéma*, 91; Stark, "Reification and Worldview."
44. Claude Pichois and Jean Ziegler, *Baudelaire* (London: Vintage, 1991), 74–81.
45. Charles Baudelaire, "Le Peintre de la vie moderne" (1863), in *Ecrits esthétiques* (Paris: Union Générale d'Editons, 1986), 360–404.
46. Jean-Christophe Royoux, "Projet pour un texte: The Cinematographic Model in the Work of Marcel Broodthaers," *Broodthaers: Cinéma*, 297–305.
47. Charles Baudelaire, *Les Fleurs du mal*, trans. Richard Howard (Boston: David R. Godine, 1982), 24.
48. Walter Benjamin, "Charles Baudelaire: Ein Lyriker im Zeitalter des Hochkapitalismus," in *Gesammelte Schriften* (Frankfurt: Suhrkamp Verlag 1991), I, 2, 509–690.
49. Stéphane Rona, "C'est l'Angelus qui sonne" (interview with Marcel Broodthaers), *+-o III*, 12 (February 1976): 18–19.
50. *Broodthaers: Cinéma*, 116.
51. Trevor Stark, "Reification and Worldview," citing Agnès Krutwig Caers, "La Vision du monde dans les Petits poèmes en prose de Charles Baudelaire," in *Lucien Goldmann et la sociologie de la littérature* (Brussels: Institut de sociologie, Éditions de l'université de Bruxelles, 1975), 133–47.
52. Charles Baudelaire, "The Queen of the Faculties," in Jonathan Mayne (ed. and trans.), *The Mirror of Art, Critical Studies by Baudelaire* (Garden City: Doubleday & Co, 1956), 233.
53. Broodthaers, "Ma mémoire est un film en couleur," trans., *Broodthaers: Cinéma*, 315.
54. Broodthaers, "Interview with Trépied," trans., *Broodthaers: Cinéma*, 320.
55. Wall-Romana, *Cinepoetry*, 19.
56. Broodthaers, "Projet pour un film," trans., *Broodthaers: Cinéma*, 313.
57. Correspondence with Wall-Romana.
58. Cinepoetry represents a more or less "underground" tradition within (Bretonian) Surrealism, as the material model of the filmic apparatus and paratexts were largely sublimated into the primacy of psychic automatism. For the complicated relationship between cinepoetry and Surrealism, see Wall-Romana, *Cinepoetry*, 136–58.
59. Ibid.
60. Royoux, "Projet pour un texte," *Broodthaers. Cinéma*, 298.
61. de Bruyn, "Cinéma modèle," 169.
62. Broodthaers, "Draft for a Text," trans., *Broodthaers: Cinéma*, 322.
63. Haidu, *Absence of Work*, 272.
64. For instance "Le Requin" (1961), "La Formule du poisson est féroce" (c.1967–68), and "L'Académie" (1968). This was pointed out by Charlotte Friling in her account of the *Plaques Académie I, Académie II* (1968). See Charlotte Friling and Dirk Snauwaert (eds.), *Industrial Poems, Marcel Broodthaers* (Brussels: Wiels/Hatje Cantz, 2021), 276–77.
65. In the introductory "Art poétique," to Broodthaers's last poetry volume *Pense-Bête* (1963–64), Broodthaers plays on the double meaning of "solitaire," at once referring to solitude and diamonds. See "The Art of Poetry," trans., *Broodthaers: Collected Writings*, 102.
66. See *Industrial Poems*, 276–77.
67. See Broodthaers, "A Cube, A Sphere…," trans., *Broodthaers: Collected Writings*, 190.
68. de Bruyn, "Cinéma modèle," 169.
69. Ibid.
70. Baudelaire, "L'Horloge," *Les Fleurs du mal*, 82.
71. Broodthaers, "Ten Thousand Francs Reward," trans., *Broodthaers: Collected Writings*, 415.
72. See Xavier Canonne, *Surrealism in Belgium 1924–2000* (Brussels and London: Mercatorfonds/Thames and Hudson, 2007).

73. See Broodthaers, "René Magritte" (1961), trans., in *Industrial Poems*, 84.
74. Ibid.
75. In 1965 or 1966 Broodthaers and Magritte themselves would shoot a similar film in Magritte's garden, titled *Broodthaers & Magritte*. (See filmography in this volume.) Although the film itself was probably left unfinished and is relatively obscure, one of its most symbolically charged images, Magritte passing a bowler hat to Broodthaers, has gained an iconic status by now.
76. "La Figure o," trans., *Broodthaers: Cinéma*, 315.
77. In 1963, Broodthaers wrote, "Magritte is famous. True to his original leanings, he continues to develop a poetic language meant to undermine the one by which we live." Broodthaers, "Beware the Challenge!" trans., *Broodthaers: Collected Writings*, 146.
78. Broodthaers, "Open letter Lignano; 27 August 1968," trans., ibid., 197.
79. See Marie-Pascale Gildemyn, "Marcel Broodthaers (1924–1976), Les (noms des) personnes" (PhD diss., University of Rennes, 2004).
80. See ibid., and Stéphanie Barron and Michel Draguet (eds.) *Magritte and Contemporary Art: The Treachery of Images* (Los Angeles and Ghent: Los Angeles County Museum of Art and Ludion, 2006).
81. Herbert S. Gershman, "Valéry, Breton and Eluard on Poetry," in *French Review* 38, no. 3 (January 1965): 334.
82. Ibid.
83. Broodthaers, "Signalisation, Düsseldorf, 19 September 1968," unpublished manuscript reproduced and translated in *Industrial Poems*, 295.
84. Broodthaers, "Literary Section, On the text by M. Foucault or on the transformation of writing into an object," in Maria Gilissen and Rainer Borgemeister (eds.), *Section Littéraire du Musée d'Art Moderne, Département des Aigles* (Brussels: MERZ, 2001), n.p.
85. Michel Foucault, *This Is Not a Pipe*, trans. James Harkness (Berkeley: University of California Press, 1982), 44.
86. Broodthaers's preliminary sketches and correspondence considering this unfinished project were compiled by Rainer Borgemeister and Maria Gilissen in *Section Littéraire* (2001). See note 84.
87. See Dirk Snauwaert, "The Figures," trans., in Benjamin Buchloh (ed.), *Marcel Broodthaers: Writings, Interviews, Photographs*, special issue of *October* 42 (Fall 1987): 127–35.
88. *Broodthaers: Cinéma*, 143.
89. Broodthaers, "La figure o," trans., ibid., 314
90. Note that Birgit Pelzer and Yves Depelsenaire have approached Broodthaers, according to Eric de Bruyn an "avid reader of Lacan," along the framework advanced by the latter philosopher. See for example Birgit Pelzer, "Die symbolischen Strategien des 'Semblant' (Schein)," in *Vorträge zum filmischen Werk von Marcel Broodthaers* (Berlin: Staatliche Museen, 2001), 45–75; and Yves Depelsenaire, *Éloge de Marcel Broodthaers* (Brussels: La Lettre volée, 2022).
91. Thomas McEvilley, "Another Alphabet, the Art of Marcel Broodthaers," *Artforum* 28, no. 3 (November 1989): 106-115.
92. Catherine David, "Le musée du signe," in *Marcel Broodthaers*, exh. cat. (Paris: Galerie nationale du Jeu de Paume, 1991), 21 (my translation from French).
93. According to Broodthaers scholar Margaux Van Uytvanck, this iconic "transaction" should be read in metaphorical terms, rather than material or historical.
94. Marcel Broodthaers, "Gesprek met Ludo Bekkers," *Museumjournaal* (15 February 1970): 66–71. French version reproduced in Gildemyn, "Les (noms des) personnes," 328.
95. Peter Bondanella, *Italian Cinema: From Neorealism to the Present* (New York: Continuum, 2001), 57.

INTRODUCTION 61

96. Hilde D'haeyere and Steven Jacobs, "Frankfurter Slapstick: Benjamin, Kracauer, and Adorno on American Screen Comedy," *October* 160 (Spring 2017): 30–50.
97. Gunning, "The Cinema of Attraction."
98. Haidu, *The Absence of Work*, 271.
99. Eric de Bruyn, "The Museum of Attractions: Marcel Broodthaers and the Section Cinéma," in Charles Esche, Tanya Leighton, and Mark Lewis (eds.), *Art and the Moving Image: A Critical Reader* (London: Tate, 2008), 115.
100. Broodthaers, "Open Letter, Antwerp, 2 December 1969," trans., *Broodthaers: Collected Writings*, 216.
101. "M is at the source of contemporary art." [...] "He unconsciously invented the modern space." Broodthaers, "A Throw of the Dice...," trans. ibid., 238 (corrected translation); Wall-Romana, *Cinepoetry*, 55–79.
102. Steven Jacobs, "CoBrA, Canvas, and Camera: Luc de Heusch Filming Alechinsky and Dotremont at Work," in Rachel Esner and Sandra Kisters (eds.), *The Mediatization of the Artist* (London: Palgrave Macmillan, 2018), 115–29.
103. Christophe Viart, "The Happy Failure: *La Pluie (Projet pour un texte)* by Marcel Broodthaers, 1969," in José Moure and Dominique Chateau (eds.), *Post-cinema: Cinema in the Post-Art Era* (Amsterdam: Amsterdam University Press, 2020), 295–310.
104. According to Manuel Borja-Villel, Broodthaers's practice created "in-between spaces." See "The Moment of Marcel Broodthaers? A Conversation," in *October* 155 (Winter 2016): 126.
105. Broodthaers, "Le D est plus grand que le T," trans., *Broodthaers: Cinéma*, 319.
106. Ibid.
107. Jean Dypréau, "Le Corbeau et le renard," in *Journal des Beaux-Arts* 1163 (15 April 1967), n. p. (my translation from French).
108. Jean Harlez's best-known film is *Le chantier des gosses* (1956–70).
109. Dypréau, "Le Corebeau et le Renard," n. p. (my translation from French).
110. Broodthaers, "Le D est plus grand que le T," trans., *Broodthaers: Cinéma*, 319.
111. Ibid.
112. de Bruyn, "The Museum of Attractions," 112.
113. Krauss, *A Voyage on the North Sea*, 45.
114. Ibid., 44.
115. Marcel Broodthaers, "Experimental Cinema and the Fables of La Fontaine. The Law of the Strongest Prevails," trans., *Broodthaers: Cinéma*, 320; P. Adams Sitney, *Visionary Film: The American Avant-Garde 1943 1978* (New York: Oxford University Press, 1979); Peter Gidal, *Materialist Film* (London: Routledge, 1989).
116. Gene Youngblood, *Expanded Cinema* (New York: Dutton, 1970).
117. See Branden Joseph and Liz Kotz (eds.), *X-Screen: Film Installations and Actions in the 1960s and 1970s* (Cologne: Walther Konig, 2004); and *Into the Light: The Projected Image in American Art 1964–1977* (New York: Whitney Museum of American Art, 2001).
118. de Bruyn, "The Museum of Attractions," 113.
119. See François Bovier, "Tony Morgan's Performative Cinema in the Age of the 'Cinematic Turn': 'Relational Films' (1969–70), 'Structural Films' (1969–70) and Produkt Cinema (1971)," *Artium Questiones* 31 (2020): 67–100.
120. de Bruyn, "The Museum of Attractions," 121.
121. Benjamin H. D. Buchloh, *Neo-Avantgarde and Culture Industry: Essays on European and American Art from 1955 to 1975* (Cambridge, Mass.: MIT Press, 2003); Alexander Alberro & Blake Stimson (eds.), *Institutional Critique: An Anthology of Artists' Writings* (Cambridge, Mass. MIT Press, 2011).
122. Jean-Louis Baudry, "Cinéma: Effets idéologiques produits par l'appareil de base," *Cinéthique*, nos. 7–8 (1970): 1–8. Translated in English as "Ideological Effects of the Basic Cinematographic Apparatus," in Philip Rosen (ed.), *Narrative: Apparatus,*

Ideology: A Film Theory Reader (New York: Columbia University Press, 1986), 286–98. See also "The Apparatus: Metapsychological Approaches to the Impression of Reality in the Cinema" (299–318) in the same volume; and Jean-Louis Comolli, "Machines of the Visible," in Teresa de Lauretis and Stephen Heath (eds.), *The Cinematic Apparatus* (London: St. Martin's Press, 1980), 122–41.

123. See Raymond Bellour, *L'Entre-Images, Photo, Cinéma, Vidéo* (Paris: Editions de la Différence, 1990); Raymond Bellour, *L'Entre-Images 2. Mots, Images* (Paris: P.O.L., 1999); Raymond Bellour, "Of an Other Cinema," in Sara Arrhenius, Magdalena Malm, and Christina Ricupero (eds.), *Black Box Illuminated* (Stockholm: Prospectus, 2003), 39–62; and Raymond Bellour, *La Querelle des dispositifs: Cinéma - installations, expositions* (Paris: P.O.L., 2012).
124. Jean-Christophe Royoux, "Projet pour un texte," trans., *Broodthaers: Cinéma*, 300.
125. "Marcel Broodhtaers," in *Documenta 5*, exh. cat. (Kassel: Documenta Gmbh, 1972), n. p. (my translation from French).
126. Barry Barker, "Marcel Broodthaers: Take the Risk with Me," last modified 23 November 2016, https://flash---art.com/article/marcel-broodthaers-2/.
127. Chaffee, "Décors" in *Marcel Broodthaers: A Retrospective*, 290–94; and Haidu, *The Absence of Work*, 228.
128. Haidu, *The Absence of Work*, 231.
129. Douglas Crimp, "This Is Not a Museum of Art," in *Marcel Broodthaers*, exh. cat. (Minneapolis: Walker Art Center, 1989), 83.
130. De Bruyn, "The Museum of Attractions," 113.
131. Chaffee, "Décors," 291. In this text, Chaffee mentions *Programme* as "one of the origins of the Décors project." *Section cinéma*, however, is not mentioned here.
132. Anny De Decker, "Fig. 1 Programme," in *Soleil Politique*, exh. cat. (Antwerp: M HKA, 2019), 127.
133. Marcel Broodthaers, interview with Marcel Broodthaers by Marianne Verstraeten," trans., in *Broodthaers: Collected Writings*, 410–11.
134. Royoux, "Projet pur un texte," in *Broodthaers: Cinéma*, 302.
135. Pavle Levi, "Cinema by Other Means," in *October* 131 (Winter 2010): 53.
136. In a letter to Franz Meyer (19 September 1974), Broodthaers discussed the design of the exhibition poster: "Here is a project for a poster accompanied by six photos. I doubt about the brown that makes up the background around a white rectangle. To 'make cinema' it would be better to use black and white letters" (my translation from French) [Kunstmuseum Archives, Basel]. In Broodthaers's poster designs that accompany the letter, cinema's role is remarkably more pronounced than is the case in the final poster, witness the omnipresence of the "films" or "film program" as a title and some drawings of film reels.
137. See Royoux, "Projet pour un texte," in *Broodthaers. Cinéma*, 309 (note 56).
138. "The exhibition, achieved by cuts [coupures] (in the intention of the artist) is parallel to the method of cinematographic editing" (my translation from French). Press file related to *L'Angélus de Daumier* accessed at the CNAC Archives, kept by the Centre Pompidou, Paris.
139. See Xavier García Bardón's essay in this volume.
140. de Bruyn, "The Museum of Attractions," 121.
141. Bruce Jenkins, "Un Peu Tard," in *Broodthaers: Cinéma*, 289.
142. See André Bazin, "The Myth of a Total Cinema," in André Bazin, *What Is Cinema*, trans. and ed. Hugh Gray (Los Angeles: University of California Press, 1967).

RENÉ AND MARCEL AT THE MOVIES
PRELIMINARY REMARKS

Bruce Jenkins

> The secret of the found object is thus the most intractable kind: it is hidden in plain sight, like Poe's purloined letter. Once found, however, the found object should, as in surrealist practices, become foundational.
> —W. J. T. Mitchell, *What Do Pictures Want?*[1]

One could imagine a gallery exhibition somewhere in which the works of two artists of the twentieth century have been displayed together and put into conversation. On one wall, a painting of a pipe that "is not a pipe" hangs next to a vacuum-formed plastic plaque embossed with letters of the alphabet, while the outline of a pipe encircles the letter H. Displayed on another wall is a series of photographic portraits. In one, the artist is seated in stark profile in front of a painting of a figure in opposing profile; next to it, there is a photo of the other artist standing in stark profile opposite a massive sculpture of a similarly posed eagle. There are other photographs of each artist in a bowler hat, or posed holding a film camera in front of their face. In yet another grouping, there hangs a painting divided into six parts with images of everyday objects, and beneath each, a written inscription misidentifying the thing; next to it is a canvas with forty-five broken egg shells in five rows and the word *moules* painted above. The gallery is filled to the brim with similar mutually referential themes and images.[2]

I have become obsessed with the relationship between the oeuvres of Marcel Broodthaers and René Magritte, two celebrated Belgian artists who were born one generation apart and whose lives intersected episodically beginning in the mid-1940s (a young Broodthaers still in his early twenties, the middle-aged Magritte pushing fifty) and continuing until Magritte's death in 1967. While this relationship has not escaped critical attention, the precise ways in which the older artist served as a mentor of sorts for the younger have largely been ignored, hiding as it were in plain sight like Poe's purloined letter, to invoke W. J. T. Mitchell's analogy.

Broodthaers & Magritte. 16mm. c. 1965–66. Camera Maria Gilissen. Courtesy of the Walker Art Center's Ruben/Bentson Moving Image Collection. © Estate of Marcel Broodthaers, c/o SABAM Belgium 2024

CENTENNIALS

While 2024 marks Marcel Broodthaers's centennial, I want to look back to another such celebration that took place in 1998, channeling the critical work the British writer and filmmaker Peter Wollen produced after visiting Brussels, then in the midst of celebrating the centennial of René Magritte. There he discovered the city "festooned with images of bowler hats, on banners, posters … There were even real bowler hats in window displays."[3] Wollen focused on the ubiquity of the bowler hat in these centennial promotions and began to examine what he termed the "discursive sources" that fed into this enduring symbol for Magritte's art.

Folded into his analysis are references to some of the several dozen home movies that Magritte made in the late 1950s and early-to-mid 1960s. For his part, Wollen succinctly captured two fundamental features of Magritte's movies: their farcical play with silent film tropes and the artist's inclusion of objects drawn from his paintings: the bowler hat (of course), but also umbrellas, tubas, and pipes. Wollen, however, is content to treat the artist's filmmaking as peripheral, much as Magritte himself preferred: "I don't make films or cinema, I make movies the good old way."[4] Nonetheless, I believe that Magritte's home movies, in their technical simplicity, lack of pretense, and loving imitation of silent cinema may well have been a significant influence on the filmmaking practice of that other, younger Belgian artist.

While there is precious little direct commentary by Marcel Broodthaers on Magritte's art, on their personal relationship, or on the kind of influence that I am claiming, we do, perhaps, have a salient parallel example of Broodthaers's take on artistic influence, this time involving another painter. In a 1973 interview with Benjamin Buchloh and Michael Oppitz focusing on his short film *Analysis of a Painting*, Broodthaers speaks about the canvas that would become the source for a significant series of his works across a range of media, so much so that decades later it would become the seminal example in Rosalind Krauss's theory of the "post-medium condition."[5] (We'll return to Krauss a little later.) Broodthaers tells his interviewers about the origins of the small maritime painting that he purchased "in a curiosity shop in the Rue Jacob in Paris."[6] He speculates that it dates from the "end of the XIXth century" and that the unsigned canvas "is the work of an amateur." When Oppitz conjectures that the artist must have lived by the coast and loved the sea, Broodthaers counters:

> I do not believe so. The amateur would rather paint a landscape that is not his own. He possibly lived in Rue Jacob and on Sundays he painted.[7]

So, too, for Broodthaers's probable assessment of Magritte's home movies. I doubt that anyone would take offense if we were to call René Magritte an amateur filmmaker or, to apply Broodthaers's turn of phrase, a "Sunday cineaste." Magritte's "minor" cinematic output may have become as foundational to Broodthaers's filmmaking as the little amateur painting in the Rue Jacob was to his art.

THE AMATEUR AND INSTITUTIONAL CRITIQUE

Let us return to Rosalind Krauss's reading of Broodthaers's filmmaking in relationship to the notion of the "amateur" that Broodthaers introduced in characterizing the painting that is central to *A Voyage on the North Sea* and a suite of related films, an artist's book, and a slide-projection piece.[8] If we bracket Krauss's slapdash history of silent cinema that lumps together the Lumière brothers, D. W. Griffith, and Chaplin, her central formal claim about Broodthaers's filmmaking is that "he replicated the primitive look of early cinema with its uneven exposures spliced together and its flickering gait."[9] While I, too, have previously written at some length about the influence of Keaton and Chaplin on Broodthaers, Krauss comes much closer here to accurately capturing the aesthetic of another Belgian filmmaker who shared these early influences—namely, René Magritte.[10]

The release of a sizeable cache of Magritte's home movies in recent years and the subsequent emergence of a modest body of critical literature focusing on them allows us now to consider these films as possible influences on Broodthaers's burgeoning film practice of the late 1960s and early-to-mid 1970s.[11] While Krauss mentions the "openness promised by early film"—an oblique reference, perhaps, to the unruliness that predated what filmmaker and theorist Noël Burch describes as the development of the "Institutional Mode of Representation"—one in fact finds such non-studio tropes in abundance in Magritte's 8mm films.[12] There is, for example, a distinct frontality to the framing of the action, with performers often looking directly into the camera lens—Magritte himself being the worst offender.[13] The editing often involves mismatched shots and overlapping action. And as the camera-arts historian Xavier Canonne concedes, these were "little amateur 8mm films that left a wide margin for improvisation."[14]

Here again we have that descriptor: "amateur," a term that film archivist Jan-Christopher Horak deployed to designate the "first American Film Avant-Garde" as a "History of Amateurs"—using the root meaning of the word to celebrate these early filmmakers as "Lovers of Cinema."[15] While the distinctive features of this "amateur" cinema were heterogeneous, the artists involved were united in their commitment to mark out a space of artistic expression beyond the narrow confines of commercial cinema. Horak then makes an invaluable distinction between this generation (active in the 1920s, 1930s, and early 1940s) and the later, far better known generation of the postwar era (Maya Deren, Stan Brakhage, et al.). As he notes, "The earlier generation viewed themselves as cineastes, as lovers of cinema, as 'amateurs' willing to work in any arena furthering the cause of film art, even if it meant working for hire."[16] Not so for the next generation, which, according to Horak, rejected "any collaboration with commercial or public interests, any utilitarian usage of the medium"—commitments that resulted in what Horak termed "a romanticized professionalization of the avant-garde project." Here, Horak, citing filmmaker and critic Jonas Mekas, offers a vivid perspective on an experimental cinema that moved well beyond any stock notions of the avant-garde, focusing on the rarely discussed institutional support that engendered the practice:

> This professionalization of avant-garde filmmaking was, of course, possible only because the institutions providing material support for the avant-garde had expanded to include university film courses (offering filmmakers a place to earn money while making their films), government and foundation grants (allowing them to finance production), and nontheatrical film exhibition within the institutional framework of museums, archives and media centers (offering filmmakers a place to show their work).[17]

Enter Marcel Broodthaers, who comes to filmmaking in the mid-1950s, more than a decade into the emergence of this new institutionalized avant-garde, which manifested itself in Belgium with, among other institutional supports, the 1949 and 1958 editions of the EXPRMNTL film festival, which also brought works of the American postwar film avant-garde to Belgian audiences. Broodthaers's film *La Clef de l'horloge* (1957) was a complex art documentary—or, as the film's subtitle calls it, a "poème cinématographique"—focusing on Kurt Schwitters's assemblages from the 1920s and 1930s (the period that saw the first generation of avant-garde filmmaking) and produced in a manner that was thoroughly consonant with that earlier mode. With its stark black-and-white cinematography and kinetic visual lexicon reminiscent of that early film avant-garde, it was a work knowingly out of time, and most especially out of step with the more professionalized forms of then-contemporary experimental film practice.[18] Its unheralded inclusion in the 1958 EXPRMNTL film competition in Brussels would provide Broodthaers with a lesson that he learned (as we say) the hard way: it was critically disregarded, and the print was lost. According to Broodthaers, "people ridiculed this effort of mine."[19] But it was an invaluable introduction to the protocols and formal concerns of the then-contemporary professionalized, institutionalized form of avant-garde cinema; this experience would have far-reaching implications for his future filmmaking, in part by deferring such production for nearly a decade. And when Broodthaers resumed filmmaking, his work reappeared, boldly insistent on disregarding the established orthodoxy, again under the auspices of the EXPRMNTL film festival.

Bringing Magritte back into the picture, I believe, reveals the ways in which Broodthaers had intentionally, and effectively, instrumentalized the amateur techniques evident in the painter's home movies into a forceful critique of the professionalized mode of the film avant-garde, then more than two decades into its ascendancy. Broodthaers, however, inverts the hierarchy Magritte had tacitly established between his painting and filmmaking by radically embracing celluloid as a primary medium for his art practice—a decision that guaranteed an even greater level of marginality vis à vis the field of contemporary art than his antiquarian filmmaking had engendered within the arena of the film avant-garde. Leaning into filmmaking and the plastic fabrication of his "industrial poems" opened up a space into which the artist would soon add new, highly critical forms of art: the installations.

As we begin to enter the established version of Broodthaers's career, here is a straightforward definition of institutional critique: criticizing art by artistic means. While this concept of Broodthaers's innovative mode of institutional critique has been predicated on his non-filmic artworks (particularly his "fiction museums") that targeted the art museum and gallery system, this anti-art strategy may well have originated in his filmic response to the institutionalization of avant-garde cinema. As I have noted, Broodthaers, for his part, found little success in this parallel universe of "experimental film," despite two attempts to gain recognition: first with the 1958 screening of *La Clef de l'horloge*, and nearly a decade later with a similarly ill-fated showing of *Le Corbeau et le renard* (1967) at *EXPRMNTL 4* in Knokke-le-Zoute, which was shown minus the printed screen that was integral to its intended presentation; the festival forced him to project the film onto a conventional movie screen. So, let me focus on the latter disappointment, which was compounded by losing out to the Canadian artist and filmmaker Michael Snow, whose film *Wavelength* received the grand prize.[20] Broodthaers called *Wavelength* "a painter's film" and went on to describe it as "a cinema of the sound object."[21] Here Broodthaers seems to be tacitly acknowledging the origins of his own cinematic practice, by contrast, as perhaps a "poet's film."

POETRY BY OTHER MEANS

In a filmed conversation with the Belgian writer and literary critic Georges Adé, Broodthaers provided a fairly meager assessment of Magritte's impact:

> The only thing he said to me was this: "Read and meditate on Mallarmé." He offered me the gift of *Un coup de dés* and *Igitur*. The poem obsessed me for 20–25 years, and now that Magritte is dead, to liberate me at least partially I believe it necessary to redo the roll of the dice on the notion of the image.[22]

While this might accurately account for Broodthaers's book *Un coup de dés jamais n'abolira le hasard* (published in 1969, the same year as the Adé interview), there is in this decades-long reckoning with what Freud would term the "burden" of Magritte's gift a larger generative cache of Broodthaers's work. I find Magritte present in much of what Krauss would term Broodthaers's post-medium practices, not least of which is the increased emphasis on filmmaking following Magritte's death in August 1967. But here it is not simply the younger artist's embrace of a particular cinematic heritage—the beloved silent comedies that Magritte recreated in his garden and sitting room with family and friends—but rather the recognition that Mallarmé's late nineteenth-century opus itself might be read as a para-cinematic work of art.

Here, I am indebted to Jennifer Wild and her study of the impact of early cinema upon the burgeoning Parisian art world in the first two decades of the twentieth century. Wild includes Walter Benjamin's analysis of Mallarmé's poem, which focused on the "vertical domain of advertising graphics in the horizontality of writing, and more generally in the book's absorption of the directional uprightness of the film screen."[23] From this perspective, we can more fully grasp what was lost in the botched screening of *Le Corbeau et le renard* in December 1967 at the International Experimental Film Competition at Knokke-le-Zoute. The organizers failed to recognize that Broodthaers's printed screen—inscribed with graphic textual extracts from La Fontaine—that served as a backdrop to the projected image was as integral to the workings of this breakthrough work as, say, Snow's intrusive sine-wave sound track was for *Wavelength*.[24]

Marcel Broodthaers and René Magritte. c. 1965–66. Photo Maria Gilissen.
© Estate of Marcel Broodthaers, c/o SABAM Belgium 2024

THIS IS NOT A PIPE

Returning to the relatively undervalued relationship between Broodthaers and René Magritte, let me point to an invaluable image captured by Maria Gilissen, a portrait of the pair taken near the end of the elder artist's life. The two seem to be gently reenacting a silent-film struggle over the ownership of a bowler hat. That hat would soon enter into the younger artist's work, both as part of the montage of color film footage inserted into *Le Corbeau et le renard* and as a pair of black-and-white static cutouts that make periodic trick film-like appearances on the shelves of the set piece that is the primary setting for the film. Far more significant is another piece of Magritte iconography—*la pipe*—that would emerge in no less than seven of Broodthaers's films, a series of "Industrial Poems" (plastic plaques) that he began producing the following year, and as an object displayed in the inner room of Broodthaers's *Section Cinéma* of the landmark *Musée d'Art Moderne, Départment des Aigles* that opened in early 1971 in Düsseldorf.[25]

It was with this suite of works depicting Magritte's image of a pipe (celebrated for its contradictory caption "This is not a pipe") that Broodthaers first fully embraced a genuinely intermedial practice, deploying this iconic object both to challenge cinema's assumed realist representations as well as to engage in the epistemic conundrums of image and word on the plastic surfaces of the Industrial Poems. While *Le Corbeau et le renard* can be read as an homage to Magritte, who passed away earlier that year, this extensive new body of work moved well beyond simple citation. Broodthaers was now actively expanding a Magrittean aesthetic by recognizing that the central elements borrowed from Magritte— image and language—could be fully realized not only on celluloid strips but equally well on vacuum-formed plastic. It was, additionally, a chance for Broodthaers to redeem the promise of his first film, *La Clef de l'horloge*, by revisiting the anachronistic production protocols of the trick film and a mise-en-scène of objects set into motion and serially displayed. He was, in other words, embarking on a voyage that instantiated the post-medium condition of his art.

All of this emerged nearly four years before the suite of works associated with *A Voyage on the North Sea* (1973–74), but always somehow hiding in plain sight.

A GODARDIAN KNOT

I have continued to ask myself why Marcel Broodthaers's films have received so little attention in the critical literature devoted to his arts practice. Even writings supposedly devoted to the film work—say, Rosalind Krauss's now canonical 1999 lecture-essay turned book, *A Voyage on the North Sea*—seem at pains to adequately describe or analyze Broodthaers's actual filmmaking. As I have noted, Krauss puts forth a woefully inadequate history of the medium, collapsing as she does the first quarter-century of film production under the descriptor "primitive." (Also, what to make of a book whose cover displays imagery from the wrong film?)[26] Perhaps Krauss's *October* colleague Annette Michelson, a seminal scholar of cinema, might have lent her expertise to that Walter Neurath Memorial Lecture in spring 1999.

The best explanation that I have come across to explain this phenomenon— the dearth of discourse on Broodthaers's films—is one gleaned, appropriately enough, from a film: Jean-Luc Godard's first feature, *À bout de souffle* (1960). This insight arrives in the dialogue during a scene late in the film as the criminal protagonist Michel (Jean-Paul Belmondo) drives through the streets of Paris at night in yet another stolen vehicle. Channeling a sociological observation from the director, Michel explains to his American paramour (played by the radiant Jean Seberg) the order of things within the criminal underworld: "No, it's normal. Informers inform, burglars burgle, murderers murder, lovers love."

To shift fields of reference from criminality to art criticism, I am tempted to extend Godard's claim about the "normal" when it comes to the critical attention paid to the art of Marcel Broodthaers: writers write, theorists theorize, philosophers philosophize. To appropriate and, in the Duchampian sense, "rectify" the title of a key painting by Magritte, let us call this "The Treachery of Words"—the mise en abyme of endless wordplay and that infinitesimal parsing of language that is the stock-in-trade of contemporary poststructuralist writers. In this text-bound world of words, images are left simply at sea.

FANMAIL FROM SOME FLOUNDER

While I have not come across any correspondence between Magritte and Broodthaers, let me offer two modest items that might represent a measure of the pair's mutual admiration and admonition. The first seems obvious: Broodthaers's imaginary interview with the painter (a journalistic fiction, perhaps not unlike his museum fictions).[27] The interview opens with the younger artist's straightforward query: "How about interviewing you for a new newspaper?" What follows, of course, is far from conventional, beginning with the presence of a certain X, to whom we are parenthetically introduced as an ever-present figure ("looks like a poet") at Magritte's interviews with a tendency to disrupt the process. This coupled with the older artist's mien ("wink of a grey eye," "diction," and an "exaggerated but otherwise appropriate politeness") has put the would-be "interlocutor ill at ease." An ambitious question about the titles of Magritte's paintings and an attempt to "retrace around your paintings the environment that has disappeared" baffles the painter. And a brief follow-up query prompts a confused response: "You have a strange way of talking." The interview concludes on safer terrain: "There are a lot of bowler hats in your paintings. Why?"

The second "communiqué" is by contrast far from obvious, and yet in reading Magritte's brief essay "Object Lesson" (1962), I find both hard-won insights and what was invaluable advice from an aging painter and amateur filmmaker addressed, perhaps, to a poet and photojournalist in his late thirties trying to forge an artistic pathway:

> It is possible to see someone tipping his hat without seeing politeness.
> It is scarcely possible to choose between two equal images unless a misplaced preference tips the balance.
> Sometimes an image can seriously accuse the viewer.
> Any object, taken as a question of a problem ... and the right answer discovered by searching for the object that is secretly connected to the first ... give, when brought together, a new knowledge.
> Comprehension of accuracy does not preclude enjoyment of inaccuracy.
> However distant we may be from an object, we are never completely separate from it.

An image unknown in the dark is called forth by an image known in the light.

Whatever lines, words, colors, are scattered on the page, the composition is always meaningful.[28]

We can, I would hope, recognize in this text from six decades ago its perspicacious purchase on Marcel Broodthaers's body of film work, the subject of this publication.

NOTES

1. The epigraph's quotation appears in W. J. T. Mitchell, *What Do Pictures Want?: The Lives and Loves of Images* (Chicago: University of Chicago Press, 2005), 114.
2. Such an array of images served as a pre-credit sequence to my symposium presentation, presented silent and without commentary. This consisted of a series of twenty or so images pairing Magritte and Broodthaers—ranging from their artworks and films to their appearances (solo and together) in front of the camera.
3. Peter Wollen, "Magritte and the Bowler Hat," *New Left Review* 1, no. 238 (January/February 2000): 104.
4. Magritte quoted in Xavier Canonne, *René Magritte: The Revealing Image* (Antwerp: Ludion, 2017), 141.
5. Rosalind Krauss, *"A Voyage on the North Sea": Art in the Age of the Post-Medium Condition* (New York: Thames & Hudson, 1999).
6. "Interview with Marcel Broodthaers on His Film 'Analysis of a Painting' by B. H. D. Buchloh and Michael Oppitz," excerpt reproduced in *Marcel Broodthaers: Cinéma* (Barcelona: Fundació Antoni Tàpies, 1997), 230.
7. Buchloh and Oppitz, "Interview with Marcel Broodthaers," in *Marcel Broodthaers: Cinéma*, 230–31.
8. The other film versions include *Analyse d'une peinture, Une peinture d'amateur découverte dans une boutique de curiosités*, and *Le même film, revu après critiques*. The artist's book, *A Voyage on the North Sea*, is a thirty-eight-page publication issued by Petersburg Press in 1973; and the slide-projection piece, *Bateau Tableau*.
9. Krauss, *"A Voyage on the North Sea,"* 43.
10. See my essays: Bruce Jenkins, "CB: Cinema Broodthaers," in *Marcel Broodthaers* (New York: Rizzoli, 1989); "Un Peu Tard: Citation in the Cinema of Marcel Broodthaers," in *Marcel Broodthaers: Cinéma*; and "The Impossible Cinema of Marcel Broodthaers," in Graeme Harper and Rob Stone (eds.), *The Unsilvered Screen: Surrealism on Film* (London: Wallflower Press, 2007).
11. The Musée Magritte has hosted on its website streaming versions of some thirty-nine Magritte amateur films. See https://musee-magritte-museum.be/en/about-the-museum/collections-mmm/archives-1. Among the recent publications that focus on Magritte's home movies, two have been of particular value for this essay: Xavier Canonne, *René Magritte: The Revealing Image* (Antwerp: Ludion, 2017); and Lucy Fischer, *Cinemagritte: René Magritte within the Frame of Film History, Theory, and Practice* (Detroit: Wayne State University Press, 2019).

12. See Noël Burch, *Correction Please, or How We Got into the Pictures* (London: Arts Council of Great Britain, 1980).
13. See, for example, *René* (1957), pairing the artist and his wife, Georgette, with Magritte demonstrating his repertoire of silly faces in medium close-ups as well as his manic mustachioed version of Chaplin's Hitler impersonation from *The Great Dictator*.
14. Canonne, *René Magritte: The Revealing Image*, 36.
15. Jan-Christopher Horak (ed.), *Lovers of Cinema: The First American Film Avant-Garde 1919–1945* (Madison: University of Wisconsin Press, 1995).
16. Jan-Christopher Horak, "The First American Film Avant-Garde, 1919–1945," in Horak (ed.), *Lovers of Cinema*, 15.
17. Jan-Christopher Horak, "The First American Film Avant-Garde, 1919–1945," in Horak (ed.), *Lovers of Cinema*, 15.
18. See Jenkins, "Un Peu Tard," 289–291.
19. Marcel Broodthaers, "Letter to Otto Hahn," 1967, in Gloria Moure (ed.), *Marcel Broodthaers: Collected Writings* (Barcelona: Ediciones Polígrafa, 2012), 176.
20. For a useful artifact of this historic moment within the experimental cinema, see P. Adams Sitney's telegram to Jonas Mekas (dated 31 December 1967), reproduced in John Klacsmann (ed.), *Retrospective: Michael Snow* (New York: Anthology Film Archives, 2021), 12.
21. Marcel Broodthaers, "Le Cinéma Expérimental et les fables de La Fontaine: La raison du plus fort," 1968, in *Marcel Broodthaers: Cinéma*, 321.
22. Broodthaers, "Le Cinéma Expérimental et les fables de La Fontaine," n. 13, 306.
23. Jennifer Wild, *The Parisian Avant-Garde in the Age of Cinema, 1900–1923* (Oakland: University of California Press, 2015), 67.
24. One can only speculate what would have happened if the same normative exhibition parameters that rejected Broodthaers's plan to project on his printed screen had been enforced for sound playback, given that Snow's signature electronic glissando was recorded on a separate 1/4-inch tape that had to be played separately alongside the film's sound track. See "Michael Snow in Conversation with Elisabetta Fabrizi and Chris Meigh-Andrews," in the *BFI Gallery Book: The British Film Institute's Contemporary Art Gallery* (London: British Film Institute, 2011), 123.
25. For the films, see *Marcel Broodthaers: Cinéma*, 94–99. For the Industrial Poems, see Charlotte Friling and Dirk Snauwaert (eds.), *Marcel Broodthaers Industrial Poems: The Complete Catalogue of the Plaques 1968–1972* (Brussels: Weils and Hatje Cantz, 2021).
26. Inexplicably, the publication's cover displays a matrix of eight images, all taken from Broodthaers's *Un Voyage à Waterloo* (1969), a film entirely unrelated to the titled subject.
27. Marcel Broodthaers, "Imaginary Interview with René Magritte," in *Marcel Broodthaers: Collected Writings*, 166.
28. René Magritte, "Leçon de choses," *Rhétorique* 7 (October 1962); reprinted as "Object Lesson," in *René Magritte: Selected Writings*, ed. Kathleen Rooney and Eric Plattner, trans. Jo Levy (Minneapolis: University of Minnesota Press, 2016), 211.

LA SÉANCE AND OTHER ASSEMBLIES

Eric C. H. de Bruyn

> But if we begin with the state, we end with the state. Let us begin instead with the popular reunions at the end of the Empire, the various associations and committees hey spawned, and the "buzzing hives" that were the revolutionary clubs of the siege.
> —Kristin Ross

LA SÉANCE

In its summer issue of 1974, the German journal of contemporary art *Interfunktionen* published an unusual artist's work by the name of "Racisme végétal: La Séance."[1] The work carries the attribution a "film de Marcel Broodthaers" and for lack of a better term might be called a cine-text. That is to say, to the extent that *Racisme végétal* can be thought of as a "film," it exists in no other shape or form than in print. It provides neither a scenario for a film that is yet to be made nor does it consist of a transcription of a film that has already been made. In fact, *Racisme végétal* is less the fictious proposition for a "film by Marcel Broodthaers" than a film program or *séance du cinéma*, and it is this polyvalent, French term—*séance*—that shall hold my attention in what follows. Séance can mean "seat," "session," or "sitting" and refers, for instance, to the meeting of a court, council, or parliament, an interval of time spent on a specific, iterative activity (e.g., a filming session or work session) or, as already noted, the performative event of a film projection. I would like to explore the intersections of both a filmic and political genealogy of the séance, particularly, but not exclusively, around the events of May '68, which allows an approach to Broodthaers's practice that is no longer framed in a strictly monographic sense. What might it mean to splice, as it were, Broodthaers's work into another type of historical *defilé*, which would not render it into the terminal point of a series in which the séance, as *Racisme végétal* implies, has become one of endless repetition, a "spectacle permanente"?

Racisme végétal is composed as a simple pamphlet in a sparse, uniform manner, if marked by certain slight inconsistencies in its layout. Leaving much

Spreads from *Racisme végétal : La Séance. Film de Marcel Broodthaers*. 1974.
Collection Ivo and Monique Van Vaerenbergh. Photo Rachel Gruijters.
© Estate of Marcel Broodthaers, c/o SABAM Belgium 2024

blank space between the lettering and images on the page, the work appears to imitate the appearance of a cheaply designed, commercial folder. The actual program is sandwiched between two identical, if mirrored photographs of a deserted beach with palm trees; a central motif within a Western imaginary of exoticism that Broodthaers would use more often in 1974, for example, in his *Jardin d'hiver* installations. Underneath this generic image of a tropical island, which appears to come straight out of a contemporary travel brochure, the ironic phrase "Racisme végétal" is printed in an overly decorative, cursive font. Perched atop the following title page, a small vignette shows Marcel Broodthaers with René Magritte, while the latter holds a film camera to his face, directly returning the gaze of the photographer. Below this photograph, the subtitle "La Séance – Film de Marcel Broodthaers" is printed, which has been broken up through the use of a discrepant set of typefaces and uneven word spacing, followed by the four numbered sections of the program: (1) *Actualités*, (2) *Complément*, (3) *Entr'acte*, (4) *Long métrage*. Finally, at the very bottom of the page, in small print, we read the description: *Spectacle permanent*.

On the subsequent pages of the program, each individual section of the film program is represented by a double spread, consisting of two movie stills, which sometimes—but not always—are drawn from the same movie. Furthermore, sometimes—but not always—this movie may be fictional in kind. As a matter of fact, in the *actualité* or newsreel section Broodthaers deliberately confuses the dualism of fictional and nonfictional film by combining a futuristic image of a rocket ship with an image of two air force pilots. Whereas the first, sci-fi image, which is clearly dated in its stylization, may seem radically out of place in a program of *actualités*, the latter could actually pass as a common component of contemporary news reports. The stills are not accompanied by any captions, which leaves the spectator guessing, and the only clue to Broodthaers's image sources is a brief, typewritten "Note de l'Editeur" at the back of the program, which reveals that, in fact, the cockpit image is drawn from Stanly Kubrick's 1964 Cold War satire, *Dr. Strangelove*. But the other image is not identified and only the most die-hard, sci-fi film buffs will recognize it as deriving from the 1936 film serial *Undersea Kingdom*.

The *complement* offers fewer difficulties, showing the well-known comedians Stan Laurel and Oliver Hardy in *Hog Wild* (1930) in a sly reference to the opening vignette of Broodthaers and Magritte (who, for once, is not shown wearing the signature bowler hat, which was also donned by the slapstick actors Stan Laurel and Charlie Chaplin). The final, *long métrage* or feature film is represented by another classic of the 1930s, the crime film *Angels with Dirty Faces* (1938), directed by Michael Curtiz and starring James Cagney and Pat O'Brien. Once more, however, it introduces another layer of historical desynchrony, including an image of three dark silhouettes against a black wall, as if referring back to the proto-cinematic device of a shadow play or the nineteenth-century parlor game of ombres chinoises.[2]

Literally interrupting this series of film stills is the entr'acte section, which substitutes the images by a simple black frame that, like a dadaist poem, is filled with fragments of advertising slogans: "Buvez le Froid … En Visitant La Ville … L'Hotel du Commerce … Plats du Jour … Chauds et Froids." On the facing page, where one might anticipate an advertising image to be shown, the only presumably documentary image is reproduced, disrupting our expectations once again. The photograph shows two women walking in a city street, during, it would appear, the 1950s. Then, just as we expect the film séance to come to an end, it is supplemented by a so-called *hors programme*, a supplement, which repeats the séance by multiplying several of the preceding film stills on one page, with the addition of the date 1973. If the *hors programme* carries a message concerning the satiation of modern reality by mass media images, the opposite page makes an even more fundamental point concerning the structural emptiness of this "permanent spectacle": whereas the frame of the *actualité* section still encloses fragments of language, the final frame is emptied of all images and words. It delimits the very whiteness of the page, a silence only interrupted by the addition of a simple inscription below the frame: *La Séance*.

Frozen into print, Broodthaers's film program has been divided into equivalent, quantifiable parts. Each segment is provided a precise, temporal measurement—5 mins, 12 mins, 10 mins, 80 mins—like a film program that is placed

Un jardin d'hiver. 1974. Installed at the group show Carl Andre / Marcel Broodthaers / Daniel Buren / Victor Burgin / Gilbert & George / On Kawara / Richard Long / Gerhard Richter, Palais des Beaux-Arts, Brussels, 1974. © Estate of Marcel Broodthaers, c/o SABAM Belgium 2024

on a loop and repeated without end. It no longer seems to matter what is presented to view: fiction and nonfiction, advertising and *actualité*, entertainment and politics have become one continuous, uninterrupted surface of projected images, which holds modern subjects apart in their common absorption by the shadows on the screen. Thus, one might propose that *Racisme végétal* adheres to a familiar assessment of the homogenizing effects of the mass media and, in particular, classical cinema, which unites the audience members in their very separateness. Here, it matters not whether one choses Theodor Adorno's model of the culture industry, Guy Debord's notion of the society of the spectacle, or even Jean-Louis Baudry's concept of the cinematographic apparatus (although Broodthaers would have been familiar, at least, with the former two). The basic argument is similar: in the darkened cinema theater, the discrete, conflictual character of actual, lived experience is erased and the public is inducted into a commodified order of semblance, where "reality becomes its own ideology through the spell cast by its own duplication" and a "poetic mystery of the product" holds sway.[3] And, thus, mainstream cinema becomes emblematic of the rationalization and administration of culture, its integration within a vertical hierarchy of state and corporate control by means of a "programmatic" logic. Yet, even if this ideological analysis of mass culture may seem all too monolithic, by 1974 the centralized, media system of "broadcasting" on which, for instance, Adorno argument relies, was already coming to an end. Furthermore, the governmental structure of Western society was undergoing a profound shift that is barely registered in Broodthaers's work, which, as I will argue, in its parodic form of critique remains focused on an older, disciplinary model of the institutional spaces of artistic and social administration.[4]

As is typical of most of Broodthaers's work, *Racisme végétal* is based on a procedure of appropriation or *détournement* of found objects. In this case, it is both the actual film stills as well as certain institutional protocols, such as the programming of cinema theaters, that is purloined by the artist. *Racisme végétal* thus operates in a kind of parasitic mode, grafting itself upon preexistent practices of social and cultural behavior. It may be tempting, in this regard, to propose an allegorical reading of the images that are assembled in this work. One might note, for instance, that Broodthaers's decision to illustrate the *actualité* section with an image of Kubrick's bitter satire of the Cold War could not have been the result of a random choice. The *faits divers* covered in the newsreels were known to serve less the purpose of public information than state propaganda and thus Broodthaers's substitution of documentary *fact* by science *fiction* is clearly a commentary on the manipulative nature of the newsreel in itself.[5] Also, as we will see, it is not insignificant that that his séance includes films from various periods, the sixties as well as the thirties of the twentieth century. Nevertheless, for all we know, an element of chance did enter into the work, depending on what Broodthaers happened to find in a local photography shop. What we do know for sure is that *Racisme végétal*'s schema of the film program was already becoming obsolete by 1974. In particular, newsreels were becoming redundant due to the rise of television. In Germany, for instance, the actual sequence of the film program, including advertising, newsreels, and documentaries (so-called *Kulturfilme*) and feature films, had been prescribed by law and this situation remained unchanged until the 1960s. However, by the end of the 1960, this law would no longer be enforced.

Racisme végétal thus addresses a phenomenon already in decline, yet in converting the film program into a memory, it also allows a return of the repressed. What was being erased, namely, with the cancelling of the extended cinema program was also the very origin of the film séance within the early-twentieth-century field of popular entertainment. Even though the film program was to operate within the field of mass culture as an "homogenizing" agent, its disparate elements are an inheritance of an older practice. The earliest film screenings, located at fairgrounds and variety theaters, consisted of one-reel *actualités* and comic sketches and these short films were inserted as one of many attractions between a series of vaudeville acts.[6] Thus, the film program, which is associated with a disciplining of the cinema audience, contains in its very structure a trace of another era in which the filmic séance formed a more heterogeneous affair. But before I pick up the trail of the film séance at the beginning of the twentieth century and situate Broodthaers's own engagement with the film screening not only as a scheduled "program" but also as a particular, if changing form of sociality, I need to address how Broodthaers himself utilized film not merely as a "method" [procédé] but as an exhibitionary form as such.[7]

Having made *La Clef de l'horloge* in 1957, Broodthaers was a filmmaker before he was a visual artist, but in the late 1950s he also organized so-called *séance-conferences* at the Palais des Beaux-Arts in Brussels, following a practice that had already been established by the ciné-clubs of the 1920s and 1930s. During these public events he presented lectures on various topics, which were supported, for instance, by the screening of films by others or a compilation of news reels, such as *Le Chant de ma génération*, which he had edited himself.[8] He also organized several film evenings during the 1970s, such as a screening of his own films on October 21, 1971, during the exhibition *Film als Objekt – Objekt als Film* at the Städtisches Museum Mönchengladbach or the presentation of a compilation film, *Rendez-vous mit Jacques Offenbach*, at the Palais des Beaux-Arts in Brussels on December 7, 1972, in which he spliced some of his films together with a newsreel and countdown leader. Unfortunately, however, we have little information on how these evenings were structured and if the audience had any active role to play. On occasion, Broodthaers seems to indicate that the film séance, as public gathering, should provide a space for debate. In the press release for the screening at the Palais des Beaux-Arts, for instance, he states that he does not want his films to be qualified as examples of an "art cinématographique," but they are "no more and no less than a painting by Meissonier or Mondrian," an object of discussion. And the opening title of *Rendez-vous mit Jacques Offenbach* declares that "this program covers the period which has seen the birth and development of inflation and its consequences," with the addition between parentheses "see the speech by Nixon, summer 1971." If Broodthaers gestures in the early 1970 toward the possibility of considering the séance not in its degraded form as a "permanent spectacle," but as a singular event that contracts the two meaning of the term—filmic performance and political gathering—then he does so only in a faint and minimal manner. However, to think of the film séance as the enactment of a participatory form of *assembly*—where, to follow Judith Butler, individual bodies become part of a concerted and collective mode of political action and debate—would not have been that unusual only a few years before, even for Broodthaers.[9]

UNE DISCUSSION INAUGURALE

May 1968 provides a convenient caesura within Broodthaers's practice, even though he had embarked upon this career as a visual artist only four years earlier. It is well-established how his museum fiction, the *Musée d'Art Moderne, Départment des Aigles*, emerged from the artist's brief participation in the occupation of the Palais des Beaux-Arts in Brussels at the end of May. The occupation, in which artists and art critics took part, followed upon a wave of other such actions taken by students in Belgium, for instance at the Université Libre in Brussels and, of course, by students and workers in France who assumed control of factories, universities, and various cultural institutions, forming public assemblies as an extraparliamentary exercise in direct democracy. This newly found freedom to assemble outside the control of the state apparatus constituted a popular form of sovereignty. As such, the assemblies contested the claims of a sovereign state to be the sole representative of "the people." Indeed, as Judith Butler argues, what defines a popular assembly is its enactment of political performativity—a convening of bodies that occupy a shared space as their own, which is always in excess of the existing means and forms of representation. The assembly, in this sense, is a séance that lacks the institutionalized form of, say, a parliamentary session or a political convention. The enactments of an assembly, furthermore, cannot be reduced to a set of verbal statements or written assertions since this would suggest the existence of a unified *program* of action, which fuses all participants within a fixed, group identity. Only if the assemblies of May '68 consisted of a "plurality of bodies" could they be truly "free" rather than conforming, in advance, to a particular set of interests or ways of acting.[10] Thus, we confront the central paradox of the assembly as a radical, constituent form of democratic power: "the people must be enacted to be represented" but once such performative event becomes institutionalized, it will "always fail to represent the people."[11]

This dilemma is all too apparent in the history of the occupation of the Palais des Beaux-Arts.[12] On May 28, an *assemblée libre* (or *volksvergadering* in Flemish) was proclaimed that was "open to everyone."[13] True to this egalitarian premise, the assembly declared in a communiqué of May 30 its solidarity with artists of all stripes, regardless of their aesthetic, disciplinary, or linguistic orientation while announcing its support of similar occupations of educational and cultural institutions, such as the actions of the students at the Université Libre in Brussels that initiated the movement of "contestation" in Belgium. Furthermore, the free assembly contested the "arbitrary" allotment of cultural funds by the state, demanded a greater self-determination of students within the educational system, and "condemned the system of commercialization of all the forms of art, considered as products of consumption," a protestation that, in retrospect, seems to have been the most futile of all.[14] In so far as a concrete plan of action went, the *assemblée libre* decided to forge separate working groups [*groupes de travail*] that would prepare the way for a future "document of critical reflection on culture and our society." Originally the occupation was planned to last only three days, however, it would ultimately last until the end of August and thus outlived most other free assemblies in Belgium and elsewhere. In the end, however, the work of the committees at the Palais des Beaux-Arts appears to have remained fruitless.

That, at least, is what the dominant narratives of the period would suggest, but perhaps we should not rush to judgment. It has become standard to characterize the free assemblies, which emerged during May '68, as inconclusive in their aims and lacking any practical course of action. In short, the spontaneous speech or *prise de parole* exercised within the free assemblies was not accompanied by an actual *prise de pouvoir*. A local Belgian newspaper such as *La Libre Belgique*, for instance, would report that the discussions of the free assembly were unable to reach any concrete consensus and became mired in a constant state of confusion.[15] This newspaper addressed a conservative, Catholic readership and might not be our most reliable source of the events; however, its coverage its typical of what would become a common representation of the presumed futility and naiveté of this contestatory moment. In retrospect, the cultural revolution of May '68 has become reduced to a mere décor of wild, disorganized celebration, a jubilant, collective "festival" or "happening.[16] But this is to discount the specific political dynamics of the assembly, which, by its very nature, must be "inconclusive." As Judith Butler has argued, an assembly can only reach a conclusion in dissolving its radical form of democracy. To decide upon a distinct political objective means the transformation of an assembly into a social *group*, which identifies with a collective form of subjectivity and, simultaneously, excludes all others from consideration. In short, we might expect that there is a counternarrative of May '68 that privileges the inconclusiveness of free speech, rather than affirming the opposite view of a cultural revolution without leaders or direction.

Maurice Blanchot has articulated one of the most radical versions of such a counternarrative, pushing the formal logic of the free assembly to its limits. Blanchot was himself a member of the Student-Writers Committees, one of the many action committees that multiplied on the margins of the free assemblies during the French May. Based on this immersive experience, he would later conceive of the spontaneous, public assembly as an "unavowable community" that remained necessarily, if distressingly so, elusive in its formation. It was not a question, he argued, of taking power and replacing it with another power. Rather, an assembly was the manifestation of a "possibility—beyond any utilitarian gain—of a being-together that gave back to all the right to equality in fraternity through a freedom to speech that elated everyone."[17] Pretending to "organize disorganization," the assemblies and committees placed the very notion of community itself under constant erasure.[18] Marguerite Duras, who was a member of the same committee as Blanchot, attested to a similar, paradoxical conception of the political gathering as one of endless deferral: "Nothing holds us together but refusal. ... We push our refusal to the point of refusing to be assimilated into the political groups that claim to refuse what we refuse."[19] It is not the *program* that identifies the assembly but the establishment of a para-political space of mutual recognition: a constitutive outside or *hors programme*, if you will, of the representational system of parliamentary democracy, which is regulated by definite protocols and divided into distinct parties.

In this light, it is not surprising that Kristin Ross in her indispensable study of the French May '68 would single out Blanchot's "actionless" action committees as the most significant manifestation of a politics of equality. In contrast to the rigid, bureaucratic apparatus of the modern state or party, the action committees followed a far more supple method of self-organization, developing their politics in situ and implanting themselves within factories, universities schools, and another social and institutional settings, without adhering to any preexistent, ideological program. Like Blanchot, Ross perceives the action committee as operating in a radically immanent manner, activating what she calls a radical "dislocation" of prevailing modes of political subjectivity that are moved out of their proper "place" within the existing order.[20] Equality, therefore, was not an objective of communal action but emerged only within the actual struggle to occupy a common space. Unlike Blanchot, however, Ross will not celebrate May '68 as a festive upwelling of a spontaneous mode of communication, where what was said mattered less than the speech act itself.

If the seizing of power was not the objective of May '68, then, to defeat another myth, it was also not about the seizing of speech, a *prise de parole*. Ross argues that to describe May '68 in terms of a grasping of either power or free speech leads either to the melancholic narrative of a failed revolution or to an apolitical representation of the events as a kind of festival or happening. To choose either of these two official narratives, Ross asserts, is to adopt the viewpoint of the state in its desire to reclaim its own legitimacy. The fact that May '68 failed to unleash a social revolution does not mean that it only achieved its opposite—an individualist "freeing" of desires—as this would reduce May '68 to a "generational conflict," which merely inaugurated a transformation of lifestyles, anticipating the rampant consumerism of later decades. Furthermore, it would integrate the events of May into an official narrative of the inevitable modernization of an authoritarian, bourgeois state, which was soon to be replaced by a postwelfare, neoliberal form of governmentality. If not a youth revolt or a symptom of cultural reform, May '68 enacted a flight from the dominant processes of social determination, whereby political subjectivity was not attached to the fixed identity of a social group (whether that of the "student" or the "factory worker") but assumed a performative aspect that emerged in the course of a struggle rather than following some preconceived demand.

Ross's reading of the political events of May '68 is a sympathetic one and it resonates strongly with Butler's later theory of the assembly, which was prompted by the uprisings of the Arab Spring and the Occupy movement during the 2010s. However, there is no need here to adjudicate the accurateness of Ross's description or reflect on the extent to which Butler's concept of the assembly coincides with that of Ross. What is useful here is to have a concept of the assembly or séance, which evades or exceeds, as Butler would say, the sovereignty of the state with its institutionalized forms of social and cultural representation. This allows a shift in perspective in regard to our conventional approach to the work of Broodthaers as a form of institutional critique. For if his *Musée* inscribes itself within a dominant order of cultural administration, if only to subvert it, then its historical diagnosis, to go back to Ross, begins with the logic of the state and ends with it. This is not to argue against the correctness of such an understanding of Broodthaers's critical strategy. Rather, I would like to ask what it could mean to not foreclose the séance all-too-soon within the institutionalized form of a "program" that would be just one more example of the inexorable logic of cultural administration. This requires that we provide an actual, historical substance to that blank frame of *Racisme végétal*, its *hors programme*, which might allow the séance to be conceived not as the representative of a programmatic logic but as indicative of a performative politics of assembly not always already inscribed within the bureaucratic order of the state.

To achieve this shift in perspective, I will need to burrow further into the exhibitionary history of film. However, first I must briefly return to Broodthaers's participation in the assembly at the Palais des Beaux-Arts and trace its immediate aftermath in his work. I have already noted how the artists' assembly became quickly associated with the official narratives of May '68. It may be tempting to view the lengthy occupation through the lens of Blanchot's concept of an unavowable community, but we lack sufficient evidence of what actually transpired there. Therefore, we are left with a dominant depiction of the occupation as being inconclusive, as noted above, and divisive, which is to say it was already separated into different "interest" groups from the start. We will see, moreover, how this characterization of the free assembly fed into the initial enactment of Broodthaers's fictional *Musée*, which was accompanied by an "inaugural discussion" of its own.

According to Jacopo Galimberti, it is possible to identify three different factions at the outset of the occupation. One was represented by the artist Roger Somville, who was a member of the Belgian Communist Party and, thus, clearly not an exponent of a nonaligned, assemblist politics. Marcel Broodthaers, who had established a much closer connection to the Belgian art world (and to the Palais des Beaux-Arts) constituted another faction, whereas there was a more "bellicose fringe," which included individuals such as the writer Tom Gutt.[21] The latter would quickly seek to ostracize Somville and Broodthaers as being too close to the "bourgeois" art market and not sufficiently trustworthy as leaders of the occupation. As a result, Broodthaers would leave the assembly, but Somville would stay till the end after, apparently, expelling the "troublemakers." We have little information about what was discussed during the first sessions of the Assemblée Libre, but Broodthaers seems to have taken on a prominent role, criticizing the lack of support for Belgian artists by the state and demanding the foundation of a museum of modern art. A week later, however, he distanced himself from the assembly, writing the first of a series of open letters that preceded the foundation of his own *Musée d'Art Moderne*. The typewritten text resembled in format, if not in its oblique style, the kind of communiqués that were circulated within the public assemblies and action committees of May '68. The letter, addressed to "mes amis," was allegedly posted from the Palais des Beaux-Arts on June 7 and formed a retort to the "contestataires," who had attacked him in the previous week:

> Calm and silence. A fundamental gesture has been made here that shines a vivid light onto culture and the aspirations of a few to control it—on one or the other side—which means that culture is an obedient matter.
> What is culture? I write. I seize speech. I am a negotiator for an hour or two. I say I. I resume my personal attitude. I fear anonymity. (I would like to control the meaning of culture.)[22]

"Calm and silence" does not function in Broodthaers's text as the mere opposite of that tumultuous irruption of speech that has become associated with May '68. Perhaps one might interpret this proclamation of "silence" as Broodthaers's attempt to detach himself from the assembly's antagonistic arena of discourse. Yet, the ironic tone of the letter suggests something else; namely, that the existence of such a space of critical detachment is illusory at best. Like the empty frame at the end of *Racisme végétal*, Broodthaers's "calm and silence" designates a discursive space that appears to be empty and free to occupy—a blank page—yet nevertheless is always already enclosed. Broodthaers's derogatory reference to "the aspirations of the few" suggests that control of a discursive space can only be achieved by the silencing of others.

It is this ambivalence of the notion of "silence" or the blankness of the page that Broodthaers would frequently exploit. One might say that he is simply pointing to the constitutive absence at the heart of any system of communication or what structural linguistics like to call the "empty signifier"; that is to say, a sign that occupies a degree zero of meaning and by this very virtue might be connected to any and all meanings. In addition to the word "silence," Broodthaers would often deploy another term—the "desert" of language—which functioned in a similar, ambivalent manner. The desert might serve as an image of cultural desolation for Broodthaers, a result of the numbing effects of the culture industry that serves up its reified fragments of language as an entr'acte. Yet, it is this very "emptiness" of the desert that provides the very basis for a typically Western imagination of an opulent space of otherness, a fata morgana of comfort, an oasis of leisure, which obscures the actual violence of a colonialist regime of conquest, the "racisme végétal" that fed its Orientalist fantasies. In the same year as *Racisme végétal*, Broodthaers would create his *Jardin d'hiver* décors where "the fundamental idea is in fact the desert ... and the absence of the desert. This desert, which is both real and symbolic [illustrative] of the current political and economic situation, but also certainly even more so the desert of reigning within our society, the desert of leisure, in the desert of the world of art."[23] Central to the *Jardin d'hiver* décors was the reproduction of engravings that illustrated popular natural history books of the late eighteenth century, such as Oliver Goldsmith's *An History of the Earth and Animated Nature*, which commonly claimed that climate was a determinant of racial character, and, of course, a plethora of potted palms.[24] Speaking of his *Tapis de sable* (1974), a solitary, potted palm tree placed on a sand surface decorated with the letters of the alphabet, Broodthaers stated that the palm tree motif has "more to do with the form of a dream, a poetic form where the palm tree becomes *détourned* from its sociological sense."[25] In a similar manner Adorno would speak of how the nineteenth-century bourgeois interior with its arrangement of objects, "greedily collected across the seas," might expand into an infinite realm of the imagination.[26] Within the bourgeois interior, as in the hothouse atmosphere of the winter garden, space appears only as Schein. The concrete world halts at its boundary, replicating the colonialist imaginary of an empty frontier or, as Broodthaers ironically proposed in a handout to his *Un Jardin d'hiver* at the Palais des Beaux-Arts, "New horizons draw themselves. I see new horizons and the hope of another alphabet."[27]

In 1974, Broodthaers appeared convinced that the political destiny of Western society has been, as it were, set in type. But in the immediate aftermath of the museum occupation, Broodthaers continued to pursue a debate about the shortcomings of the cultural politics of the Belgian state, only now he would retreat within a smaller group of acquaintances—artists, collectors, and gallerists—who were all members of the Belgian art world. The objective of these conversations, as he stated, was "to analyze the relationships Art-Society."[28] With the occupation of the Palais des Beaux-Arts already ended, he decided at the end of the summer to host a discussion at his home (which doubled as his studio) that might accommodate a larger public. From this circumstance, his fictive museum would emerge, not "as a concept, but out of a circumstance."[29] By no means, however, would this gathering and its "inaugural discussion" revive the revolutionary form of an assembly. In a film bearing this title, we see shots of the vicinity of Broodthaers's apartment, workmen unloading packing crates from a truck, which were to provide the décor of the *Musée* (as well a convenient means for the invited guests to sit upon), and fragments of the discussion that took place on the opening night. Throughout the film, segments of a handwritten text appear, written in white ink on transparent sheets, which are superimposed and, therefore, become gradually more illegible as the film progresses. This text, which characterizes the participants and summarizes the contents of the discussion, deserves to be quoted here at length:

> [*Une discussion inaugurale*] is devoted to the—tumultuous—inaugural discussion that marked the opening day: 28 September '68. In the presence of this sizeable group of people of various tendencies. A museum director, a Marxist philosopher, a revolutionary journalist, a bourgeois journalist, a dealer in progressive (avant-garde) paintings, another traditional one.
> A collector—orthodox, collector? collector or art lover [amateur]? What are the new relations that tie the artist to society? At the end of the day, is the purpose of a museum purely scientific or does it cover an art distribution system, that of the galleries; this system that mirrors capitalist society? Depending on what they represented—most of the time unconsciously—each person answered these questions with varying degrees of passion, analytical rigor, good faith, bad faith, sometimes missing the essential point altogether, with a pertinence, or with a gesture, or again by maintaining a sympathetic, aggressive, hostile, indifferent or amused silence ...
> ... a doctor with new ideas, a German student, several of them even full of the spirit we have come to know these last two or three years, a few women, finally, who take part in this violent discussion, restricted to a charming silence, perhaps, by this tenacious prejudice that men hold toward them, whereby they should be beautiful and keep quiet.
> The discussion reached no conclusion except, for a few of them, that they would do all they could to make a new cultural structure in the future that would be more independent, newer, more hospitable.[30]

Although making a gratuitous gesture toward the "tumultuous" nature of the gatherings of May '68, this text has adopted the familiar theme of the "inconclusive" nature of their *prise de parole*. The inaugural discussion, in this sense, catalogs the falling apart of the egalitarian structure of the assembly into an affirmation of individual, social types: a museum director, a Marxist philosopher, a revolutionary and a bourgeois journalist, even a German student, as if to complete the roster of possible participants in events of May.

In her important study of Marcel Broodthaers, Rachel Haidu comments that his *Musée* "imitates the mode of activist engagement so popular in 1968, occupation," which makes the "inaugural discussion" into an imitation of the assembly.[31] Yet, this imitation is cast from the position of a representative of the state, feigned as it may be, with the invitation letter to the official opening being signed "on behalf of one of the Ministers." Basing herself on Austin's speech act theory, Haidu argues convincingly that the *Musée* constituted its own fictional identity by following, almost to the letter, certain institutional rituals and linguistic conventions of cultural administration. Thus, the opening of Broodthaers's *Musée* was announced by a formal invitation card, a ceremonial speech was given by a recognized museum director, and a cold buffet was provided to a select group of artists, critics, and curators. All of this was arranged within a suitable décor, transforming the artist's living room into the semblance of a museum by the installation of packing-crates and picture postcards and addition stenciled inscriptions, such as "haut," "bas," "fragile," and "museum." However, does this example entail, as Haidu argues, that the logic of administration is prior to each and any seizure of speech? Bureaucracy, she writes, impedes any "agency-generating form of speech," which is to say that "political speech has already entered the sphere of representation: it does not—and perhaps does not ever—exist on the primal stage of dissensual confrontation that Ross proposes."[32] Certainly, the inaugural discussion appears to demonstrate as much. But for this very reason Butler has warned against reducing the performative act to the level of a mere speech act.[33] Broodthaers's *Musée* relies strongly on rhetorical devices, whereas Butler emphasizes the more primal significance of *bodies* acting in concert with each other. An assembly is more than a collection of statements. We should be wary, therefore, of parlaying the critical strategies of Broodthaers's *Musée*, which interpret May '68 in terms of the official narratives of the state, outline above, as an actual critique of the naivety of those events themselves. No doubt Broodthaers's museum fiction is adept at revealing certain processes of bureaucratization and mediatization. A film camera is clearly present in photographs of the opening of his *Musée*, which implies all the more that the inaugural discussion could not escape its own staging as a "media event." But this does not mean that there is no means of communication outside of such a "programmed" space. We might ask with Butler: "Is the action of the body separate from its technology, and is the technology not helping to establish new forms of political action?"[34]

LE CINÉMA S'INSURGE

Racisme végétal, as stated above, seems to confirm to a familiar, ideological critique of classical Hollywood cinema, which was first developed by Adorno and Horkheimer in the 1940s. Following this theoretical model, the "spectacle permanente" of mainstream cinema is one of strict division between the audience members and the screen as well as between the audience members themselves. The cinematic séance, in this regard, is an atomized one: docile bodies separated in space, the audience members only become integrated within the semblance of a homogenized world of capital.[35] Yet, if the notion of the political séance can be split between the "inconclusive" but egalitarian actions of the assembly and the "programmatic," exclusionary actions of representational politics, the filmic séance must also allow such a division between a programmed event and something *hors programme*. Obviously, one place to look would be in the early history of cinema, before the homogenizing reign of the culture industry set in. This is precisely what certain film historians began to undertake in the early 1980s, after the rise of French apparatus theory, which provided an important, ideological critique of the "voyeuristic" structure of mainstream cinema but also presented a rather monolithic view of cinematic experience.[36] In reaction to such critiques, Hansen would turn to a reconstruction of heterogeneous modes of spectatorship within early cinema, which were not (as yet) domesticated by the commercial system of classical, narrative cinema, drawing upon the theorization of a "proletarian public sphere" by Alexander Kluge and Oskar Negt.[37] What interested her was not some total subsumption of the everyday within the spectacle of capitalism but the possibility of a third, antithetical type of the public sphere, which fulfills a different function: "to provide a medium for the organization of human experience in relation to—rather than, as in the classical model, separation from—the material sphere of everyday life."[38] Marcel Broodthaers's work is above all situated in the interstices between the bourgeois public spheres, forging a parody of its ideals by emphasizing its connection to a capitalist sphere of circulation. However, one might argue that his practice is more geared to a receding horizon of the opposition between public and private, which is rooted in a bourgeois ideal of the public sphere, and that, despite all his attention to the contemporary operations of *publicité*, his artistic strategies were less well-equipped to address the intensification of the *informational* logic of the new communication media.

Whatever one might conclude in this regard, it is even more evident that Broodthaers in his post-1968 work does not directly engage with what Hansen would identify with Negt and Kluge as an alternative or counterpublic sphere.[39] Existing only in a fugitive, intermittent and peripheral mode, this third type of public sphere would flourish only in the interstices of the homogenizing grid of the culture industry. Wherever it appeared, the alternative public sphere would give expression to a set of contradictory, uneven social conditions, a form of subalternity which the culture industry sought to absorb and neutralize through its appropriation of the cultural forms of the bourgeois public sphere. Thus what defines the countersphere is a mobilization of "principles of inclusion and multiplicity, an emphasis on concrete interests and self-organization and, most crucially, an insistence on the connectedness of human experience across dominant divisions of public and private."[40] Negt and Kluge would find examples of such an alternative public sphere, for instance, in the independent communication media developed by the English working class in the early nineteenth century or Lenin's concept of "self-expression of the masses" as opposed to party propaganda. But, more apposite to our topic, they also include the protest movements of the 1960s and it is not hard to see how Ross's idea of a "dislocation" of political subjectivities during May '68 fits the bill of an alternative public sphere characterized by an interpersonal mode of connectivity that, if only for a moment, refuses any identification with those group identities, which reproduce, and are reproduced by, a capitalist system of production and the sovereign order of the state.

Hansen's own example will take us to an earlier moment. Rather than following the integration of cinema within the dominant public sphere, as Adorno and Horkheimer did, she considers what might have emerged in the gap between the two: the possibility that early silent cinema was not simply "primitive" in the sense of preceding the classical system of continuity editing, but "*because* and *counter* to its commercial orientation," it could have constituted a radically different kind of public sphere. During its first two decades, she goes on to argue, cinema had not yet institutionalize that odd conduct of "private voyeurism in public space."[41] Rather, the early film screenings had a highly exhibitionist character, informed by the rowdy environment of fairgrounds and variety theaters, which was frequented by a lower-class audience provoked and solicited by the various "attractions," rather than disciplined into a passive form of spectatorship. What was shown were one-reel *actualités* and comic sketches, accompanied by some kind of live commentary or music and interspersed with various vaudeville acts. In contrast to the classical film program, therefore, the early film séances were performative, direct as well as highly discontinuous in character.[42] All of this suggests to Hansen that what happened *in front of the screen* in early cinema must have been as important as what was depicted on the screen. It would go too far to identify the early filmic séance with an assembly, but for Hansen there could be no doubt that it was organized in a participatory and collective mode, which allowed the expression and negotiation of discordant forms of social experience. The cinema industry, in seeking cultural legitimation, would not only mimic the institutional forms of literature and theater but contribute to a broader, governmental system of disciplinary control. Those genres, modes of address, and off-screen activities that would allow for an alternative organization of public experience, Hansen observes, would be systematically eliminated, leaving us with the schema of mass culture that is *Racisme végétal*. But now, at least we can chose from two options: either we write history in a linear fashion and inscribe early cinema from its beginning within a state logic of administration, or we follow a nonlinear (and nonmonographic) approach in which the séance is not simply destined to be absorbed within a programmatic logic.

The earliest film stills of *Racisme végétal* date from the 1930s, which is precisely the decade in which, according to Hansen, the standardization and regulation of the film séance had been completed.[43] We know, however, that Broodthaers's memory of cinema reached deeper into the past. Many, for instance, have observed that his silent, one-reel films, such as *La Pluie (Projet pour un texte)* (1969), *Défense de fumer* (1969–1970), or *Ceçi ne serait pas une pipe* (1969–71), mimic the appearance and genres of early cinema, such as the comic sketch and trick film.[44] They act as so many "attractions," exploiting in short order a variety of filmic illusions that come to a head in the animated signature of *Une seconde d'eternité* (1970).

Although Broodthaers's relation to the material formats of early cinema is highly interesting, I am not concerned here with the formal character of his films as such but with the organization of his own film screenings. If we take his *Section cinéma* of the *Musée* project as a first example, it is striking that the invitation to this edition of the *Musée* stated that it was "visible uniquement au rendez-vous."[45] We have to assume, therefore, that it had little of the performative and participatory quality that Hansen imagined as part of the séances of early cinema. When Broodthaers was asked by Freddy de Vree if he wanted the *Section cinéma* to reconstitute the solitude of the museums he visited in his youth, Broodthaers, replied that he would prefer a more lively situation, "but it doesn't work, because there are not exactly crowds of people here." He worries that the fiction of his *Musée* relies only on his "personal contacts."[46] For the occasional visitors, who were mostly known to him, Broodthaers would show a program of various films, such his *Une Discussion inaugurale*, as well as a compilation of newsreels and advertisements (*Belgavox – Mode – 20th Century Fox*), street documentaries (*Brüssel Teil II*), and old slapstick movies (*Charlie als Filmstar*), which he bought from a small German distributor. The screenings made use of printed screens, such as his *Carte poétique du monde* or a white screen covered with the stenciled figs. 1, 2, 12, and A, which, for sure, provide the experience with a theatricality that opposed the absorption of the spectator within a common film theater. There is a disjunctiveness to this program which is close to the irregular alternation of reels in the early film séance, but Hansen's signaling of a potential for the alternative organization of public experience is a distant memory at best in the *Section cinéma*.

Similar to Negt and Kluge, who argued that the alternative public sphere was never submerged once and for all within the commodified sphere of mass media, Tom Gunning has suggested that the performativity of early cinema was not fully domesticated by classical cinema but went, as it were, underground. An important link between early film and Broodthaers in this regard is the ciné-club tradition, which emerged in the 1920s. Consider, for instance, Gunning's excellent description of the Dutch Film League screenings as a social practice that transformed the cinema into a laboratory space for the conducting of exercises in different modes of viewing. Often accompanied by lectures, the Film League approached the film program as mode of comparative analysis, recombining and juxtaposing different styles, genres, and periods of film.[47] Even so, if the ciné-clubs perceived themselves as a counterweight to the film industry and its submission of the medium to the commercial laws of profit, their aim was also to reterritorialize the perceptual field of cinema, if on the basis of an aesthetic rather than a monetary principle. Although the ciné-clubs would provide a showcase for certain Soviet films that were banned from public viewing, they were not exactly "revolutionary clubs." In fact, their culture of writing, lecturing, and debating the values of film as art, which insisted on the formal autonomy of the medium, is much closer to the organizational order of the classical, bourgeois public sphere.

Interestingly, Broodthaers would keep this tradition of the film lecture alive during the later 1950s, as I have already noted.[48] As such, he would, presumably, have been aware of a set of violent interventions within the orderly discussions of the ciné-club community, which took place in France and Belgium during the postwar period. In the early 1950s, members of the so-called Lettrist movement, such as Isidore Isou, Maurice Lemaître, Gil J. Wolman, and Guy Debord, began to promote what they called a *cinéma boulversante*, which was meant in Neo-Dadaist fashion to assault and uproot the conformist attitude of the general moviegoer.[49] Placing the conventions of classical cinema under erasure, Letttrism can be seen as both a culmination of the modernist aesthetics of the ciné-clubs but also as an attempt to subvert its contemplative, formalist conception of film. At first, the Lettrists proceeded by deconstructing the synchronous relation of image and sound, combining original and found footage and reworking the surface of the film by scratching, painting, or drawing on it. However, increasingly, their efforts would turn to the space in front of the screen. In Isou's first film, *Traité de bave et d'éternité* (1951), the main character is heard debating the state of cinema before a ciné-club audience. He calls for a "destruction of cinema" while he is loudly heckled by the crowd. Subsequently, Lemaître would upstage Isou by insisting that his *Le film est déjà commencé?* of 1951 is no longer to be comprehended as a film, but as a séance [his words].[50] When he projected the film, the event included various live elements, which confused the boundaries between the on- and offscreen space:

> When the audience is let in, the screening room will be dark and there will be no attendants to help people with seating. They will take their seats in an indescribable confusion ... While the spectators are still being seated, the concluding scene of a Western will be shown and the lights in the room

will then be turned on. An announcer will tell the audience to leave the room. Maurice Lemaître will then begin to read a lengthy defense of his film, which will be interrupted by shouting. The projectionist, holding a bulk of celluloid film in his hands, will appear beside the director and, accusing him of making a film in contradiction to his own ideas, begin ripping the film stock apart.[51]

If Isou recorded a fictional ciné-club debate, Lemaître staged an actual, if scripted debate in the theater. However, as Hansen observed in relation to early cinema, it takes more than a materialization of the space in front of the screen to render the theater into an assembly of dissenting bodies and voices. Guy Debord seems to have come to this very conclusion with the screening of his first film, *Hurlement en faveur de Sade* (1952), which was also his last act as a member of the original Lettrist group. When on October 13, 1952, Debord showed the film at the Ciné-Club du Quartier Latin, he included such extrafilmic elements as a fake film lecturer and scripted provocations, which had become part of the Lettrist repertoire, but he would also draw the Lettrist model of the séance to its logical conclusion:

> The soundtrack lasted only about twenty minutes ... the interruption of the sound, always quite long, left the screen and the theater in absolute darkness ... the almost constant use of press clippings, law texts, and citations with a *detourned* meaning made understanding the dialogue all the more difficult.[52]

Withdrawing both sound and image from the screen, Debord moved beyond the formalism of Lettrist cinema. In doing so, he also gestured to the political potential of the filmic séance. At the beginning of the film, a voice proclaims:

> Just as the projection was about to begin, Guy-Ernest Debord was supposed to step onto the stage and make a few introductory remarks. Had he done so, he would simply have said: "There is no film. Cinema is dead. No more films are possible. If you wish, we can move on to a discussion."[53]

It would not be until 1967, however, that the first signs of an actual *politicization* of the film séance would appear, and Broodthaers would be there to witness it. In December 1967, the fourth EXPRMNTL film festival took place at the casino in Knokke.[54] Broodthaers's own submission, *Le Corbeau et le renard*, which required a special screen on which to be projected, was not accepted by the jury. Nevertheless, it was included in an off-site screening organized by Jean-Jacques Lebel, a well-known French exponent of Happenings, whose own film had also been rejected. It is not surprising that Broodthaers's film was excluded from the competition, since even in the contemporary terms of avant-garde film, *Le Corbeau et le renard* would have registered as an unclassifiable work. In its ultimate form as a limited edition, *Le Corbeau et le renard* consisted besides the 16mm film, among other elements, of a printed screen, typographic panels, and a photographic canvas. The text on which the film is based was the result, as Broodthaers stated, of a performative exercise in *écriture personelle*, which enacted a *détournement* of La Fontaine's fable—a classical model of the French education system—into "a text made up of clichés, borrowings from elementary writing lessons and personal inventions."[55] Then, in front of a typographic representation of this text he placed a number of everyday objects "so that they would enter into a close relation with the printed characters. This was an attempt to deny as fully as possible both the meaning of the word and that of the image."[56] In his regard, as Kaira Cabañas has suggested, *Le Corbeau et le renard* might be compared to the filmic strategies of the Lettrists (or the Surrealists, for that matter). For sure, he would be familiar with their existence as Debord, among others, was in contact with Belgian Surrealists, such as Marcel Mariën. At the same time, Broodthaers described the work as a kind of "environment" and, therefore, one would also be correct to situate it within the newly burgeoning field of expanded cinema.[57] There were, in other words, more than enough reasons for the jury at Knokke to not immediately recognize the work as a legitimate "experimental film"—a judgment that Broodthaers would happily confirm: "Is it a poem? Is it painting? The film *Le Corbeau et le renard* is an exercise in reading. ... I do not like to define it as an experiment."[58] *Le Corbeau et le renard*, thus, possesses an exhibitionist aspect—it literally places words and objects on display—but there is little of the interventionist character of the Lettrist film séance.

A massive disruption of the festival program did happen due to the actions of a group of young students from various film schools in Brussels, Ulm, and Berlin, among whom were Harun Farocki and Holger Meins. The students protested against what they viewed as a lack of political content at the festival. Several film screenings were interrupted and a small brawl occurred in the central hall, yet the protests came to a head during the final event when the jury members were invited to explain their choices to a full audience. To their great consternation, Lebel took over the proceedings with a hastily organized happening—a farcical election of *Miss Expérimentation 1967*, which involved a parade of naked bodies. Meanwhile, the film students also moved in on the action by holding up placards, stating "No reality without the death of the cinema," "Cinema Muet," and "Vive Roger Pic, Chris Marker et Joris Ivens," all the while calling for a cultural revolution. Although the two interventions appeared to have been coordinated, the respective form of their *prise de parole* could not have been more different.

In the press, the students' protests were only mentioned in passing, often perceived as no more than awkward stunts. Most reviews were dominated by two themes: on the one hand, many of the films tended to assault the nervous system of the spectator (they were called, for instance, "hypnotic" and "destructive" of our real sense of time),[59] and on the other hand, the films were considered to be more "experimental" in the realm of life than on the level of the medium itself. Thus, Pierre Apraxine wrote in *Art and Artists* that many of the films undertook a "frantic assault on certain sexual taboos" but were "accompanied by a total lack of political or moral utterance" and Amos Vogel noted a "plethora of naked males and amorous frolics," while adding that the films also assailed the "the optical nerves, attacking taboos, jarring preconceptions, manipulating new techniques."[60] What emerges in the newspapers, then, is a portrayal of underground film as a celebration of alternative lifestyles, which was visceral in its sexual thematic and optical effects but depoliticized in orientation. We can already read into these film reviews, therefore, the future characterization of May '68 as a kind of orgiastic festival or generational revolt. What really happened at Knokke, however, was the emergence of a schism between experimental and militant filmmakers. Whereas EXPRMNTL had developed into a major social gathering of avant-garde filmmakers who forged a community around the filmic "experiment," this would come to an end in 1967. The German artist Birgit Hein, who was a recent convert to experimental film in 1967, would later complain that the militant filmmakers who were forged by the events of '68 were too dismissive of the political relevance of a formally innovative art of film. In her view, it was militant film that was "reactionary," as she accused it of replicating the conventions of classical cinema in its pursuit of a cinéma verité.[61] Farocki would put it more succinctly: "[Knokke was] the last time when politics and the avant-garde, aesthetics and politics, still held equal presence."[62]

In his own review, "The First Prize," of the Knokke film festival, Broodthaers barely mentions the student interventions, except for the following two paragraphs:

> The festival "was marked by several kinds of demonstrations, of which the most vehement attacked the principle of experimental film, accusing it of being escapist, and the organization of the festival with regard to the war in Vietnam. There was a bit of everything—scuffles, the satirical election of a Miss Experimentation involving a procession of naked people and an *underground* festival in a cinema in Knokke. One thing in particular touched me by the rightness of its tone. About fifty students took over the podium in front of the screen during the projection of a Japanese film which it was indeed annoying to see taking part in the competition because of its pornographic, commercial character.
> They threatened to interrupt the festival, no doubt they should have respected the rules ... Yes. The fact remains however that the students' demonstration was a generous one.[63]

Despite this slightly dismissive tone, Broodthaers did not come back from Knokke wholly unaltered. When he was asked by the film journal *Trépied* in January 1968 what his plans were for the future, he replied that he wanted to "incorporate more reality" into his work and make a film about Vietnam "based on written signs" since no compatible film had been shown at Knokke.[64] Nothing came of this idea. May '68 would intervene with Broodthaers's plans and the Vietnam film was never realized. Six years later, when asked he if had ever made a committed or "engaged" work of art, Broodthaers answered that he had done so only once, as a poet, before he became an artist, and that this was only due to the fact that his literary production remained without financial compensation. Moreover, he suggested that political agency can only be secured by a mode of withdrawal or disengagement: "I try as much as I can to circumscribe the problem by proposing little, all of it indifferent. Space can only lead to paradise."[65]

Nowhere more succinct than in his *Galerie du XXe siècle* at documenta 5 did Broodthaers draw a parallel between capitalist processes of accumulation and the cultural appropriation of space. For this installation, which concluded the activities of the *Musée*, Broodthaers inscribed on the floor, in three languages, the words "Private Property," surrounded by a protective, chain-link barrier. In the catalog he would compare the work to a "traffic sign," which calls to mind the *détournement* of an actual, "no admittance" traffic sign by students of the Université Libre in Brussels during May '68, altering its original admonishment—"ENTRÉE INTERDITE/PROPRIÉTÉ INTERDITE"—to state "ENTRÉE LIBRE/PROPRIÉTÉ DU PEUPLE." By 1972, then, the act of occupation had relapsed for Broodthaers into the logic of the state. His sign at the documenta 5 functioned as a pointed critique of the exhibitions' director, Harald Szeemann, who conducted his own "seizure of power" by forcing artists to submit to his thematic program. Broodthaers's installation was inducted into Szeemann's "Personal Mythologies" section and several other artists would join Broodthaers's protest against Szeemann's curatorial strong-arming, even though that would not prevent the rise of the independent curator in later decades. Broodthaers's strategy was to reappropriate the proprietary methods of the cultural institution, turning its principles of territorialization on its head. But where occupation once meant a gathering of bodies acting and speaking together, now only silence reigned within the roped-off space of Broodthaers.

The path that Broodthaers followed from Knokke to documenta 5 is clear. However, there is another way of describing what happened between 1967 and 1972. This genealogy of the film séance traces the slow migration of the séance from the field of experimental or avant-garde film, with its institutional apparatus of ciné-clubs, film festivals, and film museums, into the space of the street and the factories. It speaks, as it were, of the deprogramming of the film séance and its transformation into an insurgent, filmic assembly. Take, for instance, the first bulletin, *Le cinéma s'insurge*, that was published by the assembly of French film students, the États Généraux du Cinéma. It provided a rapid-fire chronicle of the unfolding events as if trying to keep up with the pace of real time:

FRIDAY MAY 17 – (Continued).
Film shot by Renault workers in the Boulogne-Billancourt factories.
Because students and workers know that film is a weapon.
Within the first ten minutes of the first session of the first general assembly, the fundamental contradiction that characterizes the current situation (image and tactics of the revolution) was revealed in full cinematic force. At the same time, the impatience for immediate action was obvious.
Trained to think before we act, we discovered how action and reflection nourished each other through immediate dialectical confrontation. Cinema enters the MOVEMENT.[66]

The *actualités* of the student/worker action committees, screened within the free assemblies, solicited their participants to assume the responsibility of revolutionary action. Yet, this direct address of cinema also seems to fall short, revealing an "impatience" of the students with the filmic message, which impedes their desire for a more spontaneous form of direct action. The dialectic between film séance and political assembly was, indeed, a highly complex one during these frantic days and we would be mistaken to suggest that there was a simple and immediate conflation between these two forms of gathering. Unfortunately, we still lack a complete history of the exhibitionary practices of militant film—its sites and publics—during the later 1960s. At best, therefore, I can offer a highly abbreviated narrative that leads from the assembly-as-film to the film-as-assembly.

In February 1967, a strike breaks out at the textile factory Rohdiaceta in Besançon and, for the first time since 1936, workers occupy a factory in France. The objective of the occupiers was not just to achieve their economic demands but to politicize the space of the factory itself. The occupation also took the form of a *cultural* contestation. In collaboration with a local "center of popular culture," which was founded, among others, by Pol Cèbe, a worker at the Rhodiaceta factor, the factory was transformed into a support for cultural activities: a disused library was refurbished, establishing a place for workers to assemble and debate, art exhibitions to be held, and film screenings, followed by discussions, to be organized. As Trevor Stark astutely observes, "By refusing the stultifying identity of the worker denied all opportunity for 'self-cultivation' and by establishing line of communication between striking workers, artists, and militant student *comités de soutien*, a community emerged that destabilized monolithic and integral categories of identity, and thereby exceeded the bounds of traditional union or party representation."[67]

In March 1967, leftist filmmaker Chris Marker receives an invitation to visit the occupied factory in Besançon. He presents a movie to the workers by

Soviet director Alexander Medvedkin, the 1935 *Happiness*, a comedy about a peasant's difficult entry into a farm collective. Later, Chris Marker returns to Besançon with Mario Marret to shoot a film, *À bientôt j'espère*, which invites the workers to speak to the camera at their own level, if focusing primarily on the organizational actions of one union delegate. *À bientôt j›espère* is shown to the workers in Besançon on April 27, 1968, but is met with a hostile reaction. During the ensuing passionate discussion, they criticize the film for distorting their lives. In particular, one woman notes that the condition of female workers is not mentioned in the film. The debate among the workers is recorded by Antoine Bonfanti, which becomes the imageless "film," *La Charnière*, in a fulfillment, it would seem, of the political aspirations of Debord's equally imageless *Hurlement*. Finally, out of Marker's awareness of *À bientôt j'espère*'s failure as a militant film, the collective film group Medvedkin is born. Following an egalitarian principle, the Medvedkin group unites professionals and amateurs, filmmakers and workers, in a collaborative process of militant filmmaking. Thus, in a document dated November 21, 1968, the Medvedkin group sets itself the goals of "giving the working class new possibilities of expression, representing through photography, film, and sound the working class condition at all levels (from alienation to militancy), practicing a new form of militant information."[68]

From the production of a film about an assembly, a séance gives birth to the production of film as an assembly. At least, that might be one possible, counternarrative to *Racisme végétal*'s schematic representation of the séance-as-program. However, I shall not pursue this line of inquiry any further, which would require closer attention to the actual circumstances in which the screenings of the Medvedkin group took place. I shall propose, therefore, another ending to this essay that returns us to the work of Broodthaers.

LA REPRISE

Among the many *actualités* made by film collectives during the events of 1968, *La Reprise du travail aux usines Wonder* has garnered particular notoriety. It was shot on June 10, 1968, by Jacques Willemont, Liane Estiez, and Pierre Bonneau, all students of the L'institut des hautes études cinématographique (IDHEC), who arrived on the scene of a worker's strike at the Wonder battery factory in Saint-Ouen, which, to their surprise, was just coming to an end. Only ten minutes long, the *La Reprise du travail* is an example of direct cinema in its purest form, a product of contingency more than design. Despite is rough, incomplete shape, it has grown in stature over time, coming to be seen as a perfect allegory of the French May. In an obvious allusion to Louis Lumière's famous *La Sortie de l'usine* of 1895, Serge Daney would even nominate *La Reprise* as the "primitive" scene of militant cinema.[69] According to this view, *La Reprise* sums up the hopes and desires of the contesting students and workers as well as their inevitable disenchantment, when the trade unions called upon the workers to return to their jobs during the course of June.

La Reprise consists of only two shots. The first is an opening shot, depicting a factory exterior festooned with a handwritten banner proclaiming "Nous ne cédons pas. Nous ne rentrons pas" and, in the foreground, the ubiquitous poster, *La Lutte continue*, produced by the Ateliers Populaires. A voice-over explains that the factory workers had voted that very morning to end their three-week strike and return to work. In the distance we hear a union official or factory manager trying to shepherd the people back through the gate. Viewed from across the street, there appears to be no immediate rush to follow this command as the people in the street continue to mill around in front of the factory building. So far, what the film students captured by chance with their camera seems to be just another public assembly, so many bodies occupying the streets in a joint protest. Yet, suddenly, the distraught cry of a woman emerges from the midst of this cluster of people. As she comes into view, we hear her denouncing the labor union and its betrayal of her hope for a better life. She adamantly refuses to reenter the factory despite the insistent efforts of a union official to coax her back into the fold: "We need to be vigilant together. Because we don't get anything alone. Your comrades decided." "No," the woman shouts, "I won't go back in, I won't! I won't put a foot in this prison again! You go in and see what a dump it is!" Then, as if challenged by this howl, this *hurlement* of the woman, each individual in the scene begins to act out certain prescribed roles: the Union Official, the Militant Student, the Factory Worker, the Company Manager. The scene assumes the character of a ready-made political theater where every person assumes their "proper" place in a restored, political order with, that is, the exception of the anonymous woman. The militant student might offer her some faint support, but *La Reprise* is clearly not only the portrayal of a worker who is betrayed but also the depiction of a women being silenced by men. "It's a victory; don't you understand," the union worker insists, becoming ever more commanding in his relation toward the woman.

Kristin Ross would single out the same film in her history of '68. "So brief, barely a narrative," she notes, before proceeding to read the film against the grain. In her view, the anonymous "no" of the woman does not signal a moment, however fleeting, in the gradual coming to power of a determinate social group—the working class. Rather, this rejection belongs to a more primal level within the ontogenesis of the political subject: "the woman, 'the people' if you will, coming into existence in the pure actuality of her refusal."[70] I tend to agree with Ross's assessment of the woman's utterance, but what is more pertinent here is that it allows us to see more clearly how the filmic séance bifurcates into the two separate genealogies that I have been tracing throughout this essay. Spreading out from the alternative public sphere of the cinema of attractions, we have on the one hand the "underground" series of interventions within the sites of cinema. There we might find the ideal of the séance-as-assembly as it was elicited, if not actualized; a convening of speaking, gesturing bodies that were moved as much by what was on the screen as by what transpired in front of it. On the other hand, we have the dominant history of the film séance-as-program, whereby everyone is assigned their "proper" place within the public sphere. It is there, reflected in the shadows on the screen that we find the familiar cast of social types: "a doctor with new ideas, a German student, several of them even full of the spirit we have come to know these last two or three years, a few women, finally, who take part in this violent discussion, restricted to a charming silence, perhaps, by this tenacious prejudice that men hold toward them, whereby they should be beautiful and keep quiet."[71] It is there, in the penumbra of a permanent spectacle that social identity undergoes endless reproduction. If, under such circumstances, an "inaugural discussion" can achieve no conclusion, that it is not due to some act of "total refusal." What is enacted *there*, rather, is not a *prise de parole* but a *reprise* of the speech act as embedded within a protocological order. And what this implied for Broodthaers, in turn, was that the only tactic of intervention that remained available to him was one of erasure, *détournement*, and withdrawal, leading him to conclude his open letter of November 29, 1968, with a feigned gesture of remorse:

> I neither wish, nor am I able to paint you a picture of the details, the sighs, the stars, the calculations of this inaugural discussion. I regret.[72]

NOTES

I would like to thank Raf Wollaert for his generous assistance in researching this essay.

1. Marcel Broodthaers, "Racisme végétal. La Séance," *Interfunktionen* 11 (1974).
2. Several of Broodthaers's slide projections, which were often shown in conjunction with his films, included illustrations of various "proto-cinematic" devices, such as magic lanterns and shadow puppets.
3. Theodor Adorno, "The Schema of Mass Culture," in J. M. Bernstein (ed.), *The Culture Industry: Selected Essays on Mass Culture* (London: Routledge, 1991), 63.
4. My point is not to conflate, say, Adorno and Foucault, but to suggest the need for a strict historicization of Broodthaers' mode of institutional critique.
5. For a contemporary critique of the ideological manipulations of the newsreel or *Wochenschau*, see Hans Magnus Enzensberger, "Scherbenwelt. Die Anatomie der Wochenschau," *Frankfurter Hefte* 4, reprinted in *Einzelheiten I: Bewusstseinsindustrie* (Frankfurt/M.: Suhrkamp, 1964), 106–33. See also Knut Hickethier, "The Creation of Cultural Identity through Weekly Newsreels in Germany in the 1950s," in Kornelia Imesch, Sigrid Schade, and Samuel Sieber (eds.), *Constructions of Cultural Identities in Newsreel Cinema and Television after 1945* (Bielefeld: Transcript, 2016), 43.

6. See, among others, Thomas Elsaesser (ed.), *Early Cinema: Space, Frame, Narrative* (London: BFI, 1990) and Wanda Strauven (ed.), *The Cinema of Attractions Reloaded* (Amsterdam: Amsterdam University Press, 2006).
7. Broodthaers, "It Is the Method that Interests Me" [1967], in Gloria Moure (ed.), *Marcel Broodthaers: Collected Writings* (Barcelona: Ediciones Polígrafa, 2013), 180.
8. *Le Chant de ma génération* no longer exists, but it appears to have consisted of a combination of scenes of the Second World War with contemporary news films. See "The Song of My Generation," in *Broodthaers: Collected Writings*, 76. A letter to the artist Livinius of 1 April 1959 provides some more insight into his film-lecture ideas. In this letter, Broodthaers announces a program, which was to include Roger Leenhardt and George Sadoul's *La Naissance du cinéma* (1950), unspecified "actualités sur les manifestations de cinéma à l'expositions," and an extract from Karel Zeman's animation film *L'Invention diabolique* (1958). His lecture was to develop the concept of film as a "succession of immobile images" and "the importance of the image in all its historical states." I thank Raf Wollaert for bringing this letter to my attention.
9. Judith Butler, *Notes toward a Performative Theory of Assembly* (Cambridge, Mass.: Harvard University Press, 2015).
10. Ibid., 164.
11. Ibid., 163.
12. For information about the occupation of the Palais des Beaux-Arts, I rely mainly on the accounts given by Rachel Haidu, *The Absence of Work: Marcel Broodthaers, 1964–1976* (Cambridge, Mass.: MIT Press, 2010); Virginie Devillez, "To Be In or Behind the Museum? Les arts visuels dans les années 68," *Bijdragen tot de eigentijdse geschiedenis* 18 (2007): 19–58; and Jacopo Galimberti, "The Occupation of the Palais des Beaux-Arts (Brussels)," in *Individuals against Individualism: Art Collectives in Western Europe (1956–1969)* (Liverpool: Liverpool University Press, 2017), 312–18. I also thank Raf Wollaert for sharing his knowledge of the events.
13. The "free assembly" was tolerated by the museum administration on the condition that it would not disrupt the ongoing programs of the museum, which already made some question the validity of its contestation from the start.
14. See the documentation, collected by Isi Fizman, in Carel Blotkamp et al. (eds.), *Museum in Motion* (The Hague: Staatsuitgeverij, 1979), 248. This dossier also includes several of Marcel Broodthaers's open letters. The working groups were organized for the fields of the visual arts, literature, cinema, animated film, cultural centers, education, urbanism, and architecture.
15. See, for instance, "Le mouvement de 'contestation'," in *La Libre Belgique* (June 4, 1968): 5.
16. On the tropes of May '68 as festival or happening, see Thomas McDonough, "Killing Property: On Festival and Revolutionary Nihilism," in *The Beautiful Language of My Century: Reinventing the Language of Contestation in Postwar France, 1945–1968* (Cambridge, Mass.: MIT Press, 2011), 135–74.
17. Maurice Blanchot, *The Unavowable Community* (Barrytown, N.Y.: Station Hill Press), 30.
18. Blanchot, *The Unavowable Community*, 31.
19. Marguerite Duras, "20 May 1968: Description of the Birth of the Students-Writers Action Committee," *Green Eyes* (New York: Columbia University Press, 1990), 57–58.
20. Kristin Ross, *May '68 and Its Afterlives* (Chicago: University of Chicago Press, 2002), 25.
21. During the war, Broodthaers had been a member of the Communist Party but was expelled in the early 1950s. As to his close relation to the Palais des Beaux-Arts, it is sufficient to note that on 31 January 1968 he took part in a conference during which Luc de Heusch's film on Magritte, *La leçon de choses*, was shown and Broodthaers screened Charlie Chaplin's *The Pawnshop*; on 6 March, he again participated in a conference, "Le Mec Art et l'art de l'objet," at the Palais des Beaux-Arts. Tom Gutt was close to Marcel Mariën and Paul Nougé, who were part of the first generation of Belgian Surrealists.

22. Broodthaers, "To My Friends…, 1968," in *Broodthaers: Collected Writings*, 189.
23. Interview with Marcel Broodthaers by Feddy de Vree, 1974, in *Broodthaers: Collected Writings*, 424.
24. Goldsmith's book first appeared in 1776, but many later editions were published in the nineteenth century and Broodthaers owned one of them.
25. Interview with Marcel Broodthaers by Marianne Verstraeten, 1974, in *Marcel Broodthaers* (Paris: Jeu de Paume, 1991), 246.
26. Theodor Adorno, *Kierkegaard: Construction of the Aesthetic* (Minneapolis: University of Minnesota Press, 1989), 43–44. Adorno uses the word *Einrichtung* which refers both to the activity of interior decoration as the setting up of an institution.
27. Broodthaers, "Un Jardin d'hiver" [1974], in *Marcel Broodthaers* (1991), 239.
28. Interview with Marcel Broodthaers by Freddy de Vree, 1969, in *Broodthaers: Collected Writings*, 228.
29. Ibid., 228.
30. Broodthaers, "In Principle the Film" [1968], in *Broodthaers: Collected Writings*, 207.
31. Haidu, *The Absence of Work*, 144.
32. Haidu, *The Absence of Work*, 146–47.
33. Butler, *Notes*, 29.
34. Butler, *Notes*, 93.
35. The classical texts are Guy Debord, *La Société du spectacle* (Paris: Buchet-Chastel, 1967) and Jean-Louis Baudry, "Cinéma: Effets idéologiques produits par l'appareil de base," *Cinéthique* 7–8 (1970): 1–8.
36. For an extensive history of the politicization of French film theory in the later 1960s, see Daniel Fairfax, *The Red Years of Cahiers du cinéma (1968–1973)* (Amsterdam: Amsterdam University Press, 2021).
37. See Miriam Hansen, "Early Silent Cinema: Whose Public Sphere?" *New German Critique* 29 (Spring–Summer, 1983): 155.
38. Ibid., 156.
39. In some of his writing of the 1950s, Broodthaers comes much closer to an acknowledgment of such alternative spheres of publicness. In the unpublished text "Expo 58," for instance, Broodthaers recounts his experience of going undercover as a journalist among the workers who were constructing the Brussels World Exhibition. He acknowledges his own discomfort at being an impostor, who nevertheless yearns for solidarity. In one telling passage, Broodthaers responds to the gestures of a carpenter, saying that it turned his thoughts in an irresistible manner to Charlie Chaplin and "the strange comfort men discover in the most difficult of situations." And again in describing a shared lunch, he states that there is "something sacred about this meal," which again reminds him of the films of Chaplin, prompting the rhetorical question: "Can you make cinema out of real life?" Marcel Broodthaers, "Expo 58," in *Broodthaers: Collected Writings*, 71–72.
40. Hansen, "Early Silent Cinema," 156.
41. Hansen, ibid., 158. Tom Gunning has proposed a more detailed periodization of early cinema, beginning with the so-called cinema of attractions (c. 1900–1908), which is more performative and participatory in nature and embedded within the field of popular entertainment represented by, for instance, vaudeville and variety theaters and the café-dansant. The cinema of attractions is followed by a transitional period (1908–1916) during which the cinema industry pursued a form of cultural legitimation within bourgeois society. This was accompanied by a standardization and regulation of the exhibition format in analogy to theater, the exclusion of live elements from the séance, and the introduction of multi-reel feature films as the main program. The classical text on the cinema of attractions is Tom Gunning, "The Cinema of Attraction[s]: Early Film, Its Spectator and the Avant-Garde," in Strauven, *The Cinema of Attractions Reloaded*, 381–88. During

the First World War, various European states would also undertake a nationalist campaign of "moral" reform in the realm of cinema in order to control the unruly, alternative public sphere of early cinema. Jennifer Wild notes how this "embourgeoisement" of cinema was met with resistance from some film exhibitors. See Jennifer Wild, *The Parisian Avant-Garde in the Age of Cinema, 1900–1923* (Berkeley: University of California Press, 2015), 140–41, 159–61.

42. There is no space to go into this topic here, but Tom Gunning, for instance, would point out that in early cinema it is "the direct address of the audience, in which an attraction is offered to the spectator by a cinema showman, that defines this approach to film making. Theatrical display dominates over narrative absorption, emphasizing the direct stimulation of shock and surprise at the expense of unfolding a story or creating a diegetic universe." Gunning, "The Cinema of Attractions," 384.

43. For a long time, into the 1950s at least, spectators could still enter and leave the cinema at will. However, that would become less and less common by the 1960s.

44. See, for instance, Rosalind Krauss, *A Voyage on the North Sea: Art in the Age of the Post-Medium Condition* (New York: Thames and Hudson, 1999), 43, where she also differentiates Broodthaers's relation to early film from the contemporary interests of other, Structuralist filmmakers.

45. The *Section cinéma* was on view from January 1971 and October 1972 in a private space in Düsseldorf. I shall not go into the history of this complex installation, as I have already discussed it elsewhere. See Eric de Bruyn, "Marcel Broodthaers and the *Section Cinéma*," in Tanya Leighton (ed.), *Art and the Moving Image: A Critical Reader* (London, Tate, 2008), 112–21, and Benjamin H. D. Buchloh, "Marcel Broodthaers' *Section Cinéma*," in *Marcel Broodthaers: Section Cinéma* (New York: Marian Goodman Gallery, 2010), 8–16.

46. Interview with Marcel Broodthaers by Freddy de Vree, 1971, in *Broodthaers: Collected Writings*, 310. Perhaps this may have contributed to Broodthaers's decision to later withdraw the *Section cinéma* from the *Musée* project. In any case, he would resolve this issue by occupying an actual art institution, the Kunsthalle in Düsseldorf, with his *Section des figures (Der Adler vom Oligozän bis heute)* the following year.

47. Tom Gunning, "Making Sense of Film," http://historymatters.gmu.edu/mse/film/film.pdf (last accessed 2 February 2020).

48. I thank Steven Jacobs for pointing out that Belgium had a rich tradition of ciné-clubs during the interwar period. One of the more interesting events was the organization by Paul Nougé, among others, of a series of film séances at the Cabinet Maldoror in Brussels in 1925. Nougé, who later would become a friend of Broodthaers, would pioneer the practice of *détournement* (even before the situationists). Although the circumstances of the Cabinet Maldoror screenings are murky, they seem to have been intended as a direct provocation of the aesthetic sensibilities of the ciné-clubs, prompting an outraged response by Pierre Bourgeois in Belgium's main modernist magazine, *7 Arts*. On ciné-clubs in Belgium, see André Thirifays, "Les Clubs de cinéma," *Reflets* (Numéro special: *Le cinéma en Belgique*) (1940): 41–50; and Daniel Biltereyst, "Ciné-clubs en het geheugen van de film: Over de eerste Belgische filmclubs en de constructie van de filmgeschiedenis," in Daniel Biltereyst and Christel Stalpaert (eds.), *Filmsporen: Opstellen over film, verleden en geheugen* (Ghent: Academia Press, 2007), 30–49.

49. My knowledge of Lettrist film relies on the following texts: Andrew V. Uroskie, "Beyond the Black Box: The Lettrist Cinema of Disjunction," *October* 135 (Winter 2011): 21–48; Kaira M. Cabañas, *Off-Screen Cinema: Isidore Isou and the Lettrist Avant-Garde* (Chicago: University of Chicago Press, 2014); and Hannah Feldman, *From a Nation Torn: Decolonizing Art and Representation in France, 1945–1962* (Durham: Duke University Press, 2014).

50. Uroskie, "Beyond the Black Box," 36.

51. Lemaître as cited by Uroskie, "Beyond the Black Box," 41.
52. Guy Debord as cited by Cabañas, *Off-Screen Cinema*, 103.
53. Guy Debord, "Howls for Sade," in *Guy Debord: Complete Cinematic Works* (Edinburgh: AK Press, 2003), 2.
54. On the EXPRMNTL film festival see Xavier García Bardón, "EXPERMNTL: An Expanded Festival. Programming and Polemics at EXPRMNTL 4, Knokke-le-Zoute, 1967," *Cinema Comparat/ive Cinema* 1, no. 2 (2013): 54–64, and Devillez, "To Be In or Behind the Museum?"
55. Broodthaers, "D Is Bigger than T" [1967], in *Broodthaers: Collected Writings*, 180.
56. Interview with Broodthaers in Trépied, in *Broodthaers: Collected Writings*, 184.
57. Broodthaers was commenting on his exhibition of *Le Corbeau et le renard* at the Wide White Space Gallery, Antwerp in 1968.
58. Broodthaers, "D Is Bigger than T," 180.
59. Peter M. Ladiges in reference to Paul Sharits and Michael Snow. Frieda Grafe, "Das Kino von Knokke," *Filmkritik* 2 (1968): 102–3.
60. Pierre Apraxine, clipping from *Art and Artists* located at the Film Anthology Archives, New York; Amos Vogel, "Goodbye Alienation, Hello Nudity," *New York Times* (21 January 1968): Section D, 15.
61. Interview of Birgit Hein by Duncan White, February 2009. Available at https://sites.dundee.ac.uk/rewind/wp-content/uploads/sites/146/2021/03/HeinTS.pdf (last consulted on 11 May 2023)
62. Harun Farocki as cited by Bardon, *EXPRMNTL*, 63.
63. Marcel Broodthaers, "The First Prize...," *Trépied* 2 (February 1968): 6–7. As reprinted in *Broodthaers: Collected Writings*, 186–87. The reference is to Koji Wakamatsu's *The Embryo Hunts in Secret* (1966).
64. "An Interview with Marcel Broodthaers by the film journal *Trépied*," *October* 42 (Autumn 1987): 38.
65. Marcel Broodthaers, Irmeline Lebeer, and Paul Schmidt, "Ten Thousand Francs Awards," *October* 42 (Autumn 1987): 43.
66. "Le Cinéma s'insurge," *Bulletin des États généraux du cinéma*, no. 1 (Paris: Le Terrain Vague, June 1968), 7. See also Sébastien Layerle, *Caméras en lutte en Mai 68* (Paris: Nouveau Monde, 2008).
67. Trevor Stark "Cinema in the Hands of the People: Chris Marker, the Medvedkin Group, and the Potential of Militant Film," *October* 139 (Winter 2012): 124.
68. "Texte Manifeste du Groupe Medvedkine de Besançon," in Layerle, *Caméras en lutte*, 285.
69. As cited by Martin O'Shaughnessy, "Post-1995 French Cinema: Return of the Social, Return of the Political?" *Modern & Contemporary France* 11, no. 2 (2003): 191. For my discussion of this film, I draw upon my "Intermittent Conversations on Leaving the Factory," in *Texte zur Kunst* 79 (September 2010): 138–45.
70. Ross, *May '68 and Its Afterlives*, 142.
71. Broodthaers, "In Principle the Film," in *Broodthaers: Collected Writings*, 207.
72. Broodthaers, "Dear Friends..., 1968," in *Broodthaers: Collected Writings*, 202

BROODTHAERS'S CINEPOETIC CONCRETIONS

Christophe Wall-Romana

Le mot MUSEUM > idée > concrétisation: objets[1]

In 1945, René Magritte gave Broodthaers a copy of the complete works of Stéphane Mallarmé, telling him this was the only book he needed to study. In 1969 Broodthaers produced his famous version of *Un Coup de dés*, Mallarmé's hapax "visual poem," by covering out its floating lines with black rectangles to crystallize its visual novelty. Broodthaers's piece has been interpreted as an emblematic gesture for a variety of new artistic outlooks from conceptual art, recuperation, *détournement*, surfaces over depth, ironic (de)commodification, the overcoming of modernism's legacy, et cetera. A few months prior to Broodthaers's first showing of his optical translation in his Literary Exhibition around Mallarmé at Wide White Space Gallery in Antwerp in December 1969, Jacques Derrida gave two momentous talks ("The Double Session,") reframing his key notion of "spacing" through Mallarmé's visual-material approach to poetry. In a 2005 essay, Jacques Rancière addressed Broodthaers's intervention on Mallarmé's poem—and, tangentially, Derrida's Mallarméan spacing. Rancière argues that Broodthaers amplified the "super-spatialization" and "thing-becoming" latent in the poem, confirming Rancière's thesis that modern esthetics made words and things fungible into each other as an epochal change in artistic representation.[2]

The present essay revisits Broodthaers's intervention on Mallarmé's poetry to suggest that Broodthaers remained strictly—albeit paradoxically—Mallarméan in a twofold way: first, by committing the matter of esthetics squarely to the perceptual encounter with matter and thingness, and second by redeploying cinema as a portable and transformative esthetic operator between the realm of language and sensible concretions. Rather than an "expanded cinema," I propose that Broodthaers's work on and around film proceeded from a "cinepoetic" esthetics transfused back or reinjected into concrete experience, words themselves, and object concretions.

THE PHONIC AND VISUAL MATTER OF LETTERS

Mallarmé is often mischaracterized as an abstract, abstruse, and cerebral poet, when he was at heart a fervent materialist of language, treasuring the thingness of words, letters, and *meter*—a cognate of matter, matrix, and mother (Latin *mater*). "It is not with ideas that poems are made," he once retorted to artist Edgar Degas, "it is with words."[3] Mallarmé was a kabbalist not in the common sense of an occult believer in magical thinking but in that of a practitioner of literality—the radical poetics of signifiers. Broodthaers embraced a similar commitment early on, although it remained embryonic, I argue, until cinema became his linchpin medium in the 1960s. In particular, Mallarmé offered poems written on fans to his wife, lover, daughter, and female friends, because the fan is a fascinatingly ambiguous device, folding and unfolding while both screening and revealing its holder's affectivity. The approved version of *Un Coup de dés* was published in unbound double pages making the book itself into a fan-like apparatus. The French for fan, *éventail*, conceals another poetic device, since it can be parsed in English (which Mallarmé taught in a high school) as "even tail," the symmetrical feathers of birds usually numbering twelve—the number of feet in the star meter of nineteenth-century French poetry: the Alexandrine. These are the kinds of material connections upon which Mallarmé's poetics hinged, inverting the power relationship between signifier and signified within the sign.[4] That last word, *signe* in French, is a homophone of *cygne*—swan—as in Mallarmé's sonnet "The Swan," staging the mirror reflection of a swan caught in ice, forming with its symmetrical mirror image a feathery fan referencing the poet's white quill confronting the blank page. *Un Coup de dés* ends on a reflection of the Big Dipper on the sea's surface, its seven stars doubled into fourteen: the number of verses of a sonnet. What I contend in this essay is that Broodthaers reprised and refashioned such transfers between language signifiers, visual esthetics, and the concrete world.

Let us examine the emblematic case of the eagle—*aigle* in French—a fetish word, concept, and image for Broodthaers. Its power comes from the Roman, Napoleonic, and Third Reich eagle emblem as foundational for European history, particularly Belgium's national formation.[5] Its iconography involves the raptor's symmetrical and winged body, and occasionally a two-headed eagle.[6] The symmetrical body of the eagle might signify for Broodthaers the uneasy history of Belgium as amalgam of Walloon and Flemish communities, contrasting with the zoomorphic ideal of Belgium: the mirror images of the Brabant lion on Belgium's coat of arms. As Sven Lütticken has shown, Broodthaers grew up in the aftermath of the Second World War overshadowed by the morphing of Germany's ancient imperial eagle into the *Reichsadler* of Nazism.[7] As it happens, the word "eagle" in French—*aigle*—is phonetically hidden in the French word for "Belgian"—*belge*—if we read it backwards: ègle[b]. Broodthaers might have been further enticed by reading the final "b" as the initial of his name.[8]

In this hypothesis, Broodthaers would have redeployed Mallarmé's signifier poetics to his own use and situation, substituting the martial eagle for the more Romantic swan.[9]

Broodthaers's use of word puns and letter recombinations is well established. For instance, in a manuscript he states that he considered "tableau" [painting] and "bateau" [boat] quasi-interchangeable as near anagrams, with "l'eau" [water] figuring in the former and sustaining the latter.[10] Broodthaers's puns and plays with letters do not carry the Orphic momentousness of Mallarmé's. Instead, they are closer to the lowbrow provocations of the Surrealists, for instance the title of their earliest journal: *Lits et Ratures* ("Beds and Erasures," a pun on the French word *littérature*). When Broodthaers makes the initial M a matrix of contemporary art by writing: "M=Model / Model / Mallarmé / Magritte / Marcel / Museum," it deflates the seriousness of artists' theoretical claims while sketching a private map of his own trajectory.[11] To understand better this vexed relationship between high art and base farce in Broodthaers's work and how it ends up centering the cinema apparatus, we will delve into the particulars of his productions, beginning with the instrumental role of *projective optics* as complement to letter recombination.

PROJECTION AND VIRTUAL ANIMATION

The conclusion of *Un Coup de dés* and the sonnet "The Swan" mediate esthetics and metaphysics through visual setups relying on parallax. The Ursa Major constellation, as Mallarmé knew, is a two-dimensional pattern of a three-dimensional array of stars very distant from each other: in the 1860s it was established that within a few thousand years that constellation would morph into a new pattern. This became for Mallarmé the index of contingency nestled into what we take to be fixed, eternal, and universal. In fine, it discloses how deep space perceived as static is inherently and disturbingly dynamic: a very slow motion-picture animating our "freeze frame" universe. Broodthaers was keenly aware of this optical, parallactic, and astronomical subtext. In a review of Belgium's 1958 World Fair, Broodthaers compares the central Atomium monument (a giant metallic molecule) to both J. J. Grandville's 1844 illustrated book *Un Autre monde* [Another World] and Jules Verne's 1865 *De la terre à la lune*.[12] Both works rely on astronomy and motion parallax, and both were crucial for pre-cinema and early cinema, since Grandville's most spectacular engravings foregrounded visual morphism while Verne's novel (via Jacques Offenbach's 1875 operetta of the same name) begat one of the earliest film masterpieces, Georges Méliès's 1902 hand-colored *Le Voyage dans la lune*. In 1973–74, Broodthaers showed eighty slide reproductions of popular images under the title "Shadow Theater."[13] Most of them address visual projection, point of view, visual motion, photography, text-image relations, and magic lantern and screen—the prototype setup for cinema.¹⁴ One image reproduces an arcane 1790 sketch by astronomer William Herschel that was the first model of the 3-D structure of the Milky Way. This suggests that Broodthaers held a lifelong fascination for motion optics and the visual animation of the macrocosm distinct from, yet contributing to, his engagement with cinema as a new media operator.

J.J. Grandville, "Le jongleur" from *Un autre monde*, 1844

While Broodthaers ostensibly thought of himself as a poet and writer until the 1960s, he ran a ciné-club during the war and came of age at a time—the mid-1940s—when many influential French-speaking poets drew on their cinephilia to renew poetic forms, yielding a second wave of cinepoetry after the first collective experiments of 1913–25.¹⁵ As several commentators have noted, the commonplace that Broodthaers was a poet who turned to visual art in 1964 overlooks the intermedial imbrications of modern poetry and visual culture at large and certainly distorts Broodthaers's own visual poetics.¹⁶ Not only are Broodthaers's early poems dreamlike, or titled dreams, but among his earliest pieces is "Projet pour un film" (1948)—a typical formula for a cinepoem envisaged as a virtual film, one that recurs in his career, shading his relation to cinema. Broodthaers's first film *La Clef de l'horloge* (1957) is subtitled "cinematographic poem," illustrating the two-way mirror between poetry and cinema. A 1958 poem titled "My Memory Is a Color-Film," mentions the poet's mental "cinematographic aptitude," which manifests as "a sudden unfolding," of "images pursuing me," and to which, he admits, "I prefer those / moments when the image turns off in me."[17] We might then ponder whether Broodthaers's art might not best be approached through cinepoetry as the center of gravity of his expansive word/image practices. This thesis that cinepoetics and projective optics constitute the matrix out of which Broodthaers's artistic activities unfolded has the advantage of offering a finer grain to Rosalind Krauss's influential interpretation of Broodthaers's work as transitioning to the post-medium "fiction" of medium-differentiality.[18] It also sidesteps the fruitless discussion of how exactly Broodthaers acquired a disposition for filmmaking per se.[19] In a piece of 1949 where he jots down ideas about art, we find this fragment: "Find texts / from the last films," another clue of the productivity of that interface.

Let us consider two examples: *L'Œuf film* (*The Egg Film*, 1965) and *Une Seconde d'éternité* (*One Second of Eternity*, 1970). The first is a cinepoem that may have germinated out of a pun, since the expression "l'œuf film" in French corresponds to the slowed down or slurred pronunciation of "*le film* [the film]," with the /f/ sound migrating to the article. The eponymous egg is then a phonic spawn disclosing a meaning that remains hidden in live motion speech. The cinepoem describes a cosmogony in which the sun is the egg yolk and the moon the eggshell—or covered in shell fragments—while stars are egg dust.[20] A variant titled "Evolution or The Egg Film" develops the same cosmogony but pits the eggshell against the mussel shell, referencing paintings by Bosch, Brueghel, and Magritte.[21] A third text of 1965, "The Eggs," proposes that the film be projected on a screen made of eggshells.[22] The second text contains several puns, likely occasioned by the fact that the French *coquille* [shell] also means "typo." Hence *évolution* [evolution] is a near anagram of *ovulation* [ovulation]; *fil* [thread] is a shortened "film" (a short film?); and the sun is painted on *écru* [ecru] rather than on the *écran* [screen]. The first two texts segue from the cosmos to the surface of the ocean, either mirrorlike, "flat as a screen," or in the form of "an ideal wave." The first two versions include the contextless expression *étoiles[,]des trains entiers* [stars(,)whole trains] which, given the striking mention in a different place of "Hitler speaking" clearly refers, via the yellow star, to the deportation of Jews by trains for the "final solution." Hence the mention of *œufs* [eggs] in the plural, which is pronounced like the letter "e" and the word *eux* [them] might point to the Shoah as part of Broodthaers's new cosmogony (*œufs entiers* [whole eggs] figures in the first version).[23]

If, according to Mallarmé, "every thought casts a dice throw," for Broodthaers, we might say, every film lays its own egg. *L'Œuf film* is something of a paradigm for all films, a kind of "Model Cinema" or *Cinéma modèle*, as printed plates (discussed below) intimate. The short *One Second of Eternity* (1970) germinated in a similar way from Broodthaers's initials M. B. tracing themselves in one second on the screen. The title comes from Baudelaire's sonnet "To a Woman Passing By," which stages a visual encounter between the male narrator and a woman walking in the street. The narrator fantasizes when glancing in a "flash" into her eyes that he can read "a hurricane" that "germinates" into a potential love consumable only in "eternity." The encounter of their gaze swells to an infinite duration from a single glance, just like a film swells out of a word, a snapshot, two letters, or a cinepoem. Broodthaers describes the film as an avowal that all artists are necessarily narcissistic, adding that "Narcissus is the inventor of cinema" since he saw his reflection on moving water, thereby establishing a chiasmus—another two-way mirror—between art-making and cinema. We should note that M. B. combines the initials of the last name of the two Symbolist poets with whom Broodthaers dialogued his entire life: Stéphane Mallarmé (S. M.) and Charles Baudelaire (C. B.).[24]

Baudelaire and Mallarmé together constitute for Broodthaers an epochal duo through which Symbolist poetics began rearticulating the visible world of modernity and the visual culture of modernism via the mediation of photography and cinema. This informed Broodthaers's exploration of cinepoetics in the late 1940s and '50s and led him back to producing an actual film anachronistically titled *Un Film de Charles Baudelaire* in 1970, in which Mallarmé figures obliquely.[25] The path Broodthaers opened is then partly genealogical—or more precisely, in media studies terms, archaeological—by returning to the emergence of cinema from photography, commenting on *Une seconde d'éternité* that its "goal is to oppose/unify static and moving images."[26] Yet this archaeological move also serves to reopen the prehistory of photocinematic medias for new artistic practices and environments through the cinepoetic paradigm itself. Let us develop this nexus by looking more carefully at what Broodthaers derived from both poets.

BAUDELAIRE, MALLARMÉ, AND PHOTO-CINÉMA

Walter Benjamin was among the first to foreground photography as a key component of Baudelaire's poetics of modernity, and subsequent scholars expanded his pioneering work.[27] Yet Baudelaire was equally fascinated by the sensorium of motion optics, specifically by how the contours of an object or scene morph over time. The clearest evidence is a long description in notes titled "Fusées" [Bobins/Rockets], where Baudelaire describes quasi-phenomenologically a "ship in motion" as "the successive multiplication and production of all imaginary curves and figures enacted in space by the real components of the object," which he compares to "an animal full of genius."[28] This passage provides an indication for the proliferation of ships and animals in Broodthaers's works as indexing auto-animated forms—the mystery of visual animation. Krauss interprets Broodthaers's book, *Charles Baudelaire, Je hais le mouvement qui déplace les lignes* (1973), titled after a verse in Baudelaire's sonnet "Beauty," as undoing Baudelaire's ideal of esthetic simultaneity, since Broodthaers's book redistributes by "dilation" across pages filled with illustration tags ("Fig. 1," "Fig. A") the poem's verses narrated by a statue.[29] Krauss argues that Broodthaers deploys "fiction" and the novel by installment to critique Baudelaire's poetry in its obsolete monumentality. These keen arguments need to be nonetheless qualified by the profound irony of the poem, and the paradoxical omnipresence of visual motion in Baudelaire's statuary.[30] "Beauty," for instance, ends with the statue describing her eyes as "pure mirrors which make all things more beautiful," implying a metamorphosis of the entire visible sphere—a shift of all visual lines. It is plain in "The Mask," a poem about a real statue by sculptor Ernest Christophe. Two male viewers approach a female statue, vaunting "the undulation of this muscular body," and especially her voluptuous and victorious mien. Yet as they get closer, they find that her face is in fact a mask concealing her real face, drenched in tears. The despair that makes her "tremble down to her knees" comes from her awareness of being condemned to live eternally—"like us," the two men conclude with angst at finitude. Not only is the statue full of vibrating lines but it requires the viewer's motion to be appreciated fully, thereby reanimating her affective life. Broodthaers, I would contend, rather than deconstructing Baudelaire's simultaneity emulates and remixes his fascination for visual motion, temporal ruptures, shifts, gaps, and diachrony.

Krauss contrasts Broodthaers's book *Charles Baudelaire* with Mallarmé's *Un Coup de dés* by arguing that the former also "questions" the ostensible simultaneism informing the latter. But this reading of *Un Coup de dés* is equally wanting. In his preface to the poem Mallarmé describes:

> The literary value [...] of this copied distance which mentally separates groups of words or words themselves, is to accelerate or else slow movement, scanning it, even summoning it according to a simultaneous vision of the Page: the latter taken as unity, as elsewhere the Verse is or perfect line. Fiction will graze and vanish, swiftly, following the mobility of writing.[31]

Certainly there is an impulse towards simultaneity, but it is at the very least in dialectical tension with motion, ruptures, blanks, speed, and the rhythmic imagination of each reader. In fact, Mallarmé was directly thinking about cinema when he wrote this preface as I have established.[32] He used specific formulations in it that are variations of draft language he penned for a statement published in 1898 regarding the use of photographic illustrations in books of literature:

> I am in favor of no illustration, since all that a book evokes must take place in the reader's mind; but, if you use photography, why not go straight to the cinematograph, whose unreeling/unfolding [*déroulement*] will replace, images and text, many a volume, advantageously.[33]

Ombres chinoises. Slideshow. 1974. © Estate of Marcel Broodthaers, c/o SABAM Belgium 2024

A broad set of sources and close associates confirm that Mallarmé closely followed the development of cinema and was actively thinking about film form when writing *Un Coup de dés*. The statement above is reproduced in the 1945 Gallimard/Pléiade edition of the *Complete Works of Mallarmé* that Magritte gave Broodthaers, and we can surmise that the latter stumbled on it and rethought Mallarmé's work via this early hint of cinepoetics. If Broodthaers did read this statement, then his blacked-out version of *Un Coup de dés* might not be simply a work of recuperation/appropriation/desacralization but a complex homage to Mallarmé's prediction that cinematic "unfolding" offers a synthesis and overcoming of the epistemic pair in the *ut pictura poesis* formula setting "images and text" as impermeable species. The black rectangles of Broodthaers's version would, in this view, connect to the black pages that figure in *Ombres chinoises* (1975) and reference the interstices between magic lantern slides, film frames, and fades to black. Both versions on *Un Coup de dés* amount to enactments of the "Exercise in poetic reading / related to classical cinematographic motion," which Broodthaers envisaged in 1967.[34]

FROM CINEPOETICS TO ANIMATED CONCRETIONS

If, as reconstructed here, cinepoetics was the matrix for Broodthaers's early works, the question becomes how and to what ends his work evolved away from it, and what relations, if any, his later work kept with it. In 1972, at the one-day event organized by Jeunesse et arts plastiques in Brussels, he showed his program-film *Rendez-vous mit Jacques Offenbach*, composed of earlier films such as *La Pluie* (1969) and *Une Seconde d'éternité* (1970). He qualified them as "works using the cinematographic support" and "artistic creations," and "reflections" but added that "this is not cinematographic art, this is [...] an object of discussion [...] these are films."[35] As Krauss points out, the rise of video art, and Structuralist cinema such as the work of Michael Snow, should be invoked to contextualize the wayward diversification of Broodthaers's moving image output as films beyond or besides cinema.[36] Nicolas Brulhart adds the genre of "artist's film," "exhibition cinema," and "open-ended apparatus" [*dispositif*] while probing the wide panorama of practices in which Broodthaers showed his film-work. He concludes that film is both "one support of expression among others" for Broodthaers, and yet also "a synthetic model" updating "an allegorical esthetics of collage, fragment and dispersion."[37] Critics plainly struggle to articulate the proper borderlands of Broodthaers's acinematic film-work.

Art theory seems to me to overshoot the playfully pragmatic register within which Broodthaers redeploys both film and cinema. By playfully I mean to circle back to wordplay as well as to the core meaning of "play" and *jeu*, having to do with a series of movements on the one hand (prescribed moves or free motions) and a refusal of social value on the other (*otium*, pretend, waste). Playspace and playtime organize an order of praxis outside of worldly praxis. My sense is that Broodthaers was deeply invested in this alt-praxis that has many historical roots (the comic genre, theater, nonsense, Benjamin's flâneur, Surrealism, Roger Caillois's theory of gaming, et cetera), and that his particular artistic passion took up the possibility of holding play as a reflection, a mirror, to better understand and intervene in real world praxis. While avant-gardes aggressively affirmed their program for a new art aiming to change the world, Broodthaers adopted the lower-agonistic project of a playful art disclosing the shaky arbitrariness and mundane contradictions hemming reality, leveraging the abundant playroom left in the interstices of social praxis. I suspect that Broodthaers decided to dilate cinepoetics precisely in that direction.

Let us consider the chiasmus title of Broodthaers's 1971 film exhibition in Mönchengladbach, *Film als Objekt—Objekt als Film*. In handwritten notes about the exhibition, Broodthaers mentions "2 types of projection (slides, films) expressed upon the same screen-object" for the "unfolding [*dépliement*] of language" with the goal of "language expressing the true," while the note ends in a double question mark: "the true??"[38] Here, film, language, objects, and screens form an iterative continuum of mutual refractions through the operations of projection and unfolding: film at one end, and the mirage of objective truth at the other. Or, per the 1973 exhibition of his films in Munich, *Images, Objects, Films, Concepts*.

While there is something makeshift or contingent about such concatenations—stating a rationale for an exhibition—some of Broodthaers's film projects provide more grain about the projection and unfolding operations. *Projet pour un poisson* (*Project for a Fish*, 1970–1971) is a case in point, its title surreptitiously concealing projection in the word "project" (this goes back to the 1948 *Projet pour un film*), while its subject, the fish, is the merest mundane being as well as a cheap working-class staple. This is one of the rare films for which Broodthaers drew several detailed storyboards, one of which shows the film's sprockets, as if the storyboard copied the inexistent film's imaginary frames. Broodthaers insists that the fish has no head *"sans tête,"* a lowbrow allusion perhaps to Max Ernst's 1929 collage *La Femme 100 têtes* or Georges Bataille's *Acéphale* journal and eponymous secret society. "Fish always seemed to me to be part of a secret society," Broodthaers muses in a note, while words like "simple," "banal," and "platitude" deflate any philosophical ambition of the enterprise.[39] Without head thus may refer more flatly to the French expression "sans queue ni tête [without head or tail]," meaning "no rime nor reason," a likely dig too at Aristotle's famous definition of diegesis as having "a beginning and middle and end." The film offers no narrative but is an attempt to present an "idea of noncommunication. The fish, itself, as an immobile film."[40] In another note, Broodthaers points to the gap between "something immobile that was already written and the comical movement which animates 24 images per second."[41] As in *L'Œuf film*, the fish is born of the film's comical staccato—from cinema's fishy sense of animation and immersion. In French, *poisson* is phonetically close to *poisseux*, which means slimy or viscous, but also *boisson* [beverage] and *poison* [poison], so it is an inherently slippery and intoxicating polymorphic signifier.[42] The follow-up book *Jeter du poisson sur le marché de Cologne* (Throwing Fish on the Cologne Market, 1973), in which the projection-project itself has been beheaded of the prefix "pro-" into *jeter* [to throw, -ject], is considered by Broodthaers "an analysis of different forms of the fish in language," while notes add that "they swim elsewhere in a world where Shark, Knife, Cook are synonyms." Not only does fish "dilate and make motion" across sounds and words, but it also does so across archetypal forms: "a cube, a ball, a pyramid, or a cylinder," and all colors of the spectrum.[43] The fish thus crystallizes the meta-cinepoetic principle, a word-sound-form in its kinetic plasticity incarnated in the simplest animal body—an animated object entirely shaped for motion. Human bodies too result from being in motion in the world, and Broodthaers wrote in his scenario for the 1964 film by Henri Kessels, *Bruegel and Goya, journalistes*: "Man too is a fish."[44] The fish also probes Mallarmé's nexus of reflection, surface, and submersion. In the stuttering *Projet pour un texte*, a failed draft meant as the theoretical support for the fish film, Broodthaers vaunts "the value of the virgin film, this white page of the filmmaker," propounding a type of "forbidden film" (which Broodthaers compares to pornography), notably "that of a shipwreck . . . without witness, without futures or glory," a direct reference to *Un Coup de dés*.[45] Perhaps Broodthaers's own version of *Un Coup de dés* submerges Mallarmé's lines by transforming them into a moving school of lexical fish whose dark backside alone is visible through the surface—darting animated concretions

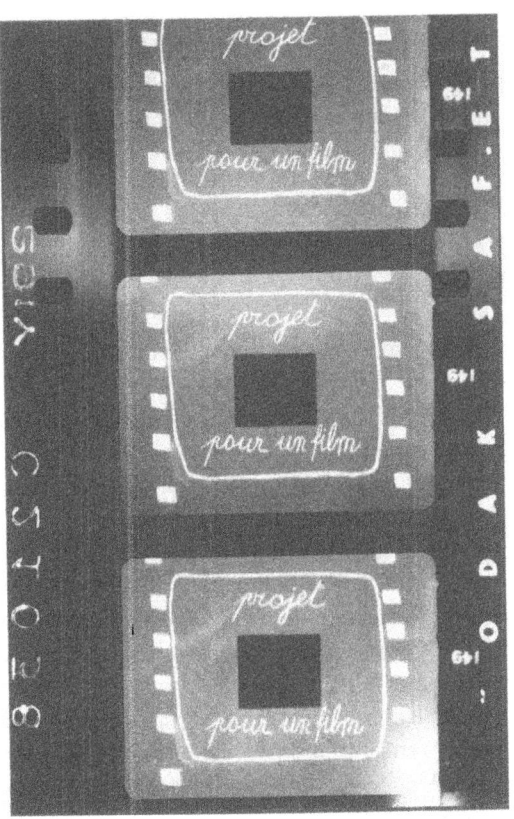
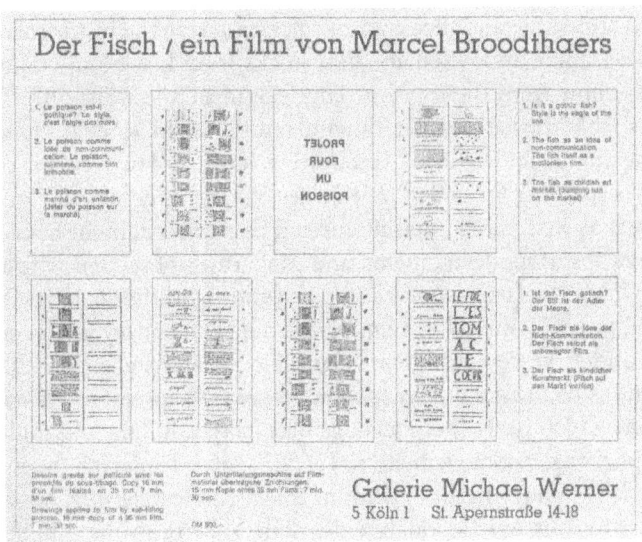

Film frames and poster related to *Projet pour un poisson*. 16mm. 1971.
© Estate of Marcel Broodthaers, c/o SABAM Belgium 2024

enacting a cinepoetic fish-film. Already in *L'Œuf film* (1965) the *pois[s]on* [fish/poison] fragments of the lexicon and imagery of *Un Coup de dés* transpire: *vagues* [waves], *écume* [spume], *mât* [mast], *étoiles* [stars], *blanche* [white].

FROM RESTRICTED TO GENERAL CINEPOETICS: DILATIONS AND CONCRETIONS

The continuum of "images, objects, films, concepts," which often deploy or strongly suggest a screen apparatus, outline a general cinepoetics that qualifies the umbrella descriptor of *installation*, a default museal category for heterogeneous objects and modalities of exhibition. We can start by looking into the *Industrial Poems*, a series of embossed metal plates that constitute a new medium displaying gnomic word-image assemblages.[46]

These plates were generated under the theoretical heading of *Cinéma modèle*, the title of an exhibition in Düsseldorf in late 1970 in which five Broodthaers films were shown: *Le Corbeau et le renard, La Clef de l'horloge, La Pipe, La Pluie*, and *Un Film de Charles Baudelaire*. In one draft announcement for the show Broodthaers writes, "CINÉMA : CE MODÈLE" [Cinema: this model], making clear the close relation between poem plates and cinema as their matrix. By early 1971, the theoretical motto of Cinema Model is replaced by the new heading *Musée d'Art Moderne, Département des Aigles, Section cinéma*.[47] Let us look at two prototype plastic plates, variants of each other, titled "CINÉMA Modèle," shown at Michael Werner Gallery in Cologne in September 1970. One is in black-and-white and the other in color, indexing the historical change in both photographic and cinematic film stocks from black-and-white to color. The plates show from the top four large commas, the word CINÉMA, two clockfaces with arms at noon/midnight, and the word Modèle. Hence twelve letters (the number of feet in an Alexandrine verse) and two cinema reels, with four pauses standing for end-stopped lines of verse (perhaps the four stanzas of a sonnet) as well frame intermittences. The noon/midnight hour points to both the 24 fps of modern cinema and Mallarmé's obsession with midnight in *Un Coup de dés* (*une toque de minuit* [midnight's bonnet/tick]) and the unfinished poem "Igitur." The twin plates, in short, convey a tacit cinepoetic program under the cover of glossy signage or advertising esthetics. We find confirmations of a sustained cinepoetic program in several of the later plates, such as one which bears "ne bougeons plus [stay still]," the old injunction of photographers against movement, or "M. B." plates displaying the final frame from the twenty-four images of the film *Une Seconde d'éternité*. Another plate, "Chez votre fournisseur (le vinaigre des aigles)" [From your supplier (eagles' vinegar)], focuses on mirror imaging and quasi-synonymy (*aigre/aigle* [acrid/eagle]). A complementary series of plastic plates foreground quasi-mirroring and anagrams such as the near-palindromic word "museum," while another

Cinéma Modèle. Vacuum-formed plate. 1970.
© Estate of Marcel Broodthaers, c/o SABAM Belgium 2024

plate shows a matrix of twelve letters surrounding a central cube that can generate the words "museum," "musée," "image," "mime," "imite [*imitate*]" and "magie [*magic*]," among many others. The plates of these series do not reproduce anything, however, as photographic plates, book plates, or film frames do. They are truly a new medium: part paintings, part rebuses, part signage, part emblems, part injunctions, part film stills, etc. They amount to novel text-image concretions of medias and experiences inviting the viewer/reader to further generate from them new experiences and meanings. This is why many of them contain arrows—as symbols of vulnerability, direction and misdirection, and more importantly dynamic vectors of becoming. Mallarméan poetics and cinema nonetheless form the bedrock of this new medium. As Broodthaers put it in 1967 in one of his deceptive anti-manifestoes about the film and attendant material of *Le Corbeau et le renard*, "Is it a poem? Is it a painting? [...] Cinema? Yes, it's a method."[48]

Some of Broodthaers's "installation" works may best be approached as what Gilles Deleuze in his book on cinema, via an analysis of Henri Bergson's duration, calls "time-images, that is duration-images, change-images, relation-images, volume-images which are beyond movement itself."[49] For such works the script that would give them a specific form and meaning remains partly virtual, partly to come, and partly the responsibility of the guest viewer animating or actualizing them. Broodthaers called some of these works "propositions," and it can be glossed in either a dialogical or a seductive context as a co-construct with the viewers. Take *Private Property* (1972) for instance, a piece in which a small mat printed with these words in three languages is encircled with four stanchions and chains.[50] It generates an immediate sensory experience of what property entails: a private reserve for which access is denied to others. At the same time, the viewer realizes that no one can access it—not even its owner—and that there is nothing to access, because the space is too small to do anything but stand there. Still, the viewer is confronted with a piece of confiscated real estate carved out of public space—an unusable black hole in the collective texture of the commons. Certainly, this can be related to Broodthaers's unease with and critique of the art market, from which he nonetheless hoped to make a living. But the efficacy of the piece is less conceptual than phenomenological: it proposes to viewers to experience virtually what ownership's gratuitous tear in the "flesh of the world" (to quote Merleau-Ponty) feels like. The relationship of this piece to cinepoetics is far from tenuous. One of the drafts connected to the *Cinéma modèle* series reads, "Theory / The Secret / Cinema is available only by appointment [*rendez-vous*]. It is pointless to show up [*inutile de se présenter*]." This statement commixes art gallery's select patronage with film theater scheduled programming. Yet cinema *is* available, and "rendez-vous" means precisely to move oneself in space with a connotation of surrender, in this case, surrendering one's presence—"inutile de se présenter." That is the key of Broodthaers's incipient theory of cinema: surrendering one's presence, not to exchange it for some fiction, but to "read between the lines" of presence through a virtual or dilatory mode of experiencing.[51] As he writes elsewhere, "my film is a rebus that you need to want to decipher."[52] Scripting a decipherment in the form of an imaginary scenario generated by the reader/viewer is a general formula for the reception of his artistic propositions—in line, again, with Mallarmé's decentered esthetic practice: "Everything takes place in the reader's mind."

FARCE AND CRAFT: MUNDANE ESTHETICS

In all his interviews and more "theoretical" statements, it is difficult to shake the sense that Broodthaers is uneasy, straining, and ultimately opting for some ironic or humorous dodge— "finir en queue de poisson [ending in a fishtail]," as the French expression has it, denoting a quick exit, a brush-off, and perhaps the suspicion of some mermaid-like abnormality. This contrasts with the format of the "letters to friends," which remains pragmatic and warm as he explains what he is up to in more pedestrian terms. During the occupation of Belgium, Broodthaers, then in his late teens, ran a ciné-club where he showed Chaplin, Keaton, Laurel and Hardy, and whatever else he could lay his hands on.[53] Like many other poets and writers, including the Lettrists,

George Bataille, Boris Vian, Henri Michaux, or Jean-Paul Sartre, being deprived of movie theaters during the occupation induced Broodthaers to attend to scenario-writing while transforming cinema into a different kind of desired object altogether.[54] Hence the first *Projet pour un film* dated 1948, ending on "the effect of a pendular motion above a desertic imagination," both a void and the minimal "philosophical toy" needed to actuate its visible animation.[55] While Mallarmé cathexed for Broodthaers this imaginary cinema, its roots are also lodged in sincere cinephilia: how moviegoing has the power to transmute grim and gray reality through an imaginary form of play.

Broodthaers was a realist and pragmatist who cited Wittgenstein, Lacan, Barthes, or Freud perhaps only to fend off his anxiety at not being well-read enough—the "bête comme un peintre [dumb like a painter]" accusation Marcel Duchamp rehashed. There is undoubtedly in his art a profoundly mundane dimension—to use an oxymoron—that attends to the materiality of his everyday life, from eggs and mussels or dealing with the gallery blurb as a befuddling and problematic genre, to larger issues like the decolonization of the Congo or the rise of advertising and mass visual culture trafficking in unreconstructed symbols like the eagle. The world, reality, and cultural manifestations around him were the craft material he remolded and reassembled for his own esthetic and intellectual necessities—what he refers to as narcissism. In this, I believe, he also saw eye-to-eye with Mallarmé, who sought all at once to transcend the mundane and disclose its profundities. It is all too obvious that the museum was a fundamentally vexed cultural apparatus for Broodthaers, not just ideologically but, we might say, viscerally and temperamentally. He was a maker of popular (in the sense of approachable) art pieces, and even his more complex idioms refused to forego an air of casual immediacy. His work is replete with funny books, punning objects, bizarre installations, assemblages of heteroclite and clashing components, a mixture of wonder and farce. He was the true twentieth-century heir of punster and caricaturist J. J. Grandville—a key source for the virtual animation of 2-D images. The mystique of his works-in-progress, remixed and never quite finding the repose of a final version, is also a kind of red herring—poisonous fish!—for art criticism to swallow hook, line, and sinker. The fishers fished, like "the sprinkler sprinkled" of early cinema. In many ways his sprawling compositions were pragmatic reflections deferring their exact philosophical yield, doubling up as extended jokes pushing their punchline further back, keeping their comic tension, waiting for the next turn of insights.

One of Broodthaers's least celebrated works is a book of simple photographs from the 1960s showing ordinary Belgians in small towns, at work, at the café, at a wedding.[56] It contains a few odd subject matters—empty but inflated shirts spinning around the wheel of a well like ghosts—yet the bulk of the snapshots present simple social events, the landscape of the everyday, the eroded affects of routine. It indexes the social origin of his playfulness, while there is nothing much playful in them. I wonder whether this documentary impulse related to his own social class was also a motivation for his anti-cinema films and cinepoetic esthetics:

> Let us imagine, in the meantime, dear sir (dear friends), the real text and the reality of the text as one world. And these routes, these seas, these clouds as though coming from a freedom and a justice.[57]

NOTES

1. Notes for *La Clef de l'horloge: Poème cinématographique en l'honneur de Kurt Schwitters*, in Manuel J. Borja-Villel and Michael Compton (eds.), *Marcel Broodthaers, Cinéma* (Barcelona: Fundació Antoni Tàpies, 1997), 24.
2. Jacques Derrida, "La Double Séance," *Tel Quel* 41 (1970): 3–43, *Tel Quel* 42 (1970): 3–45 ; Jacques Rancière, *L'Espace des mots: De Mallarmé à Broodthaers* (Nantes: Musée des Beaux-Arts de Nantes), 2008.
3. Paul Valéry, "Poésie et pensée abstraite," in *Œuvres complètes*, vol. 1 (Paris: Pléiade, 1957), 1324.
4. See Jacques Derrida, *Dissemination* (Chicago: University of Chicago Press, 1981).
5. Rachel Haidu, *The Absence of Work: Marcel Broodthaers, 1964–1976* (Cambridge, Mass.: MIT Press, 2013), xxvii–viii.
6. Jean Cocteau's play *L'Aigle à deux têtes* premiered in 1946 in Brussels, followed by the film version of the same title in 1948.
7. Sven Lütticken, "The Feathers of the Eagle," *New Left Review* 36 (2005): 109–25.
8. The French *aigle* appears in toto in the English "Belgian" (a language Broodthaers read): n aigle b ["N eagle B"].
9. Mallarmé never once used the word "aigle" in his poetry, perhaps because he defined his poetics in opposition to that of Richard Wagner, which relied on Germanic mythology. Wagner's 1893 march *Unter dem Doppeladler* [Under the Double Eagle] is one example.
10. Marcel Broodthaers, "En français les mots tableau et bateau…," in *Marcel Broodthaers: Collected Writings*, ed. Gloria Moure (Barcelona: Ediciones Polígrafa, 2012), 394–95.
11. Dorothea Zwirner, *Marcel Broodthaers* (Cologne: Walther König, 1997), 114. Cited in Alexander Streitberger, "Les Images, les mots et les choses dans l'œuvre et la pensée de Marcel Broodthaers," *Dalhousie French Studies* 80 (2009): 76.
12. M. B. [Marcel Broodthaers], "Un Autre Monde," *Le Patriote illustré* 74, no. 10 (March 1958): 389; *Broodthaers: Collected Writings*, 74–75.
13. Marcel Broodthaers, *My Ogre Book, Shadow Theater, Midnight* (Los Angeles: Siglio, 2016).
14. Of the eighty images, ten concern astronomy, six mirroring scenes; four are slides or projected images, four are photographs (showing the text: "no photography"), seven are black rectangles acting as dissolves, seventeen are sequential images (largely from comic books), and twenty-six show airborne views. Animals figure on ten images, and volcanic eruptions or explosions on twenty.
15. Christophe Wall-Romana, *Cinepoetry: Imaginary Cinemas in French Poetry* (New York: Fordham University Press, 2013), 177–256.
16. See for instance Denis Laoureux, "Broodthaers et le moule des mots," *Textyles* 40 (2011): 33–42.

17. *Marcel Broodthaers, Cinéma*, 26.
18. Rosalind Krauss, *A Voyage on the North Sea: Art in the Age of the Post-Medium Condition* (London: Thames & Hudson, 1999), 46–47 and 53.
19. Buchloh confesses in 2016, "Once again, there is a very complicated interaction because he does neither what French Lettrist and Situationist film had done in the late 1950s nor what so-called American Structuralist film does in the late 1960s. Ultimately, it is incredibly difficult to clarify where Broodthaers's model of filmmaking really came from." Benjamin H. D. Buchloh, "The Moment of Marcel Broodthaers? A Conversation." *October* 155 (Winter 2016): 133.
20. *Marcel Broodthaers, Cinéma*, 43.
21. *Marcel Broodthaers, Cinéma*, 43.
22. *Marcel Broodthaers, Cinéma*, 45.
23. This creates a curious correspondence with Georges Pérec's 1969 novel *La Disparition*, written without the letter -e-, which commentators have interpreted as pointing to the homophonic *eux* [them], meaning both Perec's Jewish family killed in the Shoah and all Jews and victims of Nazi extermination.
24. Mallarmé's name and portrait figure on Broodthaers's manuscript for the invitation to the 1970 show at Galerie Folker Skulima. *Marcel Broodthaers: Cinéma*, 128.
25. The film includes a shot of a world map with the legend "Political map of the world," an expression he used in the back on the invitation for Exposition littéraire autour de Mallarmé (1969), *Marcel Broodthaers: Cinéma*, 124.
26. *Marcel Broodthaers : Cinéma*, 128.
27. See Philippe Ortel, *La Littérature à l'ère de la photographie* (Paris: Jacqueline Chambon, 2002); and Philippe Hamon, *Imageries: Littérature et image au XIXe siècle* (Paris: José Corti, 2007).
28. Charles Baudelaire, *Oeuvres complètes*, vol. 1 (Paris: Pléiade, 1975), 664. See Marielle Macé, "Le Navire Baudelaire: Imagination et hospitalité," *Littérature* 177 (2015): 100–113.
29. Krauss, *Voyage*, 49–52.
30. See Jennifer Yee, "La Beauté: Art and Dialogism in the Poetry of Baudelaire," *Neophilologus* 102 (2018): 1–14. Emphasizing Baudelaire's staging of a "double-voiced" poetics partly via "anamorphosis" and parody in this poem and his poetry in general, Yee insists that the ideal of beauty in "La Beauté" is antithetical to them. Baudelaire, she reminds us, preferred the *ligne brisée* [broken line] of real life, which Delacroix vaunted in Rubens (11–12).
31. Stéphane Mallarmé, *Oeuvres complètes* (Paris: Gallimar/Pléiade, 1945).
32. Wall-Romana, *Cinepoetry*, 55–78.
33. Mallarmé, *Oeuvres complètes*, 878.
34. Broodthaers, *Collected Writings*, 178.
35. *Marcel Broodthaers, Cinéma*, 210.
36. Krauss, *Voyage*, 2, 24.
37. Nicolas Brulhart, "Chers amis ... histoire et esthétique du cinéma, de Marcel Broodthaers." *Décadrages* 26–27 (2014): 172.
38. *Marcel Broodthaers: Cinéma*, 192.
39. *Marcel Broodthaers: Cinéma*, 185.
40. *Marcel Broodthaers: Cinéma*, 187.
41. *Marcel Broodthaers: Cinéma*, 186.
42. Broodthaers misspels *poisson* as *poison* from *L'Œuf film* (Broodthaers: Cinéma, 43) to a drawing titled *Jeter du poison sur le marché de Cologne*, showing a bottle bearing a skull with an accompanying stem glass. Marcel Broodthaers, *Vingt fois sur le métier remettez votre ouvrage* (Dijon: ADAC, 1988), n. p. See also *Broodthaers Cinéma*, 184.
43. *Marcel Broodthaers: Cinéma*, 188–89, and 39.

44. Animals in Broodthaers bear close similarities with how poet Francis Ponge transforms animals into apparatuses of phenomenology and rhetoric. Broodthaers, *Collected Writings*, p. 126 mentions Ponge.
45. *Marcel Broodthaers: Cinéma*, 184.
46. Charlotte Frilling (ed.), *Marcel Broodthaers, Industrial Poems: The Complete Catalog of the Plaques 1968–1972* (Brussels: WIELS, Hatje Cantz, 2021).
47. *Marcel Broodthaers: Cinéma*, 132–39.
48. Broodthaers, *Collected Writings*, 180.
49. Gilles Deleuze, *Cinema 1: The Movement-Image* (Minneapolis: University of Minnesota Press, 1983), 11.
50. *Marcel Broodthaers: Cinéma*, 361.
51. Both citations figure on the handwritten mockup of the front page of the newspaper *Le Soir* reproduced in Marcel Broodthaers, *Cinéma Modèle, Département des aigles du Musée d'Art Moderne* (Winterthur: Kunstmuseum Winterthur, 2012).
52. Broodthaers, *Collected Writings*, 184.
53. Personal communication from Bruce Jenkins during the Marcel Broodthaers Film Retrospective at the Walker Art Center, 24 February 2017.
54. Wall-Romana, *Cinepoetry*, 205–38.
55. *Marcel Broodthaers: Cinéma*, 17.
56. Marcel Broodthaers, *Marcel Broodthaers in Zuid-Limburg*, in collaboration with Maria Glissen (Maastricht: Bonnefantenmuseum, 1987), 158.
57. Broodthaers, *Collected Writings*, 211 (translation corrected).

A DENOUNCED TAUTOLOGY
ON *UNE SECONDE D'ÉTERNITÉ (D'APRÈS UNE IDÉE DE CHARLES BAUDELAIRE)* (1970)

Andrew Chesher

A SYSTEMATIC USE OF DIGRESSION

> [T]he step-by-step method [...] is never anything but the decomposition (in the cinematographic sense) of the work of reading: a slow motion, so to speak, neither wholly image nor analysis; it is, finally, in the very writing of the commentary, a systematic use of digression [...] and thereby a way of observing the reversibility of the structures of which the text is woven.[1]

Broodthaers started to deploy his signature—or rather his signed initials—as a motif in 1965. In this year he made a series of drawings intended for inclusion in *Happening News*, a xeroxed magazine produced in Antwerp by a group that included the artist Panamarenko. Two of these drawings feature a swarm of handwritten M.B.s surrounding a line drawing of a broken eggshell, which itself contains a single monogram. Although they were not published at the time, remaining stored in a tube in Panamarenko's possession,[2] in February of the following year a similar drawing appeared as the frontispiece to an issue of the Brussels-based journal *Phantomas* dedicated to Broodthaers. On the outside all eggs look alike, but what hatches from them is, apparently, an individual; in this case, however, Broodthaers's signatures are reproductions from the same mold. In the ensuing years, Broodthaers painted his initials on canvases, reproduced them on prints and exhibition announcements, and inscribed them on pedestals, slide film, writing slates, and projection screens. He also produced a single 35mm film featuring his signature. Consisting of a mere twenty-four frames, *Une Seconde d'éternité (D'après une idée de Charles Baudelaire)* is the subject of this chapter.

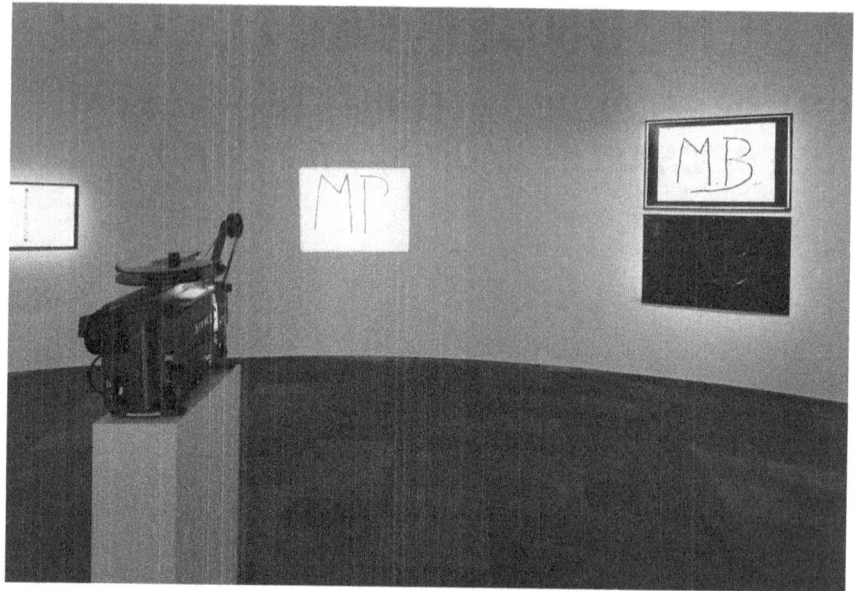

Une Seconde d'Éternité. 1970. Exhibition view "Marcel Broodthaers," Fridericianum, 2015.
© photo: Achim Hatzius © Estate of Marcel Broodthaers, c/o SABAM Belgium 2024

Une Seconde d'éternité is a looped second of celluloid, in which the artist's initials are inscribed only to disappear and recycle again and again. It was made using a simple stop-frame animation technique, Broodthaers decomposing the strokes of the pen that formed the M and the B into twenty-four linear segments. Starting at the left, from the bottom of the first stave of the M, each subsequent frame of the film adds a further segment until by the twenty-fourth frame the monogram is complete. The effect, when the film is projected on the wall of the gallery, is one of subtle vacillation: one moment the projected image reads as an immaterial inscription applied to the physical surface; the next, the image appears to objectify, in its cinematic frame, the reproduced signature itself.

The film was first exhibited at the Galerie Folker Skulima in Berlin from September 28 to November 7, 1970. Besides his film, with which it shared its title, Broodthaers's exhibition included two plaques. Titled simply *M.B.*, they reproduce the completed signature from the film's final frame in embossed plastic. As with most of his other *Industrial Poems*, this motif was conceived to have a "positive" and "negative" version.[3] Where the initials in the one appear in black relief against a white ground, its counterpart is, apart from one solitary exception, unique within the entire series of plastic plaques in being completely black.[4] The letters it represents seem to be on the verge of disappearing and would be all but indiscernible if it were not for the highlights reflected by the camber of their relief. A copy of the film mounted on a sheet of white card made up, it would seem, the third element of the exhibition. Unlike the film and the plaques, this multiple, entitled *M.B. 24 images/seconde*, was not mentioned in the exhibition announcement, possibly because it was added to the exhibition at a later stage—Broodthaers was not averse to changing and rearranging his exhibitions midstream.

Éternité joins the various slide projections, plinths, prints, and paintings in which Broodthaers deployed his initials to form a relatively discrete body of work. There are very few examples of the signature coinciding with other tropes or appearing in other contexts, although there are exceptions. The subject of the artist's signature does not play a role in any of the various sections of his fictional *Musée d'Art Moderne, Département des Aigles* (1968–72), for example. The exception that proves the rule is *Avis* (1969), a work that I will discuss in the last section of this essay and which features two signatures on the letterhead paper of his museum's *Section littéraire*. In the case of the eggshell, from which apparently the monogram originally hatched, there is, in addition to the drawings I mentioned above, the example of an exhibition invitation from 1966.[5] The fig. number symbol coincides with the signature even more rarely than the

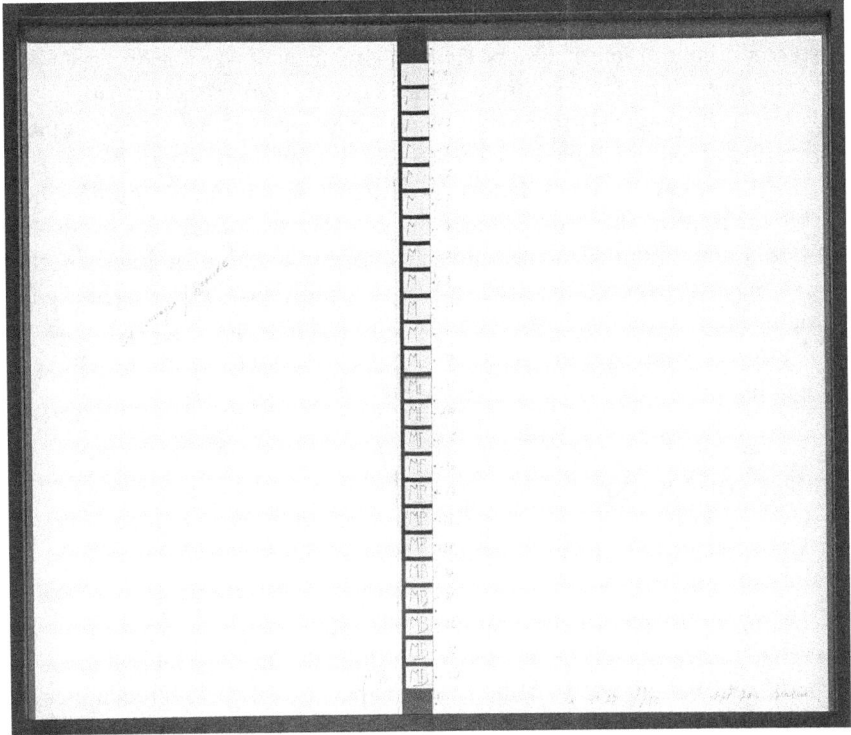

M.B., 24 images/seconde. 35mm filmstrip and pencil on cardboard. 1970.
Collection Ivo and Monique Van Vaerenbergh. Photo Rachel Gruijters.
© Estate of Marcel Broodthaers, c/o SABAM Belgium 2024

eggshell does, although Broodthaers introduced it into his work at around the same moment.⁶ I am aware of a single working sketch in which the inscription "fig. M.B." is included, and one short text, "General Theory of Art and Collection" published in an exhibition catalog in 1973, that consists of two parts, the first labeled "figure M." and the second "figure B.".⁷ Otherwise and for by far the most part, Broodthaers's initials do not intersect with the fig. numbers.

There is one other exception, although it is an instance not so much of coincidence as of indirect association: on the white card of *M.B. 24 images/seconde* on which *Éternité*'s filmstrip was presented, Broodthaers numbered each of its twenty-four frames in pencil from top to bottom. As Jean-Christophe Royoux has pointed out, this is an allusion to the symbolism of midnight, the hour of stasis, in Stéphane Mallarmé's poetry;⁸ which by turn is also echoed in the numbering system Broodthaers used most frequently with the figure number symbol: fig. 1, fig. 2, fig. 0 and fig. 12 (twenty-four hours being the completion of a day, its return to zero, and twelve being the hour of midnight on the clockface). This oblique chain of association is a good example of the intertextuality that suffuses Broodthaers's work as a whole and imbues *Éternité* no less. The Freudian term "overdetermination" could legitimately be invoked to describe it: each signifier condenses multiple meanings, and each potential meaning is displaced into multiple signifiers, such that an array of possible and even contrary meanings are stowed within *Éternité*'s twenty-four frame animation. It is this sort of compression that Broodthaers's reference to "film stock as a place for storing ideas—a rather special kind of can" should evoke in us.⁹

In what follows some of the ideas stored in *Éternité*—including the film's intertext in the nineteenth-century French poets Mallarmé and Charles Baudelaire and its condensation of themes and schemas invoked by Broodthaers's other works, in particular his other films and the slide projections featuring his signed initials—are traced by means of what Roland Barthes called "a systematic use of digression," with the aim of "observing the reversibility of the structures of which the text is woven."¹⁰

DOUBLE COMPOSITION

*24 images, the film of a second, a double subject.*¹¹

According to its parenthetical subtitle, *Éternité* is based on an idea drawn from Baudelaire. Shortly before making the film, during the winter of 1969–70, Broodthaers had attended a seminar on the poet given by the French literary theorist Lucien Goldmann.¹² Goldmann's identification of the contrast between ideal and ephemeral beauty as an essential opposition within Baudelaire's poetic universe would seem to have had a significant influence on the artist.¹³ However, though Goldmann may well have honed Broodthaers's sense for the

Où est la signature? Slide show. 1971. Installation view.
© Estate of Marcel Broodthaers, c/o SABAM Belgium 2024

poet's dialectically shifting concept, his seminar seems not to have been the first time Broodthaers encountered it. A text the artist had written around five years previously indicates Baudelaire's terms were already part of his thinking:

> The preference for eternity and the natural had ended up producing academicism, as we know. Its replacement by a preference for the ephemeral, for the artificial, for all that is false, aroused my enthusiasm as much as my poetic loyalty.[14]

Baudelaire had already alighted on this distinction in his *Salon* of 1846, where, like Broodthaers in this instance, he placed the stress on the ephemeral. "Absolute and eternal beauty," he had written there, "does not exist;" it is no more than an abstraction "creamed off from the general surface of different types of beauty."[15] In his poem *La Beauté*, published a decade later in *Les fleurs du mal*, however, the emphasis had moved to the eternal. There, beauty describes itself to the reader (us "mortals") as like "a stone-fashioned dream," "eternal, and silent as matter is timeless."[16] What beauty cannot abide, its antithesis, is "the movement that displaces the lines,"[17] which suggests temporality eroding the chiseled stasis of form.

The opposition between time and eternity surfaces in several other poems in *Les fleurs du mal*, too. *Parisian Dream*, for example, starts with an ecstatic, frozen tableau that unravels at the moment of waking. The poem's first thirteen quatrains paint a world of marble, metal, and ice that is lit from within. Its ocean has been "subdued," its waterfalls are of crystal, and it is accompanied by "a silence of eternity." In the poem's last two quatrains, however, the dreamer awakens to his squalid room and the clock striking noon, calling him back into the transient present.[18] The timepiece recurs in *The Clock*, where its ticking is likened to a droning insect announcing that it has sucked the life from the reader. Do not waste the passing minutes, the poem admonishes the reader, "They are the ore you must refine for gold!"[19] Likewise, two years after the second edition of *Les fleurs du mal* appeared, for which the last two poems discussed were written, Baudelaire described the artist's job in "The Painter of Modern Life" (1863) as being "to distil the eternal from the transitory."[20] It was in this essay that the poet described beauty as having a "double composition," its two parts being "an eternal invariable element," and "a relative, circumstantial element."[21] Without the latter, which Baudelaire located in the fashions and morals of a particular period, there would be no access to ideal beauty.

Baudelaire's doubleness finds many echoes in Broodthaers. The artist described, for example, the representations of eagles in the *Section des figures* of his fictional *Musée d'Art Moderne, Département des Aigles* (1972) as forming a "double projection," coming from art history (eternity) on the one hand and advertising or commerce (the moment) on the other, as they did. Of his *Industrial Poems* he said that they were intended to be read on a "double level," with their message not placed "completely on one side alone, neither image nor text."²² *Le Corbeau et le renard* (1967), which was projected on a screen printed tautologically with the same text that featured in the film itself, he described as a "relation between two images."²³ Finally, he wrote that *Éternité*, too, had "a double subject," which he glossed as "the meaning or meaninglessness of the relation between two languages," whether it be "that of words and that of cinema, or again, the relation between a static image and a moving image."²⁴

Writing about filmmaking the previous year in "Project for a Text" (1969), Broodthaers had expressed this last dichotomy of movement and immobility as the horns of a dilemma. The text begins by quoting a verse from Baudelaire's *La Beauté*: "I hate the movement that shifts the lines." It then goes on to list ways to avoid the displacement that cinema's movement imposes on literary form, before dismissing them and concluding, "I am cruelly torn between something immobile that has already been written and the comic movement that animates 24 images per second."²⁵ Baudelaire's line appears again in the artist's book *Charles Baudelaire: Je hais le mouvement qui déplace les lignes* (1973), where, by contrast, Broodthaers subjects it to exactly the fragmentation it expresses hatred for by dismembering and distributing it a word per page through the book's length.

What the examples listed above demonstrate is less a consistent concept than, as Barthes says of the writerly text, "the reversibility of the structures" that make up the weave of Broodthaers's work. Like all the other motifs and subjects of which he produced ever-new variations, eternity and the ephemeral did not settle into a definitive relation or take on determinate meanings. Playing on the reversible tensions between them belonged to the ironic hue of his rhetoric; their pairing also constitutes an implicit formal thread running through his cinematic work from beginning to end.

In many of the films, the contrast is implicit in the way they were made: they are moving images—shot with a cinecamera—of images, texts, or objects that are, in themselves, essentially still. In *A Voyage on the North Sea* (1973–74), for example, the static images that form its content are distinguishable from a slide projection only by the characteristic shimmer of the filmic image, a format largely followed in *Analyse d'une peinture* (1973), too. In other films, it is text that alternates between motion and immobility. *Le Corbeau et le renard* consists of close-up shots of a printed text, sometimes with objects and photos placed in front of it. Some of these shots are static, while others travel across the text. The latter, in which the text appears to move, are echoed in a sequence included in both *Une Discussion inaugurale* (1968) and some versions of *Un voyage à Waterloo* (1969), in which a Menkes transport lorry, shot through the windows of the *Nineteenth-century section* of Broodthaers's *Musée* in the Rue de la Pépinière, moves backward and forward as it parks. All we see of the vehicle are changing portions of the text painted on its side as it travels behind the apertures formed by the windows.

Une Discussion inaugurale. 16mm. c.1969.
© Estate of Marcel Broodthaers, c/o SABAM Belgium 2024

Un Film de Charles Baudelaire (1970), to take another example, consists entirely of static shots of a world map. Dates that appear as intertitles and subtitles, interspersed with words suggestive of a sea voyage, evoke the grueling creep of time. Starting on January 3, 1850, the progression through the calendar halts around the midpoint of the film. Here the same date, December 17, is repeated several times before the sequence is thrown into reverse, possibly in reference to Baudelaire's aborted journey to India after the boat carrying him was damaged in a storm rounding the Cape of Good Hope in 1841.[26] Toward the film's end, in an echo of Baudelaire's poem, a clock strikes twelve and we are left with only its monotonous ticking for the remainder. As a whole, the film thematizes the tension between the static and the temporal by pitting, in Eric de Bruyn's words, "the reversibility of a fully reified time—the abstract chronology of the clock or calendar—against the forgetfulness of an existence locked in a perpetual present."[27]

Éternité, made shortly after *Un Film de Charles Baudelaire*, could be thought of as a pendant to the latter. It, too, folds the static image into the moving and vice versa: it is both static (i.e., eternal), being as it is "projected in an endless loop," and simultaneously represents "the time of a second of cinema" (the ephemeral), which its constant cycling from inscription to erasure underlines.[28] In this way, Broodthaers's film seems to transpose into its own idiom the two sides of Baudelaire's thesis of beauty's "double composition." Turning next to Broodthaers's relation to another nineteenth-century French poet will help demonstrate the way it does this.

A CONSTELLATION

A throw of the dice / This would be a treatise on art.[29]

While *Une Seconde d'éternité*'s connection to Baudelaire is assured visibility since the poet's name appears in the film's subtitle, its relation to Stéphane Mallarmé is more obscure. On the draft for the announcement of his exhibition at the Skulima gallery, Broodthaers sketched a swift but immediately recognizable portrait of Mallarmé accompanied by the poet's name in large and deliberate cursive script.[30] In the text that went to print, however, neither the image nor name were retained. What, then, is Mallarmé's relevance to *Éternité*?

It was René Magritte, Broodthaers recorded, who had given him a copy of the typographically groundbreaking 1914 Nouvelle Revue Française edition of Mallarmé's famous *Un coup de dés jamais n'abolira le hazard*. This was in 1945 or '46.[31] Assimilating the poem seems to have taken Broodthaers some time, however. Between this initial encounter with the work and his eventual artistic response to it lay a gestation period of two decades and more. His text *Investigating Dreamland* (1960), where he described himself as being "like the phantom of Mallarmé, whom I could not understand," suggests the process was not yet complete at this time.[32] Nonetheless, Mallarmé seems here already to be a model for Broodthaers, who depicts himself, like the figure of Igitur from the poet's eponymous tale, "sitting down in a chair" and "practicing immobility."

A period of particularly intense engagement with Mallarmé began around 1969. Over the next couple of years Broodthaers repeatedly recast Mallarmé's dice, most explicitly in his redacted reproduction of *Un coup de dés* printed as an artist's book, which he presented in two exhibitions dedicated to the poet, one at the end of 1969 in the Wide White Space Gallery in Antwerp and the other a month into 1970 at the Galerie Michael Werner in Cologne.[33] Baudelaire may be the most frequently cited figure in the artist's work, but Mallarmé, whom Broodthaers described as "the founder of contemporary art," was of no lesser importance.[34]

Un coup de dés depicts a ship foundering in a storm. As it is wrecked, the ship's Master, who has let go of the helm, hesitates to cast the dice he holds in his hands instead. This scene is an allegory of the writer's situation, in which literary composition is likened to a dice throw. Whether words can be secured a meaning is uncertain in this game of chance; unless "perhaps / a constellation" (i.e., the poem's syntax resulting from the throw) can do so.[35] The significance of *Un coup de dés*'s fixing of language in a syntactical arrangement was spelled out in Mallarmé's essay *Crisis in Verse*, where he wrote, "Everything is suspended, an arrangement of fragments with alternatives and confrontations, adding up to a total rhythm, which would be the poem stilled."[36] The poem's internal order was, he mooted, capable of "eliminating chance;" in its *stillness* it would negate "the arbitrariness that remains in the terms" of ordinary speech, from which the poem must necessarily be constructed.[37] *Un coup de dés* itself, however, seems to turn away from this hope. One implication of its title, which forms a line disseminated in large capitals through a good portion of the poem's length, is that the whirlpool contingency of reading will win out against the bulwark of the constellation: "A THROW OF THE DICE / WILL NEVER / ABOLISH / CHANCE."

Shortly before staging the first of his explicitly Mallarméan exhibitions in December 1969, Broodthaers made a film entitled *La Pluie (Projet pour un texte)* (1969). Shot during the period that the *Nineteenth-century section* of his fictional museum was installed inside the building, this two-minute film features the artist sitting in the garden of his Brussels home stymied in his attempts at writing by a curtain of theatrical rain. Although it makes no direct reference to the poet, *La Pluie* clearly belongs to the series of Broothaers's meditations on *Un coup de dés*.

The affinity between the film and Mallarmé's poem is twofold. Firstly and most obviously, the scenario of Broodthaers's film is a slapstick translation of that discernable in the poem. The artist cast himself in the role of *Un coup de dés*'s Master writing in the face of the deluge that washes the ink from his sheet of paper as soon as it is applied. Like the storm symbolizing chance in the poem, the rain in the film prevails. Broodthaers, though, transposes Mallarmé's cosmic tragedy into his own comedic farce.

The correspondence does not stop there, however: the film's form also chimes with Mallarmé's poem. The other half of *La Pluie*'s "double composition" is informed by Mallarmé's revolutionary emphasis on his poem's visual dimension. Where Baudelaire, in *La Beauté*, seems to espouse the ideal stasis of metrical form, Mallarmé bridled at the linearity of conventional reading: "the back-and-forth movement of the eye finishing one line, starting another."[38]

In his *Un coup de dés*, the page rather than the line "is taken as the basic unit," which entails the paper's white expanse being "incorporated into the work itself" where it "intervenes each time an image."³⁹ Similarly, in *La Pluie* image and text from a counterpoint. The film starts with a wide shot: Broodthaers in the foreground writing on a low wooden box he uses as a desk, behind him the white-washed garden wall bearing the inscription "Département des Aigles" in black capitals. The second shot, taken from a lower angle so that these stenciled capitals appear directly beside the artist, emphasizes their juxtaposition in its tighter frame. The camera then tilts down to more words, those the artist is writing on the page in front of him. No sooner written, however, this text becomes image under the downpour that starts in the next shot, looking in no time more like a Tachist watercolor than a page of writing. At the film's end, its subtitle "projet pour un text" appears printed on top of the image of this erased writing, although this phrase only defers to yet another (although apparently unrealized) text.

These affinities notwithstanding, the intervention of the image in the text has a different value, it would seem, for Broodthaers than for Mallarmé. For the latter, the *integration* of the word with the image (the space of the page) releases it from its communicative function. *La Pluie*, however, seems to suggest the *displacement* of the word by the image—and, by turn, of the image by the text. The film's last shot illustrates this in condensed form. The final gesture of Broodthaers's pen appears to be a signature.⁴⁰ We see the hand make the characteristic flourish, but the pen's trace on the page is erased by the rain even before the gesture ends. We might conjecture that *Éternité*, made around a year later, took this concluding image as the model for its ouroboros-like cycle of inscription and erasure.

The theme of the text's negation by an image or object is an integral thread running through Broodthaers's work and, unsurprisingly, has been an emphasis in much critical commentary. Broodthaers's *Un coup de dés jamais n'abolira le hazard, image* (1969) enacts this negation by replacing Mallarmé's text with graphic bars, whose scale and placement follow that of the poem's original typography. This modified copy of *Un coup de dés* suggests Broodthaers had come to the same conclusion as Jean-Paul Sartre, who in *What Is Literature?* (1948) had written that a literary work only exists if it is read "and it lasts only as long as this act can last [...] beyond that, there are only black marks on paper."⁴¹ In Benjamin Buchloh's words Broodthaers was, in carrying out his détournement, "literally reifying and deliberately commodifying the poem's insistence on its linguistic and visual autonomy."⁴² The original instance of this apparently distinctively Broodthaersian approach to art's entanglement with the commodity has widely been identified as his sculpture *Pense-Bête* (1964), which consists of fifty copies of Broodthaers's last collection of poetry stood in a roughly formed base of plaster. For Birgit Pelzer, *Pense-Bête* "materializes the fiction of passage from one status to another," namely from unread poet to artist producing reified objects; and Buchloh adds of this—the "first performative erasure of his own poetical text"—that it seems to announce "poetry's objective historical erasure and failure to communicate any longer."[43]

Buchloh, Pelzer, and later critics who follow their lead are certainly not mistaken. Folded into these works, however, are other implications beyond their allusions to textual erasure and reification. As Jean-Christophe Royoux has pointed out, *Pense-Bête* does not only imply the immobilization of reading; the French phrase signifies a reminder, too. Therefore, the work presents an alternative: "Either one can destroy the plastic aspect of the sculpture to remobilize the movement of the lines and thus gain access to the text of the past, or one can build a new kind of writing on the memory of the buried text."[44] With this in mind, we might want to look at *Pense-Bête* afresh. It, too, might be said to possess a double subject, which comes into focus when we add to Buchloh's allusion to poetry's "historical erasure," the complement of Royoux's insight that "Broodthaers's project is to make the immobility of art mobile once again—as textuality."[45] Read in this way, the sculpture would figure not only poetry's occlusion but simultaneously its continuing relevance, in particular the relevance of what Mallarmé termed the poetic word's mobility.

Mallarmé thought that if words could be levered free from the linearity of discourse and removed from the instrumental context of speech, they would "attain a 'mobility' deriving from their innate instability."[46] In contrast to the exigencies of communication that reduce language to something like an exchange value, the mobile word is manifold, semantically capacious, and equivocal. The terms the poet used to circumscribe it evoke volatility and effervescence: whereas reality is banally "spread out like a street vendor's wares" by communicative speech, the mobile word transforms it into its "vibratory near-disappearance;" words are mobile where they "light each other up through reciprocal reflections."[47] Mobility is the quicksilver of "language playing," a kind of linguistic unconscious. In it Mallarmé saw a glimpse of the infinite; it was, as it were, a second of eternity.

How might Broodthaers's *Un coup... image* be read in Royoux's spirit not only as an immobilization of poetry but also as a remobilization of art? Perhaps the answer lies in taking a cue from how *Un coup de dés* itself developed a lesson that Mallarmé had found in the "simple maculation" of newsprint. He saw the potential for a new form of writing in the way that the inked letters were disposed on the newspaper's pages in different sizes and relations, which would derive "a spacious mobility" from their typographic image.[48] In Broodthaers's reworking of Mallarmé's poem the relations between legible text and the page's spatiality were *not only* suspended *but also* recast at another level: his graphic bars still find their significance in relation to the words they displace. If on the one hand poetry is spatially immobilized, on the other the promise of "a spacious mobility" is reintroduced at a different point. In the original poem, the white of the page "that separates groups of words from one another" seems, as Mallarmé wrote, "to speed up and slow down the movement" of reading.[49] Although the separation that Broodthaers's abstraction of the poem's typography creates is greater and the variable tempo of reading is turned into an indefinite delay, the text is not forgotten.

This brings me to the connection between Mallarméan mobility and chance. In fact, the chance that poetry's syntax will not annul has two sides. Firstly, there is the chance innate to language itself, the arbitrary association of this phonetic form with that idea. Then there is the aleatory dimension released once words have been set within the constellation of the poem. Mallarmé referred to poetry as a "superior supplement" that abolished chance of the first sort "word-by-word."[50] Poetry's stilling of speech, however, rather than ultimately ridding language of chance, transforms the word's arbitrariness into mobility, turning the *in-itself* chance of speech into the *for-itself* volatility of the poetic word (to use the Hegelian terminology that Mallarmé would have known well). So, although meaning remains uncertain in the poem's linguistic and spatial arrangement, its uncertainty changes valence: the sign's arbitrariness becomes integral to the poem's form; and, although "a throw of the dice does not abolish chance," Mallarmé believed that the constellation of the poem might yet absorb it.

A similar model of meaning, I think, could be applied to Broodthaers's work. Both the signed initials and the fig. number symbols have arbitrary connections to their referents. They attach a text (a name, a biography) to an image or object (a work, or an illustration of one). On both sides what they connect is interchangeable: this or that author with one object or another, any image with any legend. It is not by chance that Broodthaers reduced his signature to his name's initials when deploying it in his work, because initials can accommodate any number of names or words as their referents and in this sense are more arbitrary as symbols than words themselves. Broodthaers's recourse to this encompassing obtuseness demonstrates the principle. An example is found in a manuscript relating to his reworking of *Un coup de dés*, where the artist concatenates himself (Marcel) with Mallarmé and Magritte, as well as the terms Model (which Mallarmé as "forerunner of Contemporary Art" represents) and Museum—all threaded together by the letter "M."[51]

A related capaciousness is evident in Broodthaers's *Le Catalogue et la signature* (1968). This work consists of a black screen inscribed with five signatures and enclosed by a frame printed with black-and-white images of previous works. On to this signed screen eighty to one hundred slides representing Broodthaers's back catalogue were projected in rotation. Rather than the signature being applied to the object, here the object is attached to the signature: Broodthaers's initials become the overt center of the catalog's solar system and, simultaneously, an empty reference holding a potentially infinite array of works in their orbits.

One commonality between *Le Catalogue* and *Éternité* is the way in which the signature's reference to a concrete individual is displaced by its impersonal reality as a social institution. In this regard, responding to an interviewer's question about *Éternité* in 1971, Broodthaers said "the important thing is not that it's my signature or anyone else's; but the very fact of the signature."[52] Another commonality would be the way in which the reproductions in the slide carousel cycle past the static signatures on *Le Catalogue*'s screen like the second hand around a clockface.

Among the works reproduced in *Le Catalogue*'s slides are two paintings of daubed inscriptions in white and red on black grounds: *Il n'y a pas de structures primaires* and *M.B. M.B. M.B.…*, (both 1968). Signatures form each work's motif, or part of it. As such, they can be seen as being in the same vein as the drawings the artist had made for *Happening News* three years previously, where his initials had already departed from their habitual auxiliary role to become part of a rebus of sorts. Arguably, the signature's function as an index of authorship remains in all these works, but it has become distanced, nonetheless, by dint of being integrated into the work's image, its statement, rather than discretely underwriting it.

Projected on to *Le Catalogue*'s signed screen, however, the signatures from these paintings establish a new dimension: not only is the signature included as motif but it is now also applied tautologically to itself. Although the convention of the countersignature is suggested, in Broodthaers's hands the added signature—rather than shoring up the authority of the first—confers on it a Mallarméan mobility. He deployed similar doublings of the signature in a series of other works, including *24 images/seconde* (1970) in which his initials were penciled in beside the film strip. In *La Signature, série 1. Tirage illimité* (1969), another example, Broodthaers added one further signature by hand at the bottom of the screen-printed field of signed initials it reproduced. Any impression of spontaneity that the irregular rows duplicating the handwritten monogram produce fades once their uniform identity, highlighted by the addition of the original, is recognized. The unique, penciled initials themselves, by turn, juxtaposed with their serial reproduction in a print that declares itself an "unlimited edition," seem to invert into a copy, a repetition of a repetition, leached of authenticity.

A similar vacillation is set in motion between image (motif) and text (the authenticating signature) in the slide carousel work *Où est la signature?* (1971). In this case, Broodthaers drew his initials in red, blue, and black directly onto the slide film using Indian ink and felt-tip pens. These "drawings" were then projected onto a screen filled with rows of monograms very like the 1969 print *La Signature*.[53] Appearing enlarged in the image thrown by the light of the projector, the unique signs on the slides read simultaneously as reproductions. Their superimposition with the signatures inscribed on the screen underlines this equivocality: which is the authentic signature and which its image? The question of what their referents would be outside of their relation to one another seems to have been suspended, with the result that their status oscillates between reproduced signatures and signed reproductions.

An equivalent duplicity imbues *Éternité*'s animated reconstitution of the signature's inscription. Firstly, in the film the initials seem to write themselves. This farcical effect gives them the appearance of having "no signatory" (itself the hallmark of pure poetry, according to Mallarmé);⁵⁴ it implies that, like the signatures in *Où est la signature?*, they have been isolated from their indexical function and now refer in a circular fashion only to themselves.

In addition, their separate segments added frame by frame do not flow seamlessly together: slight deviances in direction, width, or alignment of the lines make the progression from one frame to the next noticeably staccato. Much hinges on this detail. We do indeed recognize the lines of the animation as tokens of the letters M and B; but, at the same time, their physical construction out of drawn lines is obtrusive: they are clearly a *drawing* simulating *writing*, the one acting as the tautological double of the other. The letters waver between these two possibilities (image and text) and so condense within themselves *Éternité*'s double subject; the signature as text seemingly superimposed with itself as image flips between letter and line, and in this way the relation found in Mallarmé between text and page, is transferred in *Éternité* into one and the same sign: *M.B.*

A DENOUNCED TAUTOLOGY

> *Slide show. My initials: M.B. are drawn onto the film.*
> *It's a projection of drawings. [...]*
> *It's a denounced tautology in the vein of L'Arroseur Arrosé*
> *(The Sprinkler Sprinkled), one of Lumière's first films.*⁵⁵

When *Une Seconde d'éternité* was shown in Berlin in autumn 1970, Broodthaers's film and the other elements of his ensemble shared Skulima's gallery with a second exhibition that the gallerist had arranged for the same period. The centerpiece of that other exhibition, *The Pencil on Paper Descriptive Works of Gilbert & George*, was a large-scale drawing called *Walking* (1970), one part of a triptych Skulima had acquired by the London-based duo that depicts them against a pastoral backdrop of trees. Each show was announced separately, which perhaps explains in part why they have rarely been associated since. Nonetheless, their coincidence is fortuitous. At the start of the final section of this chapter, where my purpose is to outline Broodthaers's deployment of tautology as trope, it offers the opportunity of a comparison.

Between the autumn of 1969 and the summer of 1970 Gilbert & George had made their first forays on the continental gallery circuit. They appeared as a singing sculpture in two major survey shows of the new conceptual art at the Düsseldorf Kunsthalle and the Städtisches Museum in Leverkusen in late 1969, and then at a series of commercial galleries in 1970, including Konrad Fischer's gallery in Düsseldorf and Art & Project in Amsterdam in May that year.⁵⁶

In the midst of this itinerary, on a weekend in mid-February 1970, both Broodthaers and Gilbert & George had participated in the fourth *Between* event at Düsseldorf's Kunsthalle. Broodthaers showed the *Section XIXe siècle (Bis)* of his *Musée d'Art Moderne, Département des Aigles*, a version and documentation of his fictional museum's first iteration, while Gilbert & George performed *The Singing Sculpture* (1969), for which they stood on a table to sing along to a recording of the music hall number "Underneath the Arches."[57] Their heads and hands were transformed by metallic makeup and they wore identical English gentleman's suits. Six months later, "the sculptors," as they were described on Skulima's announcement, appeared in the same outfits as a "living sculpture" for the first few days of their exhibition in Berlin.[58]

In their public personae, Gilbert & George sought to remove all individual and private personality from themselves.[59] Subsuming themselves under the trademark of their conjoined first names with their common first letters, and mirroring each other in their studied clothing and manners, they fitted themselves into a mold they had fashioned for themselves. It is not only the careful crafting of this exterior but more so its doubling, the copy that Gilbert is of George and George of Gilbert, that signals that this persona is a sign. George *or* Gilbert alone would hardly have the effect that their dual embodiment of the same identity produces. The pair's apparently total identification with their chosen role is also emphasized by its conflation of subject and object: they are "sculptors" who are also "sculpture."

Whereas Gilbert & George's living sculpture emphasizes a form freely chosen, Broodthaers's signatures, exhibited alongside it, suggest an alienation deriving from the artist's mercantile existence and their need for institutional recognition. One of their implications is the commodity status conferred by and on authorship; the cycling of Broodthaers's initials between inscription and erasure in *Éternité*'s loop evokes the eclipse of the artist as subject by the signifier with which they are metonymically invoked: the bureaucratic form of the authenticating signature. Likewise, in the form of the plastic plaques, which were manufactured in the same manner as municipal street signs, his initials have literally been reified as an institutional sign.[60] In contrast to Gilbert & George, when Broodthaers colluded in the production of images of himself as an art-world persona—as when he modeled a shirt in an advert for the German magazine *Der Spiegel* in 1971, and then again when he had himself photographed in a smart suit, serious glasses, and with carefully coiffured hair, looking every inch the bourgeois museum director, for an exhibition invitation in 1975—it was a self-conscious performance of a role not fully identified with, ironically foregrounding the economic and institutional structures implicit in the image.

Here a second point of comparison can be introduced alongside Gilbert & George's living sculpture by bringing Piero Manzoni's *sculture vivente* into the discussion. Again, the example comes from Broodthaers's immediate context. In February 1962 Manzoni was the subject of a solo exhibition at the

Galerie Aujourd'hui of the Palais des Beaux Arts in Brussels. Here the Italian artist met Broodthaers, signed him as a living sculpture, and issued him with a "Declaration of Authenticity" bearing his autograph. The primary subject of Manzoni's living sculpture, however, is not the person signed but the artist's signature. Indeed, it is in this encounter with Manzoni that the beginnings of Broodthaers's preoccupation with the theme is surely to be located. What the doubling of the act of signing in the signed certificate will undoubtedly have underlined for him, is that signatures themselves are tautologies of a latent sort: the signatory authenticates the signature by producing it, and the signature by turn vouches for the authenticity of the signatory in their absence. The declaration, one of many Manzoni dispensed, was of course itself an overt tautology—it says, "this person is a sculpture because I say he is one"—and as such resonates with Broodthaers's wider interest in the trope that stretches from his earlier poetry to his late *Décors*.

Seven years later, Broodthaers reproduced Manzoni's certificate on paper bearing the letterhead of his *Musée d'Art Moderne*, appending his signature as the museum's curator to the artist's. This work, *Avis* (1969), introduces a subtle but decisive change to the tautological figure. Not only does it say the same thing twice—the basic definition of a tautology—it also links together two different signatures in what appears to be a closed circuit. By countersigning Manzoni's certificate under the auspices of his museum, Broodthaers notarized the signature that vouched for his own authenticity. That is to say, the signature is reflected back on itself through the intermediary of the countersignature, which, however, by a certain reversal of the original, introduces a delay.

Returning once more to Mallarmé provides us with a third point of comparison. When Barthes, in his essay "Authors and Writers" (1960), described literary writing as an "intransitive act"—meaning that its primary object is its own language—and the author's activity as "narcissistic" and "tautological," he surely had Mallarmé in mind.[61] The poet's career was devoted to the search for a self-referential sublation of common speech into literary writing. In key works such as *Herodiade* and *Igitur*, he used the image of a figure narcissistically gazing into a mirror to symbolize this self-reflective structure within the work itself. The last stanza of his *Sonnet allégorique de lui-même* which he described as "a null sonnet reflecting itself in every way," also contains a mirror.[62] The septet of stars reflected in it echoes and fixes in a poetic image the structure of the sonnet itself, seven of whose lines end in a rhyme on the letter x. While there is no mention of a mirror in *Un coup de dés*, symmetries and reflections are nonetheless found throughout its overall form. As Jean-François Lyotard pointed out, the signified content of the poem's text is reflected in its spatial placement on the page, and this relation between text and image, in turn, is itself mirrored in the way the text's linear flow is countered by its overall chiasmic form, the latter being exemplified by the fact that it begins and ends with the phrase "a throw of the dice."[63]

Sequestered from speech within the constellation of such relationships, words, Mallarmé foresaw, would turn inward upon themselves and, refracting one another, attain the mobility he aspired to. Both *Avis* and *Éternité* could be described as constellations of a similar ilk, only ones not of words but rather of other signs also secluded from their everyday use: in *Avis*, two documents with bureaucratic pretentions and their accompanying signatures; in *Éternité*, a single monogram with a double subject in which drawing mirrors writing, and the handwritten token the institutional sign it cites, etcetera. Nonetheless, in contrast to Mallarmé, the circle between one side of the mirror and the other does not close; the work's constellation proves not to be sufficient unto itself: in *Avis*, the signatory (Manzoni, Broodthaers) is reflected in its tautological copy (Broodthaers's notice, Manzoni's certificate), *but only in the reversed form* of the signed (i.e., as signatory they are subject, but as the signed, object). The text of *Éternité*'s monogram, too, finds its double not in another text but in its obverse, an image, and a moving one at that.

This phenomenon would seem to be why Broodthaers described his signed initials projected as images as a "denounced tautology."[64] Rather than define this term, he illustrated the phrase with the example of Louis Lumière's *L'Arroseur arrosé* (1895). In this short film (an echo of which can be seen in *La Pluie*, I would suggest), a gardener finds that the water to his hose mysteriously stops. When he looks into the nozzle to find the cause, the boy who has stemmed the flow by standing on the pipe behind his back releases the pressure, with inevitable consequences.

Broodthaers's denounced tautology is the same phenomenon as that described in *Roland Barthes par Roland Barthes* as a "dislocated copy."[65] Barthes gave the example of two waiters on their night off going to another café and being waited on by a third waiter. The scene suggests to him an autonym: the served upon and serving waiters seem to refer to one another as name does to thing. Like the sprinkler and the sprinkled, they become self-referential signs; but, as the critic adds, "the roles remain inevitably separated." Just as the thing that becomes a name is no longer a thing, since it acts now as a sign, it is the difference in status that both enables and denounces the tautology: only as distinct from writing does the drawn animation function as its tautological repetition, and simultaneously, by dint of the same distinction, it also denounces the tautology. It is the second moment of this figure that Gilbert & George's living sculpture seems pointedly to avoid.

The signature that *Éternité* animates is both a text *and* an image of a text, and, as such, it is effectively "neither image nor text," Through this double subject—its suspension of meaning "between two languages"—it serves both as an acknowledgement of poetry's erasure and a transfer of its mobility to "a new kind of writing." The film generates this transposed mobility precisely by placing the immobility of the signature as alienated sign into a tautological *and* dislocated relation to itself. That is to say, as a denounced tautology *Éternité* is both a tautology *and* its denunciation. The film loop's cycling between inscription and eclipse serves as a metaphor of sorts for this and various other dislocated dualities—between drawing and writing, static and moving images, eternity and temporality, subjective sign and reified subject, et cetera—and, finally, it evokes too the mobile sign's mercurial uncertainty, what Mallarmé described as its "vibratory suspense."[66]

NOTES

Thanks to the following for sharing their research, knowledge, and memories with me: Lotte Beckwé, Marie-Pascale Gildemyn, Maria Gilissen Broodthaers, Margaux Van Uytvanck and Raf Wollaert. I dedicate this essay to my father, Michael Clifford Chesher, from whom I still have a lot to learn.

1. Roland Barthes, *S/Z* (New York: Hill and Wang, 1974), 12–13.
2. Lotte Beckwé, email to the author, 10 August 2023.
3. Charlotte Friling, "Note to the Reader," in Charlotte Friling and Dirk Snauwaert (eds.), *Industrial Poems, Marcel Broodthaers: The Complete Catalogue of the Plaques, 1968–1972* (Berlin: Hatje Cantz, 2021), 31.
4. The only other completely black plastic plaque that Broodthaers produced was a single copy of *Modèle: La pipe* (1968–69).
5. The exhibition *Je retrouve à la matière, je retrouve la tradition des primitifs, peinture à œuf, peinture à œuf* took place at Galerie Cogeime, Brussels, 27 September to 9 October 1966. Its invitation included a grid of twelve signatures alongside a monochromatic image of eight eggshells repeated three times in black, yellow, and red.
6. Dirk Snauwaert dates its first use to 1966. See Snauwaert, "The Figures," in Benjamin Buchloh (ed.), *Broodthaers: Writings, Interviews, Photographs*, (Cambridge, Mass.: MIT, 1988), 127.
7. The working sketch is a two-sided drawing in felt tip reproduced under the title *Fig. M.B.* (1969–70). See *Industrial Poems, Marcel Broodthaers*, 343. The text "Théorie générale de l'art et de la collection" was published, in German and French, in the catalog *Bilder-Objekte-Filme-Konzepte* (Munich: Städtische Galerie in Lembachhaus, 1973), 50.
8. Jean-Christophe Royoux, "Projet pour un Texte: The Cinematographic Model in the Work of Marcel Broodthaers," in Manuel J. Borja-Villel and Michael Compton (eds.), *Marcel Broodthaers: Cinéma* (Barcelona: Fundació Antoni Tàpies, 1997), 298–99.
9. Marcel Broodthaers, "D is Bigger than T," in Marcel Broodthaers, *Collected Writings* (Barcelona: Ediciones Polígrafa, 2012), 180.
10. Barthes, *S/Z*, 13.
11. Marcel Broodthaers, "24 Images...," in Broodthaers, *Collected Writings*, 281.
12. Broodthaers himself described the seminar as having taken place "in the winter of 1969–70" in his artist's book *Charles Baudelaire. Je hais le mouvement qui déplace les lignes*, (1973). See *Marcel Broodthaers: Complete Graphic Works and Books* (Knokke-Duinbergen: Galerie Jos Jamar, 1989), 101. Trevor Stark, however, has ascertained that the seminar began in January 1970. See Stark, "The Reification of the World: Poetry and Conquest in Marcel Broodthaers's Maps," *Critical Inquiry* 50, no. 3 (Spring 2024): 517.

13. Jean-Christophe Royoux was, to my knowledge, the first to comment on this. See his "Projet pour un Texte," 297–98.
14. Marcel Broodthaers, "Like Butter in a Sandwich," in Broodthaers, *Collected Writings*, 148.
15. Charles Baudelaire, "Salon of 1846," *Selected Writings on Art and Literature* (London: Penguin, 2006), 104–5.
16. Charles Baudelaire, *The Flowers of Evil*, trans. James McGowan (Oxford: Oxford University Press, 1998), 39.
17. Translation altered to a more literal rendering of Baudelaire's French: "Je hais le mouvement qui déplace les lignes," Baudelaire, *The Flowers of Evil*, 38.
18. Baudelaire, *The Flowers of Evil*, 204–9.
19. Baudelaire, *The Flowers of Evil*, 160–63.
20. Charles Baudelaire, "The Painter of Modern Life," in *The Painter of Modern Life and Other Essays* (London: Phaidon, 1995), 12.
21. Baudelaire, "The Painter of Modern Life," 3.
22. Marcel Broodthaers, "Interview with Marcel Broodthaers by Georges Adé," in Broodthaers, *Collected Writings*, 353; and "Ten Thousand Francs Rewards," 414–15.
23. Marcel Broodthaers, "Experimental in as Much as," in Broodthaers, *Collected Writings*, 178.
24. Broodthaers, "24 Images…," 281.
25. Marcel Broodthaers, "Project for a Text," in Broodthaers, *Collected Writings*, 160.
26. Stark, "The Reification of the World," 521.
27. Eric de Bruyn, "Marcel Broodthaers: Cinéma Modèle," in Gregor Jansen and Vanessa Joan Müller (eds.), *Real Presences: Marcel Broodthaers Today* (Cologne: Verlag der Buchhandelung Walter König, 2011), 17.
28. See Marcel Broodthaers, "Announcement issued by the Galerie Folker Skulima," reproduced in Manuel J. Borja-Villel and Michael Compton (eds.), *Marcel Broodthaers: Cinéma* (Barcelona: Fundació Antoni Tàpies, 1997), 128; Broodthaers, "24 Images…," 281.
29. Marcel Broodthaers, "A Throw of the Dice," in Broodthaers, *Collected Writings*, 239.
30. Similar drawings of Mallarmé appear on a number of related studies Broodthaers produced when making the film in Berlin, which are in Folker Skulima's archive. I thank Raf Wollaert for sharing them with me along with other related information from his research with Skulima.
31. Deborah Schultz and Sam Sacherhoff date this event to the year 1945. See Schultz, *Marcel Broodthaers: Strategy and Dialogue* (Bern: Peter Lang, 2007), 35, and Sacherhoff, "Literary Exhibitions," in *Marcel Broodthaers: A Retrospective* (New York: Museum of Modern Art, 2016), 137. Charlotte Friling, by contrast, has 1946. See Friling, in Friling and Snauwaert (eds.), *Industrial Poems*, 334.
32. Marcel Broodthaers, "Investigating Dreamland," in Broodthaers, *Collected Writings*, 80.
33. These exhibitions were: *Exposition littéraire autour de Mallarmé* in Antwerp 2–20 December 1969, and *Exposition littéraire et musicale autour de Mallarmé* in Cologne 20 January to 22 February 1970.
34. Marcel Broodthaers, "Ma Collection," in Broodthaers, *Collected Writings*, 305.
35. Stéphane Mallarmé, "A Throw of the Dice," *Collected Poems*, trans. Henry Weinfield (Berkeley: University of California Press, 1994), 124–45. All quotes from *Un coup de dés* are taken from this translation.
36. Stéphane Mallarmé, "Crisis in Verse," *Divagations*, trans. Barbara Johnson (Cambridge, Mass.: Belknap Press of Harvard University Press, 2007), 209.
37. Mallarmé, "Crisis in Verse," 211, 208.
38. Stéphane Mallarmé, "The Book as Spiritual Instrument," *Divagations*, 228.
39. Stéphane Mallarmé, "Preface," *Collected Poems*, 121–22.

40. This is pointed out by Bruce Jenkins, who nonetheless seems to describe a slightly different version of the film than the one I have seen. See Jenkins, "CB: Cinema Broodthaers," in Marge Goldwater and Michael Compton (eds.), *Marcel Broodthaers* (New York: Rizzoli, 1989), 93.
41. Jean-Paul Sartre, *What Is Literature?* (London; New York: Routledge, 2001), 29.
42. Benjamin H. D. Buchloh, "Marcel Broodthaers: Open Letters, Industrial Poems," in *Neo-Avantgarde and Culture Industry: Essays on European and American Art from 1955 to 1975* (Cambridge, Mass.: MIT, 2000), 108.
43. Birgit Pelzer, "Marcel Broodthaers: The Place of the Subject," in Michael Newman and Jon Bird (eds.), *Rewriting Conceptual Art* (London: Reaktion Books, 1999), 202; 203; Benjamin H. D. Buchloh, "First and Last: Two Books by Marcel Broodthaers," in Manuel J. Borja-Villel and Christophe Cherix (eds.), *Marcel Broodthaers, A Retrospective* (New York: Museum of Modern Art, 2016), 42.
44. Royoux, "Projet pour un Texte," 300.
45. Royoux, "Projet pour un Texte," 299.
46. Trevor Stark, *Total Expansion of the Letter: Avant-Garde Art and Language after Mallarmé* (Cambridge, Mass.: MIT, 2020), 137.
47. Stéphane Mallarmé, "The Mystery in Letters," *Divagations*, 233; and "Crisis in Verse," 210 and 208.
48. Mallarmé, "The Book as Spiritual Instrument," 228.
49. Mallarmé, "Preface," 121.
50. Mallarmé, "Crisis in Verse," 206; Mallarmé, "The Mystery in Letters," 236.
51. Broodthaers, "A Throw of the Dice...," 239.
52. Marcel Broodthaers, "Interview with Marcel Broodthaers by Freddy de Vree," *Collected Writings*, 312.
53. Broodthaers described the slides used in a later work, *La signature de l'artiste* (1972), as "a projection of drawings." See Broodthaers, "The Artist's Signature," *Collected Writings*, 286.
54. Stéphane Mallarmé, "The Book as Spiritual Instrument," *Divagations*, 226.
55. Broodthaers, "The Artist's Signature," 286.
56. Sophie Richard, *Unconcealed: The International Network of Conceptual Artists 1967–77* (London: Ridinghouse, 2009), 306.
57. Whereas previously mimed, this was apparently the first time they sang along. See Barbara Reise, "Presenting Gilbert & George: The Living Sculptures," excerpted from the November 1971 issue of *Art News* in Anthony McCall (ed.), *Gilbert & George: The Living Sculptures* (London: Thames and Hudson, 1993), 55.
58. Exhibition announcement for *The Pencil on Paper Descriptive Works of Gilbert & George*, reproduced in Franz Maciejewski, *Mia Casa Tu Casa: Folker Skulima, Ein Haus für die Kunst* (Heidelberg: Edition Braus, 202), 16.
59. See Carter Radcliff, "Gilbert & George and Modern Life," in *Gilbert & George 1968–1980* (Eindhoven: Municipal Van Abbemuseum, 1980), 7–35.
60. Friling, "Note to the Reader," 31.
61. Roland Barthes, "Authors and Writers," *Critical Essays* (Evanston: Northwestern University Press, 1972), 147; 145; 144.
62. Stéphane Mallarmé, *Correspondance, lettres sur la poésie*, ed. Bertrand Marchal (Paris: Gallimard, 1995), 392. Cited and translated in Barnaby Norman, *Mallarmé's Sunset: Poetry at the End of Time* (London: Routledge, 2014), 63, ftn. 15. This poem is otherwise also referred to as the "Sonnet en – yx". The translation I have referred to is Stéphane Mallarmé, "Several Sonnets," *Collected Poems*, 69.
63. Jean-François Lyotard, *Discourse, Figure* (Minneapolis: University of Minnesota, 2011), 70.
64. Broodthaers, "The Artist's Signature," 286.
65. Roland Barthes, *Roland Barthes* (London: Macmillan Press, 1977), 49.
66. Mallarmé, "The Mystery in Letters," 235.

LE CORBEAU ET LE RENARD IN KNOKKE-LE-ZOUTE
NOTES ON THE PRODUCTION AND PROJECTION AT *EXPRMNTL 4*, DECEMBER 1967

Xavier García Bardón

In December 1967, Marcel Broodthaers presented his film *Le Corbeau et le renard* (The Raven and the Fox, 1967) at the EXPRMNTL 4 festival in the seaside town of Knokke-le-Zoute in Belgium. One of the many works produced by Broodthaers in relation to the eponymous fable by Jean de La Fontaine, *Le Corbeau et le renard* comprises a series of shots of objects (such as a white boot, a black boot, a telephone, white-painted bottles covered with a handwritten text, labeled empty jars, flowers, eggs in egg cups) and photographic cutouts of objects and people (Magritte, Broodthaers, the artist's wife Maria Gilissen, their daughter Marie-Puck) placed on shelves. Behind these appears the typographic representation of a text inspired by La Fontaine. In an effort to integrate objects, texts and images, Broodthaers decided to have the film projected on a special screen "imprinted with the same typographical characters as those in the film."[1] *Le Corbeau et le renard* is a film, a text, and an object at the same time. An edition released in 1968 completes the project.

By bringing together individual and institutional histories, this chapter highlights the parallel and crossing trajectories of an intriguing parade of local and international figures such as Jacques Ledoux, Paul Haesaerts, Isi Fiszman, Jean Cayrol, Corneille Hannoset, Umberto Beni, Abel Gance, Walerian Borowczyk, Shirley Clarke, Harun Farocki, Léon Lambert, and Pierre Clémenti among others, who were all involved in a constellation of events articulated around Marcel Broodthaers's "difficult" participation to the fourth edition of EXPRMNTL. In addition, by focusing on *Le Corbeau et le renard* and its early screening history, this chapter also touches upon Broodthaers's peculiar take on a form of "expanded cinema," highlighting the material and spatial dimensions of the cinematic apparatus as well as the institutional context of film screenings.

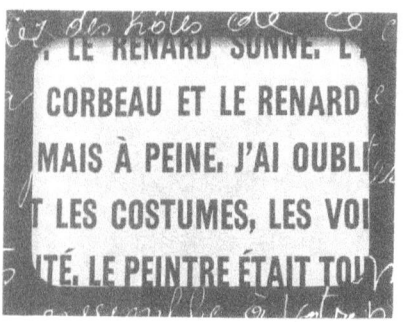
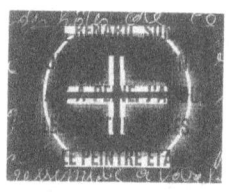

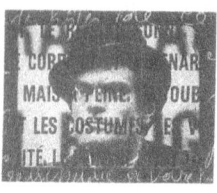

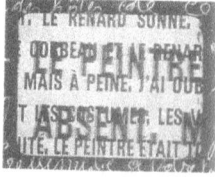

Le Corbeau et le renard. 16mm. 1967. Here, *Le Corbeau et le renard* is projected on the so-called TV-shaped screen, the smallest and lastly conceived of the three custom screens that Broodthaers designed for the film. Although this screen features the same text as the original screen used in Knokke, it is considerably smaller and furthermore surrounded by a rim of photographic canvas mounted on a wooden frame (see filmography).

"THIS MUSEUM REALLY IS A MUSEUM":
LEDOUX AND THE BRUSSELS CINÉMATHÈQUE

In July 1962, the Brussels Film Museum opened its doors—an important event both for the local cinephile community and the Cinémathèque de Belgique, which didn't have a proper venue since its creation in 1938. In the aftermath of the Second World War, screenings organized under the label Écran du Séminaire des Arts and promoted through gorgeous flyers designed by artists such as René Magritte, Paul Delvaux, and Edgard Tytgat were taking place at the Palais des Beaux-Arts. After the museum's opening, some were ready to travel from far away to catch one of its public screenings.[2] Broodthaers, who lived in Rue de la Pépinière, only a few minutes away from the museum, was a regular visitor.[3]

As the Cinémathèque's part accessible to the public, the Film Museum fulfilled two main functions: while landmark films were screened daily in its movie theater, a permanent exhibition inaugurated in 1967 informed visitors about the history of projection devices, from precinematic artefacts to state-of-the-art film machinery. "This Museum really is a museum," wrote art critic René Micha in 1981. "There you may see the main devices of the prehistory of cinema: shadow theatres, magic lanterns, kaleidoscopes, Plateau's phenakistiscope, zootropes, Marey's chronophotographic gun, flipbooks, phonoscopes, kinetoscopes, and much more."[4] The content of the Museum's display cases must have fed Broodthaers's interest in projection technology.[5]

Under the close supervision of Jacques Ledoux (curator of the institution from 1948 until his death in 1988), both areas of the Film Museum had been designed by the modernist architect Constantin Brodzki together with scenographer and designer Corneille Hannoset.[6] The two of them had already collaborated on several occasions. Hannoset, who had been affiliated with the short-lived yet influential international art group CoBrA between 1949 and 1951, was also responsible for the design of the museum's monthly leaflet, which remained practically unchanged until 2009.

In 1964, Marcel Broodthaers decided to become a visual artist. On the announcement card for his first exhibition at the Brussels Galerie St. Laurent in April 1964, Broodthaers—a poet, a journalist, a photographer, and a second-hand bookseller, aged forty—notoriously revealed the reasons for his choice. Much has been written about this card, printed on recycled magazine pages. Providing details about the economics of the gallery system in humorous phrasings, its text is considered a landmark statement in the history of the institutional critique. Yet, not much has been said about its last word. Appearing in much smaller font, and placed vertically, perpendicularly to the last line of Broodthaers's statement, it reads: "Hannoset." Broodthaers's invitation card and the Film Museum's monthly program leaflet shared the same graphic designer, and very similar fonts. Three months later, Hannoset also designed the invitation card to Broodthaers's *Sophisticated Happening*, which took place at Galerie Smith on July 23, 1964.

Both Hannoset and Brodzki were friends of Broodthaers. The artist's son, Constantin Broodthaers, was named after Brodzki, whom Marcel Broodthaers knew since 1956. Brodzki and his wife were neighbors with the Broodthaers, literally living next door, Rue de la Pépinière.[7]

EXPRMNTL

Jacques Ledoux was a rigorous archivist who contributed tremendously to the development of the discourse and technique of film preservation, not only through his activities at the Belgian Film Archives but also and notably through his involvement at the International Federation of Film Archives (FIAF). What's more, in addition to his interest in cinema's history, Ledoux devoted his energies to supporting the most adventurous ideas in filmmaking. As filmmaker, film critic, and Cinémathèque projectionist Jean-Marie Buchet put it, it was Ledoux's belief that "the films that are being made right now will always be more interesting than the films that already exist."[8] According to Amos Vogel, founder of the New York film society Cinema 16 and author of *Film as a Subversive Art*, "unlike many of the others, Ledoux had an interest in the future, he was very involved with the avant-garde, he loved it with a genuine love, and every time I saw him I realized that he had another way of seeing it."[9]

Ledoux was especially interested in experimental cinema. As curator of the EXPRMNTL film festival in the coastal town of Knokke-le Zoute (from 1949 to 1974), he put together the first event of this scale ever devoted to avant-garde filmmaking. Until the 1960s, it remained the only one of its kind. Ledoux's intention was to give visibility to new film forms as well as to facilitate connections between artists working everywhere in the world. EXPRMNTL quickly became an incomparable key place for the definition and understanding of experimental film during a critical period of its development.

Between 1949 and 1974, the festival saw five editions, spread over a period of twenty-five years. All of them were organized in Knokke's casino—except for the second edition, which took place in the context of Expo 58, on the site of the Brussels World's Fair, in April 1958. Revealing the first signs of the French Nouvelle Vague, the US Underground, the Polish young cinema, and other free radicals, its competition program combined the films—and in most cases the early works—of, among others, Agnès Varda, Peter Kubelka, Kenneth Anger, Peter Weiss, Shirley Clarke, Jean-Daniel Pollet, José Val del Omar, Walerian Borowczyk, Marie Menken, and Stan Brakhage.

It was in that context that Marcel Broodthaers premiered his first film effort, *La Clef de l'horloge (Poème cinématographique en l'honneur de Kurt Schwitters)* (1956–58). Shot during the closing hours of the Kurt Schwitters exhibition that took place at the Brussels Palais des Beaux-Arts in 1956, the film is based on Schwitters's artworks, lit up by a handheld torch lamp and framed in close shots. In order to shoot it, Broodthaers used a borrowed camera he didn't know how to use and expired film stock that he had received from the Cinémathèque.[10] With *La Clef de l'horloge*, Schwitters seems to appear for Broodthaers as the inspiring figure of a poet and a visual artist who worked both with objects and language. In the competition catalog, under a cover designed by Corneille Hannoset, Broodthaers's words shed some light on his project and answer the organizers' recurring question about the experimental nature of the work: "I believe that a film is an experiment from the moment you deal with a subject in a way that has never or rarely been approached."[11]

In December 1963, Broodthaers attended the next edition of EXPRMNTL. With lectures, concerts, public discussions, and exhibitions added to the competition screenings, EXPRMNTL 3 unfolded a much more ambitious program than its predecessor, turning into a multidisciplinary avant-garde event with experimental film at its core. US Underground films were a revelation for many attendants, most notably through the scandal raised by the censorship and subsequent private screenings of Jack Smith's *Flaming Creatures* (1963) organized by Jonas Mekas, P. Adams Sitney, and Barbara Rubin in their hotel room—on which Broodthaers wrote a text in the aftermath of the events.[12]

FREE FILM STOCK AND EGGSHELLS

In 1967, as an incentive to take part in EXPRMNTL 4, Ledoux made an interesting offer to filmmakers. Drawing on a partnership between the Cinémathèque and the Antwerp-based photochemical manufacturer Gevaert (which had merged with the German company Agfa in 1964 to form Agfa-Gevaert), the festival floated the idea of distributing free film stock (processing included) to about a hundred filmmakers from all over the world. Not only did such a deal provide valuable support to artists without financial resources, it also supplied the festival organizers with an exclusive screening program. Filmmakers and visual artists who applied for the film stock included Tony Conrad, Dore O, Martin Scorsese, Boris Lehman, Peter Weibel, Robert Beavers, Yayoi Kusama, Jud Yalkut, and Roland Lethem, among many others. Broodthaers seized this opportunity to shoot *Le Corbeau et le renard*.

To fulfill the organizers' request, Broodthaers, like any other applicant, had to submit a note of intent and a recommendation letter. A letter from Belgian art critic, filmmaker, architect, and painter Paul Haesaerts was announced by the artist.[13] A key figure in postwar Belgian cultural life through his association with his brother Luc—the director of the Séminaire des Arts (a successful cultural event series at the Palais des Beaux-Arts, comprising lectures, concerts, and the already mentioned screenings), with whom he also managed an exhibition space in the same building (the Petite Galerie du Séminaire des Arts)—Paul Haesaerts was an early exponent of the art documentary genre. Making a number of films dedicated to paintings and painters, such as *Rubens* (with Henri Storck, 1948) and the influential *Visit to Picasso* (1950), Paul Haesaerts supported the idea that art history in its written form had come to an end and would soon be replaced by moving images.[14] Although Haesaerts's letter apparently never materialized, on August 2, 1967, Broodthaers received three hundred meters (about one thousand feet, four minutes) of the 16mm Agfa-Gevaert artificial light color film stock he had applied for.[15]

Instead of one, Broodthaers had submitted two different notes of intent: *Le D est plus grand que le T* (*The D is Taller than the T*) and *Les Œufs* (*The Eggs*). In *Le D est plus grand que le T* (originally the title of a poem written before April 1967, in which Broodthaers revisited La Fontaine's fable *Le Corbeau et le renard*), the artist put forward "the idea of cinema rejecting the notion of movement. Film stock as a place for storing ideas and images—a rather special kind of can."[16] The text contained the idea that Broodthaers would further develop with his film *Le Corbeau et le renard*: filming objects, images, and words placed before a textual background. "Script: On three-color printing backgrounds, different objects stand out. They disappear, are replaced by others, reappear with and without changes."[17]

The second project is titled *Les Œufs*. Around 1965, in addition to many visual works made with eggshells (one of his signature materials until 1968 next to mussels and coal),[18] Broodthaers wrote a few texts playing with the same motif. These might be considered equally as poems or as unrealized film scripts. Such is *Évolution ou L'Œuf film* (*Evolution or The Egg Film*) published in the Belgian magazine *Phantomas* in December 1965, in which the artist suggested the idea of a film in which eggs would have been the main motif—including, he wrote, "whole eggs to be watched with special glasses, with red and white lenses, I believe, which give the illusion of emptiness."[19] For *Les Œufs*, Broodthaers also planned to modify the classic cinematic apparatus. The main idea in this case was to project a film exclusively composed of images of eggs on a screen covered with eggshells. Such a screen would probably have resembled some of Broodthaers's egg-covered canvases of the time.[20] The transcript of a short undated text relating to this project appears in the book *Marcel Broodthaers: Cinéma*, where the artist explains:

> Shadow and light are material objects.
> Shadow and light in the cinema are artificial objects.
> To attain this definition in a concrete way, the screen is altered.
> It is covered with eggshells.
> On it are projected images all of which are about the eggshell.
> Here the screen expresses its character as object
> and the confusion that links the object and its image.[21]

The alternative handwritten version of the synopsis that Broodthaers sent to the festival organizers mentions a few additional details, such as the ideal position of the viewer, but also the possibility of filming the viewing experience in order to produce a meta-film, that is, a film (screening) within a film:

> The ideal place for the viewer would be the point from which one could simultaneously see the screen, the running projection device and the objects serving as subjects. At this point, we could moreover take a shot, we would obtain a film within a film.[22]

... Or, like an egg, a form that would house another form. Interestingly, and as some critics pointed out, other films at EXPRMNTL 4 dealt with eggs.[23] *Les Souffrances d'un œuf meurtri* [The Sufferings of a Bruised Egg] (1967) for example, is described by its creator, Belgian filmmaker and writer Roland Lethem, as "a surreal fantasy about genesis, a description of the sufferings and bruises of those who conceive and are conceived."[24]

Although none of the two synopses sent by Broodthaers actually mentioned the text by Jean de la Fontaine that would lend its title to the film submitted to the selection committee, *Le Corbeau et le renard* can be seen as the combination of the two aforementioned projects: a film integrating objects, words, and images (where one or two eggs can actually be spotted) projected on a modified screen.

FROM FABLE TO FILM

Broodthaers presented *Le Corbeau et le renard* as the "logical continuation" of the earlier *La Clef de l'horloge*.[25] In both works, the artist places objects and images in an exhibition situation, used as a setting to produce the iconography of the film. In both works, the work of a poet is taken as starting point. In both works, language is key.

Shot in Brussels between May and October 1967, *Le Corbeau et le renard* is one of the many pieces produced by Broodthaers around the fable of the same title by seventeenth-century French poet Jean de La Fontaine, who based his own work on *The Fox and the Crow* by Greek writer Aesop. In the fable, it is through the power of language (a Broodthaersian theme), and specifically by the means of flattery, that the fox manages to get hold of the cheese that the crow, perched on a branch, was about to eat. Letting out a caw, the crow lets the cheese fall, and the fox eats it all. In the francophone world, this specific fable might be not only the most popular tale in Lafontaine's repertoire (in part because it stands in first position in his famous fable collection) but also the fable par excellence, which countless generations of children have had (and still have) to learn by heart.

Broodthaers's film was produced around the same time as his participation in a happening that took place in the streets of Brussels in early October 1967, during the Modern British Theatre and Poetic Show, held during the British Week. On this occasion, Broodthaers wrote the text of La Fontaine's fable on rolls of wallpaper, as the poet Umberto Beni was writing Broodthaers's own text *Le D est plus grand que le T* with chalk on the street.[26] In this happening, as in the film, the access to the text was complicated by additional layers of information.

Photographs taken by Philippe De Gobert during a happening in Brussels, 1967 © Philippe De Gobert 2024; © Estate of Marcel Broodthaers, c/o SABAM Belgium 2024

In the case of the film, shot by cameraman Paul de Fru and edited by Jean-Louis Dewert, the additional element is a large painted screen (161×218 cm), specially designed by Broodthaers, on which appear sections of the aforementioned poem. It is on that screen, altering the perception of the images, that the film is to be projected. The best description of the project is given by the artist himself:

> I took the text by La Fontaine and transformed it into what I call personal writing (poetry). In front of the typographic representation of this text, I placed a number of everyday objects (boots, telephone, bottle of milk) so that they would enter into a close relation with the printed characters. This was an attempt to deny as fully as possible both the meaning of the word and that of the image. Once the filming was over I realized that projection on a normal screen, i.e., on a simple white canvas, did not reflect exactly the image I wanted to compose. The object remained too much outside the text. For the text and object to be integrated, the screen had to be imprinted with the same typographical characters as those in the film. My film is a rebus that you need to want to decipher. It is an exercise in reading.[27]

Bearing the image of a text, the screen, a part of the film apparatus that is normally invisible, suddenly appears as an active object, constantly interfering with the projected image. Instead of neutrally receiving the visual information conveyed by the light beam, it becomes an integral part of the piece.[28] For Nicolas Brulhart, "the projected film *Le Corbeau et le renard* creates a tension between the still and the animated, the depth and the surface, the word, the image, and the thing filmed."[29] But the use of this special screen prevented the film from being shown in competition at Knokke. There was a reason for this.

TRIPLE SCREEN DISASTER

In April 1958, the second edition of the EXPRMNTL festival was scheduled to open with a tribute to Abel Gance, the pioneer French filmmaker who directed *Napoléon* (1927), one of Broodthaers's all-time favorites and a daring experiment in three-screen projection that Gance would later call Polyvision.[30] In curatorial terms, it is tempting to read Ledoux's idea as a timely reminder of the historical importance of the avant-garde, especially at this critical point in film history, when the film industry was desperately trying to regain audiences lost to television by enhancing the spectators' experience with processes such as 3D, CinemaScope, or Cinerama—which Gance had anticipated by thirty years. Next to the sophisticated Philips Pavilion, designed by Iannis Xenakis to host Le Corbusier's *Poème Électronique* (an audiovisual environment that combined multiple projections with changing coloured lights and an electronic music composition by Edgard Varèse played on more than four hundred speakers), multi-screen projections were ubiquitous at Expo 58 with such attractions as Disney's 360-degree Circarama, the Czech Pavilion's *Laterna Magika* that combined film projection and real-life performances, the US Pavilion featuring as many as twenty-five loops (shot by Shirley Clarke), and so on. In the context of EXPRMNTL itself, two works also relied on multiple projection: *Inauguration of the Pleasure Dome* (Kenneth Anger, 1957) and *Symphonie mécanique* (Jean Mitry, 1955).

Abel Gance and his assistant Nelly Kaplan were going to open the festival with *Magirama*, a three-screen compilation program bringing together on a CinemaScope-type of screen, fragments of *J'accuse* (Abel Gance, 1919/1937), alternating with four shorts, all (re)edited for Polyvision: Gance's *Auprès de ma blonde* and *Fête foraine*, Kaplan's *Châteaux de nuages*, and Norman MacLaren's *Begone Dull Care*.[31] During the screening preparations, Gance and Kaplan had to face major technical issues. In a slapstick kind of situation, a technician ripped the screen apart by placing his ladder on it. At the beginning of the screening itself, one of the projectors refused to run. The whole show had to be postponed by a few days. When it finally took place, on Saturday April 26, 1958, it was unanimously considered a failure.[32] While Gance was deeply disappointed by the disastrous experience and purportedly never talked again to Ledoux after 1958, Ledoux realized the difficulties of such a complex setup.[33] From now on, and although this clause doesn't explicitly appear in the festival regulations, all films in competition would have to be projected on the same, identical white surface. Broodthaers was aware of the incident.

SCREEN TESTS

In the catalog of films submitted to the 1967 selection jury (an in-house festival document), the technical specifications mention that *Le Corbeau et le renard* is to be projected on a "normal screen."[34] Nevertheless, in the accompanying notice, Broodthaers alludes to the distinct context in which he intends to situate it: "The film *Le Corbeau et le renard* is planned to be part of a plastic set (screen) that will bear the same title."[35]

When viewing Broodthaers's film in the context of the private preselection screenings, which took place in November and early December 1967, most members of the selection jury voted against it. Only Belgian film critic Paul Davay gave it a positive feedback, together with Jacques Ledoux, who granted it a question mark. Against the work were film critics Yannick Bruynoghe, André Vandenbunder, Roland Verhavert (also a filmmaker), and Dimitri Balachoff (also the director of Laboratoires Meuter Titra).[36] The rejection of the film was probably partly due to the fact that it was viewed on a conventional screen, depriving it of much of its strength. According to Anny De Decker, founder of the Wide White Space Gallery in Antwerp, Broodthaers was told that it was too difficult to install a special screen just for one seven-minute-long film.[37]

Nevertheless, after a first private screening organized in Paris,[38] the film was presented, again on a normal screen, in Knokke-le-Zoute on December 25 (the first day of the festival), in the context of an out-of-competition program. Works by Robert Breer (*66*, 1966), Gianfranco Barucchelo and Alberto Grifi (*La Verifica Incerta*, 1964) were presented during the same screening. *Le Corbeau et le renard* was the penultimate film in the program, sandwiched between Ursula and Franz Winzentsen's animation short *Staub* (1967) and Lam Thang Phong's fetish film *Les Disciplinaires* (1964). In a way, the rejection of Broodthaers's special screen by the EXPRMNTL 4 organizers highlights the limits of the festival. While the event challenged the limitations of the medium, it strikingly put limits to its own program. Another screening, this time on the screen prepared by Broodthaers, took place at Hôtel du Zoute, in the room of French writer Jean Cayrol, an enthusiast of Broodthaers's poetry (who, however, remained skeptical about his career as a visual artist).[39]

EXPRMNTL 4 was very chaotic, with performances and exhibitions bursting in every corner of the Casino. Some of them had been scheduled by the organizers, such as John Latham's *Juliet and Romeo* (1967) in which two actors, a blue-painted man and a red-painted woman, covered with newspaper, undressed each other; or *MovieMovie*, a project by the Dutch-based EventStructure Research Group and Sigma Projects (Jeffrey Shaw, Tjebbe van Tijen, and Sean Wellesley-Miller) in which an inflatable structure placed in the main hall of the Casino served both as a screen for multiple projections (abstract loops and Vietnam war footage) and as a bouncing castle for naked jumpers, while the improvisation group Musica Elettronica Viva played loud music. Other acts were unplanned: Yoko Ono, who had been invited to present her film *Number 4* (1967), performed her *Bag Piece* in the main hall of the Casino, for which she lay under a black cloth for several hours. French artist Jean-Jacques Lebel, one of the pioneers of happenings in Europe, organized the election of *Miss EXPRMNTL*, and so on.

UNDERGROUND MOVIES AT OUD KNOKKE

"But can you have a lively festival if you only have well-behaved people?" asked Broodthaers in his festival review.[40] Six months before May 1968, and at the height of the protests against the Vietnam War, many young people and representatives of all trends from the European Left (anarchists, provos, Maoists, ...) gathered in Knokke. In the excitement of the demonstrations that were already shaking Germany, a group of about thirty students from the Deutsche Film- und Fernsehakademie Berlin and the Institut für Filmgestaltung Ulm turned up. Some of these students—among them Harun Farocki and future Rote Armee Fraktion member Holger Meins, both studying in Berlin—together with Belgian students from La Cambre and members of the Vietnam committee of the Radio Télévision Belge, started protesting *against* the festival, most notably against what they fell as the lack of a political voice of most works.

Some filmmakers arrived in Knokke with a film that had been rejected by the festival selection jury, others came with their latest output. Toward the middle of the festival week, the US independent filmmaker and member of the competition jury Shirley Clarke was the first one to try to organize an off-festival screening. Originally planned to happen in her hotel room at Résidence Albert, it had to be relocated in the hotel corridor due to the number of attendees. Two policemen, called by the hotel management, interrupted the screening shortly after it started and had to count the members of the freshly created Hotel Corridor Film Society.[41]

At EXPRMNTL 4, Broodthaers was accompanied by Isi Fiszman, a close friend and active supporter, whom he sometimes referred to as "my collector."[42] An art lover, and an Antwerp diamond handler, Fiszman had met Broodthaers in 1964. Between June 1968 and December 1969, Fiszman, who was known for his leftist ideas, would co-write and publish the Open Letters sent by Broodthaers to renowned figures in the art world. In the summer of 1969, he would be one of the initiators of A379089 in Antwerp, an alternative space, "an anti-museum, an anti-gallery, a communication center where culture will be questioned."[43] During the 1970s, he would fund the radical leftist magazine *Pour*.

Pierre Clémenti and Marcel Broodthaers at EXPRMNTL 4, Knokke-le-Zoute, December 1967. Collection Photo Museum, Antwerp, P/1996/612/3.
© Suzy Embo/FOMU

As he was looking for a screening venue to present *Le Corbeau et le renard* in its original setup, Fiszman discovered, at a fifteen-minute walk from the Casino, a local café, the Oud Knokke, whose backroom could host about one to two hundred people. The initiative quickly took collective proportions. Together with Lebel, Fiszman rented the space and initiated an off-festival that ran parallel to the official program and whose open screenings lasted all night

Poster for the "Underground Movies" night organized at Café Oud Knokke during EXPRMNTL 4, 1967. Courtesy Cinematek, Brussels. Photo: Guy Jungblut.

long. Apart from Broodthaers's work, Lebel's *L'État normal* (1967), recent reels by Pierre Clémenti, an 8mm pornographic film by Living Theater's actor Henry Howard, and possibly *Fuses* (1967) by Carolee Schneemann were also screened, among others. To promote the event, a poster promising the screening of "Underground Movies" was hand-drawn on the backside of an official announcement for local activities, detailing the names of some of the participants.

Around 1985, Fiszman started to see Ledoux more frequently and the two of them became friends. In 1987, twenty years after EXPRMNTL 4, Fiszman gave to Ledoux the poster that he had kept since.[44] At the time, Ledoux—who was seeking ways to financially support the activities of the Cinémathèque—asked Fiszman if he could set up a crowdfunding event in the line of the spectacular *Salto/Arte* operation he had organized in Brussels in 1975. During *Salto/Arte*, in order to finance the magazine *Pour*, artists such as Joseph Beuys, Christian Boltanski, Sigmar Polke, Robert Filliou, and Panamarenko had performed real circus acts under a real circus tent. The whole show complemented an exhibition at the Musée d'Ixelles, both parts of the program being curated by Harald Szeemann. For the Cinémathèque, Fiszman and Ledoux imagined screening Abel Gance's *Napoléon* in Waterloo, on the memorial site and on the date of the historical battle. Implicitly, the project referred to the disastrous Expo 58 screening. It also paid tribute both to Broodthaers—who had passed away ten years earlier in 1976, having made at least two films, *Un Voyage à Waterloo (Napoléon 1769–1969)* (1969) and *La Bataille de Waterloo* (1975), among other works dealing with those topics—and to Gance, who had died in 1981. Artist and architect Luc Deleu would have built a tent to host this special screening. Unfortunately Ledoux was already sick at the time, and shortly after his death in June 1988 the project was abandoned.[45]

"I AM NOT A FILMMAKER"

Although unique in its attention to the screen as part of the cinematic situation, *Le Corbeau et le renard* was not the only work of its kind at EXPRMNTL 4. A few other complex experimental projection pieces were shown, although all of them also out of competition: the performative *Hawaiian Lullaby* (Wim van der Linden, 1967) in which a topless dancer appeared on stage against a Cinemascope color sequence depicting a tropical sunset and the abovementioned *MovieMovie* are two examples.[46] All of them tried to dismantle, modify, complexify, or expand the cinematic apparatus by rearranging its various elements. All of them tried to rethink the links between film and other art forms. It is interesting to consider *Le Corbeau et le renard* in this context and wonder if it was a piece of expanded cinema, or even an experimental film, after all.

Broodthaers was perfectly aware of the avant-garde film scene of the time. In the second issue of the Belgian film magazine *Trépied*, published in February 1968, the artist's often-quoted interview is accompanied by a festival review, in which Broodthaers points out his three favorite titles in the whole EXPRMNTL 4 program: *Wavelength* (Michael Snow, 1967), "the film of a painter," which won the grand prize; *Selbstschüsse* (Lutz Mommartz, 1967), "where the tool of the filmmaker is, both the director and the object," with Mommartz playing around and throwing his camera in the air while it is running; and *Le Point mort* (1967) by Jean-Marie Buchet, whose approach must have echoed some of Broodthaers's concerns ("I wanted to construct a narrative that develops in two different modes," explained Buchet, "that of words and that of images, one taking over from the other, without ever seeking to harmonize them. *Le Point mort* is therefore not a film, nor is it a literary text, although it is both at the same time").[47]

Nevertheless, on repeated occasions, Broodthaers made clear that he didn't consider himself as an experimental filmmaker. In fact, he always carefully refused any classification of his films, especially avoiding the labels "avant-garde" and "experimental." He didn't like the terms, he didn't like the idea, and was probably not interested in the context. "To define *Le Corbeau et le renard* as an experimental film?" writes Broodthaers in the text sent to the selection committee. "I prefer to define it as a fable by La Fontaine. I don't like the word experimental. Like the word war. No experimental warfare is imagined, as far as I know. I hope to have made an artist's film."[48]

In the interview with *Trépied*, Broodthaers made things clear from the beginning:

> Before I answer your question I would like to say that I am not a filmmaker. For me, film is the extension of language. I begin with poetry, then visual art, and finally cinema which brings together several different elements of art. Which is to say: writing (poetry), the object (visual art), and the image (film).[49]

In an announcement for a screening organized in 1972, again he felt the need to clarify:

> The terms "essential complements to his visual work" or even "experimental films" have appeared in the advertising for this session. They don't seem to me to be suitable for qualifying the films I want to show ... It's not cinematic art, it's ... Not more and as much as an object of discussion as a painting by Meissonier or Mondrian, these are films ...[50]

Attentive to these issues, Broodthaers, as Bruce Jenkins put it, was "equally repellent to the bourgeois defenders of orthodox high culture and to the stylish partisans of the avant-garde."[51] His was a "*counter*-counter-cinema," "suspicious of any canon." Broodthaers, adds Jenkins, had "a clear interest in avoiding absorption as 'experimental,' 'avant-garde,' or any other category of alternative practice."[52] For Nicolas Brulhart, "Broodthaers does not conceive of a relationship of continuity between film and cinema."[53] Making films doesn't make him a filmmaker. His approach to the moving image separates the film from the cinematic context, although, and especially in the case of *Le Corbeau et le renard*, it takes into account the whole cinematic apparatus, from the moment of the shooting to the moment of the projection, considering the images, their subjects (objects, texts, other images), the screen, the print, and the multiple interactions between these instances at the same time.

EXPANDING THE PROJECTION SITUATION

What Broodthaers had in mind with *Le Corbeau et le renard* was a more complex and broader work than a film that could just be projected in a cinema. From the aforementioned text submitted to the EXPRMNTL 4 selection committee, it was already clear that he envisioned his film on another plane. In the January 1968 interview given to *Trépied*, just after the festival, Broodthaers provides more details about his project:

> My film widens the frame of an "ordinary" film. It is not meant mainly, or at least exclusively, for movie theatres. For to see and be able to understand the total work that I have tried to make, not only must the film be projected on the printed screen but the spectator must also have the text. You could say this film is close to "Pop Art." It is one of those "multiples" that have been talked about for some time now as a means of distribution for art. That is why it is soon going to be shown in a gallery which has 40 copies of it made along with the screens and the books. It will therefore be exploited as a work of art, of which each copy comprises a film, two screens and a giant book. It's an environment.[54]

This environment was presented for the first time at Wide White Space Gallery in Antwerp from March 7 to 31, 1968, on the occasion of the artist's second solo show at the gallery, simply titled *Le Corbeau et le renard*.[55] In this exhibition, the film was central but other elements (texts, images) were involved, expanding the poetry of the film in three-dimensional space. The show was centered around the edition released by Wide White Space, consisting in a box (78.5×56.5 cm) covered with photographic canvas on which Broodthaers's poem had been printed. The box included a 16mm film print of *Le Corbeau et le renard*, two different screens made of photographic canvas (one, sized 95×130 cm, could be rolled up while the second one, sized 78×58 cm, was shaped as a TV screen),

Installation view of *Le Corbeau et le renard* held at Wide White Space, Antwerp, 1968.
Photo R. Van den Bempt. © Estate of Marcel Broodthaers, c/o SABAM Belgium 2024

and various prints. Forty copies were planned but only seven were made then, due to the complexity of the work. The other thirty-three copies were produced as an alternate version in 1972 and presented at another exhibition, from June 17 to 30, 1972.

Anny De Decker and Bernd Lohaus, who ran Wide White Space, had privately seen the film prior to EXPRMNTL 4.[56] On the day before the opening of the festival, De Decker had bought from Broodthaers the publishing rights of the whole set for 40,000 Belgian francs.[57] But in order to realize the edition, she also had to clear the rights from Baron Léon Lambert who, says Fiszman, had financed the film by giving 30,000 Belgian Francs.[58] A major figure in the international business scene of the time and the head of Banque Lambert, Léon Lambert was a determined art collector and a supporter of the arts, who sponsored both the Cinémathèque and EXPRMNTL. One of the festival prizes bore his name. A true cinephile, Lambert supported his favorite filmmakers (such as Gregory Markopoulos, who was awarded the Prix Baron Lambert, 2000 USD, for his film *Twice a Man* in 1963), acquired film prints for his collection (works by Markopoulos but also Yoko Ono and Takahiko Iimura for example), and regularly organized screenings in his Brussels apartment, located on the rooftop of the bank's headquarters, Avenue Marnix—barely fifty meters away from Rue de la Pépinière. In a letter dating from July 1967 and sent to friends and potential partners, Lambert had set out his intentions to provide financial support to independent filmmakers: under the umbrella of his newly created Centre Belge du Nouveau Cinéma, and in the perspective of EXPRMNTL 4, Lambert would start by helping Markopoulos finish his new film (*The Illiac Passion*, 1967) and by "financ[ing] a ten-minute experimental color document, produced under the direction of Belgian painter Broodthaers."[59] According to Fiszman, one of the first screenings of *Le Corbeau* was organized in Lambert's penthouse, in the presence of the future king and queen of Belgium, Albert and Paola.[60] Nevertheless, by the end of January 1968, for 40,000 additional Belgian francs, Wide White Space acquired from the Centre Belge du Nouveau Cinéma the negative of *Le Corbeau* and the attached rights.[61]

The connections Broodthaers made in Knokke explain the presence of the two quotes appearing on the leaflet announcing the March 1968 exhibition at Wide White Space. The first was from Shirley Clarke: "I find this film a unique experiment in adding a new dimension to cinema. Bravo." The second came from Walerian Borowczyk: "I saw *Le Corbeau et le renard*, a film which is pure poetry." Both Clarke and Polish animation director Borowczyk were members of the competition jury in Knokke-le-Zoute, where they had seen the film. Both of them had also participated, just like Broodthaers, to the 1958 edition of the festival.

In January 1968, shortly after EXPRMNTL 4, Broodthaers, asked about his plans for the future, stated, "To introduce more of the real into my efforts and make a film about Vietnam, based on the use of the written sign. In Knokke, recently, nothing along these lines has been shown."[62] "More of the real" was precisely what Farocki, Meins, the German students, and their comrades were asking for, even if they didn't exactly make the same kind of films. In May 1968, Broodthaers was in touch with the students occupying the Grand Hall at the Université Libre de Bruxelles. One of his works, *Apprendre à lire*, was exhibited among the protest banners. From late May to early June, he was actively involved in the occupation of the Palais des Beaux-Arts, acting as an intermediary between the artists occupying the building and the staff of the Palais, before distancing himself from the protesters. In June, he sent out the first of his Open Letters, a series that would address contemporary issues in the field of culture and politics. The same month, he produced his first plastic plaque, *Le Drapeau noir (tirage illimité)*, referring to the student revolts in Amsterdam, Berlin, Nanterre, Venice, Paris, Milan and Brussels. Around the same time, he wrote:

> In effect, for me the purpose is to destroy values that came into being in our times and on Western soil. I no longer want to change the world in which I live but to break it. My bombers, my atomic bombs, my diabolical inventions are already flying over the holiday spots, a bit like a remarkable anthology by Fluxus Film. Cheers and Shit.[63]

In September 1968, Broodthaers inaugurated his own critical version of a museum, the *Musée d'Art Moderne, Département des Aigles,* by opening the first of its twelve sections, *Section XIXe siècle*, at his home in the Rue de la Pépinière. The Brodzkis were among the first visitors.[64] In 1970, *Cinéma modèle*, a project under the patronage of Jean de La Fontaine, anticipated the opening of the museum's sixth section, *Section cinéma*, which opened in January 1971 at the same location in Düsseldorf, Burgplatz 12, in the basement of a house once occupied by Goethe. In *Section cinéma*, Broodthaers organized the mise-en-scène of his own take on film history, acting as the curator of a collection of objects relating to cinema, such as typical directors' chairs, an empty film reel, a rewinding table, a piano, and other artifacts that appeared as the discarded remnants of another era. Broodthaers, who sought to create a space where to deploy his approach to film in its own context, also used the space as an editing room for his current film projects. Inaugurated close to ten years after the creation of the Brussels Cinémathèque in 1962, what else was *Section cinéma* if not Broodthaers's own idea of a film museum?

—To Isi Fiszman, the storyteller

NOTES

1. "For the text and object to be integrated, the screen had to be imprinted with the same typographical characters as those in the film." "Interview de Marcel Broodthaers, notre invité au 'Hoef' le 30 janvier," *Trépied* 2, 4; reprinted in Manuel J. Borja-Villel and Michael Compton (eds.), *Marcel Broodthaers: Cinéma* (Barcelona: Fundacio Antoni Tàpies, 1997), 59 (translation 319).
2. Film directors such as Alain Resnais, Agnès Varda, François Truffaut, and other protagonists of the French Nouvelle Vague also regularly traveled from Paris to Brussels in order to see films that Ledoux privately screened at their request. Soon Mi Peten, "Entretien avec Alain Resnais," in *Revue belge du cinéma* 40 (November 1995) (special issue dedicated to "Jacques Ledoux, l'éclaireur" coordinated by Dominique Nasta), 43.
3. Maria Gilissen Broodthaers, at the symposium "Marcel Broodthaers and Cinema. Filmic Poems, Moving Scripts" organized by Raf Wollaert and Steven Jacobs (University of Antwerp), CINEMATEK, WIELS, Cinea, and Succession Marcel Broodthaers at CINEMATEK, Brussels, 18 June 2022.
4. René Micha, "Pour l'amour de l'art," *Revue Nouvelle* 73, no. 1 (January 1981): 63.
5. As a motif, this interest is obvious in a few of his films and slide projection pieces. Magic lanterns, for instance, appear in *Images d'Épinal* (1974, eighty slide projection piece) and *Les Mystères de Buffalo Bill* (1974, forty-seven slide projection piece), while the film *The Last Voyage* (1973/74) is based on hand-colored magic lantern slides.
6. A lost masterpiece of twentieth-century architecture, the original Film Museum, as designed by Brodzki and Hannoset, was demolished in 2006, as a consequence of the renovation plans of the Palais des Beaux-Arts. The museum reopened in 2009, completely redesigned by Paul Robbrecht and Hilde Daem.

7. Marie-Pascale Gildemyn, "Hommage à Marcel Broodthaers," +-0 47 (1987): 28 (see also 21 and 29).
8. "Le cinéma en train de se faire est toujours plus intéressant que celui qui a été fait." Jean-Marie Buchet, interviewed by Xavier García Bardón, Brussels, 12 November 1998.
9. Amos Vogel, *Film as a Subversive Art* (New York: Random House, 1974); "unlike many of the others": Amos Vogel quoted in Anne Head, *A True Love for Cinema. Jacques Ledoux, 1921–1988* (Rotterdam: Rotterdam Universitaire Pers, 1988), 26.
10. "La Clef de l'horloge (Poème cinématographique en l'honneur de Kurt Schwitters," in *Marcel Broodthaers: Cinéma*, 20.
11. Marcel Broodthaers, "La Clef de l'horloge," in *1958 Film EXPRMNTL Film 1958. Compétition du film expérimental. Competitie van de Experimentele Film. Experimental Film Competition. 21–27.IV.1958* (festival catalog) (Brussels: Universal and International Exhibition of Brussels 1958 / Cinémathèque de Belgique, 1958), 34.
12. Marcel Broodthaers, "Le Cinéma Expérimental et les fables de La Fontaine. La raison du plus fort," in *Marcel Broodthaers: Cinéma*, 60.
13. As mentioned in an undated summary of all applications received by the festival organizers, CINEMATEK: EXPRMNTL.1967.VI (Belgian section).
14. "Are art criticism and *written* art history not now techniques that are poorly suited to their purpose, outdated? May the image this time replace the word, may the discourse become the eloquent succession of images." Paul Haesaerts about the film *Le Monde de Paul Delvaux* (Henri Storck, 1944–46), as quoted by Paul Davay, "Cinéma et peinture à l'Écran du Séminaire des Arts," *Les Beaux-Arts* (11 March 1949): 1 (author's translation).
15. Letter from Ghislaine Bouchart, secretary of the Cinémathèque, to Marcel Broodthaers, 10 July 1967; Receipt signed by Marcel Broodthaers, 2 August 1967. Both documents held at CINEMATEK: EXPRMNTL.1967.VI.
16. Marcel Broodthaers, "Le D est plus grand que le T," handwritten project, 2 pages, CINEMATEK: EXPRMNTL.1967.VI.
17. Marcel Broodthaers, "Le D est plus grand que le T," CINEMATEK: EXPRMNTL.1967.VI.
18. For instance: *Armoire blanche et table blanche [White cabinet and white table]* (1965), *Tableau et tabouret avec œufs [Painting and Stool with Eggs]* (1966), *Sans Titre (triptyque) [Untitled (Triptych)]* (1966) or *289 œufs, 20x13=260, 2x14=28, +1=1, = 289 œufs [289 Eggs, 20x13=260, 2x14=28, +1=1, = 289 Eggs]* (1966).
19. Marcel Broodthaers, "Évolution ou L'œuf film," *Phantomas* 51–61 (December 1965): 113.
20. Such as *Mono œuf [Mono Egg]* (1965), as suggested in *Marcel Broodthaers: Cinéma*, 42–45.
21. Marcel Broodthaers, "Les Œufs," in *Marcel Broodthaers: Cinéma*, 45 (translation 319).
22. Marcel Broodthaers, "Les Œufs," CINEMATEK: EXPRMNTL.1967.VI.
23. In *Cahiers du Cinéma*, Michel Caen spotted "l'obsession clinique de l'œuf et du foetus" or "the clinical obsession with the egg and the foetus" Michel Caen, "Knokke...," *Cahiers du Cinéma* 200–201 (April–May 1968): 101. "What are we to conclude if the same primitive theme is to be found in twenty or thirty [...] productions?" asked Jean Collette in Belgian newspaper *La Libre Belgique*: "Undoubtedly, most of their authors are small-time thinkers, self-taught initiatory poets or pocket-book readers of Freud." Jean Collette, "Après le Festival de Knokke. Un bilan positif," *La Libre Belgique* (4 January 1968): 9.
24. "Une fantaisie surréaliste sur la genèse, description des souffrances et meurtrissures de ceux qui conçoivent et sont conçus." *EXPRMNTL 4*. Brussels: Cinémathèque royale de Belgique, with the help of Commission nationale belge de l'Unesco, 1967 (festival catalog), film no. 27.
25. "Its reference is *La Clef de l'horloge*, an absolutely marvelous film I made in 1958, about the works of K. Schwitters. *Le Corbeau et le renard* is the logical continuation of my undertakings." Broodthaers in an undated text reproduced in *Marcel Broodthaers: Cinéma*, 66.

26. Jacques Charlier, Dees de Bruyne, and Roland Van den Berghe also participated in the event. "Selected Chronology," in Charlotte Friling and Dirk Snauwaert (eds.), *Industrial Poems, Marcel Broodthaers: The Complete Catalogue of the Plaques, 1968–1972* (Brussels-Berlin: Wiels-Hatje Cantz, 2021), 383.
27. "Interview de Marcel Broodthaers, notre invité au 'Hoef' le 30 janvier," *Trépied* 2, 4; reprinted in *Marcel Broodthaers: Cinéma*, 59 (translation 319–20).
28. The same strategy was used by Broodthaers again in the context of *Section Cinéma*, which opened in Düsseldorf in 1971. *Une Discussion Inaugurale* (1968), *Un Voyage à Waterloo (Napoléon 1769–1969)* (1969), *Charlie als Filmstar* (1970), *Brussel Teil II* (1970), and *Belga Vox – Mode – XX Century Fox* (1970) were projected on a painted screen whose stenciled "fig. 12", "fig. 2", "fig. 1" and "fig. A" lines superimposed with the projected images "fig." is a recurring label throughout Broodthaers's whole body of work. *Le Musée et la Discussion* (1969) and *Musée Museum Haut/Bas Fragile* (1968–69) (comprising fragments of *Une Discussion inaugurale*) were projected on a hanging world map (*Carte du monde politique*). *La Promenade* (1968–69) could be projected on both. *Marcel Broodthaers: Cinéma*, 143–45; María Gilissen interviewed by Xavier García Bardón in preparation of the Marcel Broodthaers screening programs presented at the Internationale Kurzfilmtage Oberhausen on 27–28 April 2023 (see "Marcel Broodthaers. Poems as Films as Objects" / "Marcel Broodthaers. Gedichte als Filme als Objekte," 69. Internationale Kurzfilmtage Oberhausen, Oberhausen: Internationale Kurzfilmtage Oberhausen, 2023, festival catalog, 222–35).
29. Nicolas Brulhart, "Chers amis..., histoire et esthétique du cinéma, de Marcel Broodthaers," *Décadrages* 26–27 (2014): 161.
30. Gance only started using the name Polyvision after the Second World War. For a history of the filmmaker's use of the tryptich form, see: Jean-Jacques Meusy, "La Polyvision, espoir oublié d'un cinéma nouveau," *1895. Mille huit cent quatre-vingt-quinze* 31 (2000), 153–211, online version 6 March 2006, retrieved 25 August 2023, http://journals.openedition.org/1895/68.
31. Béatrice de Pastre, "Magirama – J'accuse!" *Toute la mémoire du monde: 5ème Festival international du film restauré.* (Paris: Cinémathèque française, 2017) (festival catalog), 52. *Magirama* premiered at Studio 28 in Paris in December 1957 where it played for eight weeks.
32. "The effect, at least as shown at the festival, must be considered a failure artistically. It does not blend into one visual experience, and we are reminded jarringly of the mechanical contrivance employed," writes Amos Vogel, "The Angry Young Film Makers," *Evergreen Review* 2, no. 6 (Fall 1958): 172; reprinted in Scott McDonald, *Cinema 16: Documents toward a History of the Film Society* (Philadelphia: Temple University Press, 2002), 341.
33. See correspondence between Jacques Ledoux and Abel Gance, May 1958, CINEMATEK: EXPRMNTL/1958.I.C/FRANCE. Isi Fiszman, interviewed by Xavier García Bardón, Brussels, 5 July 2016.
34. *EXPRMNTL 4. Films soumis au jury de sélection / Films voorgelegd aan de selectiejury / Films submitted to the selection jury. 1.XI.1967 – 2.XII.1967.* Brussels: Cinémathèque de Belgique, 1967 (preselection catalogue), 75.
35. "Le film *Le Corbeau et le renard* est prévu pour faire partie d'un ensemble plastique (écran) qui portera le même titre." *EXPRMNTL 4* (festival catalog), 75.
36. CINEMATEK: EXPRMNTL/1967.VIII/Selection 1967.
37. Anny De Decker, "Le Corbeau et le renard," in Lotte Beckwé and Liliane Dewachter (eds.), *Soleil Politique* (Antwerp: MuHKA, 2019), 81.
38. The screening took place 7, Quai de l'Horloge on the occasion of Broodthaers's solo exhibition *Le Corbeau et le renard*. "Selected Chronology," *Industrial Poems*, 383.
39. Isi Fiszman, interview with the author, 5 July 2016.

40. Marcel Broodthaers, [Untitled text], *Trépied* 2, 7; reprinted in *Marcel Broodthaers: Cinéma*, 61 (translation 321).
41. Elliott Stein, "Dr. Ledoux's Torture Garden," *Sight and Sound* 37, no. 2 (Spring 1968): 73; P. Adams Sitney, "Report on the Fourth International Experimental Film Exposition at Knokke-le-Zoute," *Film Culture* 46 (Fall 1967, published October 1968): 9.
42. Marcel Broodthaers, "Venise: Une biennale discutée," *Beaux-Arts* 1135 (23 June 1966): 6. Fiszman—who acquired works from Joseph Beuys, Andy Warhol, Carl Andre, and later Angel Vergara—actually rejected the words "collector" and "collecting" to define his approach to art and artists.
43. Virginie Devillez, "Je/Nous. Le cas des années 1960 et 1970 en Belgique," in Éric Van Essche (ed.), *Les Formes contemporaines de l'art engagé: De l'art contextuel aux nouvelles pratiques documentaires* (Brussels: La Lettre Volée, 2007), 20–21.
44. Probably misplaced after Ledoux's passing, the poster was only recently located. When I first met Fiszman in 2015, an investigation started that only concluded in March 2019, unfortunately only shortly after Fiszman's own passing in January 2019. The poster is now preserved in the archives at CINEMATEK together with all EXPRMNTL 4 documents.
45. Isi Fiszman, interviewed by Xavier García Bardón, 5 July 2016, Brussels.
46. Simon Hartog, "Knokkenotes," *Cinim* 3 (Spring 1969): 27.
47. Marcel Broodthaers, [Untitled text], *Trépied* 2, 6; reprinted in *Marcel Broodthaers: Cinéma*, 61 (translation 321); EXPRMNTL 4 (pre-selection catalog), 41.
48. *EXPRMNTL 4. Films soumis au jury de sélection*, 75.
49. "Interview de Marcel Broodthaers," *Trépied*, 2, 4; reprinted in *Marcel Broodthaers: Cinéma*, 59 (translation 319).
50. Announcement for the screening organized by Jeunesse et Arts Plastiques at the Brussels Palais des Beaux-Arts on 7 December 1972, reproduced in *Marcel Broodthaers: Cinéma*, 210 (my translation).
51. Bruce Jenkins, "Un Peu Tard: Citation in the Cinema of Marcel Broodthaers," in *Marcel Broodthaers: Cinéma*, 290.
52. Bruce Jenkins, "Un Peu Tard: Citation in the Cinema of Marcel Broodthaers," in *Marcel Broodthaers: Cinéma*, 290.
53. Nicolas Brulhart, "Chers amis," *Décadrages* 26–27 (2014): 162.
54. "Interview de Marcel Broodthaers," *Trépied* 2, 5; reprinted in *Marcel Broodthaers: Cinéma*, 59 (translation 320).
55. A first exhibition titled *Moules Œufs Frites Pots Charbon* had been organized from 26 May to 26 June 1966.
56. Anny De Deceker, interviewed by Xavier García Bardón, Antwerp, 13 November 2023.
57. Contract between Marcel Broodthaers and Anny De Decker, dated 24 December 1967, kindly provided by Anny De Decker. See also Anny De Decker, "Le Corbeau et le renard," in Lotte Beckwé and Liliane Dewachter (eds.), *Soleil Politique* (Antwerp: MuHKA, 2019), 81.
58. Isi Fiszman, interview, 5 July 2016.
59. "Secondly, we would like to finance a ten-minute experimental color document, produced under the direction of Belgian painter Broodthaers." Letter from Baron Lambert to René Micha (among other potential partners), 7 July 1967, MLT 07262/0043/003, Archives & Musée de la Littérature (Brussels).
60. Isi Fiszman, interview, 5 July 2016.
61. Letter from Anny De Decker to Hervé Thys (representing the Centre belge du Nouveau Cinéma), 27 January 1968, kindly provided by Anny De Decker. When contacted by Ledoux, who wanted to include *Le Corbeau et le renard* in the context of a screening

program dedicated to EXPRMNTL 4 presented at the Musée du Cinéma in February 1968, De Decker immediately was in the position to request the use of the special screen. Letter from Anny De Decker to Jacques Ledoux, 31 January 1968, provided by De Decker.
62. "Interview de Marcel Broodthaers," *Trépied* 2, 5; reprinted in *Marcel Broodthaers: Cinéma*, 59 (translation 320).
63. [Undated and unpublished text], *Marcel Broodthaers: Cinéma*, 66 (translation 321).
64. Constantin Brodzki shared his amused and amusing memories in Marie-Pascale Gildemyn, "Hommage à Marcel Broodthaers," *+-0* 47 (1987): 29.

TRAVELING WORDS AND IMAGES
FOUND POSTCARDS IN THE FILMS OF MARCEL BROODTHAERS

Deborah Schultz

Throughout his practice, Marcel Broodthaers drew on a wide range of printed matter, including advertisements, prints, and photographs as well as books and reproductions of works of art, both his own and by others. Objects were repeatedly recycled, reused, represented, and reconsidered. His work featured a wide range of items from everyday life, from eggshells and mussel shells to cooking pots, drinking glasses, and furniture; thus, "despite the conceptual expression, the pure 'style,' and the art-institutional embeddedness" of his work, it "always stemmed from everyday reality."[1] Indeed, the announcement for his first exhibition at the Galerie Saint-Laurent, Brussels, in 1964, printed over magazine pages, highlights the literal mundaneness of his materials while, simultaneously, drawing attention to the way in which the frame of art transforms things. His words—"What is it? In fact, only some objects!"—serve to strengthen his work's theoretical character while seeming to undermine it.[2]

This chapter contributes to discussions regarding the centrality of filmic practices in Broodthaers's oeuvre by exploring his treatment of found postcards through the cinematic lens. In the films under discussion here, Broodthaers evoked narratives reminiscent of the long nineteenth century while also exploring the framing structures that were central to post-Structuralism and the Institutional Critique of the 1960s and 1970s. As in other works, his anachronistic materials, methods, and references frame his critique of contemporary practices. Postcards fit into Broodthaers's interest in travel, maps, and the voyage, whether journeys made by himself, such as those articulated in the series of articles "Un poète en voyage ..." (1961), or his account of those made by others, including *Un Film de Charles Baudelaire* (1970).[3] In launching his career as an artist in 1964, he sought the "conquest of space" in formal terms regarding the space of the work and the gallery space in which the work is shown, as well as in terms of the space of the art world in which his reputation would be made.

Postcards, thus, succinctly combine words and images, acting as signs of travel and of communication with those back home. Broodthaers's use of postcards asks us to consider how words communicate, both explicitly and via underlying subtexts that can be extrapolated or imagined, especially when articulated in succinct phrases. By studying the short messages on the postcards and their associated images, he invites reflection on how we express ourselves in terms of the words that we use and the images that we choose.

FILMS OF WORDS AND IMAGES

Broodthaers made various films that originated from found postcards. These include *Histoire d'amour (Dr. Huismans)* (1969), *Chère petite sœur* (1972), *Le Mauritania* (1972), and *Ah que la chasse soit le plaisir des rois* (1972).[4] Some of these were included in compilations or séances in which a number of short films were mounted on the same reel separated by countdown leaders. These include the ten-minute sequence *Trois cartes postales* (1972) (which comprised *Histoire d'amour (Dr. Huismans)*, *Chère petite sœur* and *Paris*) and the longer twenty-eight minute sequence *Rendez-vous mit Jacques Offenbach*, first shown at the Palais des Beaux-Arts, Brussels (December 7, 1972), which comprised nine short films and fragments of films together with specially made "fig. 0," "fig. 1," et cetera, intertitles.[5] The title of the sequence repeats that of an LP of Offenbach's music produced in 1965 and 1972 in Germany, fragments of which were included on the soundtrack.

The postcard that formed the starting point for the film *Chère petite sœur* was also the basis for works in other media. In addition to the 1972 film, a negative of the postcard image was used on the invitation to the first screening of the film at the Galerie Michael Werner, Cologne, in June 1972; became the basis of an offset print edition, *Chère Petite Sœur* (1972), printed by the same gallery; and was used on posters to advertise *Rendez-vous mit Jacques Offenbach*, Brussels, 1972.

The film *Chère petite sœur* (1972) shows the image on the black- and-white postcard depicting a ship on a stormy sea with a lighthouse in the background (fig. 1).[6] On the border above the image the date is handwritten as "27-8-1901," while beneath the image an inscription reads:

> Dear little sister, this is to give you an idea of the sea during the storm which we had yesterday. I'll give you more details about it, best wishes and see you soon, Marie.[7]

In the film, close-up images of the ship are followed by images of the whole postcard against a black background. This sequencing is akin to a kind of basic animation and has the effect of suggesting the ship moving on the waves. These

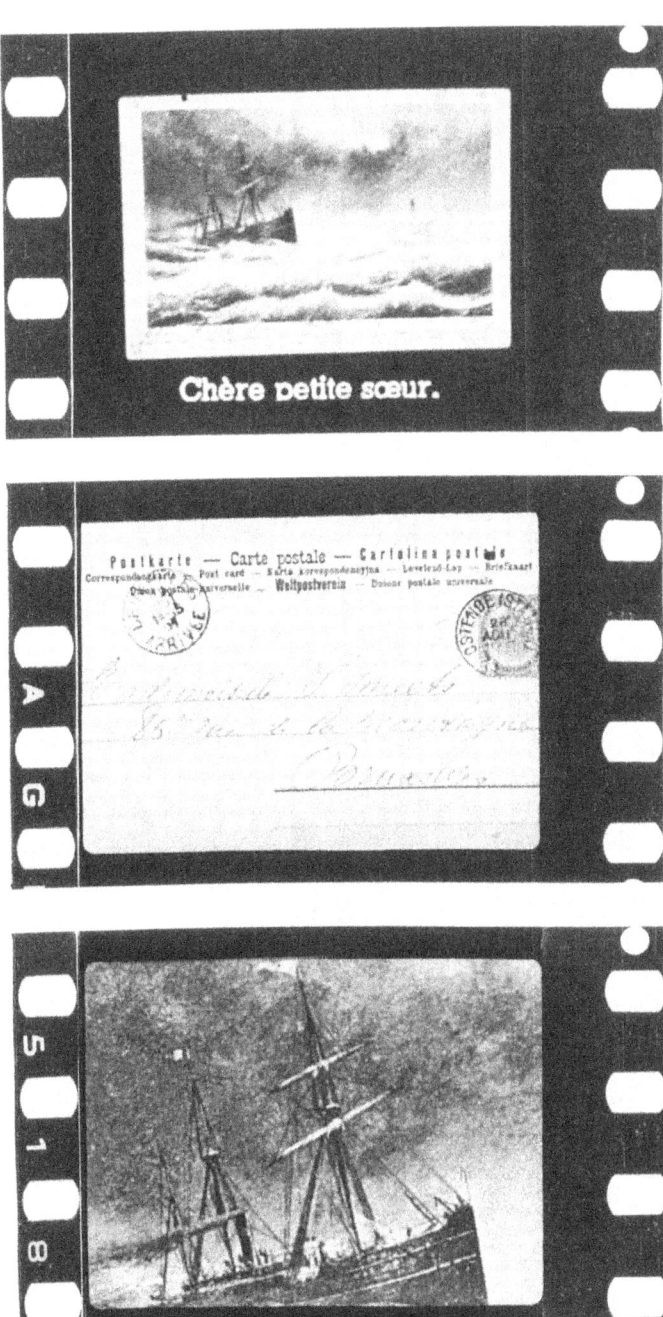

Chère petite soeur. 16mm. 1972.
© Estate of Marcel Broodthaers, c/o SABAM Belgium 2024

images of the ship alternate with the title of the film in white letters against a black background. Thus, a series of static images gives the effect of a ship moving on a stormy sea, thereby enhancing Marie's message to her sister. The words of the inscription then appear in sections, a few at a time, beneath images of the whole postcard followed by close-ups of the ship again. The words appear as printed subtitles, in white letters against a black background, rather than in their handwritten form, establishing a relationship between the handwritten and mechanical, the old and the new, that pervades Broodthaers's practice. At some points in the sequence only these subtitles appear on the screen. The address side of the card is also shown, on which the Brussels destination was written and the postmark "Ostende" was stamped.

The message on the *Chère petite sœur* postcard is brief and the image corresponds with the sender's wishes. By contrast, in the case of *Histoire d'amour* (1969), the sender expresses his regret that he is unable to find a better postcard.[8] The film focuses on the writing on the postcard, without revealing the image on the other side. The message was written by a Dr. A. Huismans to a Mademoiselle in Brussels and reads,

> You see, Mademoiselle, that I keep my word. I have only one regret—not to find here nicer cards to send to you.[9]

The card was sent from Knokke on the Belgian North Sea coast and dated "21.8.07." In contrast to *Chère petite sœur*, which begins with details, *Histoire d'amour* begins with images of the whole postcard before proceeding to detailed shots of the stamp and postmarks showing when the card was sent from Knokke and when it arrived in Brussels. Seemingly remarkably, it arrived on the day that it was sent, although this level of speed by the postal service was not unusual at the time. The camera pans across the handwritten message so closely that the material form of the original source is carefully studied and the texture of the ink on the postcard becomes the dominant image. Legible words give way to abstract marks (fig. 2). Details of the text are isolated, highlighting key words in the dialogue ("vous," "je," "c'est," "plus," "regret," "parole," "jolies") before the whole text is shown again. Then a sequence of shots is included that cuts across lines of text. As a result, a few words from a couple of lines are shown, breaking the flow of the message and effectively eliminating its comprehensibility, although some words are clearly legible. The camera ends the sequence with a long pan over the addressee, "Mademoiselle," taking in the full sweep of the capital M and the final "e."

The film ends with a sequence of five, blue-tinted postcards of the sea mainly at Ostend. In fact, six images appear in the film but the first appears to be the same as the fifth except in black-and-white. The postcards were later framed together, but only the written side of Dr. A. Huismans's postcard remains visible.[10] The image, therefore, which did not satisfy his wishes, remains an enticing mystery to the viewer. What was so bad about it? Was it of a stormy or a calm sea, or of something else? What would he have preferred to have sent? Dr. A. Huismans's text raises questions for the viewer who is unable to see the image on the other side of the postcard.

The title of *Chère petite sœur* is straightforwardly descriptive, deriving from the first words written on the postcard and of the stormy sea that is described and depicted. The title *Mademoiselle* is equally straightforward, while the 1972 title of the film, *Histoire d'amour (Dr. Huismans)*, contributes to the suggestion of a love story, which may or may not have progressed happily. The viewer might imagine that the sequence of postcard images reflects a sequence in their relationship, progressing from an image of gentle waves, building up to those of stormy seas, before ending with a calm sea. Might the stormy seas represent the passion of their amour? This, and more, possible narratives remain on the level of speculation, for the viewer has no evidence beyond what is provided, although the camera's close attention to the words on the postcards suggests intimacy, too. The name of the sender is, of course, reminiscent of that of the nineteenth-century French writer Joris-Karl Huysmans, and we can speculate whether this added another dimension to the postcard for Broodthaers, although he makes no direct reference to the writer here or elsewhere in his work.

In *Chère petite sœur* the atmosphere of the stormy sea and the close relationship between Marie and her sister are expressed powerfully and succinctly, while in *Histoire d'amour (Dr. Huismans)* the sense of regret is poignantly communicated. Viewers of these films are offered access to private correspondence between unknown people from the past and begin to imagine the back stories from the small pieces of information given. Why was Marie in Ostend in late August 1901? On a summer holiday when the weather turned inhospitable? She sent the postcard that fitted her experience of the storm. The card from Dr. A. Huismans is more mysterious. Who was the Mademoiselle in Brussels to whom he emphasized his dependability and trustworthiness in keeping his word? What became of their relationship? Was she impressed that he sent a card? Or was she too disappointed by the image? Did their relationship progress because he kept his word, regardless of the quality of the postcards on offer?

Postcards have a starring role in a few other films by Broodthaers. An unrealized 1963 project, titled *Les Cartes postales* (Postcards), was based on postcard photographs of children from ca. 1900 juxtaposed with images of anti-contraceptive laws from the 1960s.[11] Interestingly, the film *Paris* (1971) in the sequence *Trois cartes postales* does not include any actual postcards.[12] In contrast to *Chère petite sœur* and *Histoire d'amour (Dr. Huismans)*, in *Paris*, static images are replaced by moving film as the camera pans from the Eiffel Tower to the Seine with subtitles of the word "postcard" appearing on the screen in various languages. The film then cuts to a train on a bridge and again the camera pans from right to left, following the train over the bridge while words for "postcard" continue as subtitles. The film *Mauritania* (1972) takes as its starting point a postcard of the early twentieth-century British ocean liner. The film shows the whole postcard as well as close-ups, studying the image in detail.[13] Finally, *Ah que la chasse soit le plaisir des rois* (1972) includes a postcard of wild birds that became part of the offset print edition *Comment va la mémoire et La Fontaine* (1973).[14] In this film, a few details of the postcard image are shown, however, neither the image nor the handwritten message and address side of the postcard are studied in great detail. Instead, the film features a range of printed material relating to hunting, of which the postcard provides one example. Other images include colored prints of wild birds; paintings or prints deriving from paintings of foliage, a boat on water, two flying ducks targeted by two hunters and, toward the end of the film, hunting dogs; printed targets, one of which includes a simple image of a flying bird and a hare while another includes a simple image of a bird; a modern advertisement for a rifle with the image cropped to include some of the advertising text; and a series of three instruction images for shooting. Thus the material ranges from targets used for shooting practice to representations of the actual targets of hunters (i.e., wild or gamebirds or hares) as well as images of the tools used to hunt (including dogs as well as guns).

In addition to this collection of source materials, *Ah que la chasse soit le plaisir des rois* features a range of film techniques. The camera remains still throughout the film; however, animation is suggested through a sequence of images of the target featuring a flying bird and a hare; a target of a fly gradually comes into focus; the camera zooming into a target image of another bird; and

Untitled (Material used for the filming of *Mauretania*). Postcard. 8,7×13,7cm. c. 1972. © Estate of Marcel Broodthaers, c/o SABAM Belgium 2024

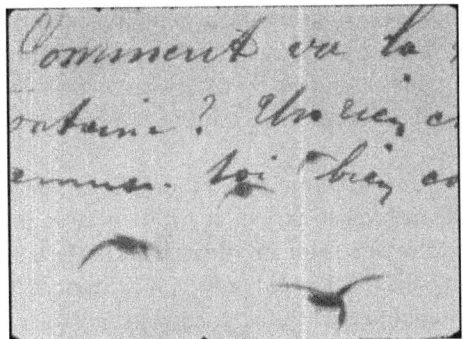
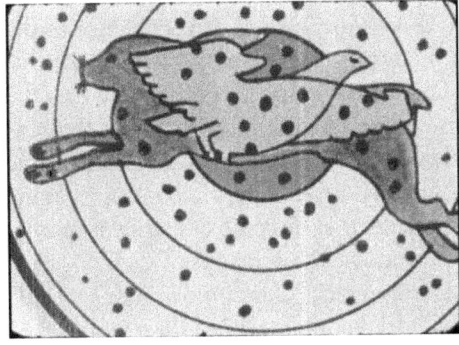
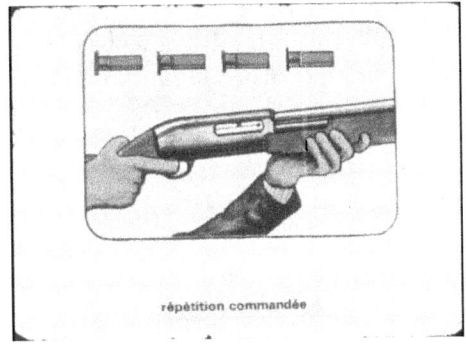

Ah que la chasse soit le plaisir des rois. 16mm. 1972. Courtesy Cinematek.
© Estate of Marcel Broodthaers, c/o SABAM Belgium 2024

many of the images gradually getting lighter and darker as they fade into and out of the film. Details as well as whole images are shown, including the eye of a bird cropped to resemble a target. The title of the film, a line from a scouts' song, together with the old painted images of animals and nature and the old postcard with a message handwritten elegantly in ink referring to La Fontaine, are countered by modern images of guns and shooting instructions. The contrasting aesthetics reinforce this distinction; whereas the old images are largely colorful and derive from handmade production methods such as drawing, painting, and printmaking, the new images have a machine aesthetic with hard, clear lines and simplified forms. Broodthaers, thus, positions romantic notions of hunting and childhood innocence against cold images of modern day reality. A similar combination can be found in the exhibition *Décor: A Conquest* at the ICA, London (1975), in which he set out the contrasting tools of combat in the nineteenth and the twentieth centuries.

Although each film lasts only three or four minutes, duration plays its part in focusing the viewer's attention on the words as well as on the spaces between them. Duration was part of the discourse of many filmmakers in the late 1960s and 1970s, a number of whom—from Michael Snow, Hollis Frampton, to Andy Warhol—made their films deliberately slow or used a static camera as a means of signaling their critical exploration of the medium. According to Justin Remes, "To be radical [...] was to be *slow*. A stubborn resistance to the pace of spectacle and money-driven modernization seemed the only creative option."[15] In Broodthaers's films, a static camera enables and encourages the viewer to take their time to explore the materials slowly together with the camera and to consider the possible subtexts of the words and images. At the same time, film, in contrast to other media, enabled Broodthaers to control what the viewer looks at and for how long. Film meant that he could construct a specific viewing sequence, leading the viewer to study certain details of each postcard for a specific period of time. As Remes comments, "One could argue that static films are even more insistent on spectatorial contemplation than is traditional visual art."[16] In Broodthaers's practice, films are constructed of still images, books can no longer be read (see his last edition of poems that he embedded in plaster, *Pense-Bête*, 1964), and museums are composed of reproductions rather than original works of art.

MEDIUM SLIPPAGE AND SPECIFICITY

At first glance, then, the source materials for these films look very slight; they are just a few old postcards. However, from these limited ingredients, Broodthaers's considered camerawork opens up new dimensions for the viewer's imagination. We can understand why Paul Éluard described postcards as "trésors de rien de tout" or "insignificant treasures" and compiled his own collection of nearly five thousand items.¹⁷ In contrast to the dematerialization taking place across much Conceptual Art, objects and materials supported rather than detracted from the communication of Broodthaers's ideas. While for Joseph Kosuth, for example, "there is always something hopelessly real about materials" that prevents them from functioning as bearers of abstract ideas, for Broodthaers it was precisely the realness and specificity of materials that added to the multilayered complexity of his works in which the material and the imaginative, fact and fiction, were always closely interrelated.¹⁸ Eric de Bruyn thus locates Broodthaers's practice within "post-minimal film [...] an expanded field of filmic practice that cannot be defined in terms of the film *medium* alone."¹⁹ Indeed, Broodthaers finds a way to combine the distinctly visual elements of film with narrative implications and wider cultural resonances.

Through this close attention and camerawork, the words on the postcards are translated into the visual subject of a film as one medium slips into another. Broodthaers "used his film practice as a mode of production and as a visualization device, paradigmatic of the uncertain, interstitial spaces that interested him."²⁰ With regard to the postcard films, these spaces were, literal and acutely visual, spaces on the material page, while he equally explored the metaphorical spaces between how words and images communicate. Words become visual forms by the animated camera that reads and rereads them, translating them from still objects into a moving medium, although it is always the camera that moves, not the subject, that is, the inanimate postcards. A few years earlier, regarding *Le Corbeau et le renard* (1967) Broodthaers commented that "the book becomes a film, the film becomes a painting (the screen)."²¹ In the same text, he also stated bluntly, "This is not a film," thereby contradicting what was in front of the viewer.²² He began the 1968 *Trépied* interview by stating, "Before answering your question I would like to say that I am not a filmmaker," while in a text for the screening of *Rendez-vous mit Jacques Offenbach* he described the films as "artistic creations" and, therefore, part of his artistic practice, rather than "essential complements to his plastic works" or even "experimental films."²³ As de Bruyn writes, his filmic practice causes "the boundaries between the different media to become permeable and diffuse. These boundaries are not deleted but dislocated in a dialectical play of negotiation without end."²⁴ Thus, the films are good examples of the intertextuality of Broodthaers's work, exploring not only what film can be but also how words and images communicate. Rather than one medium eliminating another, they coexist and the ambivalent balance of power between the image and the text is highlighted. Jacques Derrida's comment on postcards could equally apply to Broodthaers's practice as a whole. As he wrote in his 1980 book *The Post Card*, "What I prefer, about post cards, is that one does not know what is in front or what is in back [...] Nor what is the most important, the picture or the text, and in the text, the message or the caption, or the address."²⁵ Expectations are continually challenged as ambivalence and uncertainty prompt new ways of thinking.

In the postcard films in particular, the studied attention of the camera gives significance and value to words that might otherwise appear unremarkable or mundane. With regard to *Le Corbeau et le renard*, Liesbeth Decan argues that "by means of tracking shots of certain words or phrases, and by alternating this technique with close-ups of a certain object or a photographic image, the meanings of the words and the objects/images begin to interact and shift."[26] The same might apply to many of Broodthaers's other films, including those with postcards in which the camera extracts individual words from the written message and asks the viewer to study them alone. Interestingly, whereas in *Le Corbeau et le renard* and various other works "Broodthaers was very fond of undermining the legibility of his works," the inverse might be said, to some extent, of the postcard films in which the camera clearly and repeatedly reads the handwritten words.[27] The films act as points of dialogue between media in which each is explored in depth and in relation to one or more other media. To paraphrase Robert Smithson's comment on one of his own exhibitions, words are *both* to be looked at and to be read as well as being the semiotic source of reflection on how language is structured and communicates.[28]

Broodthaers's films of postcards were made in a similar way to those of paintings such as *Analyse d'une peinture* (1973) and *A Voyage on the North Sea* (1973–74); for both, the starting point was a nineteenth-century oil painting by an amateur artist of a fishing fleet at sea.[29] In each of these films, the camera explores the surface of the painting, focusing on details as well as abstract close-ups. Painting is explored via film as one medium studies, or even consumes, another. In the case of *A Voyage on the North Sea*, the painting is coupled with a black-and-white photograph of a modern yacht. In an interview with Broodthaers on *Analyse d'une peinture*, Michael Oppitz comments that in this film "the actor is a picture."[30] The equivalent could apply to the postcard films, in each of which a postcard has the starring role. In the interview, Broodthaers argues that the film both represents a particular painting and painting is also the subject of the film. In the same way, the postcard films both represent postcards and have postcards as their subject. By exploring the images slowly and thoroughly, the films invite the viewer to reflect on postcards as representations of a very particular, and, even in the 1970s, increasingly historic form of communication.[31]

For Rosalind Krauss, the sequence of images in the film *A Voyage on the North Sea*, from views of the whole marine scene to the close ups of the canvas weave, "might suggest that the narrative summoned [...] is an art historical one, telescoping [...] the story of modernism's exchange of the deep space necessary to the visual narrative for an increasingly flattened surface that now refers only to its own parameters, the 'reality' of the world supplanted by the reality of the pictorial givens."[32] In other words, the sequence of images might seem to trace the development of modernism, from the illusionistic representation of a fishing fleet, to abstract close ups of the materials used to construct that illusion, both the paint on canvas and the grain of the reproduced images. However, any suggestion of a linear temporal narrative is soon disrupted as full views of the boat are followed by shots of the yacht and back to the boat in no apparent order. Thus, "in successive moves, Broodthaers scrambles the account of a modernist progression."[33] A challenge to linear temporal sequencing is equally evident in the postcard films in which the camera moves from full frame representational images to abstract close-ups of the materials, or vice versa, and back again.

This challenge to chronology pervades Broodthaers's practice in which the historic or anachronistic counters the modern. Postcards highlight his predilection for the outdated and play a double role in various other works by simultaneously depicting the historic while signaling modern means of image reproduction, circulation, and accessibility. Examples include his extensive museum project, the *Musée d'Art Moderne, Département des Aigles* (1968–72). In the first stage, the *Section XIXème siècle* (1969), postcards represented well-known nineteenth-century oil paintings on the walls of the fictive museum or formed the basis of color slides projected onto packing crates.[34] Similarly, postcards of seventeenth-century paintings featured in the *Section XVIIème siècle* in Antwerp (1969), making a connection between the works depicted and the city in which they were displayed.[35] The title of these sections succinctly combined old and new, the *XVIIème* or *XIXème siècle* with the *Moderne*.

The museum project, in relation to the 1968 Institutional Critique discussions taking place in Paris, Brussels, and elsewhere, explored the framing structures of art, which included the museum signage, the packing crates to transport the artworks, a ladder to hang them, and so on. All the elements of a museum were in place apart from what is usually the main focus for visitors, the works of art. Instead, original, unique paintings that are conventionally considered valuable were replaced by color postcard reproductions, that is, mass-produced items of little intrinsic individual value. As Decan comments, "By exhibiting art reproductions in a gallery," Broodthaers seems to "have carried [...] to the limit" Benjamin's analysis that "to an ever-increasing degree, the work reproduced becomes the reproduction of a work designed for reproducibility."[36] Decan is referring here to Walter Benjamin's seminal essays "Little History of Photography" (1931) and "The Work of Art in the Age of Its Technological Reproducibility" (1936), while Douglas Crimp has argued that the reproduction contributes to the aura of the original, thereby reminding us that the original is unique. Through the "presence" of reproductions the "absence" of the original is made all the more apparent. As Crimp writes, "The museum has no truck with fakes or copies or reproductions. The presence of the artist in the work must be detectable; that is how the museum knows it has something authentic."[37] Broodthaers, of course, challenged precisely this order of things. Establishing his own (fictive) museum, he displayed slides, postcards, and other reproductions that defied the institution's usual raison d'être. On the invitation to his solo exhibition at the Galerie Gerda Bassenge und Benjamin Katz, Berlin (1969), he asked, explicitly and rhetorically, "Is a postcard which reproduces an image of Ingres worth several million?"[38] In other words, where does value conventionally derive from? Why is the uniqueness of an object valued more highly than its image?

Susan Stewart has pointed out that the postcard has little value in its own materiality (until, for example, it becomes rare). Its value lies in its role as evidence of what we have seen, when we send the card to someone else, or keep it for ourselves as a souvenir or aide-mémoire. According to Stewart, "We do not need or desire souvenirs of events that are repeatable. Rather we need and desire souvenirs of events that are reportable, events whose materiality has escaped us, events that thereby exist only through the invention of narrative."[39] Marie sent the postcard depicting the stormy sea to report her experience to her sister, to share her experience with her, to provide a material form of the event, and to create a lasting narrative of it. The sea was stormy and Marie thought of her little sister. The case of Dr. A. Huismans and his Mademoiselle is somewhat different. Nothing had happened that he wished to communicate to her. The event was his thinking of her and keeping his word. The postcard, the viewer may conjecture, was a sign of that thought and that trustworthiness, providing material evidence of both; Broodthaers's title *Histoire d'amour* prompts the viewer to imagine that it was intended to contribute to the development of their relationship. Stewart refers to examples in which postcards act as reminders for those who have been somewhere or for the recipients who may vicariously enjoy something of the sender's experience. With regard to Broodthaers's works, we, as viewers, many years after the postcards were sent, are far removed from the senders' original experiences. Perhaps this explains why our imagination so swiftly begins to fill in the many gaps and why the works are so evocative, leading us to fantasize about the wider contexts in which these postcards first existed. Indeed, with the very succinct messages on the postcards, which tell us little, we are forced to turn to our imagination.

The value acquired by the postcards and their effect on the viewer's imagination may also relate to their small and seemingly insignificant materiality. The postcard's size means that, according to Stewart, it can easily be "enveloped by the body [...] appropriated within the privatized view of the individual subject."[40] Perhaps this is what makes it so appealing and accessible? Indeed, the postcard needs to be small, insignificant, diminished in scale in order to be consumable, while its "impoverished and partial" form means that "it can be supplemented by a narrative discourse." The example given by Stewart is useful: "The plastic replica of the Eiffel Tower does not define and delimit the Eiffel Tower for us in the way that an architect's model would define and delimit a building."[41] Similarly, if its form was more extensive or impressive, its narrative potential would be reduced.

A postcard that has not been sent is simply another mass-produced item. It has not been chosen or handled by a sender or a receiver. When a handwritten inscription is added, the mass-produced item becomes singular. The indexical mark of the sender's pen affirms the presence of person and place and gives the postcard a unique aura: this person was there and sent the postcard as evidence that s/he was thinking of someone. Stewart has pertinently commented on "the disappointment we feel in receiving a postcard from the sender's home rather than from the depicted sight."[42] We want to know that the person thought about us and made the effort to send us a postcard when s/he was away, rather than back home. Thus, the postcard acquires an authenticity in becoming "the point of origin for narrative."[43] As the receiver has no direct experience of the place of its origin, the sent postcard's narrative value shifts from being a reminder of a place or of an experience to evidence of an event (i.e., that the sender thought of the receiver).

Nowadays, the activity of sending and receiving postcards has significantly diminished, with texting and emailing taking its place. Postcards have become antiquated, a means of communication that is no longer effective. Whereas in the early twentieth century, post could arrive on the day it was sent, this is no longer the case. Today, lacking the immediacy of a text, WhatsApp message or equivalent, the postcard has largely become socially irrelevant. However, what the contemporary digital message gains in immediacy, it lacks in texture and substance. In its diminished yet material form, the mass-produced postcard is made uniquely resonant by one person's handwritten message to another.

COMMERCE AND SENTIMENT

Postcard production was an extensive commercial business in the late nineteenth and for most of the twentieth century, when billions of postcards were widely produced and consumed in Europe alone. Those in Broodthaers's films were sent during the "Golden Age of the picture postcard," their popularity having grown rapidly during the 1890s and reaching a peak between 1895 and the start of the First World War, when the tourist industry was significantly disrupted and by which time camera innovation was starting to enable amateurs to produce their own photographic souvenirs.[44] At its height the industry was so extensive that, in 1903, "a British newspaper predicted that within ten years Europe would be buried beneath postcards, as a result of the new 'postcard cult.'"[45] Affordable for the average tourist, postcards circulated widely, sent from one place to another thanks to extensive and well-functioning postal services. A form of communication at a particular moment in time, they were not usually intended to have an afterlife or, to reference Igor Kopytoff, a "biography" beyond the relationship between the sender and the recipient.[46] Indeed, the value that we imagine the postcard had for the recipient would seem to preclude subsequent commercial circulation. Instead, we expect the postcard to remain among the possessions of the recipient, valued, even cherished, as a sign of attention and affection from someone close to them that would then be passed on to their descendants.

However, when we read the words written by Marie or, in particular, by Dr. A. Huismans and imagine a meaningful sentiment behind them, we have no evidence to support our twenty-first-century imagination. A German author, observing his fellow travelers, wrote in 1901 of how the tourist "digs deep into his pocket, brings out his purse and buys, more or less grudgingly, 2, 4, 6, 10, or 20 postcards, according to the number of friends and family. Instead of enjoying the marvelous view of the landscape [...] the tourist sits down and with an unusable pencil scribbles some unreadable lines."[47] Despite his criticism of the practice, the author "admitted having written and sent fifty-two cards at the last stop [of a cruise] in a Norwegian harbor."[48] This example is not unusual. The number of postcards an individual traveler often sent was staggering. Despite their relative affordability, the cost of the postcards and postage must have added up for the average tourist, and yet the craze was too powerful to resist. It is highly possible that both Marie and Dr. A. Huismans sent many postcards, thus rendering the act more of a conventional, even ritualistic, tourist activity rather than something that was always singular or deeply meaningful. Sending a postcard was often a "sign of life" or a response to a collector's request, neither of which required a lengthy or intimate discourse for which a letter, enclosed in an envelope, would be more appropriate. For a postcard to perform its role "to confirm, mobilize, or strengthen social relationships," a short message, or no message at all, was all that was required.[49] It was not unusual for tourists to be commissioned to send postcards to collectors and the Mademoiselle might well have been one such a collector, hence Dr A. Huismans's regret at not finding something better for her.

Interestingly, the postcards focused on in *Chère petite sœur* and *Histoire d'amour (Dr. Huismans)* are representative of two different phases of postcard production: the postcard from Marie to her sister, sent in 1901, was designed to have the address and stamp on one side (then, interestingly, considered the recto) and only an image on the other side (or verso). This is why Marie squeezed her message into the margin beneath the image, whereas, in 1907, Dr. A. Huismans's postcard had a designated space for a message to the left of the address. Although he could have written more, a short message remained the cultural norm. When postcards were first produced, the brief writing style seemed impolite or even vulgar for some, while for others it felt liberating.[50] There was no longer the space for the lengthy phrases and flowery language that were expected in more formal letter writing.

While some of Broodthaers's films consist of observations of and commentaries on contemporary life, the postcard films do so at an angle, exploring cultural practices in the past such as postcard writing through the investigative lens of the contemporary camera. In doing so, he invites the viewer to consider the "social life," to draw on Arjun Appadurai's term, in which the postcards existed.[51] Indeed, as T. S. Eliot wrote, "Even the humblest material artefact, which is the product and symbol of a particular civilization, is an emissary of the culture out of which it comes."[52] With speed and mobility of central importance to modernity, postcards—which were quick to buy, write, send, and receive—became immensely popular, providing the opportunity to communicate with loved ones elsewhere or satisfying the urge to collect something modern and decorative. Appreciating the extent of the widespread postcard craze helps us today to understand the cultural and communicative value of postcards then as well as how such intimate possessions might end up recirculating in commercial domains. Perhaps unsurprisingly, when people amassed thousands of postcards in their own collections, their descendants might not feel the need, or have the space, to keep all of them.

Reading the message from Dr. A. Huismans to his Mademoiselle through this historic lens, the wording seems far less intimate and meaningful. Nevertheless, perhaps the messages were not just the fulfillment of a conventional or contractual obligation but actually meant something? Were the words written hastily in order to catch the post in time? Or were they carefully chosen to communicate the author's feelings? As Bjarne Rogan writes, "These inscriptions are almost void of information but they are still messages with a strong expressive value."[53] Drawing on communication theory, Rogan identifies postcard messages as relating to two distinct forms of communication: "linear," in which information is communicated, and "circular [...] to confirm or mobilize an already existing social relationship."[54] These two postcards would seem to fit these two theories neatly, with Marie's a good example of a linear form of communication while Dr. A. Huismans fits the circular definition. However, if circular communication relates to "people who have a fairly close social relationship, the purpose of such communication acts being to *confirm* or mobilize an already existing social relationship" then either Dr. A. Huismans and his Mademoiselle were already close or his postcard contradicts this theory. This ambivalence is, perhaps, central to our fascination with this postcard in particular. There is always the possibility of a deeply meaningful relationship behind a short message, just as there is behind a short digital message.

For readers today, these postcard messages, taken out of the context in which they were sent, seem cryptic, intriguing, and mysterious. The tension between the imagined intimacy of the message and its public exposure, traveling un-enveloped, heightens our interest. As Derrida has commented, "What I like about postcards is that even if in an envelope, they are made to circulate like an open but illegible letter."[55] The sender can only communicate in a limited number of words. Although addressed to an intended readership, postcards are physically readable to all who might see them, traveling envelope-less and uncovered. But their messages often communicate little to those outside of their intended readership, especially when they seem to be just a fragment of a longer conversation. As Sanae Tokizane has commented, "The postcard is generally unreadable simply because its message is forced to be curt and fragmental. It is, as it were, an encoded note, which can be deciphered only by someone who shares the code."[56] This tension between legibility, illegibility, coded and ambivalent messages pervade these postcard films. Broodthaers deliberately mines these qualities through his studied camerawork, which may not enable us to understand what the message means, but we are in no doubt as to what was written.

In this respect, they relate to his imaginary interviews, such as with René Magritte (1967), his problematic interviews, such as his "Interview with a Cat" (1970), his one-sided dialogues such as his Open Letters (1968–72), and his one-sided conversations such as with Jeremy Bentham in *Figures of Wax* (1974). In each of these, communication is disrupted. Broodthaers also gave many actual interviews during his career, although his responses were often carefully scripted, cryptic, contradictory, or insincere. Also worth mentioning here is his performance *Speakers' Corner* (1972), in which he held up a blackboard with words written on it but remained silent, at odds with the expectations of the audience. Nevertheless, dialogue was a highly productive aspect of his practice, forming the starting point for many of his own works that provide his response—both celebratory and critical—to the works of others. His self-conscious strategy for artistic success meant that he located himself in the art world in relation to those around him and his works are underpinned by and filled with references to artists and writers, both predecessors and contemporaries.[57]

In the 1960s and 1970s, postcards were used in a number of art projects, often signifying a mundane, anti-elitist, democratic format in which to promote ideas over material form. Indeed, the un-envelopedness of the message equally signified a free and open form of expression beyond the commercial parameters of the art world. Postcards—both found and specially made—were used in mail art, including by Fluxus artists such as Robert Filliou with whom Broodthaers hung out at Daniel Spoerri's restaurant and gallery in Düsseldorf, just along Burgplatz from his *Section cinéma*, and whose practice Broodthaers was familiar with. For Spoerri, Filliou, and their associates the chance element was central to their practice, and this would have resonated with Broodthaers too. Postcards also formed part of the output of Conceptual artists, including Eleanor Antin, who produced a series of fifty-one photo-postcards, *100 Boots* (1971), and On Kawara, who famously sent two a day for his series *I Got Up* (between 1968 and 1979). Richard Hamilton, whom Broodthaers got to know while living in the UK, providing a text for Hamilton's print *Flower-Piece Progressives* (1974), also used the medium in a number of works. These include *A Postal Card – For Mother from S.M.S. No. 1* (1968), which derived from a mass-produced sepia postcard of a crowded beach at Whitley Bay in the north of England. A foldout accordion from the middle of a facsimile of the postcard comprised eight images of a detail of the postcard image viewed in increasing close-up. The details became progressively more pixelated, with the figures bordering on the illegible.

CONCLUSION

Broodthaers's postcard projects tap into a current fascination with the lives of so-called ordinary people. In recent years the "biographical turn" has developed in the humanities, the use of narrative has been foregrounded in history, and oral history is now an established discipline. The lives of unknown individuals, as opposed to established public figures, are now perceived as having significant value in contributing to our wider understanding of history. Items such as found postcards as well as diaries and snapshot photographs are good examples of easily overlooked items of everyday life that were previously considered of little historic value. However, such ephemera, "embroiled in the pleasures and politics of mutual social relations," provide an insight into the ways in which people lived their lives.[58] Due to its accessibility, an item like a postcard crosses social divides in time and space. It is, in fact, its very ordinariness and seeming insignificance that makes it such an authentic trace of specific cultural practices in the past.

In the films I have discussed, Broodthaers investigates these qualities of the mass-produced postcards too, while also evoking narrative possibilities instigated by the words written on them. His camerawork studies the form of the postcards, covering every detail of their material existence. At the same time, the literalness of what is shown over and over again—ink on paper—counters this immaterial imaginative dimension. In these films that take postcards as their starting point, Broodthaers produced layered, textured, and nuanced works that relate to experimental or avant-garde cinema while remaining at a critical distance from it. As in much of his practice, the films blur the distinction between fact and fiction, between the reality of their existence and their potential narratives.

NOTES

1. Liesbeth Decan, *Conceptual, Surrealist, Pictorial: Photo-Based Art in Belgium (1960s–early 1990s)* (Leuven: Leuven University Press, 2016), 40.
2. Marcel Broodthaers, Announcement for *Moi aussi je me suis demandé si je ne pouvais pas vendre quelque chose*, Galerie Saint-Laurent, Brussels, 1964: "Ce que c'est? En fait, des objets."
3. An account of these films within the thematic context of maps and travel in Broodthaers's work can be found in my book, *Marcel Broodthaers: Strategy and Dialogue* (London: Peter Lang, 2007).
4. The framed source material for all four of these films is in the MACBA Collection, Barcelona, on long-term loan from the Jost Herbig Collection; see links from https://www.macba.cat/en/art-artists/artists/a-z/broodthaers-marcel.
5. See Manuel J. Borja-Villel, Michael Compton, and Maria Gilissen, *Marcel Broodthaers: Cinéma* (Barcelona: Fundació Antoni Tàpies, 1997), 204 (for *Trois cartes postales*) and 208–9 (for *Rendez-vous mit Jacques Offenbach*).
6. *Chère petite sœur* (1972), 16mm, black-and-white and toned, 4 minutes, Brussels.
7. "Chère petite sœur, celle-ci pour te donner une idée de la mer pendant la tempête que nous avons eue hier. Donnerai détail à ce sujet, bonne amitié et à bientôt. Marie."
8. The film *Mademoiselle* (1971) 16mm, color, sound, 3 minutes, Brussels, seems to be virtually identical to *Histoire d'amour (Dr. Huismans)* (1969) 16mm, color, silent, 3 minutes, Brussels; the only differences seem to be that sound was added and the name was changed when the film was included in *Rendez-vous mit Jacques Offenbach* (1972). The Jeu de Paume exhibition catalogue also list *C'est-je-parole-regret* (1971), 16mm, color, silent, 7 minutes, which is likely to be a longer version of the same film as the title refers to the main words written on the postcard; see Catherine David and Véronique Dabin, *Marcel Broodthaers* (Paris: Galerie nationale du Jeu de Paume, 1991), 316.
9. "Vous voyez, Mademoiselle que je tiens parole. Je n'ai qu'un regret: c'est de ne pas trouver ici de cartes plus jolies à vous adresser."
10. See http://www.macba.cat/en/material-de-rodatge-de-mademoiselle-3911.
11. I am grateful to Maria Gilissen for this information.
12. *Paris* (1971) 16mm, color, silent, two minutes, Paris. In the David and Dabin catalog, the film is titled *Paris (Carte postale)*; see David and Dabin, *Marcel Broodthaers*, 316. The MACBA collection contains a forty-seven-second version titled *Tour Eiffel*; see https://www.macba.cat/en/art-artists/artists/broodthaers-marcel/tour-eiffel.
13. The David and Dabin catalog states that two versions were made of *Mauretania (Avec mer)* (1972): *Mauretania (AOX – XOA)* and *Mauretania (Fig. o – Figures Fig. A)*, 16 mm, color, ca. two minutes, Düsseldorf; see David and Dabin, *Marcel Broodthaers*, 316. The MACBA version of *Rendez-vous mit Jacques Offenbach* begins and ends with three still images of the Mauretania postcard, with the camera progressively closer to the postcard.
14. *Ah que la chasse soit le plaisir des rois* (1972), 16mm, color, silent, 8 minutes, Brussels.
15. Justin Remes, *Motion[less] Cinema: The Cinema of Stasis* (New York: Columbia University Press, 2015), 23.
16. Remes, *Motion[less] Cinema*, 20.
17. Paul Eluard, "Les plus belles cartes postales," *Le Minotaure* 3–4 (December 1933); quoted in David Prochaska and Jordana Mendelson (eds.), *Postcards: Ephemeral Histories of Modernity* (University Park: Penn State University Press, 2010), 133. The phrase "trésors de rien de tout" has also been translated as "treasures of nothing."
18. Joseph Kosuth, "Four Interviews," *Arts Magazine* (February 1969): 23, quoted in Liz Kotz, *Words to Be Looked At: Language in 1960s Art* (Cambridge, Mass.: MIT Press, 2007), 186.

19. Eric de Bruyn, "The Expanded Field of Cinema, or Exercise on the Perimeter of a Square," in Museum Moderner Kunst Stiftung Ludwig Wien and Matthias Michalka (eds.), *X-Screen: Film Installations and Actions in the 1960s and 1970s* (Cologne: Verlag der Buchhandlung Walther König, 2003), 160.
20. Manuel J. Borja-Villel and Christophe Cherix, "I Am Not a Filmmaker: Notes on a Retrospective," in Manuel J. Borja-Villel and Christophe Cherix (eds.), *Marcel Broodthaers: A Retrospective* (New York and Madrid: The Museum of Modern Art and the Museo Nacional Centro de Arte Reina Sofia, 2016), 18.
21. Marcel Broodthaers, cited in Borja-Villel, Compton, and Gilissen, *Marcel Broodthaers: Cinéma*, 52.
22. Borja-Villel, Compton and Gilissen, *Marcel Broodthaers: Cinéma*, 52.
23. "Interview de Marcel Broodthaers, notre invité au 'Hoef' le 30 janvier," *Trépied* 2 (February 1968): 4–5; reproduced in English in Gloria Moure (ed.), *Marcel Broodthaers: Collected Writings* (Barcelona: Ediciones Polígrafa, 2012), 184. Marcel Broodthaers, "Marcel Broodthaers: Films" in Borja-Villel, Compton, and Gilissen, *Marcel Broodthaers: Cinéma*, 210.
24. De Bruyn, "The Expanded Field of Cinema," 159.
25. Jacques Derrida, *The Post Card: From Socrates to Freud and Beyond* (Chicago: University of Chicago Press, 1987), 13.
26. Decan, *Conceptual, Surrealist, Pictorial*, 32.
27. Decan, *Conceptual, Surrealist, Pictorial*, 32.
28. Robert Smithson described his exhibition at the Dwan Gallery, New York, 1967, as consisting of "Language to Be Looked at and/or Things to Be Read." See Kotz, *Words to Be Looked At: Language in 1960s Art*, 2.
29. Borja-Villel, Compton, and Gilissen, *Marcel Broodthaers: Cinéma*, 226.
30. B. H. D. Buchloh and Michael Oppitz, "Interview with Marcel Broodthaers on His Film Analysis of a Painting," *Interfunktionen* 11 (November 1973); reprinted in Borja-Villel, Compton, and Gilissen, *Marcel Broodthaers: Cinéma*, 230.
31. Susan Hiller began collecting postcards of rough seas in 1972 for her project *Dedicated to the Unknown Artists*. At around the same time she saw Broodthaers's show at the Jack Wendler Gallery, London. In 2009 she produced two works that pay homage to Broodthaers work, with particular reference to the contrasting seas in *A Voyage on the North Sea*. They are *Voyage on a Rough Sea: Homage to Marcel Broodthaers*, in which rough seas are depicted, and *Homage to Marcel Broodthaers: Voyage*, depicting yachts on calm seas. I am grateful to Andreas Leventis, associate director, Lisson Gallery, for this information.
32. Rosalind Krauss, *A Voyage on the North Sea: Art in the Age of the Post-Medium Condition* (London: Thames & Hudson, 2000), 52.
33. Krauss, *A Voyage on the North Sea*, 52.
34. See *Marcel Broodthaers: Slide Projections* (Eindhoven: Stedelijk Van Abbemuseum, 1993). Postcards also featured in various other works, including *Untitled (Cartes postales concernant la peinture du XIX siècle)* (1968) comprising twenty-six postcards in a frame (see https://www.moma.org/collection/works/186774) and the offset lithograph edition *Musée-Museum* (1972) (see David and Dabin, 25), both of which related to the museum project, as well as the diptych *Les Très Riches Heures du Duc de Berry* (1974–75) (see David and Dabin, 284), which comprised a stenciled painting and a frame of twelve postcards of pages from the celebrated illuminated manuscript.
35. The *Musée d'Art Moderne, Département des Aigles, Section XIXème siècle* took place for a year at the artist's Brussels home on Rue de la Pepinière (1968–69), while the *Musée d'Art Moderne, Département des Aigles, Section XVII siècle* was exhibited at art center A 37 90 89, Antwerp (1969).

36. Decan, *Conceptual, Surrealist, Pictorial*, 36–37, referring to Walter Benjamin, "Little History of Photography" (1931) and "The Work of Art in the Age of Its Technological Reproducibility" (1936), in Michael W. Jennings, Brigid Doherty and Thomas Y. Levin (eds.), *The Work of Art in the Age of Its Technological Reproducibility, and Other Writings on Media* (Cambridge, Mass.: Belknap Press of Harvard University Press, 2008), 24.
37. Douglas Crimp, "The Photographic Activity of Postmodernism," in *On the Museum's Ruins* (Cambridge, Mass.: MIT Press, 1993), 112.
38. Decan, *Conceptual, Surrealist, Pictorial*, 36.
39. Susan Stewart, *On Longing: Narratives of the Miniature, the Gigantic, the Souvenir, the Collection* (Durham: Duke University Press, 1993), 135.
40. Stewart, *On Longing*, 136–38.
41. Stewart, *On Longing*, 136.
42. Stewart, *On Longing*, 135.
43. Stewart, *On Longing*, 136.
44. Bjarne Rogan, "An Entangled Object: The Picture Postcard as Souvenir and Collectible, Exchange and Ritual Communication," *Cultural Analysis* 4 (2005): 1.
45. Rogan, "An Entangled Object," 4.
46. See Igor Kopytoff, "The Cultural Biography of Things," in Arjun Appadurai (ed.), *The Social Life of Things: Commodities in Cultural Perspective* (Cambridge: Cambridge University Press, 1986), 64–91.
47. Rogan, "An Entangled Object," 9.
48. Rogan, "An Entangled Object," 9.
49. Rogan, "An Entangled Object," 19.
50. See Rogan, "An Entangled Object," 14–18.
51. See Appadurai (ed.), *The Social Life of Things*.
52. Rogan, "An Entangled Object," 3, quoting T. S. Eliot, *Notes towards the Definition of Culture* (London: Faber & Faber, 1948), 92.
53. Rogan, "An Entangled Object," 15.
54. Rogan, "An Entangled Object," 15.
55. Derrida, *The Post Card*, 12.
56. Sanae Tokizane, "What Postcards Want to Say," *International Journal of Human Culture Studies* 28 (2018): 119.
57. This is the central argument of my book, *Marcel Broodthaers: Strategy and Dialogue*.
58. Catherine Zuromskis, *Snapshot Photography: The Lives of Images* (Cambridge, Mass.: MIT Press, 2013), 12. I have found Zuromskis's book on snapshot photography valuable as a counterpoint to discussions on the function of postcards and their role in works of art.

MARCEL BROODTHAERS'S UNDERGROUND CINEMA
AU-DELÀ DE CETTE LIMITE (1971)

Charlotte Friling

Au-delà de cette limite is largely based on Marcel Broodthaers's observation of the graphic shapes of the text featured on the famous Parisian metro signs—*Au-delà de cette limite vos billets ne sont plus valables* ("Beyond this limit, tickets are no longer valid") and *Limite de validité des billets* ("Limit of ticket validity"), which are indicators of the boundaries of exchange, circulation, legal and social norms. Thus, the film continues Broodthaers's speculations on reproduced, printed, projected, and materialized text and typography, also exemplified in his series of "industrial poems" or visual rebuses on plastic plaques (1968–72).[1] Both the "industrial poems" and the film take street or public signs as their point of departure. A significant example is the plaque *Rue René Magritte Straat* (1968), with its background of a brick wall and its bilingual street sign as homages to Magritte, described by Broodthaers as follows: "The bricklayer, up against the wall. The man of letters, to the letter."[2]

Like the plaques, *Au-delà* is a poetic exercise in reading. Both challenge the viewer's understanding of language and meaning while reflecting on the limits of communication and on the power of words and surfaces, as demonstrated by Jacques Rancière in *L'Espace des mots: De Mallarmé à Broodthaers*.[3] The film occupies a particular place in Broodthaers's filiation with Stéphane Mallarmé (the inventor of "modern space"), actualizing the latter's poetics of a spatialized text and aiming at a form of "personal (poetry) writing." *Au-delà* addresses the deconstruction of the limits of language, the rules by which power manifests itself, and on the formation of subjectivity and poetics.

In addition, *Au-delà* reveals itself to be an important element in Broodthaers's *Musée d'Art Moderne, Département des Aigles* (1968–72), his critical project aimed at exposing and reformulating institutional constraints. The film is situated at the intersection of three of his fictional museum's twelve "sections," namely the *Section financière* (Autumn 1971), the *Section cinéma* (its first installment from January 1971 to January 1972), and the *Section des figures (The Eagle from the Oligocene to the Present)* (Summer 1972).

Mainly filmed in Paris, *Au-delà* explores the iconic and mythical reputation of the city's underground—the Métropolitain—in the aftermath of May '68, aware of its symbolic legacy in numerous literary, artistic, and cinematic works from Dadaism to the New Wave, including *Le Métro* (Georges Franju and Henri Langlois, 1934), *La Première nuit* (Georges Franju, 1958), and the ciné-vérité manifest *Chronique d'un été* (1961) by Jean Rouch and Edgar Morin. Furthermore, familiar with the theories of French structuralist and poststructuralist thinkers from Lacan to Foucault, Broodthaers acknowledges the deconstruction of principles and structures on which laws, categories, and norms operate. *Au-delà* exemplifies certain Lacanian concepts as well as the poet's continuous preoccupation with linguistics and image/text relations with vehicles of authority and power, a preoccupation he pursued intensely while preparing his *Section des figures*.

Au-delà occupies a specific place in Broodthaers's *Section cinéma*, which ran (in two installments) from January 1971 to October 1972 and included the production and editing of films such as *Belga Vox-Mode-20th Century Fox*, *Charlie as a Filmstar*, or *Brüssel Teil II* (all 1971), as well as a series of screening

Au-delà de cette limite. 16mm. 1971. Courtesy Cinematek.
© Estate of Marcel Broodthaers, c/o SABAM Belgium 2024

programs.⁴ The film stands out because of its unique tone and use of montage, its analysis of the "plastic" reproduction of texts and typographic characters in public signage, and its study of the effects of objectification by the institutional apparatus on individual and artistic speech.

Au-delà de cette limite is a silent 16mm film in black-and-white, made in the winter of 1971. One version is listed in the landmark book *Marcel Broodthaers: Cinéma* (1997) as having a duration of seven minutes and thirty seconds.⁵ This chapter departs from the description of a second, longer version (8'50"), kept at Cinematek in Brussels, marked by a different arrangement of sequences. I also look at the various sequences that were cut by Broodthaers from the final versions, and which are reproduced and described in the 1997 book. Basically, the film consists of the following materials: footage of the Paris metro and its immediate surroundings; still images taken inside the Paris metro and the ubiquitous enamel signs; still images of a Bahnhof Bellevue sign outside the eponymous Berlin S-Bahn station; and French text fragments printed in various places in the image.

Rather than employing or experimenting with the new image technology of video (available in the early 1970s and harnessed by many conceptual artists working at the time), Broodthaers kept using celluloid. With this low-budget and low-tech film, Broodthaers reveals his interest in the medium's ability to achieve his intended poetic strategies and sensitivity. Cinema's specificity as an art of montage is central in *Au-delà*. Inserted as subtitles, the text acts as another layer of perceptual montage, writing, reading, and interpretation. Language is at the heart of the film, whether filmed or inserted onto the celluloid by the artist in postproduction.

Broodthaers constructs his film with a simple montage of both moving and still images: on the one hand, animated, sequenced, projected, temporalized cinematic images; on the other, fixed, single, nontemporalized photographic prints. Crucially, the latter are not mere static stills that have been inserted but rather *filmed* photographic stills. Maria Gilissen emphasizes the fact that Broodthaers insisted on these photographs being filmed.⁶ Rather than using freeze-frames as traces that transmit a sense of eternity, Broodthaers's camera actively scrutinizes, questions, and activates the photographic images, alternating frontal shots, zooms, and tracking shots that move over their flat surfaces. In so doing, Broodthaers seems to refer to the practice of inserting stills in films or documentaries to illustrate a situation when no moving image is available, typically of a diegetic, narrative, formal, or discursive nature. By making moving images from still images, Broodthaers explores the limits of cinema and photography's creative forms, moving away from their original purity while increasing their expressive possibilities. It is perhaps also a reflection on the second of cinema being made up of twenty-four (still) images: "And here I am, cruelly torn between something immobile that has already been written and the comic movement that animates 24 frames per second."⁷

The film consists of various sequences or chapters, a montage of alternating static and moving images: (1) Title (filmed photograph) and Opening sequence (moving image); (2) Inside and outside the metro (moving image); (3) From Paris to Berlin (filmed photograph); (4) Poem (filmed photograph); (5) Inside and outside the metro (filmed photograph) and "Limite juridique" (moving image); and (6) Repetition of poem (filmed photograph).

TITLE AND OPENING SEQUENCE

The title sequence delves straight into the crux of Broodthaers's project, its profound engagement with language and linguistics, and the exploration of the interplay between image and language. It introduces both the concept of the objectification of text and the possibilities of bringing text alive through the medium of film, transforming straightforward or frontal text into something more heterogeneous that calls for different modes of perception.

The first seconds of the film are close-ups of a filmed photograph of a sign in the Paris subway. At first, we see groupings of capital letters (LIM, DE), isolated and abstracted by the camera, reduced to their graphic aspects, freed of their semantic charge. As mere shapes or sounds, they become actors of a visual and poetic puzzle. The next fragments feature words such as "de validité" and "des billets," allowing the viewer to recompose the full statement featured on the sign "Limite de validité des billets."[8] At once static and dynamic, this "text sequence" presents *Au-delà* as an experiment revolving around the construction and deconstruction of language. The hesitation between material and literary sign, legibility and illegibility, signifier and signified pervades the rest of the film and recalls both the book and film version of *Le Corbeau et le renard* (1967), a spatialized play with reproduction, representation and text, and a rebus reminiscent of the reading exercises set up by his "industrial poems."

This sequence is followed by a more classic and dynamic cinematic opening scene, consisting of footage shot from a moving train with a handheld camera, recording Paris's Haussmannian façades along the tracks, and passing above an overhead train or metro bridge. The film's title now appears in the conventional form of inscriptions engraved on the celluloid, in lower case, by means of subtitles or intertitles, positioned on the top part of the screen and above the fast-moving landscape: "Au delà de cette limite les billets ne sont plus valables." Next, a static shot looking out from a station shows curving train tracks.

From the start, Broodthaers points to the two levels or surfaces carrying text that he explores throughout the film: the standardized sign or legal warning as preexisting images "in" the film, on the one hand, and the poet's subjective voice, on the other, placed "above" or over of the image, engraved into the celluloid strip. Broodthaers undermines what is expected of both layers. He breaks up the sentences carried by the first layer to highlight a personal reading. Then, playing with font, size, position, and using repetitions, he disrupts and creates a distance vis-à-vis the second.[9] This binary dynamic recalls that of the plastic plaques, produced almost consistently as a false positive-negative pair or as two slightly different versions or interpretations of the same motif.

A shift of signifiers occurs, from the warning sign intended for travelers (inside the metro) to the film screen/projection itself carrying a message for viewers. Both film and text are support and subject at once, referring to their own limits. This echoes René Magritte's painting *La Condition humaine* (1933), which shows a painting in front of a window, seen from inside a room, depicting exactly the part of the landscape hidden by the painting, "au-delà." Magritte writes, "The tree in the painting therefore hid the tree behind it, outside the room. For the viewer, it was both inside the room, on the painting, and outside, in thought, in the real landscape. This is how we see the world. We see it outside ourselves and yet we only have a representation of it inside us. In the same way, we sometimes place in the past something that is happening in the present. Time and space then lose that crude meaning that only everyday experience can take into account."[10]

INSIDE AND OUTSIDE THE METRO

The camera then descends the stairs into a hall featuring various signs, including "Limite de validité des billets," which is also repeated as an intertitle. The repetition is an illustration of the cacophony of messages and advertisements found in public space, their ubiquity and overlap making them illegible, annulling their authority and aura. Other signs such as "Passage interdit" ("No Entry") can be seen, fixed in clearly visible places of passage (corridors, turnstiles, et cetera) and in the flow of commuters. This flow is for instance evoked in the silent short 16mm film *Le Métro* (1934) by Franju and Langlois, which features similar shots of moving trains and commuters coming and going through the corridors, passing each other, going up and down the stairs, in perpetual motion. However, in Broodthaers's film, a sentiment of control, containment, and claustrophobia prevails, in contrast to the fluidity and freedom of movement conveyed by the images filmed from the moving train. It recalls Michel Foucault's studies on the mechanisms of power and regulation, with which Broodthaers was acquainted at the time. Yet Broodthaers was not systematically aligned with his positions, as illustrated by *Ceci est une pipe*, a planned publication project of the *Section littéraire* of his *Musée d'Art Moderne, Département des Aigles* (initiated in 1969, eventually cancelled in 1972), in reaction to Foucault's essay "Ceci n'est pas une pipe" (1968), an interpretation of René Magritte's famous painting *La trahison des images* (1929).

The motif of the white ceramic tiles, typical of the Paris metro, appears here for the first time and will become a leitmotiv of the film. However, Broodthaers's film draws as much attention to the enamel signs, which could be seen all over the Paris subway in the 1960s and 1970s. A ticket was and still is valid for several journeys as long as you stay within the circulation area of the metro. Once you leave the designated area, however, the ticket expires, and you need a new ticket to reenter the metro. The expression has been so popular that it appears, as is or with variations, in several films or novels at the time, such as Romain Gary's book *Au-delà de cette limite votre ticket n'est plus valable*, published in 1975. The phrase became a *lieu commun* or a commonplace, mere information or communication, accepted by all passive users without being challenged rhetorically. Broodthaers, however, disrupts and activates the phrase, starting with its use as the title of his film.[11]

Paris is the obvious setting of most of the film. Invited to exhibit at Galerie Yvon Lambert (15 Rue de l'Echaudé, in the 6th arrondissement), Broodthaers, who had met Lambert through Niele Toroni shortly before, proposed to produce and screen *Au-delà*. Since the opening of his first Paris gallery in 1965, Lambert acted as a pioneer in championing Minimal and Conceptual Art in France, showing artists such as Carl Andre, Lawrence Weiner, Daniel Buren, and Robert Ryman among others.[12] It is unclear which of the two known versions of the film was projected at the gallery. In a letter to Lambert dated November 25, 1971, Broodthaers writes that the film is still in the making and mentions time and financial constraints:

> The film will be finished just in time. It will cost more than expected. That is, it will cost *me* more. The subject is thin ... so I must support it without greed. That is to say that I want to keep the 15% I get from each sale. I will never again agree to such a low flat-rate production price.[13]

Jean Harlez, who acted as a cameraman for various other films by Broodthaers, traveled from Brussels to Paris for a day of shooting. Maria Gilissen photographed specific locations and details of the settings.[14] Yvon Lambert recalls being present during the filming of sequences in the Saint-Germain-des-Prés or Odéon metro, close to his gallery and an iconic area of the May '68 uprisings in Paris. No strict script had been shared with them beforehand, and all three remember that much of the filming was improvised on the spot, camera on the shoulder, with barely any budget and very little time.

The "exhibition" opened on December 15 and ran for about a month. Broodthaers wished to present this new film in an otherwise empty space, playing with the limits of its format, language, and conventions.[15] *Au-delà* is neither entirely "cinema" nor a "work of art," but closer to what Jean-Christophe Royoux coined "exhibition cinema," made for a specific context and space.[16] In an interview conducted by the ORTF (Office de Radiodiffusion-Télévision

Française), Broodthaers points out that the film is meant as a "plastic experience" and that the way it is screened (directly on the wall) questions the gallery wall as a limit.[17] He concludes that all "limits, walls, gallery walls, prisons, and limitations are intolerable." Although inspired by French avant-garde films, the film was not meant to be screened in a regular cinema theater. It was to be presented in a commercial gallery space and, arrestingly, as an unlimited multiple:

> On the other hand, I absolutely want it to be presented as an *unlimited edition*. Otherwise it would lose its logic ... those few minutes ... I think we should agree on how to defend it. An unlimited edition cannot be sold at a high price (alas). That is to say, it is likely to be bought by cultural associations which could then not only use it as they see fit but also insert it in ridiculous programs. No public screenings without my approval. This is the promise that should be extracted from any potential buyer. It's up to you to let him know. Beyond a certain limit, even banknotes are no longer valid.[18]

Despite his apparent concerns about the financing, distribution, and sale of this ambitious film, Broodthaers almost sabotaged the gallerist's duty to sell it, his conditions making it highly unlikely to attract a buyer. And indeed, Lambert failed to sell a single copy.[19]

"What should we think of the relationship linking art, advertising and commerce?" Broodthaers asked in March 1971 in *Der Spiegel*, in which he appears in a Van Laack shirt advertisement, signing "M.B. (le directeur)."[20] In May–June, the "Service Financier" of his *Musée d'Art Moderne, Département des Aigles* conceived a publication project in which Broodthaers imagined the announcement of a sale contract for a kilogram of gold as an ingot, stamped with an eagle motif, planned to finance his *Musée*. It was followed by the announcement, in October, of the *Section Financière Musée d'Art Moderne 1970–1971 à vendre pour cause de faillite* (for sale due to bankruptcy) at the Cologne Art Fair. That same year, Broodthaers's plaque *Section publicité* announced the "Service Publicité" (Advertising department), a further function and discursive "site" of his *Musée* that was a comment on the strategies of the culture industry. Broodthaers displaces the usual way of consuming "cinema" by projecting his film in the white cube of a gallery space rather than in the black box of the cinema theater. His desire to control a certain experience of the work is clear, as his demand to cater it to a specific audience ("no public screenings without my approval"). Presented as the only artwork in the gallery, its format as a democratic multiple or an "unlimited edition" paradoxically eludes the status of the reified, unique work of art.

This concept of the multiple brings to mind one of Broodthaers's iconic vacuum-formed "industrial poems," *Le Drapeau noir (tirage illimité)*, the first version of which was produced in June 1968 as an open edition witnessing the protests rattling Europe at the time (Amsterdam, Berlin, Nanterre, Venice, Paris, Milan, and Brussels are listed on the plaque). Despite its playful design and rebus-like aspect, the plastic plaque carries a noticeable political accent. *Au-delà* carries a whiff of nostalgia, like a bitter farewell to the fervor of May '68. The artist's request to distribute it as an unlimited edition recalls his wish for the unlimited plaque "to spread indefinitely the wavelength of the poem" and to indicate "pure intention."[21]

After the sequence that focuses on warning signs, the camera records ordinary people, anonymous passersby: two boys in trench coats intriguingly exchanging something, men and women walking up and down the stairs, probably at different metro stations. The only recognizable "actor" seems to be Broodthaers himself, who makes a very discrete cameo appearance, filmed from behind several times, holding a briefcase walking up the stairs, then buying a ticket. This scene can be read as a metaphor for a transaction, for knowingly participating in this regulated, constricted game. Once Broodthaers moves away, the camera crosses the cashier's gaze, first frontally, then from behind a gate further away. This unplanned *regard caméra*, considered a mistake in classical cinema, draws the viewer into the film, inducing an awkward sense of reality.

Au-delà cannot be labeled as Nouvelle vague cinema, though it uses some of its codes, such as a pseudo-documentary mode, location shooting, an unstable handheld camera, and improvisation by amateur actors, reminding viewers that they are watching a film. The film has its "hero," *je* (I), who soon finds himself in a tragic situation ("*à la limite de la folie, de l'internement*"), stuck between restrictive rules and dreams of independence. An homage to Jean Vigo's film *Zéro de conduite* (1933) is tangible, a depiction of a repressive and bureaucratized establishment in which surreal acts of rebellion occur.

Broodthaers's film evokes a sense of incarceration created by imposing boundaries, especially in the footage of metallic railings and gates that block people from entering without their ticket and warning them of exclusion once they are outside the "system." There is a clear "in" and a clear "out." As demonstrated by his plaque *Le Drapeau noir*, Broodthaers rarely fails to address the social and political moments in which his work is made.[22] In *Au-delà*, he might also point to the more personal context of his illness and own mortality. In French, *l'au-delà* also stands for the afterlife, the "beyond" in which the tickets, even the banknotes he mentions in his letter to Lambert, are no longer useful.

Suddenly we find ourselves outside, the camera eventually emerging from the metro into the street, recording a busy Parisian crossing and the apparent "free" movement of cars and people. The title "Limite de validité" appears, positioned higher up, closer to the center of the screen, partly covering the faces of pedestrians, somehow obstructing the fleeting promise of escape. The film then takes us back into another station that features a visually different *Limite de validité* sign, in a different font and mounted in a more contemporary light box. It is filmed as a backdrop to a little handwritten advertising sign and mannequin with sweaters on sale at a "Record price of 9.95 Fr," a nod to Pop Art's critical and subversive use of advertising imagery and motifs that inspired some of Broodthaers's works.

FROM PARIS TO BERLIN

After these various scenes with moving images, the montage switches back to filmed photographs of signs (introducing movement in a still image), making sure that the film's spectators understand they are looking at a still image, like in the very first sequence of the film. The camera moves across the surface of the print, zooming in on an overexposed part of a sign, where some letters, when isolated, dissolve and become difficult to decipher. The focus is on blurry patches around the letters "CET" and "DE," both materialized and dematerialized linguistic signs. The shots seem to remind us: this is not a sign, but an image of a sign.

The following shots in the montage exploit another photograph, of which we first see the clear word fragment "elle," in a notably different font than in the previous sign.[23] The camera then moves to the right or "east," allowing viewers to read the rest of the word, "ellevue." The succeeding shots are long shots of that same photograph, first a full view of a sign "Bahnhof Bellevue," then a full view of that sign attached to an elevated track of the suburban train station/S-Bahn bridging a road. The viewer is thus transported from Paris to Berlin's Hansa Quarter (in the exclusive diplomats' quarter) through a simple montage trick. In 1971, Bahnhof Bellevue marked a significant border itself, as it used to be the last station where trains coming from West Berlin would call before reaching Bahnhof Friedrichstrasse, located in East Berlin. Another view of a corner building behind the bridge/viaduct and some trees closes the Berlin sequence, which, in contrast to the Paris sequence, is only based on photographs and does not contain moving images.

The messages from the metro signs "Limite de validité…" and "Au-delà…" are repeated as titles in both French and German, both in lower and upper case, either at the bottom of the screen or positioned more centrally. These deliberate choices are reminiscent of Broodthaers's publication designs, particularly his invitation card for Yvon Lambert's presentation of *Au-delà*. Typical of the poet, the card's layout has a classic look, carefully orchestrated, with a very particular choice of fonts and use of lower and upper cases: on one side of the card, above the address, date and opening hours, the title "Au-delà de cette limite vos billets ne sont plus valables" appears in lower-case Anglaise font, while on the other side of the card, a "poem" is printed in capital letters, a block that is reminiscent of the rectangular shape of a projection screen.

> At the limit... the self... the subject. At the limit of a theory of birds, cabbages, stakes. At the limit of passion, madness, internment. The old one? The new one? At the limit of identical objects. Below. Beyond.

Do the birds refer to the eagles? The cabbages to the imposed diet? And the stakes to picket lines or some sort of strike/setback? He mentions all these in his letter to Lambert:[24]

> A lot of worries. A trip to Berlin to pick out some eagles in the museums. My liver hurts. I have trouble sticking to a strict diet. A permanent fatigue obscures all my plans. Maria helps me in this particular case, but she too is difficult. Of course she is. Finally this film will be finished.[25]

The film was made in a complex context, marked by the artist's fragile health and his many projects to develop his *Musée d'Art Moderne*. It is during his trip to Berlin that winter to visit museums and collections, looking for eagles for his upcoming exhibition *Section des figures* (*The Eagle from the Oligocene to the Present*) at the Städtische Kunsthalle Düsseldorf (May–July 1972), that he took—or asked Maria Gilissen to take—photographs. Some were subsequently used in an early version of *Au-delà*.

Outtake negatives reproduced in the 1997 book dedicated to Broodthaers's cinema show a zoo cage in the Jardin des Plantes in Paris, with the sign "Bison d'Amérique." Maria Gilissen and Jean Harlez remember the Jardin as being a destination Broodthaers insisted on filming during their short stay in Paris. The botanical garden, zoo, and Museum of Natural History were already closed when they got there, but Broodthaers asked Harlez to take some views from outside the gates. These reinforce the feeling of incarceration, inclusion, and exclusion.

The outtakes also include photographs of the Pergamon Museum in (then) East Berlin, its imposing façades and signs—"Museum" and "Pergamon Museum"—presenting the museum as an authoritative institution, a conditioned "container," or collection of the exotic. Other photographs show Broodthaers entering and leaving the metro through a full-height metal turnstile gate flanked by metal rods, much like bars of a zoo cage, and restricting access to those who are "authorized." Finally, more stills show the artist entering and leaving Galerie Yvon Lambert, in which one can distinguish a handmade sign "Limite de validité des billets." The scene was filmed by Broodthaers during *Au-delà*'s screening in the gallery and planned as footage for another short film by the artist.[26]

Broodthaers plays on the word "billets," which means both tickets and bank notes. In his letter to Lambert, he writes, "Beyond a certain limit, even banknotes are no longer valid."[27] Broodthaers suggests parallels between conditioned systems, spaces of power and spectacle such as the film theater, gallery, museum, zoo, and metro. They recall Broodthaers's engagement with Foucault's thought as well as his quote: "You direct a museum the way you direct a hospital, the way you direct a prison."[28] Eventually, Broodthaers decided to erase these recognizable places and representations of himself from the version of the film described here.

POEM

The "graphic knot" sequence in *Au-delà* focuses on the image, on surface, and text. It's a filmed analysis of a photograph featuring a sign attached to a tiled metro wall. The latter acts as a background to intertitles that add up to an increasingly confusing text, or "poem":

> Below beyond, At the limit ... the self ... the subject, At the limit of passion, madness, internment, At the limit ... the self ... the subject, Below beyond, Below beyond, At the limit of identical objects, Legal limit, Legal limit.

The use of lower and upper case, the position of the words on the screen, and the particular rhythm recall Stéphane Mallarmé's strategies for the spatialization of words in his 1897 graphic poem *Un coup de dés jamais n'abolira le hasard*. In his exhibition *Exposition littéraire autour de Mallarmé* at the Wide White Space Gallery in Antwerp (January 1969), Broodthaers refers to this canonical text. In *Au-delà*, he attempts to go beyond Mallarmé's innovative and experimental approach to poetry, transferring his exploration of the relationship between words, silence, and the white spaces from page to screen.

This key sequence appears twice in the film, being repeated as the final sequence, and recalls the poem on the Lambert invitation card. The sentence used in the film is a nevertheless slightly different version, as Broodthaers leaves out the suggestive sentence "At the limit of a theory of birds, cabbages, stakes" and the questions "The old one? The new one?" It is unclear which of these two versions of the poem was written first, or when they were composed: whether before inspiring the production of the film, or after, sparked by the film's content and images. The whole sequence has language at its crux, with a complex layering of existing texts (public signs) and a specially written text (poetic intertitles). Jacques Rancière described Broodthaers's point as follows:

> It is this limit to the power of words and surfaces that Broodthaers's film devoted to the famous Parisian metro plaque, "Au-delà de cette limite les billets ne sont plus valables," emblematizes. The filmed sign is like a response to the collage of bus tickets on Schwitters's canvas. A ticket is not a material of life that can be recycled into an element of artistic form, like the old-fashioned catalogues or magazines that Surrealism was fond of. It

is nothing but a title that allows one to move within the limits of a closed and defined system bordered by two gates. Beyond their signifying value, words are no longer valid and the surface that bears them does not change them into anything else.[29]

In this part of the film, the camera explores the surface of a photograph of a "Limite de validité" sign against a wall of the Paris metro, paying particular attention to the structure of that wall as a backdrop to both the sign and the poem. The sequence opens with a close-up of the blank tiled wall with its typical graphic linings. The intertitle "Au-delà de cette limite vos billets ne sont plus valables" appears in upper case—as if it were the title of the sequence—while the camera moves down the wall. The camera stops and another title appears, "En deçà, Au delà" ("Below, beyond"), positioned left and right on the screen, facing each other. These indications or opposite directions, of a below and an above/beyond, are visualized and implemented in the metro scenes alternating between inside and outside, people walking up and down, as well as in the camera movements, moving in and out, up and down, right to left and back, and across a photograph. Broodthaers plays with what Walter Benjamin calls cinema's distinctive visual techniques: "Its lowerings and liftings, its interruptions and isolations, its extensions and accelerations, its enlargements and reductions."[30] The restlessness of the camera as well as the repetitions and superpositions of words create a state of confusion as to their order, meaning, value, and authority, disorienting readers while also emancipating them from the rigidity of an imposed language in favor of an intuitive, empirical experience.

The camera zooms in on the metro sign, dissecting the sentence into fragments: "Limite de, validité, billets." The last shot shows, in small letters in the lower right corner of the sign, the inscription "Email Laborde" ("Enamel Laborde"), the name of the company that produced the signage. The name recalls the well-known Clinique de Cour-Cheverny also named de la Borde, a French center for "institutional psychotherapy" founded in 1953, focusing on group dynamics and the relationship between patients and doctors. This interdependency suggests the linguistic concept of signifier and signified, the two complementary sides of the concept of the linguistic sign developed by de Saussure and subsequently by the Structuralist school. Félix Guattari, disciple of the psychiatrist and psychoanalyst Jacques Lacan, practiced all his life at la Borde as a philosopher and psychoanalyst.[31] This reference resonates with Broodthaers's interest in Lacan's seminars and writings, and with his use of terms like "*à la limite*, folie" and "internement."[32] Broodthaers's poem and entire final concept for the film might even have been triggered by this coincidence, and thus written after the shooting in Paris.

The next title, "A la limite ... le moi ... le sujet" is positioned more centrally on the screen, using the tiles as background. The repetition of the three dots reflects hesitation, perhaps a shortage of breath. Broodthaers touches upon Lacan's notion of the subject, *le moi*, the self. Who is "me"? The "hero," narrator, artist? A work by Broodthaers dated 1967–71 features a photographic print in a mirror-glass frame on which he wrote with a black marker: "Á la limite ... le moi... le sujet. Á la limite d'objets identiques. En deçà. Au-delà." The negative print showing Broodthaers from the back dates back to his 1967 "literary happening" in the streets of Brussels, an early incarnation of his work *Le Corbeau et le renard*. The text clearly links both works. This snapshot was also used by the artist for the photographic canvases *Apprendre à lire* and *Apprendre à parler*, which were respectively displayed in the Université Libre de Bruxelles during the student occupation in May 1968 and the exhibition *La Collection privée de Marcel Broodthaers* at Galerie 44 in Brussels (Autumn 1968), where it was juxtaposed to a series of copies of *Le Drapeau noir (tirage illimité)*. The trajectory from the fable of *Le Corbeau et le renard* to *Au-delà* is evident, as is their common theme of flattery, discourse, and rhetoric. On another related object dating from 1971, the artist wrote with India ink on film stock "M.B. ... Au-delà de cette limite les billets... Au-delà En deçà... Á la limite ... L'ancienne? La nouvelle? Au-delà de ... En deçà," next to a series of M.B. initials. The repetition of the artist's signature, of the *moi*, recalls his work around Narcissus, "the inventor of cinema."[33]

Zooming out, a full shot of the metro sign follows, before a close-up again of the tiles, which serves as a background for the title "Á la limite de la passion, de la folie, de l'internement." Beyond its reference to la Borde, the statement also echoes the idea of narrative intrigue developed by Broodthaers in the film *Crime à Cologne*, also dated 1971. It was filmed in a gallery (Michael Werner) in a specific, recognizable geographical location (Cologne) and with a similar focus on text and suspense in part of the film (close-ups of words on pages of a book by John Blackberry and a man holding a gun).[34]

The titles "Á la limite... le moi... le sujet" and "En deçà, Au delà" appear and disappear while the camera moves in different directions, at different speeds, trying to exit the grid. It hits the words "limite de" from the sign, interrupted by a new title that seems to echo the former inscription "Á la limite d'objets identiques." The camera then moves diagonally across the tiles, before going back to the sign, hovering over it to allow viewers to read it until the end: "Limite de validité des billets." The sequence ends as it began, with a shot of blank metro tiles, like a visual pause or moment of silence, allowing one to catch one's breath before continuing reading.

The motif of the metro tiles recalls the Magrittean brick wall motif, the tracing of an itinerary on a map, or an impenetrable grid or fence, from which the nervous camera tries to find an exit. It recalls the plaque *Liberté* (1968), a unique work featuring a brick or tiled background, each tile enclosing a letter of the alphabet. On top of that grid, the word "liberté" (freedom) appears in large letters across the entire surface. The rebus *Société* (1969) also comes to mind, with its grid containing loose, evocative but imprisoned words and signs. Like these plaques, the focus on words or "mots-idées" in *Au-delà* recalls Mallarmé's famous words: "It is not with *ideas* that one makes verses, it is with *words*" ("Ce n'est pas avec des *idées qu'on fait des vers, c'est avec des mots*").

INSIDE AND OUTSIDE THE METRO

The next sequence starts with a static photograph, taken inside the metro, of people, their shadows, and a sign "Limite de validité …," filmed frontally, without the camera moving. It is followed by moving images shot at the station exit. We see a "Metro" sign, traffic signs, and the top of the stairs leading above ground, accompanied for a brief period by the term "Limite juridique" in lower case. The camera, now positioned at the top of the stairs, looks back to a large "Metro Austerlitz" sign (close to the Jardin des Plantes), then toward a busy Parisian street after a rain shower, its cars, passersby, and leafless trees. Austerlitz is a reference to one of the key engagements of the Napoleonic Wars, often cited as a tactical masterpiece.

For the end of this sequence, Broodthaers returns to the symbolic overhead train bridge, like the one filmed in Paris in the opening sequence or the one photographed in Berlin at Bahnhof Bellevue. We see trains passing and crossing overhead and cars crossing below it, moving in opposite directions. The scene is marked by a dialectical dynamic, with the camera going down at the beginning ("en deçà"), looking up at the end ("au delà"), with the bridge as a space of transit, voyage. The intertitle "Limite juridique" reappears superimposed on this view on the city, but this time in upper case and for a notably long time. Font, size, punctuation, duration: all play a role in how the message is communicated and the poem is read.

The camera eventually tilts up slowly to film the top of a building and treetops, eventually tilting further to show only the blank sky, over which we see the inscription. Unlike the blank metro tiles background made with still photographs, this one is filmed, free of the limiting grid, beyond the legal limits. The limit of the film's title can thus be understood in two ways with different, even opposing implications. On the one hand, it can be seen as an insurmountable horizon, an impassable wall. On the other hand, the boundary is the line that can be crossed and moved. The first, shorter version of the film ends here. In the second version, the camera tilts down a bit and treetops reappear, as if the title is reconnected to a specific place. It is followed by the very last sequence of the film, which is a repetition of the "poem" sequence (sequence 4).

CONCLUSIONS

Au-delà de cette limite coincides with Broodthaers's project for the *Musée d'Art Moderne, Département des Aigles* (1968–72) and it was made under the aegis of his *Section cinéma*. These years were also marked by a large output of films as well as "industrial poems" and "open letters." Certain aspects of the film can be linked to Structural cinema, which Broodthaers was familiar with, for example the work of Hollis Frampton, in particular his *Word Pictures* photographs (1962–63) that prefigure his film *Zorns Lemma* (1970), which features an alphabet composed of words that appear on street signs. Likewise, Chris Marker's *La Jetée* (1962), another experimental masterpiece constructed as a "photonovel," left a mark on Broodthaers. With its dialectic between still and moving images and its fascination for texts and inscriptions, *Au-delà* also tallies with some of Broodthaers's own films made around the same time, such as *Projet pour un poisson* (1970–71), *Analyse d'une peinture* (1973), and his three films involving postcards (*Histoire d'amour*, 1971; *Chère petite soeur (La Tempête)*, 1972; *Paris*, 1972). Nonetheless, *Au-delà* has a particular place in his filmography. Although one of the most conceptual works, it contains a certain "dramatic" structure and recognizable "spatial sequences." It marks the transition from his poetic films, in which signs, writing, and images are the main subject matter that are submitted to a dynamic mobilization through montage, to films in which straightforward photo-mimetic images are confronted with graphic signs as well as printed, reproduced, or written texts. The film even emphasizes a dialectical relation between static, frontal signs and the multidimensional images of "the real," to which Broodthaers adds a narrative of historical and allegorical relations, as in some of his later films such as *Crime à Cologne* (1971), *Un Jardin d'hiver* (1974), *Figures of Wax* (1974), or *Berlin oder ein Traum mit Sahne* (1974–75).

"This is not cinematographic art," Broodthaers claimed, contesting the use of certain terms applied to his work such as "essential complements to his plastic œuvre" and "experimental films." "No more and no less an object of discussion than a painting by Meissonier or Mondrian, these are films."[35] In conclusion, *Au-delà* is a film that takes the shape of a poem, and a poem that takes the shape of a film. It resonates as much with the "linguistic turn" operated by Conceptual Art in the late 1960s as with the paradigm shift that took place from the work of art as a field of spontaneous individual gestures made by a liberated or uninhibited "self" to the clearly organized constructions and structures of a society of industrial productivity, repetition, and forced standardization. Broodthaers's unorthodox position, however, consists in his insistence on the value and strength of the ambiguity of the non-homogeneous and of the fluidity of language, this in contrast to a move toward a uniformity of meaning, of language as information, and of communication by means of administrative and computer technologies. This resounds with American art critic Thomas McEvilley's essay "Another Alphabet," in which he insists on Broodthaers's questioning of category systems randomly dividing nature and culture, and on his critical eye toward the Hegelian distinction between the two: "Broodthaers suggests that the Madness of nature may be saner than the Work of culture" and that "human Work—the human effort to control and manipulate nature—is seen as itself rooted in nature, dependent on it."[36]

In the film, Broodthaers confronts the insistence on the legal value of the transaction of communication or circulation in a system of text with the randomness of reality and subjectivity. *Au-delà* illustrates a catharsis of the limited, static, and restrictive language of protest, politics, or legal prose, transformed into an unconstrained, unexpected, and personal poetic flow. His *Museum* fiction—particularly its Cinema section—reflects on how any enterprise of individual "underground" poetics collides with the codes, limits, and regulations to which any transaction of exchange is reduced. It is no longer "Sous les pavés, la plage" ("Below the cobblestones, the beach") but below the cobblestones, the Metro.

NOTES

I wish to thank Dirk Snauwaert for the kind help and essential feedback he provided during the writing of this essay. I am also grateful to Steven Jacobs and Raf Wollaert for bringing particularly insightful references to my attention.

1. See Charlotte Friling and Dirk Snauwaert (eds.), *Industrial Poems, Marcel Broodthaers: The Complete Catalogue of the Plaques, 1968–1972* (Brussels / Hamburg: WIELS / Hatje Cantz, 2022).
2. Friling and Snauwaert, *Industrial Poems, Marcel Broodthaers*, 84.
3. Jacques Rancière, *L'Espace des mots: De Mallarmé à Broodthaers* (Nantes: Musée des Beaux-Arts de Nantes, 2005).
4. *Marcel Broodthaers: Cinéma* (Barcelona: Fundació Antoni Tàpies, 1997), 140–53.
5. *Broodthaers: Cinéma*, 202.
6. Maria Gilissen, conversation with the author, 5 September 2022.
7. Marcel Broodthaers, "Projet pour un texte," in *Broodthaers: Cinéma*, 91 and 184–85.
8. It is interesting to note that the version of the film described in *Broodthaers: Cinéma* opens in the reverse order, namely with its title. This is followed by a sequence showing details of the same metro sign, with no mention of the sign *Limite de validité*.
9. Rachel Haidu takes a similar stance on Broodthaers's use of text and subtitling as a subversion of "the usual functions assigned to language by the film medium." See Rachel Haidu, *The Absence of Work: Marcel Broodthaers, 1964–1976* (Cambridge, Mass.: MIT Press, 2010), 271–72.
10. René Magritte, manuscript of his lecture "La ligne de vie," *Combat 3* 105 (10 December 1938), translated from the French: "Je plaçai devant une fenêtre vue de l'intérieur d'une chambre, un tableau représentant exactement la partie de paysage masquée par ce tableau. L'arbre représenté sur ce tableau cachait donc l'arbre situé derrière lui, hors de la chambre. Il se trouvait pour le spectateur à la fois à l'intérieur de la chambre sur le tableau et à la fois, par la pensée, à l'extérieur, dans le paysage réel. C'est ainsi que nous voyons le

monde, nous le voyons à l'extérieur de nous-mêmes et cependant nous n'en avons qu'une représentation en nous. Nous situons, de la même manière, parfois dans le passé, une chose qui se passe au présent. Le temps et l'espace perdent alors ce sens grossier dont l'expérience quotidienne tient seul compte."

11. Broodthaers lists similar *lieux communs* on a film strip illustrated in *Broodthaers: Cinéma*, 203: "Les billets ne sont plus valables, être copains comme cul et chemise, changer d'avis comme de chemise, vendre jusqu'à sa dernière chemise" (1971, India ink on film stock).
12. Broodthaers was subsequently shown by Yvon Lambert on several occasions during his lifetime: *Actualité d'un bilan* (1972, group exhibition in which he presented the first of eight multipart paintings, titled *Série en langue française (Série de neuf peintures sur un sujet littéraire)* in a new body of work later titled *Peintures littéraires* (1972–75); *A, B, C – Paysage d'automne* (the work *Paysage d'automne*, originally conceived as an edition of 140 was eventually sold "en bloc" as a unique piece, perhaps "sabotaging" the gallerist's (and his) commercial interests) and *Deux films de Marcel Broodthaers: 1. Une peinture d'amateur découverte dans une boutique de curiosités; 2. Le même film revu après critiques* (both solo exhibitions in 1973).
13. *Broodthaers: Cinéma*, 200.
14. Jean Harlez, conversation with the author, 23 August 2022.
15. Broodthaers and his wife Maria Gilissen attended the opening screening in Paris. During his stay, he allegedly filmed *Au-delà* being screened in the empty gallery. Maria Gilissen, conversation with the author, 5 September 2022.
16. Jean-Christophe Royoux, "Projet pour un Texte: The Cinematographic Model in the Work of Marcel Broodthaers," *Broodthaers: Cinéma*, 302.
17. Marcel Broodthaers, ORTF recorded interview, Herman and Nicole Daled Papers, partial gift of the Daled Collection, III.78. Museum of Modern Art Archives, New York.
18. *Broodthaers: Cinéma*, 200.
19. Yvon Lambert, conversation with the author, 18 January 2023.
20. Marcel Broodthaers, *Der Spiegel* (22 March 1971): 166.
21. Friling and Snauwaert, *Industrial Poems*, 44.
22. Broodthaers often cites Jean Vigo, father of social cinema in the 1930s, friend of Charles Dekeukeleire, for whom Jean Harlez worked. See also Bruce Jenkins, "Toward a Social Cinema," *Millennium Film Journal* 1 (Winter 1977–78): 23.
23. In the version studied in *Broodthaers: Cinéma*, Broodthaers films the detail "ILLE" from "BILLETS", then the fragment "ELLE", from "BELLEVUE," moving from France to Germany, from "il" (he) to "elle" (her).
24. See also his first open letter from 7 June 1968, written in the context of great cultural turmoil, in which he positions the "self" or "Je dis je" (I say I), and suggests his dire financial situation: "Je n'ai pas de revendications matérielles à formuler bien que je me saôule avec de la soupe aux choux" (I have no material claims to make, though I get drunk on cabbage soup).
25. *Broodthaers: Cinéma*, 200.
26. Maria Gilissen notes that this sequence was not filmed for *Au-delà de cette limite*, but for another short (lost) film that was shot inside his exhibition at Yvon Lambert and was to be titled *Deux films*. Maria Gilissen, conversation with the author, 5 September 2022.
27. *Broodthaers: Cinéma*, 200.
28. "Marcel Broodthaers. L'Angelus de Daumier," Atelier de Création Radiophonique, included in Gloria Moure (ed.), *Marcel Broodthaers: Collected Writings* (Barcelona: Polígrafa, 2012), 460–61.
29. Rancière, *L'Espace des mots*, 20–21.
30. Walter Benjamin, "The Work of Art in the Age of Mechanical Reproduction," in *Illuminations* (New York: Schocken Books, 1969), 237.

31. I thank Xavier García Bardón for bringing this reference to my attention. The creation of the Clinique de la Borde was part of a movement to reform psychiatry that developed in France in the postwar period, based on a radical critique of asylums and a fight against segregation. The movement sought to humanize psychiatry and profoundly transform the hospital through an emphasis on group dynamics and the relationship between caretakers and cared-for. Other cases exist from which Broodthaers's interest in (anti-)psychiatry clearly transpires: in 1962, he dedicated an article to the Club Antonin Artaud, while in 1970, he mentioned the experimental psychiatrist R. D. Laing as an advocate for "the uselessness of art."
32. Broodthaers attentively read and reflected on Lacan's *Écrits*, published in 1966.
33. "1 seconde pour Narcisse ..." (1970), in *Broodthaers: Collected Writings*, 282. See the film *Une Seconde d'éternité* and related plastic plaque *M.B.* (both dated 1970).
34. *Broodthaers: Cinéma*, 196–97.
35. Marcel Broodthaers, "Marcel Broodthaers: Films" (text written on the occasion of the screening of his films organized by Jeunesse et arts plastiques in Brussels on December 7, 1972), in *Broodthaers: Cinéma*, 210.
36. Thomas McEvilley, "Another Alphabet: The Art of Marcel Broodthaers," *Artforum* 28, no. 3 (November 1989): 106–15.

BROODTHAERS, BENTHAM, AND PYGMALION
FIGURES OF WAX (1974)

Steven Jacobs

STILLNESS

Many if not all of the films by Marcel Broodthaers in one way or another deal with still images: paintings, photographs, postcards, magazine illustrations, maps, inscriptions, magic lantern slides, et cetera. In so doing, his films relate closely to the art forms, imagery, and materials he was working with as a visual artist. But his filmic explorations of still images also resonate with the ubiquitous images of stasis we find in contemporaneous experimental films as well as in the modernist art house cinema of the 1960s and 1970s. Like the film experiments by Andy Warhol, Yoko Ono, Michael Snow, and Hollis Frampton or the feature films by Robert Bresson, Michelangelo Antonioni, and Alain Resnais among many others, Broodthaers's cinema seems to be marked by a resistance to speed, ignoring movement and dynamics—phenomena that often had been presented as essential characteristics of the cinematic medium.[1]

Furthermore, despite his somewhat idiosyncratic use of the film medium, Broodthaers's interest in cinematic stasis also invokes various thematic issues of contemporaneous avant-garde and modernist cinema, such as a fascination with the motif of the statue coming to life (or its opposite, the petrification of a living being). Focusing on his 1974 film *Figures of Wax*, this chapter discusses Broodthaers's take on the film medium's capacities in dealing with the interaction between stillness and motion, the dead and the living, and processes of animation and mortification. In so doing, this chapter also attempts to throw a new light on Broodthaers's reliance on Surrealism—a staple in Broodthaers criticism and scholarship—through an analysis of his cinematic exploration of the tropes of the wax figure and the mannequin doll.

Stasis definitely marks *Figures of Wax*, a film made in London in 1974.[2] Shot in 16mm in color with a soundtrack featuring piano music and a voice-over commentary, the film (Broodthaers's longest) has a somewhat "professional" look that differs clearly from several of the more deskilled films he made earlier.[3] The film features the wax statue of British utilitarian philosopher Jeremy Bentham

(1748–1832), put on display in a cabinet in a corridor of University College London.[4] To be precise, the wooden showcase does not contain a wax statue in the strict sense but holds the actual stuffed and preserved body of Bentham to which a wax head showing his features was added. With some amazement, Broodthaers observed that "the skeleton serves as the *ossature* (Ha! Ha!), to construct a wax figure."[5] In addition, the cabinet contains Bentham's mummified head, which was cooked in an oven according to Bentham's own instructions, based on an interpretation of Maori practices. When the result was disappointing, the "statue" was completed with a wax head by French anatomical sculptor Jacques Talrich, who based his portrait on various paintings and sculptures of the philosopher.[6] Broodthaers's first interest in Bentham and the idea for the film were triggered by his fascination with his mummy rather than with his philosophical theories. However, by the time he requested permission of the UCL to make the film, he was already familiar enough with Bentham's ideas, suggesting an approach that would be completely in line with "Jeremy Bentham's eccentric genius."[7] Furthermore, turned into an exhibit in a display case, Bentham must have attracted the attention of the director of the *Musée d'Art Moderne, Département des Aigles*, who had expressed his interest in exhibition infrastructure such as packing crates, vitrines, labels, and signage in many of his works of the early 1970s.

Figures of Wax. 16mm. 1974. Courtesy of the Walker Art Center's Ruben/Bentson Moving Image Collection. © Estate of Marcel Broodthaers, c/o SABAM Belgium 2024

Bentham's taxidermized corpse particularly features in the middle and main section of the film. A series of medium shots, close-ups, and extreme close-ups show us details of the body and attire of the philosopher. Only at the end of the film does Broodthaers provide us with a master shot, offering a view of the quite banal and generic university corridor in which the cabinet is situated. On an adjacent wall, we can see the 1829 Bentham portrait painted by Henry William Pickersgill. In the very last shot of the film, Broodthaers's camera scans the details of this painted portrait, by means of a vertical panning shot starting at the philosopher's face, moving downward and ending at the painting's label attached to the lower part of the gilded frame, marking the end of the film. Broodthaers's exploration of the pictorial surface of the portrait is reminiscent of some of his earlier films that focus on paintings, such as *La Clef de l'horloge: Poème cinématographique en l'honneur de Kurt Schwitters* (1957–58), *Analayse d'une peinture* (1973), and *Voyage on the North Sea* (1973–74), fragmenting the original image by means of a close-up, scanning the texture of the paint, and drawing our attention to material and institutional components such as the frame and the label of the painting.

WAX FIGURES

In *Figures of Wax*, the Pickersgill painting's flatness, emphasized by the close position of the camera and the reflection of light on the texture of the paint, is also juxtaposed to the "real" and bodily presence of the painter's sitter. *Figures of Wax* unmistakably plays on the uncanny associations of Bentham's preserved body, which are already announced in the old-fashioned Gothic font of the opening credits. The wax figure is, of course, a staple in Gothic fiction—its origins closely connected to the terror of the French revolution, which also marked the life and works of Madame Tussaud, who was imprisoned for three months and awaited execution.[8] She allegedly made death masks of famous victims of the revolution before she traveled with her collection to Britain and eventually founded her famous museum in Baker Street, London, in 1835, shortly after Bentham's death. One of the main attractions of her museum was a Chamber of Horrors, combining victims of the revolution and newly created figures of murderers and other criminals whose wax faces were often "taken from life," in the sense that they were cast from death masks taken by Tussaud herself. Broodthaers's film on Bentham was probably inspired by his fascination of such wax museums. In 1961, he referred explicitly to Madame Tussaud in his poetic travel report to London published in *Les Beaux-Arts*, linking her museum to the era of the French revolution and Napoleon.[9] First and foremost, however, his fascination with such wax figure cabinets tallies perfectly with his general interest in nineteenth-century strategies of visual display such as magic lanterns, world exhibitions, zoos, winter gardens, and museums. Throughout the nineteenth century, houses of wax, also known in French as *cabinets des figures* developed into a popular form of visual entertainment. The 1880s and 1890s saw a real boom of these museums after the opening of the Musée Grévin in Paris.[10]

Highly popular until far into the twentieth century, wax figure cabinets also provided the theme of an entire subgenre of horror films, starting with Maurice Tourneur's *Figures de Cire* (1914) and Paul Leni's *Wachsfigurenkabinett* (1924) and an unstoppable series of Hollywood adaptations, including *Mystery of the Wax Museum* (Michael Curtiz, 1933) and the 3D spectacle *House of Wax* (André De Toth, 1953), each of them emphasizing the uncanny and morbid associations of the wax figures.[11] The uncanny effect of wax figures is not only the result of their inherent connections to death, it is also related to the fragility of wax—the deterioration or destruction of the wax figures is a recurrent motif in these films that often dwell on the imagery of melting wax figures. In 1971, British artist Peter Dockley made a short film entitled *Cast* that consists entirely of human wax figures slowly melting.

Furthermore, the uncanny effect of wax statues is inherently linked to the hyperrealist characteristics ascribed to these statues, an element that certainly fascinated many Surrealist writers and artists. In Belgian Surrealist circles of the late 1920s, the journal *Variétés*, for instance, included some photographs of the Musée Spitzner, an anatomic museum created in the middle of the nineteenth-century that presented wax casts of human bodies as well as monstrosities.[12] In the twentieth century it developed into a cabinet of medical curiosities at fairgrounds, such as the annual Foire du midi (Fair of the Midi, close to the South station) in Brussels. In *Variétés*, the photographs of the Spitzner cabinet were juxtaposed to paintings by Antoine Wiertz depicting acts of suicide and bodies opening tombs and coffins, emphasizing their morbid associations. In the 1930s and 1940s, Paul Delvaux, whom Broodthaers photographed in his studio while touching a skeleton, made several works referring to the Musée Spitzner, and we can only wonder if the young Broodthaers might have seen it.[13]

STATUES, SURREALISM, AND CINEMA

Like for Broodthaers, the Surrealist fascination with wax figures is part of a larger interest in humanoid objects such as puppets, dolls, ventriloquist dummies, classical statues, and mannequins that Broodthaers expressed in various media such as the (posthumously published) book *Statues de Bruxelles* (which he made in collaboration with photographer Julien Coulommier) as well as the two-minute film *Monsieur Teste* (1974/75), which features a suited mechanical doll (or ventriloquist dummy) named after the protagonist of Paul Valéry's 1894 novel about a man who experiences nothing special, does virtually nothing, and is not very talkative.[14] The film, initially titled *Mouvement*, hypostasizes the confrontation between the lifeless puppet and the dynamic medium of film, alternating static shots in which the figure turns its head from left to right with panning shots of the immobilized head. When a succeeding long shot reveals the entire figure sitting in a chair in front of a curtain and reading the French weekly magazine *L'Express*, the movement of the camera from side to side echoes the motion of the figure's head as he peruses the journal.

Broodthaers's uncanny figures of the wax statue and the dummy are reminiscent of the Surrealist fascination for the mannequin—an object that plays an important role in another section of *Figures of Wax* and that will be discussed in a following paragraph. A type of utilitarian sculpture, the mannequin is a conventional artists' prop, a dressmakers' dummy, and a familiar figure of fashion display. It became a Surrealist icon through its emphatic presence at the 1938 *Exposition internationale du Surréalisme* but, at that time, it was already associated with Giorgio de Chirico's paintings and Eugène Atget's photographs, two touchstones of an earlier Surrealist sensibility. Due to their functional resemblance to living bodies, mannequins possess an uncanniness that is, in the words of Susan Felleman, "overdetermined, deriving from their displacement from dressmaker's shop, window display, or studio prop into Surrealist tableaux, often erotic, strange, and magical."[15]

Troubling the boundary between the animate and inanimate, the mannequin also tallies with the Surrealist's fascination for Pygmalion, the mythic Cypriot sculptor who was able to bestow life upon his statue of a perfect female, turning cold ivory into warm flesh.[16] The Pygmalion motif (the dream of the statue coming to life) as well as its opposite such as fantasies in which living beings are turned into stone as in the myths of Medusa, Niobe, Aglauros, Echo, and Atlas, particularly fascinated filmmakers as the film medium itself is based on the animation of the still image. Not coincidentally, film pioneers such as Georges Méliès (often applauded by the Surrealists) cherished the motif of the statue coming to life, as if making explicit the differences between the static art of sculpture and the new dynamic art of film.[17] With *Pygmalion et Galathée* (1898), Méliès also authored one of the first film adaptations of the Pygmalion myth, and one of his films contains a wax mannequin. In *Le Diable géant ou le Miracle de la Madonne* (1901), for instance, a wax Madonna statue comes to life to banish a hyperactive devil.

The Pygmalionist effects of cinema were particularly taken up by Surrealist and Post-Surrealist filmmakers, interested in exploring the boundary between the animate and the inanimate themed with echoes of ancient mythology and classical sculpture: *L'Âge d'or* (Luis Buñuel, 1930), *A Study in Choreography for the Camera* (Maya Deren, 1945), *Ritual in Transfigured Time* (Maya Deren, 1946), *The Potted Psalm* (Sidney Peterson and James Broughton, 1946), *Dreams That Money Can Buy* (Hans Richter, 1947), *Four in the Afternoon* (James Broughton, 1951), and *The Pleasure Garden* (James Broughton, 1953) all contain key scenes involving statues coming to life or scenes in which the hermetic immobility of statues is emphasized by their confrontation with living and moving or dancing bodies. In particular, living sculptures pervade the oeuvre and writings of Jean Cocteau, who repeatedly referred to the idea that Russian composer Modest Mussorgsky had already proposed in the 1880s: an art that "will express itself by statues that are moving."[18] The films of his so-called Orphic trilogy—*Le Sang d'un poète* (1932), *Orphée* (1950), and *Le Testament d'Orphée* (1959)—connect living statues as well as the petrification of living beings with death, the underworld, and the hereafter. Statues are even closely related to Cocteau's persona. In *Le Testament d'Orphée*, he is turned into a moving statue with the eyes of a Roman sculpture while *Le Sang d'un poète* opens with a prelude in which Cocteau himself appears as something of a sculptural hybrid. It comes as no surprise then that Cocteau was also attracted to wax figures—in *Le Musée Grévin* (Jacques Demy & Jean Masson, 1958), he staged a remarkable encounter with his own wax image.

Finally, the Pygmalionist dream of the statue coming to life also defines various forms of "performance" and "body art" that marks the European neo-avant-gardes of the 1960s and 1970s. Gilbert & George, for instance, presented themselves as "living sculptures" in various group shows in 1969 and 1970 that also included works by Broodthaers.[19] Last but not least, Broodthaers himself was famously declared a certified "scultura vivente" by Piero Manzoni on the occasion of the Italian artist's solo exhibition in Brussels in February 1962.[20]

INTERVIEW WITH A CORPSE

Cocteau's confrontation with his wax effigy brings us back to Broodthaers's encounter with a wax figure. In 1964, in the first year of his career of a visual artist, Broodthaers created *En souvenir de Cocteau*, a tribute to the French poet, artist, and filmmaker who had died the previous year, consisting of a collage containing various forms and objects, including a small torso evoking a fragment of a white classical statue. In *Le Sang d'un poète*, Cocteau's voice-over inquires, "Is it not crazy to wake up statues so suddenly from the sleep of centuries?" One could ask this question when watching Broodthaers's *Figures of Wax* as well.

In the film, Bentham's mummified body is fragmented by means of a series of close-ups. This filmic fragmentation, however, does not really mobilize Bentham's body. The editing rhythm is rather slow and steady. Broodthaers does not try to animate Bentham by means of camera movements, montage, or light effects in the way some mid-century art documentaries on sculpture such as *Visual Variations on Noguchi* (Marie Menken, 1945), *Thorvaldsen* (Carl Theodor Dreyer, 1949), and *L'Enfer de Rodin* (Henri Alekan, 1957) attempted to set in motion sculptures by Noguchi, Thorvaldsen, or Rodin respectively.²¹ On the contrary, Broodthaers rather emphasizes the stillness of the philosopher's body, confronting it with his own bodily presence, sitting in front of the philosopher, asking him questions, smoking, and reading a newspaper. However, the interaction between the artist and the philosopher is minimal. The setup is somewhat reminiscent of the scenes showing static characters in the vicinity of statues in modernist arthouse cinema of the 1960s.²² Films such as *Viaggio in Italia* (Roberto Rossellini, 1954), *Le Mépris* (Jean-Luc Godard, 1963), *L'Année dernière à Marienbad* (Alain Resnais, 1961), and *Gertrud* (Carl Theodor Dreyer, 1964) present their characters in static poses evoking a sculptural presence while statues are explored by a highly mobile camera, their juxtaposition or approximation invariably resulting in an enigmatic atmosphere.

Broodthaers plays on a similar mood of mystery, stressing Bentham's immobility as well as his hermetic muteness. Without the use of direct sound but with the help of subtitles, we see Broodthaers talking to the lifeless body of Bentham, making futile and absurd attempts to interview the deceased philosopher. While the voice-over commentary instructs us on Bentham and his philosophy, we are looking at a silent film whose protagonist is not able to talk. Broodthaers asks the philosopher:

> If you have a statement to make
> please do so
> If you have a secret
> tell me
> or a special message
> give an indication.
> If you wish to protest.
> I promise to keep it
> ... Or ...
> you prefer to dream?
> a new statement
> a secret
> a special message
> a protest
> or an artistic idea ...
> a dream.

While an initial version of the screenplay contained a full dialogue in which Bentham marveled at the apparatus of cinema and desires to see a film, Bentham, in the actual film, does not answer any of Broodthaers's questions and remains silent—a fact that is emphasized by a panning shot starting at Broodthaers's mouth with his moving lips to the mute, dumb face of Bentham.²³ In addition, the silence and noncommunication of the philosopher is emphasized by

Broodthaers using his mouth to smoke a cigarette in front of the indifferent Bentham. Despite the attempts at interaction and despite his representation through the dynamic medium of film, Bentham remains still, mute, aloof as a mysterious statue.

The setup evokes the conventions of a television interview but it is also completely in line with the imaginary interviews that Broodthaers created in his capacities of both writer and artist: his 1967 imaginary interview with René Magritte, his 1970 audio-interview with a cat, and his encounter with the just-deceased poet Marcel Lecomte, whose profile is contained in a dozen of canopic-like preserve jars next to a coffin in *Le Salon noir* (1966), Broodthaers's installation at Galerie Saint Laurent in 1966.[24] The interview with Bentham isn't thus Broodthaers's first encounter with the Dead, enforcing the necromantic associations that are inherently connected with mummies and wax figures.[25]

Consisting of his skeleton padded out with hay and dressed in his clothes with a wax head fitted with some of his own hair, Bentham combines the wax figure, the Surrealist mannequin, the uncanny mummy, and the statue—because that is what he actually is. A utilitarian philosopher, Bentham conceived the usefulness of people after their death. In his pamphlet *Auto-Icon; or Further Uses of the Dead to the Living*, Bentham suggested that all persons could become their own statue or "Auto-Icon," a monument to themselves.[26] Bentham's body thus establishes its own statue, his "Auto-Icon." He became his own image—a fact that must have appealed to Broodthaers as Bentham became an imprint or a cast of himself, like a mussel and a mold (*le moule* and *la moule* in French). Bentham's auto-icon might be an icon or symbol but is first and foremost an index—it is interesting to note here that both Julius von Schlosser and André Bazin saw the wax figure and the death mask (often made in wax), with their indexical relation to the deceased, as among the origins of photography and film.[27]

BRANDSCAPE MANNEQUINS

Last but not least, *Figures of Wax* (the plural in the title is significant) connects Bentham's immobile body, which only features in the film's middle section and its final shots, to other bodies, including that of the artist himself, situated in the streets of London. These scenes connect the mummified philosopher from the Enlightenment, enclosed in a time capsule set aside in a university corridor, to the everyday spaces of the contemporary city, though the voice-over warns us that "although this film was made between the two elections of 1974, any identification with reality is entirely incidental and is not the intention of the author." Both the Bentham scenes and the street sequences are connected through the continuous soundtrack with a voice-over commentary as well as piano music (played by Broodthaers himself) consisting of scales and variations on extracts

Figures of Wax. 16mm. 1974. Courtesy of the Walker Art Center's Ruben/Bentson Moving Image Collection. © Estate of Marcel Broodthaers, c/o SABAM Belgium 2024

from Beethoven's *Mondscheinsonate* (1800) and Chopin's *Marche funèbre* (1827), which connects to the morbid image of the philosopher's body.[28] A significant part of the film consists of footage of the London city center, reminiscent of 1970s color street photography by artists such as William Eggleston, Stephen Shore, and particularly Joel Meyerowitz, who often visualized pedestrians isolated in the bright light of the afternoon sun.

Broodthaers tellingly focuses on mannequin dolls, a Surrealist staple evoking a fetish, both in the Freudian and Marxist sense of the term, linking desire to consumerism. Like Bentham's body enclosed in his cabinet, the mannequins are locked in the window displays of shops, their frozen bodies juxtaposed to those of passing pedestrians in the middle of the metropolitan bustle. By juxtaposing Bentham's body to these mannequins, *Figures of Wax* takes up the argument that Broodthaers already developed in his 1961 travel report of London, in which he links the wax figures at Madame Tussaud's to the luxury shops in Bond Street:

> Bond Street: an ideal place for meditating on glorious artistic alienations. [...] Bond Street is an artery lined with luxury boutiques. Before it crumbles into ruin under the pressure of peripheral poverty and the power of time—let's wait a bit longer—it should be put in Madame Tussaud's. Minks scurry along the pavements in autumn and winter, and silk umbrellas in every season.[29]

Given this perspective, the film title does not only refer to Bentham but also to the mannequins, which are not only still and lifeless but are also petrified images of commodified women. Their presence is telling in a film in which the voice-over tells us that Bentham advocated for the right to vote of every adult, including women. Broodthaers even deploys the Pygmalionist powers of cinema, intercutting close-ups of the dolls with close-ups of faces of "real" women in static poses.

Furthermore, Broodthaers presents the mannequins and the shop windows as strategies of visual display. They are objects of our gaze, but they also organize, structure, and focus it. Broodthaers plays on this by also including close-ups of the eyes of the mannequins as well as an over-the-shoulder-shot of a mannequin: we are looking at the street from within the shop window, as if we and the mannequin are able to return the gaze of a man who is looking inside.

Both types of beings, mannequins on the one hand and shoppers on the other, occasionally interact not only through the film's editing that evokes the eyeline matches of classical cinema but also by visual echoes. The stripes of a scarf of a passing woman recurs for instance in those of one of the pieces of clothing worn by a mannequin.

By drawing our attention to mechanisms of visual display, Broodthaers emphasizes the interdependency of mannequins and shop windows. Like mannequin dolls, shop windows are instruments of commodity fetishism, cherished by early modernists such as Eugène Atget, whose photographs of mannequins in display windows feature in various Surrealist journals, such as *La Révolution Surréaliste* and *Variétés*. Stéphane Mallarmé, one of Broodthaers's key points of reference, expressed his amazement at shop windows and the new visual culture of merchandising in an 1892 essay entitled "Étalages."[30] Not much later, Marcel Duchamp's ready-mades, another key reference for Broodthaers, pointed at the similarities between the display of commodities in shop windows and the isolation of the artwork in the modern museum. Since the late nineteenth century, shop windows became an inherent part of the new environment of the modern, industrial metropolis. Its broad avenues, lined with the new facilities of consumption such as shop windows and department stores, not only facilitated the optimal mobility of persons and commodities, they also changed the city into a spatial and visual system of control and surveillance.

A realm subjected to an all-encompassing gaze or an omnipresent eye is a theme that Broodthaers addressed in his sculptural installation *La Tour visuelle* (1966), consisting of a stack of magazine cutout eyes encased in glass jars. For Broodthaers, there is a close connection between the conception of Jeremy Bentham's famous Panopticon, drawings of which are shown briefly in the film, and the development of modern capitalism and its reliance on visual display—*Figures of Wax* explicitly connects the optical devices of the panopticon and the shop window. Made in 1974, the film coincides with the rediscovery of Bentham's panopticon by authors such as psychoanalyst Jacques-Alain Miller and philosopher Michel Foucault, who both understood the panopticon not as a building type but rather as a mechanism of power.[31] An eminent practitioner of the so-called institutional critique of museums highly interested in the institutionalized and disciplinary conventions of art and its display, Broodthaers must have been intrigued by Bentham's panopticon, an optical device that is also an instrument of control and social conditioning, invented at the start of industrial capitalism. As the voice-over commentary states, Bentham was a major source of inspiration for John Stuart Mill and David Ricardo, who laid the foundation of classical liberalism.

Figures of Wax situates Bentham, enclosed in his cabinet and separated from the everyday like an Egyptian mummy in his sarcophagus, in a realm marked by consumer capitalism, where, according to Karl Marx's famous phrasing, "all that is solid melts into air." Broodthaers dwells on the reflections of moving traffic in mirroring surfaces—a staple shot of numerous city symphonies such as Walther Ruttmann's *Berlin: Die Sinfonie der Großstadt* (1927). In particular, the film focuses on the eerie reflections in the shop windows and on a landscape marked by a surface culture consisting of empty signs. *Figures of Wax*, for instance, contains footage of a man carrying a sign and a woman carrying a stack of newspapers; there are inscriptions everywhere, in line with Broodthaers's fascination for texts, words, letters, inscriptions, and writing attempts in most of his films. "Take Left," a sign marked on the street surface appears at the beginning of the film. Not unlike Hollis Frampton's evocation of New York in *Zorns Lemma* (1970), inscriptions appear on pavements, façades, buses, and windows, most notably a window of a discount shop entirely covered by inscriptions—in several shots, Broodthaers focuses on texts written on glass panes, a motif that recurs in *Crime à Cologne* (1971) and *M.T.L. (D.T.H.)* (1970). In his city symphony of postindustrial London, urban space is transformed into a *brandscape*, a landscape of empty signs, exemplified by the inserts of the US dollar, British pound, and Deutschmark signs, emphasizing the modern metropolis as the site of the circulation of money—as Georg Simmel defined the modern metropolis in his influential 1903 essay "Die Großstädte und das Geistesleben."[32] For Simmel, who also wrote *Philosophie des Geldes* in 1900, the hyperstimulation of the senses associated with modern city life was inherently connected with the reorganization of urban space in the service of capitalism, which stimulated the increasingly faster circulation of people, ideas, goods, and commodities. Shot not only on location on the pavement of the shops in Oxford Street but also near the roundabout at Moorgate, in the heart of London's banking district, *Figures of Wax* explicitly links the footage of the city of money and commodity fetishism to the phantasmagoria of the wax figure by the newspaper that Broodthaers is holding while attempting to interview Bentham. It is a copy of *The Guardian* of February 9, 1974, with a headline stating "World Money Disorder Sets Gold and Silver Soaring," evoking a world affected by rampant inflation, rising oil prices, and social unrest after the dissolution of the Breton Woods agreements in 1971. It is the condition of late capitalism determined by a financial regime of freely floating fiat currencies that Broodthaers perfectly addressed in works featuring exchange rates, such as *Poème-Change-Exchange-Wechsel* (1973) consisting of a series of tables of signatures. Highly interested in the decorative fate of reified art objects, Broodthaers, an avid reader of György Lukács and student of Lucien Goldmann, merges consumer capitalism of the 1970s with the uncanny sphere of mummies and wax figures.[33] Enclosed in his cabinet, the embalmed philosopher seems to enjoy his spectral presence in the streets of London filled with consumers and mannequin dolls. Given this perspective, films such as *Figures of Wax* and *Monsieur Teste* seem to resonate less with the utopian dreams of the industrialized modernity than with, as Eric de Bruyn has noted, "fantasies of an automated, post-labor future ushered in by the digital networks of neoliberal capitalism."[34] Rather than a Pygmalion who brings wax figures and mannequins to life, Broodthaers emphasizes the sedation of the shopping pedestrians in the London streets.

NOTES

1. On slowness and stasis in experimental and modernist cinema, see Justin Remes, *Motion(less) Pictures: The Cinema of Stasis* (New York: Columbia University Press, 2015).
2. The most detailed discussions of *Figures of Wax* can be found in Cathleen Ann Chaffee, "Figures of Wax: Marcel Broodthaers in Conversation with Jeremy Bentham" (master's thesis, Courtauld Institute, University of London, 2001); and Shana G. Lindsay, "Mortui Docent Vivos: Jeremy Bentham and Marcel Broodthaers in *Figures of Wax*," *Oxford Art Journal* 36, no. 1 (March 2013): 93–107. See also "Figures of Wax," in *Marcel Broodthaers: Cinéma* (Barcelona: Fundacio Antoni Tapies, 1997), 268–75.
3. The film's credits further mention: Camera: Clive Meyer and John Hardy; Editing: Noel Crain; Commentary: Charlotte Hardman.
4. Bentham's preserved body in a cabinet can still be found today at University College London, although it has been relocated a few times since 1975. Today, the location of the cabinet is not the same as the one shown in the film. See "The Auto-Icon: Bentham's Mortal Remains Have Been at UCL since 1850," https://www.ucl.ac.uk/culture/auto-icon/auto-icon.
5. Marcel Broodthaers in a letter to Jost Herbig (20 May 1973), included in *Marcel Broodthaers: Cinéma*, 274.
6. Chaffee, *Figures of Wax*, 13.
7. Chaffee, *Figures of Wax*, 3.
8. On Madame Tussaud, see Pamela Pilbeam, *Madame Tussaud and the History of Waxworks* (London: Continuum, 2006); and Kate Berridge, *Madame Tussaud: A Life in Wax* (New York: HarperCollins, 2006).
9. Marcel Broodthaers, "Un poète en voyage ... à Londres," *Journal des Beaux Arts* 942 (23 June 1961): 11. English translation in Gloria Moure (ed.), *Marcel Broodthaers: Collected Writings* (Barcelona: Ediciones Polígrafa, 2013), 56.
10. On wax figure cabinets, see Roberta Panzanelli (ed.), *Ephemeral Bodies: Wax Sculpture and the Human Figure* (Getty Research Institute: Los Angeles, 2008) and the theme issue "Theorizing Wax: On the Meaning of a Disappearing Medium" of *Oxford Journal* 36, no. 1 (March 2013).
11. Vito Adriaensens, "Anatomy of an Ovidian Cinema: Mysteries of the Wax Museum," in Steven Jacobs, Susan Felleman, Vito Adriaensens, and Lisa Colpaert, *Screening Statues: Sculpture and Cinema* (Edinburgh: Edinburgh University Press, 2017), 84–100.
12. See *Variétés* 1, no. 4 (August 1928). On the Musée Spitzner, see Pierre Spitzner, *Catalogue du musée anatomique anthropologique et ethnographique du Dr P. Spitzner* (Paris: Dr P. Spitzner, 1896); and Christiane Py et Cécile Vidart, "Les musées d'anatomie sur les champs de foire," *Actes de la recherche en sciences sociales* (1985): 3–10.
13. See Marc Rombaut, *Paul Delvaux* (New York: Rizzoli, 1990), 28–29; and David Scott, *Paul Delvaux: Surrealizing the Nude* (London: Reaktion Books, 1992), 60–64. Broodthaers photographed Delvaux in 1966. Broodthaers also wrote on Wiertz, see Marcel Broodthaers, "Wiertz Museum" (1974) in *Broodthaers: Collected Writings*, 443.
14. Paul Valéry, *Mr. Teste* (Paris: Gallimard, 1926).
15. Susan Felleman, "The Mystery ... The Blood ... The Age of Gold: Sculpture in Surrealist and Surreal Cinema," in Jacobs et al., *Screening Statues*, 46–64.
16. Victor Stoichita, *The Pygmalion Effect: From Ovid to Hitchcock* (Chicago: University of Chicago Press, 2008). See also Kenneth Gross, *The Dream of the Moving Statue* (University Park: Penn State University Press, 2006).

17. Steven Jacobs and Vito Adriaensens, "The Sculptor's Dream: Living Statues in Early Cinema," in Jacobs et al., *Screening Statues*, 29–45; Lynda Nead, *The Haunted Gallery: Painting, Photography, Film c. 1900* (New Haven: Yale University Press, 2008).
18. Jean Cocteau, "Good Luck to Cinémonde" (1953) and "The Myth of Woman" (1953), in André Bernard and Claude Gauteur (eds.), *Jean Cocteau: The Art of Cinema* (London: Marion Byars, 1992), 34 and 123.
19. Both Broodthaers and Gilbert & George participated in an event at Düsseldorf's Kunsthalle in February 1970 and in the Sulima gallery in Berlin in the autumn of 1970.
20. Isabelle Graw, "The Poet's Seduction: Six Theses on Marcel Broodthaers's Contemporary Relevance," *Texte zur Kunst 103* (September 2016): 48–73.
21. Steven Jacobs, "Carving Cameras on Thorvaldsen and Rodin: Mid-Twentieth-Century Documentaries on Sculpture," in Jacobs et al., *Screening Statues*, 65–83.
22. Suzanne Liandrat-Guiges, *Cinéma et sculpture: Un Aspet de la modernité des années soixante* (Paris: L'Harmattan, 2002); Steven Jacobs and Lisa Colpaert, "From Pompeii to Marienbad: Classical Sculptures in Postwar European Modernist Cinema," in Jacobs et al., *Screening Statues*, 118–36.
23. "Figures of Wax," in *Marcel Broodthaers: Cinéma* (Barcelona: Fundacio Antoni Tapies, 1997), 271.
24. Marcel Broodthaers, "Interview imaginaire de René Magritte," *Journal des Arts Plastiques* 30 (January 1967), included in *Broodthaers: Collected Writings*, 164–66; Marcel Broodthaers, "Interview with a Cat" (1970) in *Broodthaers: Collected Writings*, 288–89; *Marcel Broodthaers - Le salon noir 1966* (Venice: Palazzo Grassi, 2014).
25. Chaffee stipulates that Bhikhu Parekh's *Bentham's Political Thought* (1973), of which Broodthaers owned a copy, contains a dialogue between Bentham and an imaginary interviewer. See Chaffee, *Figures of Wax*, 10.
26. Jeremy Bentham, "Auto-Icon; or Further Uses of the Dead to the Living. A Fragment," posthumously published in 1842. See also C. Haffenden, "Every Man His Own Statue: Bentham's Body as DIY Monument," in *Every Man His Own Monument: Self-Monumentalizing in Romantic Britain* (Uppsala: Acta Universitatis Upsaliensis, 2018), 40–91. See also Alessandra Violi, "Glass, Mixed Media, Stone: The Bodily Stuffs of Suspended Animation," in Alessandra Violi, Barbara Grespi, Andrea Pinotti, and Pietro Conte (eds.), *Bodies of Stone in the Media, Visual Culture, and the Arts* (Amsterdam: Amsterdam University Press, 2020), 261–76.
27. See Julius von Schlosser, "History of Portraiture in Wax," in Roberta Panzanelli (ed.), *Ephemeral Bodies: Wax Sculpture and the Human Figure* (Getty Research Institute: Los Angeles, 2008); and André Bazin, "Ontologie de l'image photographique" (1945), in *Qu'est-ce que le cinéma?* (Paris: Cerf, 1976), 11–19.
28. Chaffee, *Figures of Wax*, 9.
29. *Broodthaers: Collected Writings*, 56.
30. Christophe Wall-Romana, *Cinepoetry: Imaginary Cinemas in French Poetry* (New York: Fordham University Press, 2013).
31. Jacques-Alain Miller, "Jeremy Bentham's Panoptic Device" (1973), *October 41* (Summer, 1987): 3–29; Michel Foucault, *Surveiller et punir: Naissance de la prison* (Paris: Gallimard, 1975).
32. Georg Simmel, "Die Großstädte und das Geistesleben" (1903), in *Georg Simmel: Gesamtausgabe*. edited by Otthein Rammstedt (Frankfurt am Main: Suhrkamp, 1995), vol. 7, 1, 116–31. See also Georg Simmel, *Philosophie des Geldes* (Leipzig: Duncker & Humblot, 1900).
33. In 1969–70, Broodthaers attended Lucien Goldmann's seminar at the University of Brussels. See also Chaffee, *Figures of Wax*, 16.
34. Eric de Bruyn, "Marcel Broodthaers," *Artforum* 55, no. 9 (May 2017).

IN THE EYE OF THE STORM
BERLIN ODER EIN TRAUM MIT SAHNE (1974)

Raf Wollaert

> Should freedom ever—which God forbid—vanish from the entire world,
> a German dreamer would discover her again in his dreams.
> —Heinrich Heine

"The definition of Berlin is as fragile as that of Art," Marcel Broodthaers wrote in an unpublished note from 1974 that bears the arcane title "BERLIN, EVERYTHING or The Eye of the Storm, *Feuilleton*."[1] Penned at the time he stayed in this city in the context of a DAAD artist residency, the statement ties the artist's biography to the prime concern haunting his work and thought toward the end of his life: art and the artist's autonomy, jeopardized by the entwined forces of reactionary politics and reification. Broodthaers's Berlin residence, spanning between April 1974 and March 1975, coincides with a critical stage in his oeuvre, which saw the development of a series of wayward retrospectives, known as the *Décors*. Showcasing earlier works along appropriated objects in ever changing, site-specific constellations, they radically defy the retrospective's typical aim to consolidate and merchandize the artist's oeuvre and persona. At the same time, this so-called *Décor* period also yielded one of the artist's most intriguing films, titled *Berlin oder ein Traum mit Sahne* (Berlin or a Dream with Whipped Cream) (1974).

In this film, an ostensible portrait of Broodthaers's life in Berlin informs a strongly allegorical and intertextually coded critique of art's degeneration into commodity or cultural-political maneuvering. Since the structural powers at the root of this disenchantment are his primary target, *Berlin*'s significance falls squarely within the institutional critique that the artist embarked upon with *Musée d'Art Moderne, Département des Aigles* and revamped under the aegis of *Décor*. That Broodthaers presented a slapstick-infused allegory to channel his stand is in itself rather unremarkable—others of his late films, such as *Eau de Cologne* and *Figures of Wax*, produced in the same year, blend lighthearted comedy with symbolical depth too. Moreover, the film features many of the artist's usual tropes, such as the bourgeois interior, the potted palm tree, the parrot, maps, or nautical imagery. What sets *Berlin* apart is its contemplation of

Broodthaers's familiar concerns and themes through the prisms of his precarious health condition—making it perhaps one of his most personal films—and that of German Romanticism, a motif that only recurs sporadically throughout his late work. By unravelling this intricate mesh of sub- and intertexts and reconstructing the context of Broodthaers's Berlin residency, this essay analyzes *Berlin*'s critical agenda.

"I AM AT THE END OF THE WORLD. FINALLY ... THERE ARE BARGES"[2]

After a journey that had taken him over the North Sea and twice across the iron curtain, Broodthaers arrived in April 1974 in the Berlin apartment that would serve as his abode for about a year. Located as he was on the banks of the Spree that picturesquely winds through the city, barges passing down the river must have been among the first things that he would notice at his new home base. It was the second time that Broodthaers settled in Germany, after having lived in Düsseldorf between 1970 and 1972. Since he had traded the latter for London, a return to Germany seemed all but likely, as he hoped that "no one would notice him there for at least two years."[3] This resolution, however, soon turned out to be beyond Karl Ruhrberg, the former director of the Düsseldorf Kunsthalle, who invited him to participate in the DAAD (Deutscher akademischer Austauschdienst; German Academic Exchange Service) artist-in-residence program in Berlin. Broodthaers accepted, yet only on the condition that he would be allowed to live outside the artists' community—Künstlerhaus Bethanien, still existing today—that Ruhrberg recommended him to join. Broodthaers would imagine his stay differently, "perhaps in the old-fashioned way," providing the following reason:

> I am really in need of solitude. I am not in marvelous health. (I don't drink, a factor that makes life in the kind of micro-society that would develop in these studios quite difficult.) Solitude also allows more direct contact with the city (and I am already scared at the thought of these discussions on art and their uses.)[4]

Despite these reservations, he nonetheless did already suggest some avenues to explore when staying in Berlin:

> But I do desire to spend some time in Berlin. I would like to make a film there about museums (mainly Charlottenburg and the basements of Dahlem where they work on collections and restorations), on museums and museography as I conceive it—from a double negation. I don't know what form this project could take. I'll have to see. There is also the Island of Peacocks [Pfaueninsel] the romantic of which could be depicted as a

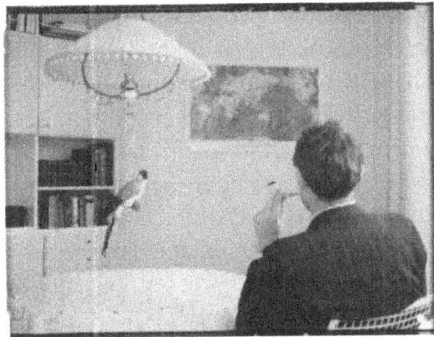

Berlin oder ein Traum mit Sahne. 16mm. 1974. Courtesy of the Walker Art Center's Ruben/Bentson Moving Image Collection. © Estate of Marcel Broodthaers, c/o SABAM Belgium 2024

character, or better still as a fundamental décor of the city. In short, attempting a synthesis of the city and isolation, not with a dramatic perspective, but with all the positive things isolation can bring in relation to the technological development of cities at the heart of the economic circuit.[5]

Broodthaers's proposal fully aligns with his usual imagery and concerns. However, none of the sites mentioned would eventually appear in *Berlin*, which essentially ended up being a kind of *Kammerspielfilm*, since the lion's share of its plot unfolds within the living room of his apartment. Nevertheless, "a synthesis of the city of the city and isolation" would still make for a proper caption. Also, the romantic atmosphere Broodthaers mentioned definitely seeped into the film. The only two characters it features, namely "the artist," Broodthaers himself, and "the girl," played by his daughter Marie-Puck, first enter the picture as *Rückenfiguren*, a staple of (German) romantic painting. The former daydreams at the sight of a map of the ocean floor, while the latter beholds the Spree through an open window. As the constant, urban traffic flow outside levels off to a hypnotic murmur, sporadically interrupted by the bellowing horn of a ship, the artist and the girl remain mired in boredom, engaging in mundane activities under the golden light of a lazy late summer afternoon. The film's mild color palette, in harmony with Jörg Jeshel's gentle cinematography, imparts it with a decidedly painterly ambiance, which begs the question to which extent this domestic reverie paints an accurate picture of Broodthaers's life in Berlin. Like its cast, the film's dramatic action is kept to a minimum, as it remains basically limited to a succession of two isolated slapstick gags, interspersed with long takes from the window showing barges gently floating down the river.

THE SPIRIT OF *DÉCOR*

The first sequence of *Berlin* revolves to a large extent around the two characters' interactions with a limited set of props punctuating the living room: the girl can be seen watering and moving a potted palm tree, while the artist smokes a pipe. Ultimately, the scene has its comic denouement in the latter's bewilderment over an egg found on the lace-covered table he is sitting at, supposedly left by a stuffed parrot perched above it. These props fulfill a significant dual purpose. At first sight, they enter the stage as unmistakable clichés of bourgeois decoration and divertissement from the fin-de-siècle era,[6] while at the same time revealing obvious connections to other works by the artist, previously featured as either exhibits or props in films. Recurring as a hallmark in almost every *Décor*, the potted palm tree is the example par excellence in this sense.[7] In fact, the ambiguous role of the objects in *Berlin* exemplifies Broodthaers's concept of the "spirit of the décor," that is to say his intention "to restore the object, [either a previous work or found object such as the palm tree,] to its real function and not to transform it into a work of art."[8] This strategy is fundamental to the critical enterprise of the aforementioned series of exhibitions he staged during his final years. Broodthaers affirmed that using objects as film props indeed qualifies as giving them such a "real function."[9] In two films created during the same period, *Un Jardin d'hiver (A B C)* (1974) and *La Bataille de Waterloo* (1975), the exhibition space itself actually served as the film set, while the latter exhibit consisted almost entirely of rented props from a film set warehouse.

Obviously, the filmic connotation of the word "décor"—a film set—cannot go unnoticed in this context. Many scholars, including Cathleen Chaffee and Rachel Haidu, have emphasized the evident cinematic dimension of the *Décor* retrospectives and their intrinsic entanglement with Broodthaers's cinema. Film assumed a key role within these exhibitions, while some of the latter even developed out of an initial project for a mere screening.[10] According to Haidu, "the *Décors* provide a framework in which apparently autonomous objects such as films are broken down into a system of art production that recursively points to the relation among exhibition, production, reproduction, and retrospective. [...] Cinema, itself a crucial medium for Broodthaers, is in the *Décors* mobilized to reset the terms of experience of 'a work.'"[11]

Broodthaers's remediation of the (art) object and exhibition through cinema works in two ways, since, many times, the latter would not only fulfill the role of a (suggested) film set but in some cases also that of a screening venue. *Un Jardin d'hiver (A B C)* was both shot and screened in the staged environment it was named after, a winter garden assembled of folding chairs, palm trees, nineteenth-century zoological prints, and a closed-circuit video allowing visitors to observe themselves circulating the exhibition space on a monitor.[12] As the exhibit's objecthood collapses into representation, the public finds itself beholding and performing at once. This defamiliarization effect was further exacerbated through the mise en abyme that emerged as soon as this film was projected on a tripod screen placed at the center of the very environment it represented.

Cinema provides only one example of the *Décors*' general deployment of multiple *dispositives* utilizing a form of feedback to refract the exhibition's monolithic experience into a myriad of simultaneous perspectives, in an effort to undercut the beholder's panoptical oversight.[13] This approach appears to resonate with the practices of Post-Minimalist artists such as Dan Graham and Bruce Nauman, whose criticism, like that of Broodthaers, addressed the repressive aspects of established institutions and the emerging mass media society. Their environments, too, subjectify the passive spectator as an active performer by returning their gaze through mirrors and video feedback.[14] However, if Graham and Nauman only moderately confused Minimalism's "presentist" or "literalist" phenomenology through the injection of a "just past" or "immediate future,"[15] and furthermore remained indebted to its slick aesthetics overall, Broodthaers's *Décors* stand out by their radical insistence on the historical preconditions of both objecthood and spectatorship. As the direct heirs of the *Musée d'Art Moderne*, the *Décors* offer an archaeology of the formalized interactions between the artist and public that take place within the walls of the museum. Within this critical endeavor, the transcendental subject is transformed into a figure of historical and political contingencies.

Though never noted before, there may well be a similar, albeit more subtle, reflexive dimension to *Berlin*'s initial presentation during *Invitation pour une exposition bourgeoise*, the *Décor* exhibition that concluded Broodthaers's Berlin residency and opened at the Nationalgalerie in February 1975. As in *Un Jardin d'hiver*, a puzzling overlap between the film's site of production and display is crucial in this regard. Significantly, instead of the exhibition hall or an assembled environment, the actual museum cafeteria, known as the "Erfrischungsraum" (Refreshments Space) served as the venue where *Berlin* was first screened.[16] It is at this point that the film's second scene becomes significant.

COFFEE AND CAKE

After a brief afternoon slumber, the artist straightens himself back up at the table, apparently to honor an über-German tradition: the typical afternoon indulgence of "Kaffee und Kuchen" (coffee and cake). As the girl retrieves pastries and a tray of whipped cream from a liquor cabinet, the artist dons his reading glasses and opens the newspaper. Oddly enough, a whole crowd seems to have suddenly gathered outside the view of the camera, since the once serene ambiance on the soundtrack has yielded to the off-screen din of a busy Konditorei (pastry shop). This second sequence culminates with the image of the artist unruffled trying to read his newspaper through his glasses, now entirely covered with a generous coating of whipped cream. According to Bruce Jenkins, this sight gag serves a "metonymic signifier" for the cream pie trope in slapstick cinema, a genre Broodthaers also referenced in several other works such as *La Pluie* (1969), *Eau de Cologne* (1974), or *Figures of Wax* (1974). Obviously, the coffee and cake ritual that the artist performs solitarily in his living room parallels the activities of many a museumgoer either before or after visiting an exhibition. The lively soundtrack of *Berlin*'s second scene supposedly reflected the animated museum cafeteria rather than the placid atmosphere of Broodthaers's apartment. As the film's already confused diegetic and non-diegetic soundtracks are blended with the actual ambient noise of its screening location with Surrealist panache, the fourth wall is effectively breached. Even beyond the confines of the exhibition hall, the museum visitor is thus subjectified as the performer of a formalized social custom, which is highlighted once more by *Berlin*'s closing scene showing middle-class locals entering a typical outdoor café surrounded by palm trees.

However, in addition to serving as an alienating device and a slapstick trope, the artist indulging in *Kaffee und Kuchen* also channels a very personal, deeply melancholic subtext. Despite *Berlin*'s distinct documentary semblance, it is, in fact, unlikely that the artist would have actually enjoyed cream-topped pastries as an afternoon treat. It is clear from his letters and the accounts of his contemporaries that when arriving in Berlin, Broodthaers was already greatly affected by a lingering liver condition that restricted him from consuming alcohol or rich foods like pastries. Art critic Pierre Sterckx recalls how Broodthaers would "confront the forbidden delights that had become poisonous to him" by selecting a typical Brussels patisserie as the place to meet journalists.[17] He considered this a gesture of witty defiance, rather than one of outright cynicism. Nevertheless, there is no question that Broodthaers's strict diet placed a strain on his social life and mobility during his time in Berlin. As mentioned in the letter to Ruhrberg, the doctor's order to abstain from alcohol contributed significantly to his self-imposed isolation, as he knew all too well that artist gatherings were often heavily boozed. Although he would always approach the art scene with a certain distance, wary to be absorbed by any reductive form of collective movement, *Berlin* particularly depicts how his apartment had become a true hermitage. Given this perspective, the film's peculiar conflation between private and public, as materialized by the comical transformation of liquor cabinet into a pastry counter and the apartment into a coffee bar or dining hall, is all the more telling. Broodthaers's "synthesis of the city and isolation" may align with the demands imposed by his fragile health but is definitely at odds with the prevailing philosophy of artist residencies, which typically encourage immersive engagement with the local artist scene and the specific traits of the environment. The DAAD artist-in-residency program was no exception to this, as it was conceived to "promote what has always been a matter of course in artistic centers: intense communication, pluralist offerings, and critical debate."[18] After all, the program's primary objective was to revive West Berlin's cosmopolitan allure and restore its once-thriving avant-garde artist society, which had suffered from the cultural desertification under the Nazi regime and the city's subsequent isolation from the Western world due to Cold War geopolitics.[19] Needless to say that such an incentive toward "the confrontation with the local scene, encounters with colleagues, and discussion" appears utterly irreconcilable with Broodthaers's desire to exactly steer clear of the artist community and evade every discussion on art.[20] Thus, through its portrayal of this tension between isolation and exchange, *Berlin* does have a documentary value when it comes to the artist's biography.

THE LAST VOYAGE

As expressed in the letter to Ruhrberg, Broodthaers believed that solitude, rather than social exchange, would allow him to connect with the city that after all held great appeal to him. This conviction evokes the image of the flâneur, who relishes blending in with the urban crowd while at the same time retaining a sense of detachment from it. However, his illness would often render him greatly immobile. Moreover, his photographs from this period suggest that his strolls were mostly limited to the immediate surroundings of this residence.[21] Instead of the mentioned romantic sites, they essentially depict the same elements that the artist would observe through his apartment's windows, that is the scenery of the Spree River, which is minutely portrayed in *Berlin*. Broodthaers's fascination with the river and its barges becomes evident from the very moment he set foot in the city, which is clear from their frequent appearance in his writings during that period. Interestingly, a letter to Belgian painter Émile Salkin, one of his longtime friends, casts this fixation within the artist's overall penchant for maritime themes. While fishes, stormy seas, and water in general feature prominently in Broodthaers's (filmic) oeuvre at large, this interest may be expressed most paradigmatically in the famous book and film edition *A Voyage on the North Sea* (1974). In the first part of the letter to Salkin, written in December 1973 while Broodthaers was confined to a London hospital bed, he reveals, obviously referring to the latter work, that he is busy "fabricating a little travel novel in images."[22] It appears that he failed to mail the letter promptly, as a brief, second passage was added as late as April 1974, thus after he had already moved to Berlin: "I live on the banks of the Spree, where petrol barges pass by."[23] Interestingly, along with his place of residence, Broodthaers's penchant for nautical imagery seems to have shifted from seafaring to inland navigation. In the light of this letter in which he also speaks out about his health prospects, which, he admits, look "rather awful,"[24] the figure of the ship becomes the object of *Sehnsucht*, simultaneously offering a source of distraction while frustratingly symbolizing the freedom of movement that the artist precisely lacked at that time. The image of Broodthaers that is conveyed here, by the way, is strikingly reminiscent of one of his other films conceived in the same period: *The Last Voyage* (ca. 1972–76).[25] As a silent succession of early twentieth-century magic lantern slides that were originally meant to illustrate an eponymous folk song, it shows the final moments of an old, bedridden man staring through a window that opens onto ocean. Assisted by his daughter, he contemplates both his life— the paraphernalia in his room suggest a sailor's past—and destiny through a galleon at sea disappearing behind the horizon along with a setting sun: "I shall go out with the tide lass, Out on the turn of the tide, Far over there, beyond the sea, Where there is waiting a Home for me; I'm not afraid of the thought, dear lass, Dark through the deep and wide, His love will steer me, Home, when I go, Out on the turn of the tide!"[26]

For the elderly man as much as Broodthaers, the window may be considered a para-cinematic framing device introducing the (minimal) movement of ships in a stilled environment. In this sense, the latter becomes a structural figure to investigate the crux of cinema, perpetually hovering between stasis and motion. This thread informs the artist's filmic oeuvre at large, yet intriguingly manifests

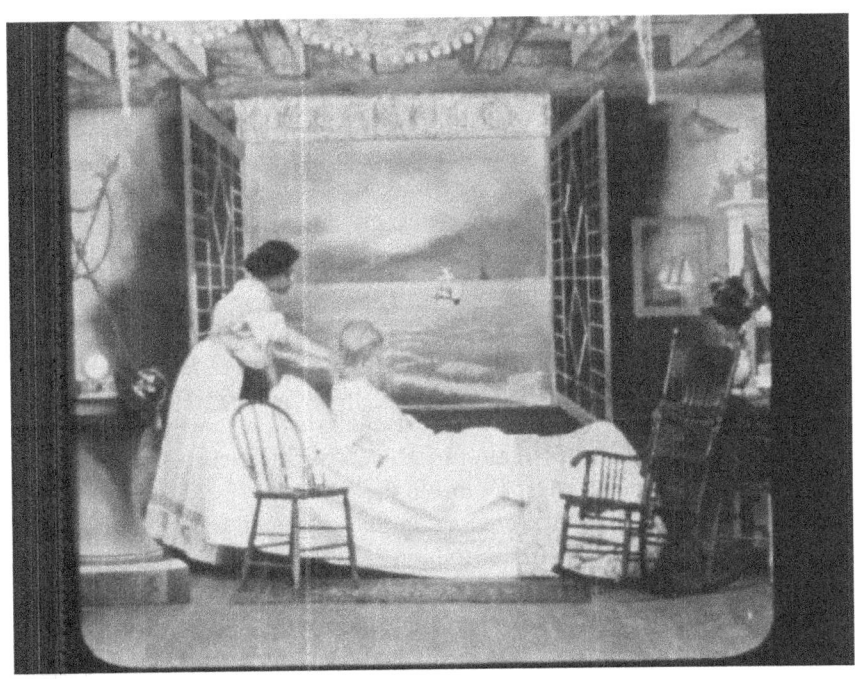

The Last Voyage. 16mm. 1972–76. © Estate of Marcel Broodthaers, c/o SABAM Belgium 2024

itself in entirely different styles within *A Voyage on the North Sea* and *Berlin*. In a similar vein to *The Last Voyage*, the former, whether as film or bioscopic book,[27] relies primarily on montage to suggest a dynamic unfolding of a series of static images—a common strategy of the artist and furthermore a basic procedure within the arsenal of Structural Cinema and some directors associated with the Rive Gauche. In *Berlin*, by contrast, the scenes depicting barges are devoid of any editing. By their exasperatingly slow passage through the film's *plan-séquences*, they almost seem to be caught in standstill, as such tallying with the ambiance of summer boredom enveloping the film at large. Similar to David Lamelas's ongoing *Time as Activity* series (1969- …) in which the hustle and bustle of various global cities is presented as a figure of pure duration, Broodthaers's long takes of barges paint a portrait of time, rather than the city.[28]

In addition to this biographical subtext and Structural dimension, the Spree and its barges lie at the root of an intricate intertextual network, allowing for different correspondences to sprout from the same figure(s). Three works that the artist engaged with when envisaging *Berlin* deepen the film's semantics and critical import significantly: *L'Atalante* (aka *Le Chaland qui passe* after the popular song by Lys Gauty that featured in the film) (1934) by French filmmaker Jean Vigo;[29] Edgar Allan Poe's famous short story *MS. Found in a Bottle* (1833); and, perhaps of even greater renown, *Die Lorelei* (1824) by Heinrich Heine. Jenkins was first to point out that the barge traffic on the Spree, together with the soundtrack of *Berlin*, signals an undeniable reference to Vigo's feature film, which is widely considered a masterpiece of early sound cinema. That Broodthaers initially seemed to fancy "Le Chaland qui passe" as a title for *Berlin* makes this even more obvious.[30] Thus, in Broodthaers's imagination the Spree flowed seamlessly into the French canals, while he was probably oblivious to the German "überlaufer" film *Unter den Brücken* (Under the Bridges, 1944–46) by Helmut Käutner, which, obviously inspired by *L'Atalante*'s plot, style, and imagery, portrays a love story set on a barge sailing down the Spree and Havel Rivers. *L'Atalante*, for its part, tells the story of the honeymoon of boatman Jean and country girl Juliette aboard of the eponymous barge. Once anchored in Paris, a tension soon arises between the newlyweds: whereas Juliette craves for a taste of the vibrant metropolis, Jean seems destined to dwell on the French canals for the remainder of his life. The conflict is only resolved when both lovers' longing gazes meet, as in a dream, below the water line. Jenkins argues that "in *Berlin*, Broodthaers reprises the themes at the heart of the Vigo film— the links between imagination, faith, and freedom—and condenses them into the Keatonesque figure of the dreaming artist."[31] These motifs too may well have resounded with the artist's inner turmoil, being an "itinerant artist," yet impeded from exploring the place where he moored.

MS. Found in a Bottle adds another intriguing, if more oblique perspective to the intertextual field that *Berlin* opens onto. In October 1974, about a month after the film had been shot, Broodthaers presented the edition *The Manuscript*

Found in a Bottle at the Berlin René Block Gallery. Consisting of an empty, "ordinary bottle, used for Bordeaux wine" on which "the manuscript" and "1833" are printed,[32] it provides a direct reference to Poe's best-known short story, as is explained on a sheet wrapped around the bottle. The latter's header suggests that it was found "on the green beach of the Spree," which in turn provides a reference to a namesake novel by Hans Scholz that was adapted into a television series extremely popular in Germany during 1960s.[33] Of course, the figure of the empty bottle too may well be carried by the gloomy tide of the artist's biography that had apparently taken a similar fateful course as the seemingly rudderless ship that the tale's narrator unwillingly boarded. As an absent, but no less powerful message, it is tossed to an anticipated, "fictitious audience" at an instant of imminent doom.[34] Within this dismal scenario, the empty bottle also becomes a signifier of Broodthaers's isolation, not only writerly but also social, as another nod to his prohibition on drinking—significantly, once the map of the ocean floor hanging in the Berlin apartment was exhibited as an artwork, it received the title *Drinking the Last Drop at the Bottom of the Ocean – To your Health: Map of the Ocean Floor*.[35] Finally, "The Eye of the Storm," the title of this essay, may well be informed by the maelstrom that ultimately swallows Poe's ghost ship. On the other hand, the empty bottle can also act as a metonym for Broodthaers's *Décor* enterprise at large, in which the artist's lifelong emphasis on issues of institutional reception, merchandising, mediation, and canonization, in short, the context of the "autonomous" artwork, turned inward and reached a very pinnacle against the horizon of a looming death: "It used to be: read this, look at this. Today it is: allow me to present ... "[36] Finally, the question of *Nachleben* (afterlife) takes center stage in Broodthaers's reading of Heine's *Lorelei*, providing the framework for the remainder of this essay.

WHILE READING THE *LORELEI*

Rather than visiting the picturesque sights of Berlin, Broodthaers immersed himself in some literary monuments of Romanticism. He mentions reading the work of authors such as Achim von Arnim and Clemens Brentano, "with a view on the Spree."[37] In this way, also the *Lorelei* caught his attention once again.[38] No doubt the greatest cliché of so-called Rhine Romanticism, Lorelei refers to the steep cliff rising high above a treacherous bend in the river where many a ship was wrecked. In Brentano's ballad titled "Lore Lay" (1801), the folklore surrounding the rock first condensed into the figure of a legendary enchantress bearing this name. However, it was Heinrich Heine's "Die Lore-ley" (1824), telling the story of a siren luring sailors into their deaths, that would eventually come to embody the contemporary Lorelei myth. Taking root in German collective memory, the Lorelei became an icon of German nationalism and, as such, the subject of an extensive visual culture, yielding prints, postcards,

Spreads from *En lisant la Lorelei. Wie ich Die Lorelei gelesen habe*. 1975.
Collection Ivo and Monique Van Vaerenbergh. Photo Rachel Gruijters.
© Estate of Marcel Broodthaers, c/o SABAM Belgium 2024

maps, et cetera, which spans more than two centuries by now. Broodthaers drew on this popular cult for the artist book *En lisant la Lorelei: Wie ich Die Lorelei gelesen habe* (1975) (While reading the Lorelei). Although only published after his passing, the book's concept and design go back to 1974 and most likely developed primarily during his Berlin stay, as such running parallel to *Berlin*.[39] In Broodthaers's imagination, the Rhine and the Spree intertwined with one another. This is further evidenced by the book project's remarkable emphasis on barges whose "infinite humming"—part of his daily experience in Berlin—has come to override the murmuring sound of the Rhine's currents and a nearby waterfall.[40] What's more, some authors have mentioned the Lorelei and other myths involving Romantic creatures, such as Undine, Wili (Giselle), and mermaids in general, as a subtext for the *amour fou* that underpins *L'Atalante*'s plot—an intertextual connection that Broodthaers too may well have perceived.[41] As such, *En lisant la Lorelei*, which may be said to convey Broodthaers's reception of the myth, presents a key document that allows to grasp some of the crucial concerns underlying *Berlin*. For this reason, it is worth a detour.

In *En lisant la Lorelei*, popular imagery related to the Lorelei's tourist fetishization is juxtaposed with stock exchange tables taken from newspapers on the one hand, and partially overworked decals depicting a group of people gathered around the television screen on the other. Additionally, an elementary love story, apparently between Heine and the Lorelei herself, is recounted by means of the same imagery. Finally, it contains a reproduction of Heine's famous poem in French and German, alongside a preface by Broodthaers. At first glance a heterogenous and hermetic rebus, the artist book essentially represents a visual "essay," conceived as a case study on the Marxist principle of reification. Though not mentioned literally, this specific theoretical angle is clear from Broodthaers's preface, which channels the notion by invoking its spiritual father—Lukács[42]—and principal effect, the degeneration of authentic, subjective experience into consolidated figures of authority and commerce. According to Lukács apologist Lucien Goldmann, with whom Broodthaers attended a seminar in 1969–70, "the process of reification, as the inevitable consequence of the market economy, extends over and penetrates into the interior of all non-economic sectors of thought and effect. Religion, morality, art, literature's [...] authenticity in the capitalist world is *hollowed out from the inside* by the appearance of an autonomous economic system that takes hold of all manifestations of human life."[43] Formulated as such, the notion of reification allowed Broodthaers to add theoretical cachet to his preexisting and definitely romantically informed lamentation over modernity's disenchantment propelled by the erosion of culture into commodity, which he saw exemplified by the Lorelei's commercially driven mythification and its plethora of mass-produced tourist imagery.[44] What makes the Lorelei such a fascinating site for a (cursory) survey of reification is the topos's embodiment of the dynamic's ultimate perversion: its recuperation of Romanticism itself—according to Broodthaers, "Historical romanticism has degenerated into a process of destruction"—which originally emerged as the alleged counterreaction to early capitalism and the rationalism of the Enlightenment. Nostalgia, formerly a symptom of Romantic idealism and resistance, has now become a token of bourgeois bad taste, the Lorelei a "prêt-à-porter." *En lisant la Lorelei* thus offers a paradigmatic insight into Broodthaers's pessimism about culture under late capitalism, no doubt informed by the neo-Marxist underpinnings of Adorno's *Culture Industry* and Debord's *Society of the Spectacle* arguments, which he appeared to subsume under the notion of reification toward the end of his career. However, in addition to a paradigmatic example of the artist's thinking at the time he envisioned *Berlin*, the book can also be read as an arresting allegory on his fate as an artist, which gains an unexpected significance when slid over *Berlin*.

THE END OF ART

> Let's go back one hundred fifty years. Back then, it was still legitimate that Heinrich Heine wanted to overcome Romanticism with irony. He did not marry the "Lorelei."[45]

In the preface of *En lisant la Lorelei*, past and present are bridged, as Broodthaers ponders the legacy of Heine, with whom he may have identified in more than one way. Like him, he found himself as an "itinerant" artist living as an expat in a foreign city.[46] In hindsight, Heine's ambiguous status of an intermediary between the Romantic and modern era, which Lukács discusses at length in the essay "Heine as a National Poet" (1935),[47] may even be said to resonate with Broodthaers's oft-assigned place at the bridgehead of postmodernism. By means of a typical Broodthaersian time warp, his contemporary predicament is set off against Heine's historical one. As such, the latter's "Ende der Kunstperiode" (End of the Art Period), by which he sought to bid farewell to Romanticism's idealist detachment and political sterility and at the same time fashion himself as a harbinger of the modern era,[48] suddenly offers an anachronistic but fascinating framework for Broodthaers to approach the current impasse he thought art was caught in. In an unpublished note related to *En lisant la Lorelei*, he observed how the heritage of Romanticism resurfaced in contemporary art:

> We, artists [...] develop toward a bizarre status of a divine order that accords [us] (innocently?) a secret as a piece of universal truth. This evolution toward the recognition of the artist by society appears to be inscribed in a destiny, at once moral and common. A heritage that undoubtedly stems from Romanticism [...][49]

Cover design by Broodthaers for *Studio International*, no. 970 (October 1974). © Estate of Marcel Broodthaers, c/o SABAM Belgium 2024

With these words, Broodthaers no doubt targeted the shamanism of Joseph Beuys, whom he would criticize repeatedly.[50] Less obviously, however, his concerns may also have been addressed to some of the standard bearers of Conceptual Art,[51] whom he accused of a similar idealism as Heine did concerning his Romantically indebted contemporaries (at least in Lukács's view). Moreover, he had diagnosed early on how Conceptual Art's utopian aesthetics of dematerialization proved equally prone to reification. As Benjamin Buchloh and Eric de Bruyn have shown, Conceptual Art's recourse to the media and logic of a "totally administered world," resulting in an "aesthetic of administration," had turned the artwork into the latter's very mimesis.[52] Conceptual Art has notoriously been associated with the notion of the "end of art" because of the sweeping erasure of traditional aesthetic experience it advocated,[53] a rhetoric to which Broodthaers responded through his contribution in two art periodicals published in the same year *Berlin* was shot. While the cover he designed for the October issue of *Studio International* read "FIN[e] [a]RTS," alluding to the French word for end, *fin*, he published a brief notice (*avis*) in *Interfunktionen*:

> an artistic theory will be functioning for the artistic product in the same way as the artistic product itself is functioning as advertising for the order under which it is produced. There will be no other space than this view according to which, etc. ...[54]

Exposing the false disinterestedness of a model of "Art as Idea as Idea" is one thing. Resolving the question of how to escape from this cul-de-sac is quite another. Or to raise the issue in Broodthaers's terms: How to evade the trap of reification, given the latter's power to lure any countermovement into serving its own agenda?

Typically for Broodthaers, this topical question is framed within a historical context. As the above quote suggests, Heine's deployment of irony, of which "Die Lore-Ley" can be considered a prime example, inspired him in this case. Many accounts have cast Heine's remodeling of the Lorelei into a story about a treacherous siren as a cautionary tale, an allegory in other words, about the dangers lurking beneath Romanticism's escapist idyll. According to Lukács, Heine's principle of irony is meant to "destroy the bourgeois illusions about an ostensible harmony."[55] Broodthaers's persistent depiction of the Lorelei as a mermaid is in sync with this reading. In his version of the Lorelei, Heine himself appears as a character. His Oddyssean refusal to marry the Lorelei is cast as a metaphor for the author's rejection of Romanticism, which Broodthaers, still true to Lukács' account, judged to be an essential condition for the political commitment necessary to open up a new era in literature.[56] Nevertheless, a century and a half later such strategy had lost its effectiveness, if it was ever effective at all. For history has taught that Heine's rejection of Romanticism, however fierce it was, did not prevent his legacy from equally being "hollowed out," as exemplified by the current eclipse of his poem's critical dimension by exactly the idealist spirit that it sought to subvert. According to literature scholar Albert Béguin, whose work Broodthaers was apparently aware of, "the banal Romanticism that was to spread and become vulgarized to the point of lulling asleep the German bourgeoisie, borrowed its poetic paraphernalia from Heine."[57] As Broodthaers saw the inescapable omnipotence of reification confirmed in its smooth harnessing of both Romanticism and Heine's riposte to the latter, refracting the contemporary "end of art" through the lens of Heine's "End of the Art Period" provided anything but a brighter outlook, leaving him in utter pessimism about the fate of art in general, and the prospect of his oeuvre in particular. Of course, this melancholic mood is silhouetted even more sharply against the bleak light of his impending mortality.

A DUCK ON THE SPREE

It is important to note that Broodthaers's concern over the destructive effects of reification on art's autonomy and critical potency is not limited to specific cases but informs his oeuvre as a whole. According to art historian Trevor Stark, who approaches his practice from this perspective, Broodthaers "transformed the political compromises and financial entanglements of culture under capitalism into his medium."[58] This may be especially true for the final stage of his career, witness an increased number of references to Lukács and reification, of which *En lisant la Lorelei* provides only one example. For Broodthaers, however, reification extended further than the "transformation of art into merchandise,"[59] as its forces compromised the artist's persona and political integrity too. Only weeks after shooting *Berlin*, he empathically tackled this issue in the inaugural speech he gave at the opening of the *Catalogue-Catalogus* exhibition at the Brussels Palais des Beaux-Arts, the first *Décor* retrospective organized after Broodthaers was awarded the Robert Giron Prize. Addressing the audience and jury members, he stated:

> You lose your name, you are not mister Broodthaers for example, or comrade Broodthaers, or [just] Broodthaers, you progressively become *a* Broodthaers [...] that is to say that I become myself an object, that is to say that I think that on a critical level, things are progressively refused to me.[60]

This fear of losing his identity and becoming critically silenced resonates particularly within the context of the cultural politics underpinning the DAAD residency. Founded in 1963, barely two years after the Wall had literally inscribed in stone West Berlin's isolation from the rest of the Western world, an American-funded "artist import" program marked the beginning of the DAAD artist-in-residence program.[61] Parallel to commodities such as food, fuel, or medical supplies, artists were now flown in from the West, with the aim of providing a cultural lifeline to this symbolically important exclave. As participating in the program involved generous (institutional) support, numerous renowned international artists smoothly found their way to the city. In Broodthaers's case, the DAAD not only took care of his apartment and health insurance but also bore the production costs of *Berlin*.[62]

However, the flip side of this policy implied a compliant and politically indifferent role for the artist depending on the tutelage of this kind of cultural politics.[63] In his 1973 lecture, titled "The Artist's Freedom of Speech in our Society," the German novelist Günter Grass warned that amid the geopolitical détente of the early 1970s, art's critical dimension might easily be ignored or even be the price to pay for the primarily economically motivated rapprochement (between the West and the East) at the root of "peaceful coexistence."[64] According to him, capitalist liberalism, as the alleged opposite of Soviet authoritarianism, by no means guaranteed genuine artistic freedom, a stance he sharply articulated as follows:

> The freedom of the arts is only possible where social and individual human rights are respected; wherever a relative freedom of art or a privileged status of the artists is bought, artists evade social conditions, which are usually latent grievances, and isolate themselves as an elite; content with a

playground-freedom, their art, splendid and concealing, adorns restraining conditions, the artist being the whore of altering powers.[65]

Broodthaers would no doubt have supported Grass's concerns over artistic freedom, as exemplified by the critical questions he raised on occasions of institutional recognition, whether it be the award of the Giron Prize or the DAAD residency. Regarding the latter, he wondered "what art ends up being if the artist wears a ceremonial dress."[66] In a surprisingly similar vein to Heine's irony (as seen from Lukács's perspective), he contended that "highlighting the contradictions that are part of bourgeois society" seemed the only way to avoid ending up as a piece of décor himself, or, as he put it piercingly, "a duck on the Spree."[67] In keeping with Grass, he acutely experienced freedom of speech's fragility, as it came under increasing pressure amid the economic and political hardship gripping the era. In addition to inflation that he would often refer to, Broodthaers lost sleep over West Germany's curtailment of civil liberties in the wake of the Red Army Fraktion's terrorist guerilla plaguing the country.[68]

Surprisingly, no such political stands explicitly feature in *Berlin*, making the film appear anything but political. Retreated to his allotted apartment, Broodthaers is portrayed indulging in the sweet delights of bourgeois life, content to contemplate its clichés and enjoy the view of passing barges, while the "peripeties of history" remain well outside the frame.[69] *Berlin*'s only reference to current events on the political stage is provided by the newspaper that is depicted. The headline of that day (August 28, 1974) concerns a rather ordinary partisan vaudeville unwinding in the backwash of the so-called Guillaume affair, an espionage scandal that had forced Willy Brandt to resign as a chancellor earlier that year; news Broodthaers would never have caught through his cream-clouded lenses.[70]

THE EYE OF THE STORM

In the end, the critical import of *Berlin* and its subtitle evoking a dream narrative remains ambiguous.[71] Like Heine, Broodthaers was greatly skeptical of the emancipatory potential of the dream. According to Karl Ruhrberg, he "wanted reality instead realism," by which he sought to underscore a political engagement that does not tolerate idealist escape hatches.[72] However, similar to Heine, who spent his final years shackled to his so-called *Matratzengruft* (mattress tomb), for Broodthaers too, the dream may have become "the symbol of poetry, of freedom of the spirit, of a transfigured universe, where suffering, carnal life, torture and physical pleasure are spiritualized,"[73] to use Béguin's words. Nevertheless, *Berlin* more likely depicts a nightmare than a dream. Behind its idyll lurks a bitter satire that exactly depicts what Broodthaers sought to defy with all courage of despair: isolation, resignation, reification. Citing Béguin a final time, one could argue that "the romantic dream that denied a reality too brutal, is denied in turn through the intervention of an irony that no longer has anything to do with the sovereign games of the free spirit."[74] Although probably not intended in this way, this too qualifies as the "double negation" that Broodthaers mentioned in his letter to Ruhrberg.

Under the guise of slapstick, irony is thus employed as a means of resistance. Breathing life into inanimate objects like the stuffed parrot and leaving the artist stone-faced at once, it taps into the sociocritical dimension that has been ascribed to it since the 1920s, which was especially emphasized by the champions of Frankfurter critical theory (Benjamin, Kracauer, Adorno), whose critique of the culture industry underpins Broodthaers's (late) oeuvre.[75] In *Berlin*, the commodification of his own art and the political detachment of the artist are the prime targets of his mockery. Often, these effects coincide with institutional recognition, which may be said to find its most concrete embodiment in retrospectives. Unsurprisingly, then, Broodthaers's institutional critique took a personal turn when his star rose toward the end of his life. Furthermore, this critical stance gained special urgency in the face of a looming death, a critical trigger for any oeuvre's reification.

Broodthaers's late *Décor* practice, of which *Berlin* is part, does not just touch on these issues but can also be seen as an attempt to subvert it: the "spirit of the décor" is literally conceived to undo the eclipse of use value by exchange value that traditionally takes place within the exhibition room. As discussed earlier, *Berlin* contributed to this endeavor by turning art objects into film props. However, like *En lisant la Lorelei*, *Berlin* also presents a critical allegory on the fate of art under capitalism, in this case imbued with a significant biographical overtone. As the natural expression of a melancholic worldview according to Walter Benjamin, "allegory is the antidote to myth."[76] Without delving into the specifics of this argument, it is advanced here as a model for the critical enterprise of the *Décors* in general and *Berlin* in particular.[77] For allegory provided Broodthaers a strategy that allowed him to contemplate and elude, albeit temporarily, the twofold shipwreck of imminent reification and death. As such, Berlin, both the film and the city, present a fleeting mirage in a turbulent world, "the eye of the storm."

NOTES

This chapter is partly based on archival research conducted at the archives of the DAAD Berliner Künstlerprogramm and the Staatliche Museen zu Berlin, which I would like to thank for their cooperation. Additionally, I would like to express my gratitude to Margaux Van Uytvanck, Ivo Van Vaerenbergh, and Johan Smets for providing me access to some materials that were fundamental to my argument.

1. Marcel Broodthaers, "The Eye of the Storm," trans., in Gloria Moure (ed.), *Marcel Broodthaers: Collected Writings* (Barcelona: Ediciones Polígrafa, 2012), 447.
2. *Broodthaers: Collected Writings*, 446.
3. Michael Compton, "In Praise of the Subject," in Susanne Pfeffer (ed.), *Marcel Broodthaers; Exhibition History 1964-75 and Selected Works 1957-75* (Kassel: Fridericianum Koenig Books, 2020), 37.
4. Marcel Broodthaers, "Dear Karl Ruhrberg," trans. in *Broodthaers: Collected Writings*, 377.
5. Broodthaers, "Dear Karl Ruhrberg," 377.
6. Several scholars, such as Michael Oppitz, Thomas McEvilley, and Rachel Haidu, to name only a few, have noted how Broodthaers's *Décors* convey a postcolonial critique through his distinct choice of objects. The potted palm trees, world maps, and stuffed exotic animals represent more than anachronistic references to fin-de-siècle bourgeois interiors and serve as unmistakable tokens of nineteenth-century Western imperialism and colonialism.
7. Likewise, the close relationship between the world map of the ocean floor and *Carte du monde poétique* (1968) or *Un Film de Charles Baudelaire* (1970) cannot have gone unnoticed for a contemporaneous audience (familiar with Broodthaers's oeuvre). The parrot(s), finally, having only been introduced under the form of a (found) image in the book accompanying *Un Jardin d'hiver* (I), would only later become one of the most recognized figures in Broodthaers's work, after significant appearances in the exhibitions *Ne dites pas que je ne l'ai pas dite – Le Perroquet / Zeg niet dat ik het niet gezegd heb – De Papegaai* (Wide White Space, September 1974) and *Éloge du sujet* (Kunstmuseum Basel, October 1974). The parrot(s) also occurred in the *Invitation pour une exposition bourgeoise* in whose context *Berlin oder ein Traum mit Sahne* premiered, making it the only object to feature in both the film and the exhibition.
8. Marcel Broodthaers, audio interview, c. late 1975, in *Avant-Garde in Belgium, 1917–1978*, vol. 3, *Apprentissage et filiation* (Brussels: Sub Rosa, 2009), CD, quote translated by Cathleen Chaffee.
9. Ibid.
10. This was for instance the case in *Éloge du sujet* held at the Kunstmuseum Basel in the fall of 1974.
11. Rachel Haidu, *The Absence of Work* (Cambridge, Mass.: MIT Press, 2010), 233.
12. For a more detailed account, see Manuel Borja-Villel, Michael Compton, and Maria Gilissen (eds.), *Marcel Broodthaers, Cinéma*, exh. cat. (Barcelona: Fundació Antoni Tàpies, 1997), 240–9.
13. Other of such specular *dispositives* include the exhibition catalog, the mirror, editions, etc.
14. See Eric de Bruyn, "From Jersey City to Cybernetics," in Dan Graham, *Video – Architecture – Television: Writings on Video and Video Works 1970–1978* (Zürich: Lars Müller Publishers, 2013), n. p.
15. Ibid.
16. Heinz Ohff, "Ein Traum mit Sahne: Marcel Brodthaers [sic] in der Neuen Nationalgalerie," *Tagesspiegel* (28 February 1975).
17. Pierre Sterckx, "Une anecdote peu connue de la vie et de la pensée de Marcel Broodthaers," in *Joseph Beuys, Marcel Broodthaers, Robert Rauschenberg, Andy Warhol*, exh. cat. (Paris: Galerie Isy Brachot, 1989), 14–15 (my translation from French).
18. Jürgen Harten, "Die Zukunft einer Chance," in Karl Ruhrberg and Thomas Deecke (eds.), *30 Internationale Künstler in Berlin; Gäste des Deutschen Akademischen Austauschdienstes; Berliner Künstlerprogram; Beethovenhalle Bonn 14.-27.12.1973*, exh. cat., ed. Karl Ruhrberg and Thomas Deecke, 1973, n. p. (my translation from German).
19. Ibid., see also Roland Wiegenstein, "Eine erwachsene Institution," in ibid., n. p.

20. Karl Ruhrberg, "Notiz zur Ausstellung," in ibid., n. p. (my translation from German).
21. Some of these photographs are collected in Maria Gilissen and Susanne Lange (eds.), *Marcel Broodthaers: Texte et photos*, exh. cat. (Göttingen: Steidl, 2003), 368–83. In "Das Wort Film?," published in the exhibition catalog of *Invitation pour une exposition bourgeoise*, Broodthaers appears to express his regrets over the fact that he was unable to explore Berlin more intensively: "Berlin was a special city for me. There are more bridges here than in Venice. But there are also very different groups of people. I would have liked to have known more about that." See "The Word Film?" trans., in *Broodthaers: Collected Writings*, 464.
22. Marcel Broodthaers, letter to Émile Salkin (December 1973–April 1974), reproduced in *De la collection Marie-Puck Broodthaers*, auction catalog (Paris: Artcurial, 2023), 92–93 (my translation from French).
23. Ibid.
24. Ibid. A few months after the shooting of *Berlin*, Broodthaers had to undergo a critical surgery, whose uncertain prospects made him cruelly aware of his mortality. On the occasion of *Invitation pour une exposition bourgeoise*, which had to be postponed because of the surgery, Ruhrberg tellingly expressed that "the most pleasant thing about this exhibition was the fact that the latter could take place in the presence of the artist." See Jürgen Hart and Karl Ruhrberg, "Kunst und Literatur ... Welches Gesicht bleibt Verborgen? Der belgische Künstler Marcel Broodthaers," *MAGAZIN KUNST* 15, no. 2 (1975): 75 (my translation from German).
25. *The Last Voyage*, initiated by Broodthaers and posthumously finished by Maria Gilissen, is named after and consists of an early twentieth-century series of seven magic lantern slides, illustrating an eponymous song. According to art critic Hans Theys, it recounts "the story of a father who, on his deathbed, points through the window at a ship and tells his daughter it is the one that will carry away his soul." See Hans Theys, "The Lie of Waterloo," 1996, accessed July 27, 2023, http://hanstheys.ensembles.org/ensembles/text-material?item=20747.
26. Refrain from "The Last Voyage," song by Clifton Bingham, music by Stanley Gordon. *The Last Voyage*, music score (London: Charles Sheard & Co., 1907), n. p.
27. The term "bioscopic books" encompasses artist's books that translate cinema's kinetic and time-based sensorium into the format of the book and reading experience. Concerning this genre, *A Voyage on the North Sea* can be considered a textbook example and a special case at once. See Tine Guns, Inge Ketelers, and Isolde Vanhee (eds.), *Bioscopic Books*, exh. cat. (Ghent: Grafische Cel, Luca School of Arts, 2021).
28. *Time as Activity* encompasses a series of films, shot in various cities across the globe, in which Lamelas addresses time as a substance. *Time as Activity – Düsseldorf* marked the beginning of the four-decade series. It consists of three stationary, three-minute shots showing different places of the city at different times of the day. Through their narrative insignificance, duration itself becomes the film's prime medium. Since 1968, Broodthaers and Lamelas were close and would regularly feature in the same group shows. For a detailed account of Lamelas's cinema practice, see Chema González and Yolanda Romero (eds.), *David Lamelas: en lugar de cine; in place of film*, exh. cat., (Granada: Centro José Guerrero, 2011).
29. In attempt to make *L'Atalante* more popular, Gaumont changed the film's title to *Le Chaland qui passe* (after the popular Lys Gauty song) upon its theatrical release. It is possible Broodthaers only knew the film under the latter title.
30. Both the catalogs of the exhibtions *Catalogue-Catalogus* (Palais des Beaux-Arts, Brussels) and *Éloge du sujet* (Kunstmuseum, Basel) refer to *Berlin* as *Le Chaland qui passe*.
31. Bruce Jenkins, "Un Peu Tard: Citation in the Cinema of Marcel Broodthaers," in *Cinéma*, 293.
32. For the full text, see *Exhibition History 1964–75 and Selected Works 1957–75*, 568.

33. Michal Ron, "MUSEUM / enfants non admis': Arriving Late to Marcel Broodthaers," *The Garage Journal: Studies in Art, Museums & Culture* 3 (2021): 225–26.
34. As such, the work cycles back to *Pense-Bête*. The semantics of *Ms. Found in Bottle* appear to resonate with the way he looked back on his entry in the artworld in the 1974 text "Ten Thousand Francs Reward": "Until that moment [*Pense-Bête*] I had lived practically isolated from all communication, since I had a fictitious audience." See *Collected Writings*, 417.
35. *Exhibition History 1964–75 and Selected Works 1957–75*, 536–37.
36. "Ten Thousand Francs Reward," trans., *Broodthaers: Collected Writings*, 418.
37. Quote from a note reproduced in Philippe Cuenat's brilliantly elaborated study on the artist book *En lisant la Lorelei: Wie ich die Lorelei gelesen habe*. See Philippe Cuenat, *Marcel Broodthaers, Autour de la Lorelei* (Geneva: Mamco, 1997), 68 (my translation from French).
38. Broodthaers's engagement with Heinrich Heine's conception of the Lorelei reaches at least back as far as 1971, when he presented *Project for an Uninhabited Island in the Rhine: Museum Island* (1971) at the Düsseldorf Kunsthalle, a project documenting the proposal to raise an artificial "museum island" built on one thousand cement bags in the Rhine river at the foot of the famous rock. The work featured in the group show *Between 6* (1971) at the Düsseldorf Kunsthalle. For a detailed account, see Renate Buschmann, *Chronik einer Nicht-Ausstellung; Between 1969–73 in der Kunsthalle Düsseldorf* (Berlin: Reimer, 2006), 227–30.
39. Cuenat, *Autour de la Lorelei*, 162–63. In fact, the better part of the imagery that was used for the book first surfaced in *Éloge du sujet*, Broodthaers's second *Décor* exhibition that opened at the Basel Kunstmuseum in October 1974, only weeks after *Berlin* was shot.
40. Ibid., 77 (my translation from French).
41. See for example Barthélemy Amengual, *Monde et vision du monde dans l'oeuvre de Vigo* (1966), cited in Anne-Gaëlle Saliot, *The Drowned Muse* (Oxford: Oxford University Press, 2015), 282–83; Jean-Max Méjean, *L'Atalante de Jean Vigo* (Rome: Gremese, 2017), 40.
42. György Lukács advanced his seminal approach to the phenomenon of reification in *History and Class Consciousness* (1923).
43. Lucien Goldmann, *Recherches dialectiques* (Paris: Gallimard, 1972), 68, as cited by Trevor Stark in his excellent online lecture "Marcel Broodthaers, Between Poetry and Reification," Youtube, May 17, 2021, 41:35, https://www.youtube.com/watch?v=oB6Vjk5wVOc&ab_channel=CalgaryInstitutefortheHumanities.
44. According to Richard Westerman, Lukács's early work betrays a clear reliance on neo-Romantic thought. "For many of Lukács's critics, then, *History and Class Consciousness* represents a Marxian reinterpretation of the essentially neo-Romantic outlook of his early years." Despite fueling widespread criticism, Lukács's Romantic anti-capitalism may have been the prime reason for Broodthaers to acquaint himself with his thinking. See Richard Westerman, *Lukács's Phenomenology of Capitalism: Reification Revalued* (Cham: Palgrave MacMillan, 2019), 4–13.
45. Note reproduced in Cuenat, *Autour de la Lorelei*, 81 (my translation from French).
46. Heine spent the last twenty-five years of his life living as an expatriate in Paris.
47. See Georg Lukács, "Heine as a National Poet," trans. in *German Realists in the Nineteenth Century*, ed. Rodney Livingstone (Cambridge, Masss.: MIT Press, 1993). Broodthaers was likely aware of the essay and appears to refer to it in the preface of *En lisant la Lorelei*: "Whether Heine's voice followed the course of modern thinking or the opposite has been the subject of a debate that took place in the 1930s with Georg Lukács" (my translation from French).
48. See Jochen Schmidt, "Heines Geschichtskonstruktionen: Das 'Ende der Kunstperiode' und das Ende der Kunst," *Zeitschrift für deutsche Philologie* 127, no. 4 (2008): 499–515.
49. Note by Broodthaers related to *En lisant la Lorelei*, reproduced in Cuenat, *Autour de la Lorelei*, 68 (my translation from French).

50. See for example Broodthaers's 1972 open letter to Beuys: "Mon cher Beuys," Düsseldorf, 25 September 1972, published under the title "Politik der Magie? Offener Brief von Broodthaers an Beuys," *Rheinische Post* (3 October 3 1972).
51. The opening sentence of Sol Lewitt's *Sentences on Conceptual Art* resonates particularly well with the mystic status of the artist that Broodthaers discerns: "1 – Conceptual Artists are mystics rather than rationalists. They leap to conclusions that logic cannot reach." In a 1969 open letter addressed to David Lamelas, Broodthaers had already criticized this stance by reversing Lewitt's *Sentences*. See "My dear Lamelas...," trans., *Broodthaers: Collected Writings*, 215.
52. See Benjamin H. D. Buchloh, "Conceptual Art 1962–1969," *October* 55 (Winter 1990): 105–43; Eric de Bruyn, "Cinéma Modèle," *Texte zur Kunst* 29 (March 1998): 33–49.
53. Most famously by Arthur Danto and Mel Ramsden.
54. "View...," trans., *Broodthaers: Collected Writings*, 432.
55. Georg Lukács, *Heinrich Heine: Poète national*, trans. Jean-Pierre Morbois, p. 80, 5 November 2023, available at http://amisgeorglukacs.org/2017/02/geor g-lukacs-realistes-allemands-du-19e-siecle.htmlkiwi.com/0/56/34/64/20191001/ ob_2cbbd7_georg-lukacs-heinrich-heine.pdf (my translation from French).
56. In two preliminary versions of the preface, Broodthaers relates Heine's refusal to "marry the Lorelei" to a distinctly political position. For instance, he states, "Heinrich Heine did not marry the Lorelei which broke his heart as a poet, and he became the political poet that we love." Reproduced in Cuenat, *Autour de la Lorelei*, 81 (my translation from French).
57. According to Cuenat, Broodthaers once recommended the book to Yves Gevaert, assistant at the Belgian "Association for Exhibitions" with whom Broodthaers would work together for his two 1974 Palais des Beaux-Art shows. See Cuenat, *Autour de la Lorelei*, 186. "The banal Romanticism": Albert Béguin, *L'Âme romantique et le rêve* (Paris: José Corti, 1939), 313, cited in Cuenat, *Autour de la Lorelei*, 187. Cuenat relates Béguin's criticism to Guy Debord's semantics: "The spectacle is the guardian of sleep." Ibid. (my translation from French).
58. Stark, "Marcel Broodthaers, between Poetry and Reification," 19:33
59. Ibid.
60. Marcel Broodthaers, unpublished transcript of a speech delivered on the occasion of his acceptance of the Robert Giron Prize, Palais des Beaux-Arts, Brussels (26 September 1974), private collection (my translation from French).
61. See Wiegenstein, "Eine erwachsene Institution," n .p.
62. This is attested by *Berlin*'s (initial) title card and was confirmed by Maria Gilissen in a conversation with the author on 6 June 2019.
63. The expansion of the *culture industry* from the 1960s on went hand in hand with the spread of this model, which often generated public friction between the radicalism of artists and the conservative policies advocated by institutions. Daniel Buren and Hans Haacke's "fiascos" at the Guggenheim Museum, as well as the latter's work removal from *Projekt '74. Kunst bleibt Kunst*, to which Buren and Broodthaers reacted, provide relevant examples to this context. See Deborah Schultz, *Marcel Broodthaers; Strategy and Dialogue* (Bern: Peter Lang, 2007), 237–74.
64. Günter Grass paraphrased by Jürgen Harten in, "Zukunft einer Chance," 65. Günter Grass, *Der Bürger und seine Stimme: Reden, Aufsätze, Kommentare* (Darmstadt: Luchterhand, 1974), 165 (my translation from German).
66. Broodthaers, "The Eye of the Storm," 447.
67. Broodthaers, Robert Giron Prize speech; Broodthaers, "The Eye of the Storm," 447.
68. In an open letter, dated 25 November 1974, addressed to the Berlin Senate, Broodthaers took the tribune to publicly contest a further infringement of civil liberties by the West German state in the wake of the murder of the state court president Günter von

Drenkmann by a left-wing extremist splinter group. This attack, which is referred to in the letter as "the tragic events of November," shocked the German public and prompted the government to strengthen several legal measures. Open letter consulted at the DAAD Archives Berlin.

69. Broodthaers, "To Be a Straight Thinker," 469.
70. Although this newspaper article most likely appears coincidentally in the film, it is worth noting that Brandt's resignation no doubt struck Broodthaers. For one thing, he paid tribute to Brandt for having established the freedom of expression necessary to set up the exhibition *The Eagle from the Oligocene to the Present* (Kunsthalle Düsseldorf, 1972). What's more, many of his contemporaries implicitly or explicitly recall the artist's admiration for Brandt. While according to Ruhrberg, "Brandt represented the embodiment of hope for Broodthaers," Lynda Morris argued that "Broodthaers chose to leave [Düsseldorf] because of the attitude that brought about the downfall of Brandt." Klaus Staeck, for his part, remembered Broodthaers's fear of an "election victory for the Reactionaries." See respectively Marcel Broodthaers, *Der Adler von Oligozän bis Heute*, exh. cat., vol. 1 (Düsseldorf: Kunsthalle Düsseldorf, 1972), 4; Karl Ruhrberg, "Die Bilder und die Worte," in *Marcel Broodthaers*, exh. cat. (Cologne: Museum Ludwig, 1980), 8 (my translation from German); Lynda Morris, "The Museum of Modern Art in Oxford 1965–1975," in *Genuine Conceptualism* (Ghent: Herbert Foundation, 2014), 153; Marie-Pascale Gildemyn (ed.), "Hommage à Marcel Broodthaers," in +-0, 47 (1987), 33.
71. It should be reminded that the dream narrative is a staple with the post-Surrealist avant-garde cinema of the 1940s and '50s, represented, among others, by Maya Deren, Kenneth Anger, or Luc de Heusch. Broodthaers's cinematic endeavors seem far removed from this approach.
72. See Ruhrberg, "Kunst und Literatur ... Welches Gesicht bleibt verborgen?" 77.
73. Béguin, *L'âme romantique et le rêve*, 325 (my translation from French).
74. Ibid., 325–26.
75. See Hilde D'Haeyere and Steven Jacobs, "Frankfurter Slapstick: Benjamin, Kracauer, and Adorno on American Screen Comedy," *October* 160 (Spring 2017): 30–50.
76. Walter Benjamin, "Central Park," trans. Lloyd Spencer and Mark Harrington, *New German Critique* 34 (Winter 1985): 46. Interestingly, reification and allegory are closely related in Benjamin's vision, as he argued that "the devaluation of the world of objects in allegory is outdone within the world of objects itself by the commodity." Ibid., 34. According to Thijs Lijster, "one could [even] translate the dialectical poles of allegory, devaluation, and sanctification into a dialectic of reification." Lijster, "'All Reification Is a Form of Forgetting': Benjamin, Adorno, and the Dialectic of Reification," in Samir Gandesha and Johan F. Hartle (eds.), *The Spell of Capital: Reification and Spectacle* (Amsterdam: Amsterdam University Press, 2017), 59.
77. Casting Broodthaers as an "allegorist of the avant-garde," Benjamin Buchloh was the first of series of (primarily American) scholars (Douglas Crimp, Rosalind Krauss, Rachel Haidu, etc.) to read Benjamin's theories in the former's work, which still represents an important approach to his oeuvre. See Buchloh, "Marcel Broodthaers: Allegories of the Avant-Garde," *Artforum* 18, no. 4 (May 1980): 52–60. This essay analyzes concrete instances of allegory in Broodthaers's late work and filmmaking.

FILMOGRAPHY

Raf Wollaert

The cinema of Marcel Broodthaers followed "the same generative principles" that governed his artistic practice as a whole. Therefore, no filmography can claim the status of a definitive account, as this endeavor precisely seems to be at odds with the artist's strategies to thwart any form of consolidation. Within the filmic realm, Broodthaers's practice of constant rearrangement and repurposing finds its counterpart in a frantic reediting that, to some extent, was carried on after his passing. As a result, only a minority of the artist's films comes without alternative edits or titles nowadays, which forces a number of choices upon anyone venturing to chart or show this work. Because these choices varied over time and from historian to historian, curator to curator, et cetera, the default entropy of Broodthaers's filmic oeuvre appears to have increased to the point that the ambition of a faithful historical reconstruction is only hardly imaginable—at least if this ever was or is the point at all.

This filmography seeks to keep the middle between a chronological filmographic account and an inventory of the films existing today. On the one hand, it is based on the comparing and combining of the multiple filmographies drafted during Broodthaers's lifetime and after his death, of which the 1989 Walker Art Center and 1997 Fundació Tàpies exhibition catalogs, respectively edited by Bruce Jenkins and Manuel Borja-Villel, provided the most vital instances. Hans Theys's contributions to this domain were also of a particular significance. On the other hand, this filmography came about through the minute examination of some of the main institutional collections of Broodthaers's films. Cinematek (Brussels) plays a historic role in preserving an almost comprehensive collection extending all the way to the smallest rushes. Also the collection of films assembled by Jost Herbig and his family during Broodthaers's lifetime played a crucial role in shaping this filmography. Preserved without posthumous reedits, it served as a key reference corpus. Until recently, these films were held on long-term loan at the MACBA (Barcelona), where they were consulted. Other key institutions include the Walker Art Center (Minneapolis), the Hoffmann

Foundation (Basel), and Centre Pompidou (Paris). The extensive holdings of Maria Gilissen were not systematically accessed.

The result of this exercise is the below list of titles corresponding to those mentioned and showed during Broodthaers's lifetime and still existing today, albeit, in some cases, under (slightly) different edits and titles. Whenever possible, the earliest given titles, adapted to French spelling (if applicable), are indicated. The same applies to the film gauge, although it should be mentioned that the original format is hardly determinable, since extensive copying has made it so that many titles exist on both 16 and 35mm today. The notes added indicate not only the alternate titles under which a specific film is circulating (whether accurate or not) but also whether or not it requires a custom screen. Despite Broodthaers's "expanded" understanding of cinema, this filmography sticks to his works on film stock, thus excluding cinepoems, scenarios, film projects, and lost films (all of which are to some extent included in the abovementioned exhibition catalogs). Although Broodthaers's cinema may resemble his prolific slide projection practice in its marked reliance on the still image, and even if his films were often shown in conjunction with them, these too are not covered in the below list. (For an inventory of the latter corpus, see Anna Hakkens, *Marcel Broodthaers: Projections* (Eindhoven: Stedelijk Van Abbe Museum, 1994.)

Although this filmography remains nonexhaustive, a limited number of films were added to the 1997 Fundació Tàpies exhibition catalog, including the first (nonexhaustive) list of films on which Broodthaers collaborated as a writer. On the other hand, in an effort to bring order to some confusion that has arisen, films and fragments that were either completed or shown frequently during Broodthaers's lifetime have been differentiated from posthumous edits. This classification, however, is by no means intended to assume a prescriptive character. It should be stressed that the selection and categorization that this filmography draws upon are anything but exempt from discussion and historical critique. It is in the first place conceived as an aid for the screening and research of Broodthaers's cinema, which will not cease to fascinate future generations of cinephiles and scholars.

FILMOGRAPHY

1. FILMS BY MARCEL BROODTHAERS

La Clef de l'horloge (poème cinématographique en l'honneur de Kurt Schwitters)
1957, 16mm, b/w, sound, 7'
Technical assistance: Guy Hekkers and Marc Marchal

La Clef de l'horloge was shot in 1956 during a Kurt Schwitters retrospective that ran at the Brussels Palais des Beaux-Arts between October 13 and November 11. Apparently, a soundtrack was only added in 1958. In the end, Broodthaers dated the film 1957.

Le Corbeau et le renard
1967, 16mm, color, silent, 7'
Camera: Paul and Michel De Fru

Requires being projected on one of the following three painted screens: a large painted canvas (161 x 218 cm), a roll-up photographic canvas (90×130 cm), and a TV-shaped, photographic canvas mounted on wood (61×81 cm). The latter two were part of two eponymous editions distributed in 1968 and 1972 by Wide White Space Gallery, Antwerp.

Also known as *Le Corbeau et le renard (D'après La Fontaine)*.

Musée d'Art Moderne, Département des Aigles, section XIXe siècle: Une Discussion inaugurale
1968, 16mm, b/w, silent, various lengths

Various versions of this film exist, each featuring a (slightly) different edit and length. Additionally, there are many rushes and raw edits with the same subject, which makes it impossible to delineate a definitive selection of versions. Apparently, Broodthaers conceived a three-part film documenting the activities of the *Musée d'Art Moderne, Département des Aigles, Section XIXe Siècle: I. Une discussion inaugurale, II. Voyage a Waterloo* (See "Films by Broodthaers, posthumously finished") *III. Le temps d'une journée (The Time)* (the latter remaining unidentified). See *Broodthaers: Cinéma*, 145. In (at least) one copy titled *Département des Aigles*, s.d., 16mm, b/w, silent, 14', scenes of the first two parts are integrated into a single edit.

Fragments circulating under the titles *Marie-Puck parlante; Promenade; Écriture; Musée haut bas fragile;* and *Tableau Magritte* are usually included in the edits subsumed under *Une Discussion inaugurale*.

Also known as *Une discussion inaugurale,* and (possibly) *Écran museum section 19e siècle; Département des Aigles Figure*.

Le Musée et la discussion
1969, 16mm, b/w, 12'
Requires a world map as a screen.

Note: *Le musée et la discussion* too draws on the thesaurus of fragments making up the edits (subsumed under the title) of *Musée d'Art Moderne, Département des Aigles, section XIXe Siècle: Une discussion inaugurale.*

According to the 2010 *Section Cinéma* exhibition catalog (New York: Marian Goodman), this film was only occasionally projected on an altered world map hanging next to a stenciled wall. The former was turned into the artwork titled *Carte du monde poétique* (1968). However, according to the 2016 *Broodthaers: A Retrospective* exhibition catalog (New York/Madrid: MoMA/Reina Sofia), the film was projected on *Carte utopique du monde* (1968).

The fragments *Ombre arbre sur mur*; and *James Puck Piet* are related to this film. Also known as *Musée-Museum*.

La Pluie (projet pour un texte)
1969, 16mm, b/w, silent, 2'
Camera: Jean Harlez; Cast: Marcel Broodthaers

Also known as *Projet pour un texte*.

La Pipe (René Magritte)
1969, 16mm, b/w, silent, 5'
Camera: Jean Harlez

Some sources date this film 1968–69.
In 1971, this film was shown on the screen of a projection box with the inscription "Abb. 1." (See *Marcel Broodthaers: Cinéma*, 176–79.)

La Pipe (Figure noire); La Pipe (Figure blanche); Ceci ne serait pas une pipe
1969–1971, 16/35 mm, b/w, silent, 2'20"

All three abovementioned films consist of the same edit drawing on takes from *La Pipe (René Magritte)*. They differ from one another considering the content and color of their subtitles that were added in 1971, as indicated by the variations of their titles.

Apparently, *Ceci ne serait pas une pipe* also exists in an English, significantly longer version: *This Wouldn't Be a Pipe,* 1969–72, 16mm, b/w, silent, 7'.

La Pipe (Gestalt, Abbildung, Figur, Bild)
1969–72, 16mm, b/w with blue tinting, 4'20"

This film's edit draws entirely on takes from *La Pipe (René Magritte); La Pipe (Figure noire);* and *La Pipe (Figure blanche),* supplemented by an additional layer of surtitles added in 1972.

La Pipe satire
1969, 16mm, b/w, silent, 3'
Camera: Jean Harlez; Cast: Marcel Broodthaers, Maria Gilissen

This film (partly) draws on takes from *La Pipe (Magritte).*
This film does not appear in any filmography prior to 1989.

Défense de fumer
1969, 16mm, b/w, silent, 30"
Camera: Jean Harlez; Cast: Marcel Broodthaers

This film draws on two takes from *La Pipe satire.*
This film does not appear in any filmography prior to 1989.

Un Film de Charles Baudelaire [French version]
1970, 16/35 mm, color, sound, 7'
Camera: Jean Harlez

Un film de Charles Baudelaire exists in two versions: a first, French version and a second, English version that differ from one another as to the content and language of their subtitles. According to the 1997 Fundacío Tàpies exhibition catalog, the French version was not shown during Broodthaers's lifetime.

Un Film de Charles Baudelaire [English version]
1970, 16/35mm, color, sound, 7'
Camera: Jean Harlez

Un film de Charles Baudelaire exists in two versions: a first, French version and a second, English version that differ from one another as to the content and language of their subtitles. Although commonly known as *A Film by Charles Baudelaire,* the latter, translated title appears not to have been in use during Broodthaers's lifetime.

Also known as *A Film by Charles Baudelaire*; *Un Film de Charles Baudelaire (Second Version)*; *Un film de Charles Baudelaire (Carte politique du monde ou Système de signification)*.

La Lune
1970–72, 35mm color, silent, 2'30"

This film appears related to the development of *Un Film de Charles Baudelaire* [English version]; see *Broodthaers: Cinéma*, 124.

This film does not appear in any filmography prior to 1989.

Also known as *Une image de la lune*.

M.T.L. (D.T.H.)
1970, 16mm, color, silent, 4'30"
Camera: Jean Harlez

Sources contradict each other as to whether or not this film requires a custom screen. According to Broodthaers's contemporaries, *M.T.L (D.T.H.)* was first projected on the painted windowpane of the gallery, which also constitutes its very subject. Although the film was projected on a regular screen at subsequent screenings during Broodthaers's lifetime, a posthumous reconstruction of the gallery window is held in a public collection (whose dimensions, however, are not faithful to those of the original windowpane.)

In 1972, Broodthaers himself shot a new sequence for the film. See *Broodthaers: Cinéma*, 112–15.

Une Seconde d'éternité
1970, 16/35mm, b/w, silent, 1"
Camera: Wenzel

Also known as *La Signature*; *Ma signature*; *Ma signature comme seconde*; *Une Seconde d'Eternité (D'après une idée de Charles Baudelaire)*.

Films shown at *Section Cinéma*, January 1971–October 1972:

Musée d'Art Moderne, Département des Aigles, section XIXe Siècle: Une Discussion inaugurale
1968, 16mm, b/w, silent, various lengths

See entry above.

According to the 1997 Fundació Tàpies exhibition catalog, and the 2010 *Section Cinéma* exhibition catalog (New York: Marian Goodman), this film was supplemented by *Un Voyage à Waterloo (Napoléon 17969–1969)*, see below: "Films by Broodthaers Posthumously Finished." This is contradicted by the fact that the edit in which *Un Voyage à Waterloo* exists today appears to have been only produced after Broodthaers's passing as it is not mentioned in any film program presented during Broodthaers's lifetime. Most likely, fragments on which the latter film was based were indeed shown, albeit not (yet) in the edit that corresponds with this title nowadays. As mentioned, some edits having the activities of the first section of the *Musée* as a subject combine takes stemming from *Une discussion inaugurale* and *Un Voyage à Waterloo*.

Requires a custom screen: Marcel Broodthaers. *Écran Fig. 0, Fig. 1, Fig. 2, Fig. A.* (1971) See *Belgavox – Mode – 20th Century Fox*.

Charlie als Filmstar
1971, 16mm, b/w, silent, 2'30"

Appropriated film. Its footage concerns an 8mm copy distributed by *Globus Film* of the 1914 Mack Sennett production of *The Masquerader* by Charlie Chaplin.

Requires a custom screen: Marcel Broodthaers. *Écran Fig. 0, Fig. 1, Fig. 2, Fig. A.* (1971) See *Belgavox – Mode – 20th Century Fox*.

Brüssel Teil II
1971, 16mm, b/w, silent, 2'20"

Appropriated film. Its footage concerns an 8mm copy distributed by *Globus Film*. In one collection, this film is preceded by *Brüssel Teil I*.

Requires a custom screen: Marcel Broodthaers. *Écran Fig. 0, Fig. 1, Fig. 2, Fig. A.* (1971) See *Belgavox – Mode – 20th Century Fox*.

Belgavox – Mode – 20th Century Fox
1971, 16mm, b/w, sound, 8'30"

Requires a painted screen. Appropriated/found-footage film.

The four above films were originally projected on a whitewashed brick wall bearing stenciled "Fig."- signs. On subsequent occasions, the films were projected on a special screen whose layout was based on the latter wall and which is (generically) titled *Fig. 0, Fig. 1, Fig. 2, Fig. A* (1971). This screen comes in different versions (titles) and sizes. See *Broodthaers: Cinéma*, 172. Apparently, this screen lent its name to the compilation of *Charlie als Filmstar, Brüssel Teil II*, and *Belgavox – Mode – 20th Century Fox*, namely 1898–1971. *Fig. 0, Fig. 1, Fig. 2, Fig. A (These and other films)*. 16mm, b/w, 1971.

Le Musée et la discussion
1969, 16mm, b/w, 12'

Requires a world map as a screen. See entry above.

The 2010 *Section Cinéma* exhibition catalog mentions *Promenade* (1968) as an additional film projected during *Section cinéma*. In fact, it is a short rush that is (partly) included in *Le musée et la discussion*, and, as such, unlikely to have been projected as a separate film as part of the *Section cinéma* program.

Le Poisson
1970–71, 16/35 mm, b/w, silent, 7'35"
Camera: Jean Harlez

According to the 1997 Fundació Tàpies exhibition catalog, two rare variations of this film exist: *Le poisson est tenace* and *Exercice*. See *Broodthaers: Cinéma*, 181.

Also known as *Le Poisson (projet pour un film)*, *Projet pour un poisson (projet pour un film)*.

Crime à Cologne
1971, 16/35mm, b/w, silent, 1'30"
Camera: Jean Harlez; Cast: Marcel Broodthaers, Jule Herbert (Kewenig)

Some sources mention a soundtrack for this film.
Also known as *Krimi in Köln*.

Au-delà de cette limite
1971, 16mm, b/w, silent, 7'30"
Camera: Jean Harlez

According to the 1997 Fundació Tàpies exhibition catalog, several separate outtakes cut from the final edit still exist.

Also known as *Au-delà de cette limite vos tickets ne sont plus valables*.

0-X
1971, 16mm, b/w, silent, 3'

This film does not appear in any filmography prior to 1977.

Paris
1971, 16mm, color, silent, 2'

This film is part of the so-called Postcard Films series, including *Histoire d'amour (Dr. Huismans)*, *Paris*, and *Chère petite soeur*. These also feature in a compilation film titled *Trois cartes postales* or *Cartes postales* (1971–72).

Also known as *Carte postale I "La Seine"*; *Tour Eiffel*; *Paris (La Seine), (Carte postale I)*.

Histoire d'amour (Dr. Huismans)
1971–72, 16mm, color, sound, 3'

This film is part of the so-called Postcard Films series, including *Histoire d'amour (Dr. Huismans)*, *Paris*, and *Chère petite soeur*. These also feature in a compilation film titled *Trois cartes postales* or *Cartes postales* (1971–72).

Also known as *Histoire d'amour (Dr. Huysmans)*; *Mademoiselle*; *Carte postale II "Mademoiselle."*

C'est-je-parole-regret is related and perhaps identical to *Histoire d'Amour (Dr. Huismans)*.

Chère petite soeur
1972, 16mm, b/w, color, 5'

This film is part of the so-called Postcard Films series, including *Histoire d'amour (Dr. Huismans)*, *Paris*, and *Chère petite soeur*. These also feature in a compilation film titled *Trois cartes postales* or *Cartes postales* (1971–72).

Also known as *Carte postale III Chère petite soeur*; *Chère petite soeur (la tempête)*; *La Tempête*

Mauretania
1972, 16mm, color, silent, various lengths

Two variations of this film (differing from one another concerning content of its subtitles) exist: *Mauretania (AOX-XOA)* and *Mauretania (Fig.0-Figures-Fig. A)*.

Although this film depicts a postcard, it appears not to have been included in any compilation comprising the above three "Postcard Films."

Some sources mention a soundtrack for this film.

Also known as *Mauretania (avec mer)*.

Ah que la chasse soit le plaisir des rois
1972, 16mm, color, silent, 6'30"

The notes to some clippings of the material that Broodthaers used for shooting these films suggest a connection to the film *Die Farbe/La couleur/The color* (1972), 16mm, color, 2', first mentioned in 1989.

Also known as *La chasse*.

Rendez-vous mit Jacques Offenbach
1972, 16mm, b/w and color, sound, c. 30'

This is (largely) a compilation film comprising (successive) takes from: *La Pipe (figure blanche)*; *Chère petite soeur*; *Histoire d'amour (Dr. Huismans)*; *La Pluie*; *Une Seconde d'éternité*; *Crime à Cologne*; and *Ah que la chasse soit le plaisir des rois*, supplemented by rushes, such as *Gare centrale* and *Écriture*, countdown leaders, and white "Fig."-subtitles on black leader.

An alternative version of this film exists and includes the above films preceded by fragments of *Mauretania*; and *Un Film de Charles Baudelaire* [English version], while ending with *Mauretania (AOX-XOA)*.

Only some parts of this film have a soundtrack. The film was (eventually) named after the title of a compilation LP of Jacques Offenbach that was (occasionally) used as an external soundtrack for the film.

Analyse d'une peinture
1973, 16mm, color, silent, 7'

Under the alternative title of *Une peinture d'amateur découverte dans une boutique de curiosités*, this film was later spliced together with an alternative edit bearing the title *Le même film revu après les critiques* (1973), 16mm, color, silent, 5'. The resulting compilation reel was titled *Deux films*. According to the 1997 Fundació Tàpies exhibition catalog, the latter was accompanied by a record *Bruitage Cinéma (vol. 1, Mer – Plage – Vent – Tempête – Orage)* fulfilling the role of an external soundtrack, similar to *Rendez-vous mit Jacques Offenbach*, see *Broodthaers: Cinéma*, 232–33.

This film is identical to *Une peinture d'amateur découverte dans une boutique de curiosités*.

A Voyage on the North Sea
1973–74, 16mm, color, silent, 4'15"

This film draws on the same fragments as *Analyse d'une peinture*, supplemented by images of a modern yacht taken off the shore of Ostend.

Also known as *Un voyage en Mer du Nord*.

Un Jardin d'hiver (A B C)
1974, 16/35mm, color, sound, 7'
Camera: Paul De Fru; Cast: Marcel Broodthaers

Eau de Cologne
1974, 16/35mm, color, sound, 2'
Camera: Paul De Fru; Cast: Marcel Broodthaers, Jule Herbert (Kewenig)

Berlin oder ein Traum mit Sahne
1974, 16mm, color, sound, 13'
Camera/sound: Jörg Jeshel; Cast: Marcel & Marie-Puck Broodthaers

Also known as *Le chaland qui passe*.

Figures of Wax
1974, 16mm, color, sound, 16'
Camera: Clyve Myer and John Hardy; Editing: Noël Cronin; Commentary: Charlotte Hardman; Piano: Marcel Broodthaers; Cast: Marcel Broodthaers

Also known as *Jeremy Bentham* and *Figures of Wax (Jeremy Bentham)*.

Monsieur Teste
1974–75, 35mm, color, silent, 2'

According to Maria Gilissen, this film was supposed to be part of the unfinished *Mouvement-Living Pictures* film project that Broodthaers envisaged toward the end of his life. Other related rushes supposedly include *Chasseur*; *Victoria-montre cheval*; *Billiard*; *Parlement*; *Slip-test (dissolves)* and *New York (Part 1)*.

La Bataille de Waterloo
1975, 16/35mm, color, sound, 11'
Camera: Martin Bell; Editing: Noel Cronin; Sound: Richard King

This film officially premiered about one year after Broodthaers's death, on February 8, 1977, at the London Tate Gallery.

Also known as *Un vice*.

2. FILMS BY BROODTHAERS, POSTHUMOUSLY FINISHED

Objet
1967–84, 16mm, b/w, silent, 10'
Camera: Jean Harlez, Editing: Jean-Louis Dewert & Maria Gilissen

The fragment *Cercueil-Freeze* is supposedly related to this film.

Signalisation
1968–85, 16mm, b/w, silent, 6'
Editing: Jean-Louis Dewert & Maria Gilissen

Un Voyage à Waterloo (Napoléon 1769–1969)
1969–85, 16mm, b/w, silent, 13'
Camera: Jean Harlez; Editing: Maria Gilissen

The Last Voyage
1972–76, 16mm, color, silent, 4'

This film was supposedly found as an in-camera edit by Broodthaers.

Kassel Wilhelmshöhe (Herkules mit Kaskaden)
1972–84, 16mm, b/w, silent, 5'30"

Speakers Corner
1972–87, 16mm, b/w, silent, 8'
Camera: Maria Gilissen; Cast: Marcel Broodthaers

According to the 1997 Fundació Tàpies exhibition catalog, this film was shot in connection with Broodthaers's *Neuf peintures, Série anglaise* exhibition taking place at Jack Wendler Gallery in London (1–22 December 1972). As the initial print turned out to be of poor quality, it was apparently abandoned only to be reedited and supplemented by still photographs later, see *Broodthaers: Cinéma*, 222.

The MoMA holds a video version of the film stemming from the Daled collection, which supposedly came with the work exhibited in the abovementioned show (*Neuf peintures, Série anglaise*): *Do You Have a Tongue in Your Mouth?* (1972), b/w, sound, 6'25."

New York (Part 2)
1973–84, 16mm, b/w, silent, 14'10"
Cast: Marcel Broodthaers

3. UNFINISHED FILMS AND RUSHES BY BROODTHAERS

Mont des Arts
1964, 16mm, color, silent, 4'

Broodthaers & Magritte
c. 1965–66, 16mm, color, silent, 1'
Camera: Maria Gilissen

Also known as *B. Magritte, Magritte (Home Movie)*.

Pompei
1972, 16mm, color, silent, 2'

New York (Part 1)
1973–75, 16mm, color, silent, 1'

Some fragments of this film are related to *La lune*. (See entry above)
According to Maria Gilissen, this film was part of the unfinished *Mouvement-Living Pictures* film project that Broodthaers envisioned toward the end of his life. Other related rushes supposedly include *Chasseur; Victoria-montre cheval; Billiard; Parlement;Slip-test (Dissolves);* and *Monsieur Teste*.

Slip-test (Dissolves)
16mm, color, silent, 6'

According to Maria Gilissen, this film was part of the unfinished *Mouvement-Living Pictures* film project that Broodthaers envisioned toward the end of his life. Other related rushes supposedly include *Chasseur; Victoria-montre cheval; Billiard; Parlement; New York (Part 1);* and *Monsieur Teste*.

4. FILMS TO WHICH BROODTHAERS COLLABORATED AS A WRITER

Un certain Saint-Tropez (1959)
Directed by Patrick Ledoux; Text: Marcel Broodthaers

Monaco (1959)
Directed by Patrick Ledoux; Text: Marcel Broodthaers

Un deux trois qui a la balle? (1959)
Directed by Patrick Ledoux; Text: Marcel Broodthaers

Les Quatres saisons (1959)
Directed by Philippe Collette; Text: Marcel Broodthaers

Dimanche (1960)
Directed by Costia de Renesse; Text: Marcel Broodthaers

Le Poirier de Misère (1961)
Animation Film. Animated and directed by Jean Coignon; Dialogues: Marcel Broodthaers

Festival international de jazz (1962)
Directed by Patrick Ledoux; Text: Marcel Broodthaers

Bruegel et Goya, Journalistes (1964)
Directed by Henri Kessels, Screenplay: Marcel Broodthaers

French and Dutch versions of this film exist. According to the 1997 Fundació Tàpies exhibition catalog, Broodthaers also wrote the initial commentary, only to be later replaced by a text from the hand by Jean Raine in the French version of the film. Broodthaers's commentary supposedly persists, albeit translated, in the Dutch version of the documentary.

CONTRIBUTORS AND EDITORS

ERIC C.H. DE BRUYN is professor of Modern and Contemporary Art in the Department of Art History at the Freie Universität Berlin. He is an editor of *Grey Room* and has curated programs at the MuMOK in Vienna, Musée Pompidou in Paris, and the Whitney Museum in New York. His writings on contemporary art and media have appeared, among other places, in *Artforum, Art Journal, Grey Room*, and *Texte zur Kunst*.

ANDREW CHESHER gained his PhD from Chelsea College of Arts in 2007, where he is a senior lecturer on the Fine Art BA course. His research focuses on Neo–avant-garde and postconceptual practices with a special emphasis on philosophical analysis, in particular phenomenology and critical theory. His essays include: "Phenomenology After Conceptual Art," published in *Analecta Husserliana: The Yearbook of Phenomenological Research* (2018), "Reconfiguring the Lifeworld: Spatial Experience in the Universe of Technical Images," in *Time, Space and Mobility* (2018), and "Desublimating the Gestalt: Towards an Archaeology of Robert Morris's Anti Form," in *Zeitschrift für Ästhetik und allgemeine Kunstwissenschaft* (2021). He has given academic papers at international conferences in recent years in Switzerland, Germany, Poland, Belgium, and various parts of the UK. He has also directed documentaries on modern music, including *Knots and Fields: Darmstadt and the Legacies of Modernism* (made with David Ryan) (2010) and *Changing the System* (on Christian Wolf) (2007), which have been screened at Kettles Yard in Cambridge, UK; the ISSUE Project Room in New York; Internationales Musikinstitüt Darmstadt, Germany; and Centre d'Art Contemporain Genève, Switzerland as well as other institutions in North America and Europe.

XAVIER GARCÍA BARDÓN teaches at École de Recherche Graphique and Université Libre de Bruxelles. A former film curator at BOZAR (Brussels, 2004–20), he has worked with numerous institutions such as Centre Pompidou Paris, International Film Festival Rotterdam, Cinémathèque française, WIELS, Oberhausen Kurzfilmtage and Cinematek, among others. He has curated Marcel Broodthaers screenings for the National Museum of

Modern and Contemporary Art, Korea (Seoul, 2014) and SHHH silent film festival (Ostend, 2021). García Bardón holds a PhD in Film Studies from Université Paris 3 Sorbonne Nouvelle (2017) with a research on the history of the Knokke-le-Zoute EXPRMNTL film festival, and a Master in History from UCLouvain (1999).

CHARLOTTE FRILING studied art history and art criticism at Central Saint Martins in London, the University of Oxford, and Columbia University, New York. After her work experiences at Yvon Lambert and the Hamburger Bahnhof - Staatliche Museen zu Berlin, she became an associate curator at WIELS (Brussels) in 2013, where she worked on exhibitions of Franz Erhard Walther and Mark Leckey. Together with Dirk Snauwaert she co-curated the exhibitions *Atopolis* (Mons 2015, European Capital of Culture), *The Absent Museum* (WIELS's tenth anniversary, 2017), and *Convex / Concave* (TANK, Shanghai, 2019). She also co-curated the exhibition *Industrial poems, Open Letters*, focused on Marcel Broodthaers's plastic plaques (WIELS, 2021 & MASI Lugano, 2022).

STEVEN JACOBS is an art historian specializing in the relations between film, architecture, and the visual arts. His publications include *The Wrong House: The Architecture of Alfred Hitchcock* (2007), *Framing Pictures: Film and the Visual Arts* (2011), *The Dark Galleries: A Museum Guide to Painted Portraits in Film Noir* (2013), *Screening Statues: Sculpture and Cinema* (2017), *The City Symphony Phenomenon: Cinema, Art, and Urban Modernity between the Wars* (2018), and *Art in the Cinema: The Mid-Century Art Documentary* (2020). His other research interests focus on Belgian modern art, particularly the work of late modernist painter Raoul De Keyser. He teaches at the Department of Letters at the University of Antwerp and at the Department of Art History at Ghent University.

BRUCE JENKINS is Professor of Film, Video, New Media, and Animation at the School of the Art Institute of Chicago. Prior to coming to SAIC, he was Stanley Cavell Curator at the Harvard Film Archive. Jenkins previously served as Curator of Film/Video at the Walker Art Center, Minneapolis where he collaborated on exhibitions devoted to Chantal Akerman, Marcel Broodthaers, Bruce Conner, Chris Marker, William Klein, and the Fluxus Group. He has written exhibition catalog essays for the Museum of Contemporary Art, Sydney; the Renaissance Society, Chicago; Museo Reina Sofía; the Guggenheim Museum; the Tate; and Wexner Center, among others. His critical writings have appeared in *Artforum, October, Mousse*, and *Millennium Film Journal*. He has authored a book-length study on the work of Gordon Matta-Clark; edited a volume of writings by Hollis Frampton; and written the principal essays for monographic publications on Michael Snow,

Matt Saunders, and Basim Magdy. His most recent project was as principle coauthor of *The Films of Andy Warhol Catalogue Raisonné: 1963–1965* (Whitney Museum of American Art and Museum and Yale University Press, 2021). The latter volume received the 2022 Kraszna-Krausz Moving Image Book Award.

DEBORAH SCHULTZ is a Reader in Art History at Regent's University London. Her research explores word-image relationships, photographic practices, and archives, and the representation of memory in twentieth-century and contemporary art. She completed her PhD thesis at the University of Oxford on *Marcel Broodthaers: Strategy and Dialogue* (published Bern and Oxford, 2007). Other recent and forthcoming relevant publications include *Photo Archives: The Place of Photography*, edited with Geraldine Johnson (London, 2023); "The (Re)constructed Self in the Safe Space of the Family Photograph," in *Picturing the Family*, Silke Arnold-de Simine and Joanne Leal (eds) (London, 2018); "Proximity and the Viewer in Contemporary Curating Practices," in "On Proximity," special issue of *Performance Research*, June 2017; and 'Investigating the Unknown: Crossing Borders in Contemporary Art," in *Crossing Borders: Transition and Nostalgia in Contemporary Art*, Ming Turner & Outi Remes (eds) (Taipei, 2015).

CHRISTOPHE WALL-ROMANA is Professor and Samuel Russell Chair in the Humanities in the Department of French and Italian at the University of Minnesota. His work focuses on cinema as a cognitive, epistemic, and esthetic matrix, mostly in the French-speaking domain. He is the author of *Cinepoetry: Imaginary Cinemas in French Poetry* (Fordham, 2012), and *Jean Epstein: Film Philosophy and Corporeal Cinema* (Manchester, 2013). He is currently at work on a book in media archaeology addressing the role of racial formation and astronomical ideas in the emergence of photography and cinema provisionally titled *Imaging the Unseen*. He has translated books by Judy Blume, Philip K. Dick, Norbert Wiener, W. S. Merwin, Jean Epstein, and recently, together with Joe Hughes (University of Melbourne), the course notes of Gilbert Simondon titled *Imagination and Invention* (University of Minnesota Press, 2022).

RAF WOLLAERT recently gained his PhD on the subject of the cinema of Marcel Broodthaers at the University of Antwerp (Belgium). Since 2019, he dedicated multiple projects to the artist, including the LP edition *La Lumière manifeste*, a number of film screenings, as well as an international symposium. His most recent lectures were delivered at Princeton University, the Chelsea College of Arts in London, and the Akademie der Künste in Berlin. Currently, Wollaert is a Fulbright visiting scholar affiliated with the Broodthaers Society of America and New York University.

INDEX

66 (1966) 155

À bientôt j'espère (1968) 98
À bout de souffle (1960) 70
Adé, Georges 68
Adorno, Theodor W. 79, 86, 89, 90, 234, 239
Aesop 44, 151
Âge d'or, L' (1930) 211
Ah que la chasse soit le plaisir des rois
 (1972) 170, 174–175, 254
Akerman, Chantal 54
Albert II, King 162
Alechinsky, Pierre 43
Alechinsky d'après nature (1970) 43
Alekan, Henri 212
Analyse d'une peinture (1973) 20–21, 129,
 178, 203, 254, 255
Andre, Carl 78, 194
Angels with Dirty Faces (1938) 77
Anger, Kenneth 148, 154
Année dernière à Marienbad, L' (1961) 213
Antin, Eleanor 184
Antonioni, Michelangelo 207
Apraxine, Pierre 95
Aristotle 114
Arroseur arrosé, L' (1895) 137, 140
Asher, Michael 48
Atalante, L' (1934) 230, 233
Atget, Eugène 211, 217
Au-delà de cette limite (1971) 36, 41, 56,
 189–206, 252
Auprès de ma blonde (1956) 154

Balachoff, Dimitri 154
Barker, Barry 49
Barthes, Roland 24, 25, 41, 55, 119, 126, 129,
 139, 140
Barucchelo, Gianfranco 155

Bassenge, Gerda 180
Bataille, Georges 119
Bataille de Waterloo, La (1975) 49, 50, 158,
 225, 256
Baudelaire, Charles 16, 17, 25, 26–31, 32, 34,
 36, 41, 55, 109–111, 116, 123–132, 169, 249,
 250, 254
Baudry, Jean-Louis 48, 79
Bazin, André 54, 214
Beavers, Robert 149
Beethoven, Ludwig van 216
Begone Dull Care (1949) 154
Béguin, Albert 236, 238
Belgavox – Mode – 20th Century Fox
 (1971) 91, 251
Bellour, Raymond 48, 54
Belmondo, Jean-Paul 70
Beni, Umberto 145, 152
Benjamin, Walter 27, 28, 48, 68, 110, 113, 179,
 200, 239
Bentham, Jeremy 49, 56, 184, 207–220, 255
Bergson, Henri 117
Berlin: Die Sinfonie der Großstadt
 (1927) 217
Berlin oder ein Traum mit Sahne (1974) 39,
 49, 50, 56, 203, 221–244, 255
Between Showers (1914) 39
Beuys, Joseph 158, 235
Blackberry, John 201
Blanchot, Maurice 41, 42, 83, 84
Boltanski, Christian 158
Bonfanti, Antoine 98
Bonneau, Pierre 98
Borgemeister, Rainer 15
Borja-Villel, Manuel 16, 245
Borowczyk, Walerian 145, 148, 162
Bosch, Hieronymus 109
Brakhage, Stan 66, 148

Brandt, Willy 238
Breer, Robert 155
Brentano, Clemens 231
Bresson, Robert 207
Breton, André 29, 34, 218
Brodzki, Constantin 147, 148, 163
Broodthaers, Constantin 148
Broodthaers, Marie-Puck 224, 247, 255
Broughton, James 211
Brueghel, Pieter 18, 109, 114, 259
Bruegel et Goya, journalistes (1964) 18, 114, 259
Brulhart, Nicolas 113, 153, 160
Brüssel Teil II (1971) 91, 190, 251
Bruynoghe, Yannick 154
Buchet, Jean-Marie 148, 159
Buchloh, Benjamin 15, 24, 25, 28, 65, 133, 134, 235
Buñuel, Luis 211
Buren, Daniel 48, 55, 78, 194
Butler, Judith 81, 82, 84, 88

Cabañas, Kaira 94
Cagney, James 77
Calligraphie japonaise (1955) 43
Caillois, Roger 113
Cameraman, The (1929) 39
Canonne, Xavier 32, 66
Cast (1971) 210
Caught in the Rain (1914) 39
Cayrol, Jean 145, 155
Cèbe, Pol 97
Ceci ne serait pas une pipe (1969–71) 34, 35, 91, 248
Chaffee, Cathleen 49, 225
Chaland qui passe, Le (1934) 230, 255
Chant de ma génération, Le (1959) 80
Chaplin, Charlie 39, 40, 47, 53, 65, 77, 91, 118, 251
Charles Baudelaire, Je hais le mouvement qui déplace les lignes (1973) 110–111
Charlie als Filmstar (1971) 39, 40, 91, 251
Charnière, La (1968) 98

Châteaux de nuages (1956) 154
Chère petite sœur (1972) 56, 170–173, 182, 203, 253, 254
Christophe, Ernest 111
Chronique d'un été (1961) 190
Chomette, Henri 23
Chopin, Frédéric 216
Cinéma Modèle (1970) 15–17, 19, 35, 41, 43, 50, 52, 109, 116–118, 163
Clair, René 37
Clarke, Shirley 145, 148, 154, 156, 162
Clef de l'horloge, La (1957) 16, 17–20, 23–24, 25, 33, 35, 41, 43, 67, 70, 80, 108, 116, 148, 149, 151, 209, 247
Clémenti, Pierre 145, 156, 158
Cocteau, Jean 212
Coignon, Jean 14, 259
College (1927) 39
Collette, Philippe 14, 258
Comolli, Jean-Louis 48
Compton, Michael 15
Conrad, Tony 149
Corbeau et le renard, Le (1967) 16, 17, 34, 36, 41, 43–46, 50, 56, 68–70, 93, 94, 116, 117, 129, 145–167, 177, 178, 192, 201, 247
Corbusier, Le 153
Costa, Pedro 54
Coulommier, Julien 210
Crime à Cologne (1971) 41, 42, 201, 203, 218, 252, 254
Crimp, Douglas 28, 50, 179
Curtiz, Michael 77, 210

Daney, Serge 98
Darboven, Hanne 29
Davay, Paul 14, 154
David, Cathérine 36
Dean, Tacita 54
Debord, Guy 79, 92–94, 98, 234
de Bruyn, Eric 13, 15, 16, 25, 29, 31, 45, 46, 50, 55, 131, 177, 218, 235
Decan, Liesbeth 178, 179
de Chirico, Giorgio 211

de Decker, Anny 154, 161
Défense de fumer (1969–70) 91, 249
De Fru, Paul 14, 152, 247, 255
Degas, Edgar 106
de Haulleville, Eric 29
de Heusch, Luc 14, 43
Dekeukeleire, Charles 14
de La Fontaine, Jean 16, 17, 44, 69, 94, 145, 150–153, 159, 163, 174, 176, 247
Deleuze, Gilles 42, 117
Delvaux, Paul 18, 147, 210
Demy, Jacques 212
Deren, Maya 66, 211
Derrida, Jacques 42, 105, 177, 183
De Sica, Vittorio 37
De Toth, André 210
de Vree, Freddy 91
Dewert, Jean-Louis 152, 256
Diable géant ou le Miracle de la Madonne, Le (1901) 211
Dine, Jim 33
Disciplinaires, Les (1964) 155
Discussion inaugurale, Une (1968) 87, 91, 129–130, 247, 248, 250, 251
Dockley, Peter 210
Dr. Strangelove (1964) 77
Dore O 149
Dotremont, Christian 14, 43
Dotremont: Les Logogrammes (1972) 43
Dreams That Money Can Buy (1947) 211
Dreyer, Carl Theodor 212, 213
Duchamp, Marcel 37, 39, 71, 119, 217
Dumont, Fernand 29
Duras, Marguerite 83
d'Ursel, Henri 14
Dypréau, Jean 44

Eau de Cologne (1974) 221, 226, 255
Edison, Thomas 25
Eggleston, William 216
Egoyan, Atom 54
Eisenbahnüberfall, Ein (1972) 53–54
Eliot, T. S. 183

Éluard, Paul 34, 176
Enfer de Rodin, L' (1957) 212
En lisant la Lorelei. Wie ich die Lorelei gelesen habe (1975) 231–234, 237, 239
Entr'acte (1924) 37
Epstein, Jean 23
Ernst, Max 114
Estiez, Liane 98

Fantômas (1913–14) 12, 24, 32, 36
Farocki, Harun 94, 95, 145, 155, 162
Felleman, Susan 211
Fête foraine (1956) 154
Feuillade, Louis 12, 53, 54
Figures de Cire (1914) 210
Figures of Wax (1974) 13, 49, 56, 184, 203, 207–220, 221, 226, 255
Filliou, Robert 158, 184
Film als Objekt—Objekt als Film (1972) 80, 113
Film de Charles Baudelaire, Un (1970) 16, 17, 24–31, 34, 36, 41, 110, 116, 130, 131, 169, 249, 250, 254
Film voor Lucebert/Lucebert, tijd en afscheid, Een (1962/1967/1994) 43
Fiszman, Isi 145, 156, 158, 161, 162, 163
Flaming Creatures (1963) 149
Fluxus 23, 46, 54, 162, 184
Foucault, Michel 25, 34, 35, 42, 48, 190, 193, 199, 217
Four in the Afternoon (1951) 211
Frampton, Hollis 23, 42, 176, 203, 207, 218
Franju, Georges 190, 193
Freud, Sigmund 68, 119, 126, 216
Fuses (1967) 158

Galimberti, Jacopo 85
Gance, Abel 145, 153, 154, 158
Gauty, Lys 230
Gertrud (1964) 213
Gilbert & George 29, 55, 78, 137, 138, 140, 212
Gildemyn, Marie-Pascale 15, 33

Gilissen, Maria 64, 69, 145, 191, 194, 198, 246, 249, 256, 257, 258
Godard, Jean-Luc 13, 54, 70, 213
Goldmann, Lucien 28, 41, 126, 218, 233
Goldsmith, Oliver 86
Gordon, Douglas 54
Goux, Jean-Joseph 36
Graham, Dan 29, 46, 225
Grandville, Jean Ignace Isidore Gérard 27, 107, 108, 119
Grass, Günter 237, 238
Greenaway, Peter 54
Griffith, D. W. 65
Grifi, Alberto 155
Guattari, Félix 200
Gunning, Tom 25, 39, 91, 92

Haesaerts, Paul 14, 18, 145, 149, 150
Hamilton, Richard 184
Haidu, Rachel 15, 30, 41, 49, 88, 225
Hamoir, Irène 29
Hannoset, Corneille 145, 147, 148, 149
Hansen, Miriam 89, 90, 91, 93
Happiness (1935) 98
Harlez, Jean 14, 44, 194, 198, 248, 249, 250, 252, 256
Hawaiian Lullaby (1967) 158
Head Guy, The (1930) 39
Hein, Birgit 95
Heine, Heinrich 221, 230, 231, 233–236, 238
Herschel, William 108
Histoire d'amour (Dr. A Huismans) (1971) 56, 170–173, 180, 182, 203, 253, 254
Hog Wild (1930) 77
Horak, Jan-Christopher 66
Horkheimer, Max 89, 90
House of Wax (1953) 210
Howard, Henry 158
Hurlement en faveur de Sade (1952) 93, 98
Huyghe, Pierre 54
Huysmans, Joris-Karl 173

Illiac Passion, The (1967) 162
Inauguration of the Pleasure Dome (1957) 154
Investigating Dreamland (1960) 131
Isou, Isidore 92, 93
Ivens, Joris 94

J'accuse (1919/1937) 154
Jardin d'hiver (A B C), Un (1974) 49, 50, 77, 78, 86, 203, 225, 226, 255
Jenkins, Bruce 15, 16, 33, 53, 55, 159, 160, 226, 230, 245
Jeshel, Jörg 224, 255
Jetée, La (1962) 203
Juliet and Romeo (1967) 155

Kaplan, Nelly 154
Katz, Benjamin 180
Käutner, Helmut 230
Kawara, On 78, 184
Keaton, Buster 39, 53, 65, 118, 230
Kessels, Henri 14, 19, 114, 259
Kiarostami, Abbas 54
Kluge, Alexander 89, 90, 91
Kopytoff, Igor 181
Kosuth, Joseph 34, 177
Krauss, Rosalind 20, 28, 45, 46, 65, 66, 68, 70, 109, 110, 111, 113, 178
Kubelka, Peter 148
Kubrick, Stanly 77, 79
Kusama, Yayoi 149

Lacan, Jacques 35, 41, 119, 190, 200, 201
Ladri di biciclette (1948) 37
Lam Thang Phong 155
Lambert, Léon 145, 161, 162
Lambert, Yvon 194–199
Lamelas, David 29, 230
Langdon, Harry 39
Langlois, Henri 190, 193
Last Voyage, The (ca. 1973–76) 228–230, 256
Latham, John 155

INDEX

Laurel and Hardy 39, 77, 118
Lautréamont, Comte de 37
Lebel, Jean-Jacques 93, 94, 155, 156, 158
Lecomte, Marcel 214
Ledoux, Jacques 145, 147–148, 149, 153, 154, 158
Ledoux, Patrick 14, 258, 259
Lehman, Boris 149
Lemaître, Maurice 92, 93
Leni, Paul 210
Lenin, Vladimir 90
Lethem, Roland 149, 151
Levi, Pavle 52
Lohaus, Bernd 161
Lukács, György 28, 218, 233–238
Lumière, Louis and Auguste 25, 53, 65, 98, 137, 140
Lütticken, Sven 106
Lyotard, Jean-François 139

McCall, Anthony 46
McEvilley, Thomas 36, 203
MacLaren, Norman 154
Mademoiselle (1971–72) 173, 253 See also: *Histoire d'amour (Dr. A. Huismans)*
Magritte, René 14, 17, 29, 32–37, 39, 55, 63–73, 77, 105, 107, 109, 112, 131, 135, 145, 184, 189, 193, 201, 214, 247, 248, 249, 257
Mallarmé, Stéphane 27, 36, 37, 42, 43, 55, 68, 105–122, 126, 131–137, 139–141, 189, 199, 202, 217
Man Ray 37, 39
Manzoni, Piero 55, 138–140, 212
Marey, Étienne-Jules 24, 147
Mariën, Marcel 94
Marker, Chris 54, 94, 97, 98, 203
Markopoulos, Gregory 161, 162
Marret, Mario 98
Marx, Karl 217
Masson, Jean 212
Mauritania, Le (1972) 174, 253–254
M.B. 24 images/seconde (1970) 125–126, 136
Medvedkin, Alexander 98

Meins, Holger 94, 155, 162
Meissonier, Ernest 81, 159
Mekas, Jonas 66, 149
Méliès, Georges 54, 107, 211
Menken, Marie 148, 212
Mépris, Le (1963) 213
Merleau-Ponty, Maurice 118
Métro, Le (1934) 190, 193
Meyerowitz, Joel 216
Micha, René 147
Michaux, Henri 119
Michelson, Annette 70
Mill, John Stuart 217
Miller, Jacques-Alain 217
Mitchell, W. J. T. 63
Mitry, Jean 154
Mommartz, Lutz 46, 159
Monde de Paul Delvaux, Le (1946) 18
Mondrian, Piet 81, 159, 203
Monsieur Teste (1974–75) 210, 218, 255, 258
Morgan, Tony 29, 46
Morin, Edgar 190
MovieMovie (1967) 155, 158
M.T.L. (D.T.H.) (1970) 218, 250
Musée Grévin, Le (1958) 212
Mussorgsky, Modest 212
Muybridge, Edward 24, 25
Mystery of the Wax Museum (1933) 210

Napoléon Bonaparte 106, 202, 209
Napoléon (1927) 153, 158
Nauman, Bruce 46, 225
Negt, Oskar 89, 90, 91
Nixon, Richard 81
Noguchi, Isamu 212
Nougé, Paul 14
Number 4 (1967) 155

O'Brien, Pat 77
Œuf Film, L' (1965) 29, 55, 109, 114, 116, 150
Offenbach, Jacques 107, 170
Oldenburg, Claes 33
Ombres Chinoises (1974) 112

One Week (1924) 39
Ono, Yoko 155, 161, 207
Oppenheim, Dennis 46
Oppitz, Michael 65, 178
Orphée (1950) 212

Panamarenko 55, 123, 158
Paola, Queen 162
Paolozzi, Eduardo 24
Payday (1922) 39
Pelzer, Birgit 133, 134
Peterson, Sidney 211
Pickersgill, Henry William 209
Pipe, La (1969) 16, 17, 23, 31–37, 44, 47, 69, 116, 248–249
Pipe (Gestalt, Abbildung, Figur, Bild), La (1969–72) 34, 249
Pipe satire, La (1969) 32, 33, 249
Plato 48
Pleasure Garden, The (1953) 211
Pluie, La (1969) 12, 16–17, 23, 37–39, 41–43, 91, 113, 116, 132, 133, 140, 226, 248, 254
Poe, Edgar Allan 30, 63, 230–231
Point mort, Le (1967) 159
Polke, Sigmar 158
Poirier de misère, Le (1961) 14, 259
Pollet, Jean-Daniel 148
Potted Psalm, The (1946) 211
Première Nuit, La (1958) 190
Projet pour un film (1948) 29, 41, 108, 114, 119
Projet pour un poisson (1970–71) 55, 115, 203, 252
Pygmalion et Galathée (1898) 211

Racisme végétal: La séance (1974) 75–80, 84–86, 89, 91, 98
Rancière, Jacques 105, 189, 199
Rauschenberg, Robert 24
Remes, Justin 176
Rendez-vous mit Jacques Offenbach (1972) 50, 80–81, 113, 170, 177, 254
Renoir à Picasso, De (1950) 18

Reprise du travail aux usines Wonder, La (1968) 98
Resnais, Alain 11, 207, 213
Ricardo, David 217
Richter, Hans 37, 211
Rimbaud, Arthur 37
Ritual in Transfigured Time (1946) 211
Rodin, Auguste 212
Rogan, Bjarne 183
Ross, Kristin 75, 83, 84, 88, 90, 99
Rosselini, Roberto 213
Rouch, Jean 190
Royoux, Jean-Christophe 16, 27, 29, 52, 126, 134, 194
Rubens (1948) 150
Rubin, Barbara 149
Ruhrberg, Karl 222, 227, 238–239
Ruttmann, Walther 217
Ryman, Robert 194

Sadoul, Georges 11, 24–25
Salkin, Émile 228
Sang d'un poète, Le (1932) 212
Sartre, Jean-Paul 42, 119, 133
Schneemann, Carolee 158
Scholz, Hans 231
Schwitters, Kurt 17, 18, 19, 23–25, 36, 67, 148–149, 199, 209
Selbstschüsse (1967) 159
Scorsese, Martin 149
Scram! (1932) 39
Seberg, Jean 70
Seconde d'éternité, Une (1970) 41, 55, 91, 109–110, 113, 116, 123–144, 250, 254
Section Cinéma (1971–1972) 12, 16–17, 31, 35, 45, 46–48, 49–54, 69, 91, 116, 163, 184, 190, 203, 248, 250–252
Segal, George 33
Sennett, Mack 39
Sharits, Paul 42
Shaw, Jeffrey 155
Shore, Stephen 216
Simmel, Georg 218

Sitney, P. Adams 446, 149
Skulima, Folker 124, 131, 137–138
Smith, Jack 149
Smithson, Robert 178
Snow, Michael 46, 68, 69, 113, 159, 176, 207
Sollers, Philippe 42
Somville, Roger 85
Sortie de l'usine, La (1895) 98
Soupault, Philippe 29
Spoerri, Daniel 46, 184
Stark, Trevor 15, 25, 26, 30, 97, 236
Staub (1967) 155
Steamboat Bill Jr (1928) 39
Sterckx, Pierre 227
Stewart, Susan 180–181
Storck, Henri 14, 18, 29, 150
Study in Choreography for the Camera, A (1945) 211
Symphonie mécanique (1955) 154
Szeemann, Harald 96, 158

Talrich, Jacques 208
Tapié, Michel 44
Testament d'Orphée, Le (1959) 212
Thirifays, André 14
Thorvuldsen (1949) 212
Toroni, Niele 194
Tour visuelle, La (1966) 19, 217
Tourneur, Maurice 210
Traité de bave et d'éternité (1951) 92
Trois Cartes Postales (1972) 170, 173, 253
Tussaud, Marie 209, 216
Twice a Man (1963) 161
Tytgat, Edgard 147

Undersea Kingdom (1936) 77
Unter den Brücken (1944–46) 230

Val del Omar, José 148
Valéry, Paul 34, 210
Vandenbunder, André 154
van der Keuken, Johan 43
van der Linden, Wim 158

van Tijen, Tjebbe 155
Varda, Agnès 148
Varèse, Edgard 153
Verhavert, Roland 154
Verifica Incerta, La (1964) 155
Verne, Jules 107
Viaggio in Italia (1954) 213
Vian, Boris 119
Vigo, Jean 11, 196, 230
Visual Variations on Noguchi (1945) 212
Vogel, Amos 95, 148
von Arnim, Achim 231
von Schlosser, Julius 214
Vormittagsspuk (1928) 37
Voyage à Waterloo, Un (1969) 129, 158, 247, 251, 256
Voyage dans la lune, Le (1902) 107
Voyage on the North Sea, A (1973–74) 20, 22–23, 65, 70, 129, 178, 209, 228, 230, 255
Vrijman, Jan 43

Wachsfigurenkabinett (1924) 210
Wall-Romana, Christophe 17, 28, 29, 42, 55, 105
Warhol, Andy 23, 176, 207
Wavelength (1967) 46, 68, 69, 159, 196
Weerasethakul, Apichatpong 54
Weibel, Peter 149
Weiner, Lawrence 194
Weiss, Peter 148
Wellesley-Miller, Sean 155
Werner, Michael 116, 132, 170, 201
werkelijkheid van Karel Appel, De (1962) 43
Wiertz, Antoine 210
Wild, Jennifer 68
Willemont, Jacques 98
Winzentsen, Ursula and Franz 155
Wittgenstein, Ludwig 119
Wolman, Gil J. 92
Wollen, Peter 64
Word Movie (1966) 42

Xenakis, Iannis 153

Yalkut, Jud 149

Zéro de conduite (1933) 196
Zorns Lemma (1970) 42, 203, 218

www.ingramcontent.com/pod-product-compliance
Lightning Source LLC
Chambersburg PA
CBHW061709300426
44115CB00014B/2611